Study Guide

GLEITMAN, FRIDLUND, REISBERG
Psychology
Sixth Edition

Study Guide

GLEITMAN, FRIDLUND, REISBERG
Psychology
Sixth Edition

JOHN JONIDES
UNIVERSITY OF MICHIGAN

PAUL ROZIN
UNIVERSITY OF PENNSYLVANIA

W • W • NORTON & COMPANY • NEW YORK • LONDON

Layout and composition by Roberta Flechner Graphics

Permission and credits appear on page 259, which constitutes an extension of the copyright page.

ISBN 0-393-92462-9 (pbk.)

W. W. Norton & Company, Inc., 500 Fifth Avenue, New York, NY 10110
    www.wwnorton.com

W. W. Norton & Company Ltd., Castle House, 75/76 Wells Street, London W1T 3QT

1 2 3 4 5 6 7 8 9 0

CONTENTS

ACKNOWLEDGMENTS

The authors would like to thank Caroline Arnold, Jason Fabozzi, Elizabeth Gross, Georgia Larounis, Jennifer Lerner, Laura Lowery, Maureen Markwith, Linda Millman, Deborah Reyher, Amanda Thomas, Nathan Witthoft, and Barbara Zeeff for their contributions and valuable suggestions.

In the course of developing the sections entitled "Investigating Psychological Phenomena" for each chapter, we have had occasion to seek the advice of colleagues and students who have particular expertise in the areas in question. We would like to acknowledge the help of Lyn Abramson, Henry Gleitman, Aaron Katcher, Charles G. Morris, Lorraine Nadelman, Harriet Oster, Christopher Peterson, Martin E. P. Seligman, W. John Smith, Marjorie Speers, and Edward Stricker. We also thank Walter Love and Jeannie Morrow for special assistance in field testing a number of the activities that we have included.

Thanks to Kim Yi, Marian Johnson, JoAnn Simony, and Roberta Flechner for their hard work in turning this edition's manuscript into a book.

Finally, we thank Cathy Wick, April Lange, Andrea Haver, Aaron Javsicas, and Jon Durbin for their advice throughout the development of the text in its various editions.

The authors of this guide are listed in alphabetical order on the title page.

TO THE STUDENT

This study guide is designed to help you to understand and apply the material presented in *Psychology*, Sixth Edition, by Henry Gleitman, Alan Fridlund, and Daniel Reisberg. Each chapter in the study guide corresponds to one in the textbook. There are four sections in each study guide chapter: Learning Objectives, Programmed Exercises, Self-Test, and Investigating Psychological Phenomena. The first three sections will help you determine the essential ideas of the chapter as well as give you experience with possible test questions. The fourth section, Investigating Psychological Phenomena, allows you to extend your knowledge of some issues raised in the text. This section will also give you a feeling for how the data used by psychologists are collected, and how theories are tested in psychology. Let us briefly review the function of each of these sections.

LEARNING OBJECTIVES

We have provided an outline of the key issues discussed in each chapter. Each entry in the outline refers to a basic fact, theory, or relationship that you should have learned from the chapter. These entries are listed in order of occurrence in the chapter and are arranged under the same headings used in the chapter. It may be useful to read the learning objectives before reading the chapter, as well as after. They will help to orient you to the major issues, or the "big picture," of the chapter.

PROGRAMMED EXERCISES

For each chapter of the text, we have provided fill-in-the-blank questions. These questions test your basic knowledge of the key words and concepts of the chapter. These questions are very straightforward and can be looked up and verified in the text. So that you will know whether you are correct, the answer has been provided on the right side of the page. Be sure to cover that side of the page with your hand or a piece of paper as you do the exercises.

To facilitate locating the answers in the text, the programmed exercises are also arranged under the major headings of the textbook, and they follow the order of presentation in the text. This allows you to see which fact or theory pertains to which major point of the chapter.

SELF-TEST

For each chapter in the text, we have prepared a self-test composed of multiple-choice questions. They also follow the order of the text. In general, these questions are more difficult than the fill-ins, though both types of questions cover the range of materials presented in the text. The multiple choices sometimes highlight subtle distinctions, ask for some amount of integration, or test your ability to apply some of the material in the text.

Since multiple-choice questions are commonly used in examinations, and since they can also be very instructive, we will spend some time in this section discussing how to answer them. We will also describe and illustrate some different types of multiple-choice questions used in this study guide.

First, some basic strategies. Most multiple-choice questions on examinations, and in this study guide, have four or five choices. On most examinations there is a penalty of −1/3 point for wrong answers of four-choice questions, and −1/4 point for wrong answers on five-choice questions. This would mean that wild guessing should net a score of zero. But if you can eliminate even one choice, it pays to guess among the remaining alternatives.

Read each question carefully. Try to understand the *point* of the question. Read through the alternatives. The answer may be obvious to you. If not, try to eliminate some of the choices. You may be able to eliminate choices on the following grounds:

1. The choice is inherently inconsistent, illogical, or actual nonsense (e.g., word salad: a bunch of usually relevant terms combined in a meaningless way).

2. The choice makes sense and may even be true, but it is not an *answer* to the question.

3. On the basis of your knowledge, the choice is just the wrong answer to the question.

Get used to sorting out sense from nonsense and relevant from irrelevant answers. These skills will stand you in good stead in many of your activities outside of this course. Work with the remaining choices (if more than one choice remains), and do the best you can to determine the best fit between the question and the answer.

We will illustrate a number of different types of multiple-choice questions, all represented in this study guide. For each example we will indicate the correct answer and add comments on some of the incorrect choices.

Straight factual questions. Many multiple-choice questions simply ask for your knowledge of facts: names, definitions, and basic concepts.

1. The Prime Minister of Great Britain at the end of World War II was
   a. Neville Chamberlain.
   b. Winston Churchill.
   c. Harold Wilson.
   d. Sir D. Winter.
   e. Anthony Eden.

Comment: This is a very straightforward question. You know it or you don't. The answer is *b*, Winston Churchill. The other names were selected to make the question somewhat difficult: three of the other choices were prime ministers of Great Britain at the beginning or after the war, and one, Sir D. Winter, is a fictitious name.

2. The best way to describe inflation is
   a. increase in the gross national product not accompanied by increased unemployment.
   b. a general increase in prices.
   c. a decrease in the money supply.
   d. a decrease in the value of the monetary system, when associated with a gross national product.
   e. another form of recession.

Comment: This question is more difficult than 1. This is in part because the choices are more difficult. The correct answer is *b*. Answers *a*, *c*, and *e* are just wrong. Though *a* is consistent with inflation, it does not define it. Item *d* is inherently wrong; that is, it is sort of nonsense. What does it mean to decrease the value of the monetary *system* as opposed to money? And everything is associated with some gross national product. Keep your eyes open for nonsense. There is a lot of it in the world.

Evaluating evidence for a theory. In this type of question you are asked to judge whether particular results (real or hypothetical) support a particular theory (or which theory would be supported or opposed by a particular result). The theory and/or results may have been presented in the text, or they may be introduced in the question. The question tests both your knowledge of the materials, and your progress in understanding how to evaluate evidence. This type of question is often formulated in the negative—"Which of the following would be evidence against theory X?"—simply because it is usually easier to come up with results supporting major theories than results opposing them. We will assume, for the next sample question, that you have read in some text or other that Yentzel claimed that the crime rate increases as population mass and density increase. (Yentzel is a fictitious name.)

3. Which of the following would be evidence against Yentzel's theory? (Note: We assume that New York is larger than Philadelphia, which is larger than Tucson.)
   a. Philadelphia has a crime rate higher than Tucson.
   b. A few cities with increasing population also have increasing crime rates.
   c. A few cities with decreasing population have an increase in crime rate.
   d. Philadelphia has a lower crime rate than New York.
   e. The ratio of murder to robberies is lower in New York than in Tucson.

Comment: The correct answer is *c*, because this result is opposite to what would be predicted by Yentzel's theory. Answers *a*, *b*, and *c* are supporting evidence for the theory. Answer *e* is irrelevant: the theory says nothing about the types of crime, and *e* says nothing about the overall crime rate. (Note another clue to the right answer: *b* and *c* are opposites, so it is likely that one is evidence against the theory. However, clever exam writers know about this and sometimes put in opposites that are irrelevant to the question to keep you on your toes.)

Extending a principle or theory to a new situation. This type of question tests your understanding of a principle, theory, or concept by asking you to apply it to a situation other than those presented in the text.

4. If the saying "a stitch in time saves nine" were applied to medicine, one would recommend
   a. reducing the amount of sewing in surgery.
   b. increasing the cost of medical insurance.
   c. increasing the frequency of checkups.
   d. increasing the number of physicians.
   e. making prescription drugs available over the counter.

Comment: The correct answer is *c*. To answer the question, one must understand the saying and translate it into medical terms. This translation would be something like, Medical precautions can lead to avoidance of major illnesses. Alternative *a* is irrelevant to the *real* meaning of the saying and simply follows the *literal* meaning. Answer *b* would not lead, in any direct way, to avoidance of illness. But *b* is a sort of correct answer, since one might assume that increasing the cost of medical insurance would lead to increased coverage. The answer says increasing the cost, not the amount of insurance. Answer *c* relates directly to the saying, More checkups should lead to early discovery of illnesses that might prove harmful if allowed to develop. While *d* might well cut down the rate of illnesses, it is not a direct way of arriving at prevention. Lastly, *e* is irrelevant to the issue raised in the saying.

Relating different ideas or facts, or integrating materials. This type of question often involves materials from different sections of a chapter, or perhaps from different chapters (we have refrained from the latter, since we don't know the order in which you will be reading the chapters in the book).

5. The president of the United States is related to the electoral college as a U.S. Senator is related to*
   a. his or her own college faculty.
   b. the voters of his or her state.
   c. the members of the House of Representatives.
   d. the state of his or her electors.
   e. the state of his or her voters.

Comment: The correct answer is *b*. The electoral college is the group of people who actually elect the president. The voters of a senator's state are the people who elect the senator. Item *a* is totally wrong and simply a play on the word college. Item *c* is factually wrong. Item *d* is wrong and doesn't make too much sense, and item *e* is a reversal of the correct answer and has no relation to the question.

INVESTIGATING PSYCHOLOGICAL PHENOMENA

For each chapter of the text, we have presented one or two activities or experiments. These activities build upon concepts or theories presented in the chapter and extend and deepen your knowledge and understanding of these concepts or theories.

─────────────

*This type of relation is often stated as "president of the U.S.: electoral college::U.S. Senator: _____"

The activities give you an opportunity to understand something about the progress of psychology as a science. While the text emphasizes our current understanding of psychology, the activities emphasize the process through which we arrive at this understanding. How is the theory tested? How do psychologists get data to describe basic relations or test theories? How do they analyze the data? We hope to give you a feeling for how progress is made, while at the same time indicating the problems and difficulties associated with the serious study of something as complex as the human mind.

We have attempted to provide you with a variety of activities. Some emphasize the generation or testing of theories, others emphasize data collection or analysis. We have tried to cover the major methods of data collection used by psychologists: among all the activities are included examples of the experiment, the questionnaire, direct observation, and the interview. In many cases we provide data from studies we have done with introductory psychology students as a base for comparison with the data you collect. In each activity in which you collect data, we guide you through some analysis of the data and get you to try to interpret the data and relate it to issues raised in the text. If your instructor wishes to include the activities as part of the course, he or she may ask you to tear out the report (data) sheet pages, and hand them in. These sheets are duplicated at the end of the book in Appendix 2. Otherwise, you may consider these activities as a less formal extension of your education in psychology.

We have tried out all of these activities on undergraduate students like yourselves. We have included only studies that work out for the great majority of students. Of course, with people as variable as they are, all the studies that you do on one or a few students will not show the same results. But we expect that most of you will get most of the predicted results.

Many of the most important phenomena in psychology cannot be included in these activities because they must be measured under controlled conditions that you could not easily arrange. Some involve expensive equipment, like timers that can time thousandths of a second, or panels of lights and switches. Some important relations are not striking enough to be seen in one or a few participants. We have tried to find, for each chapter, at least one activity that can be appreciated within the limits under which you will be working. We require no equipment other than pencil, paper, some sort of second indicator (stopwatch, digital watch with second indicator, or a watch with a second hand), and materials presented within this study guide. We have limited the time demands on you for any activity to less than one hour. In all but a few cases, we have limited the number of participants to a very few. At the beginning of each activity, we indicate the equipment involved and the time demands it will make on you and the participants.

These activities are designed to be both educational and entertaining. We hope that you find that they meet these goals.

CHAPTER 1

Introduction

Learning Objectives

THE SCOPE OF PSYCHOLOGY

1. What is psychology? What is it a science of?

Watching the living brain
2. What makes the measurement of blood flow relevant to the study of the brain?

Memory errors
3. Be able to cite a factor that can render an eyewitness's memory false.

Innate capacities
4. What technique has been used to tell us about the innate perceptual abilities of infants?

Displays and the evolution of communication
5. How is social interaction in animals mediated by displays? How do displays differ from one animal to another? Give examples.

Complex social behavior in humans
6. How are humans more complex in their social behavior than other animals?

A SCIENCE OF MANY FACES

7. Discuss the range of phenomena studied by psychologists. What are some important questions to ask about emotions?

Emotion as a subjective experience
8. Describe how feelings are often determined by judgments and context.
9. Describe the experiment by Schacter and Singer that demonstrates the ambiguity of internal states.

Emotion and cognition
10. What role does interpretation play in understanding emotions?
11. Give examples of how emotion colors cognition, such as memory.

Emotion and biology
12. Give some examples showing the relationship of the amygdala to fear.

13. What are some of the biological effects of emotion outside the brain?

Emotion and social behavior
14. What does the study of smiling tell us about the social expression of emotion?

Emotion and human development
15. Describe a phenomenon demonstrating early empathy for emotional states among infants.

Emotion and culture
16. What is the evidence about the universality of emotions?

Emotion and pathology
17. Describe the range of emotions encountered in various pathologies.

Perspectives on psychology
18. What fields have contributed to the development of psychology? What are psychology's approaches to the study of the individual?

THE SCIENCE OF PSYCHOLOGY

19. What differentiates psychology from the approaches to study of the mind (e.g., philosophy, religion)?
20. Name some of the techniques used to study phenomena by psychologists.

THE SCIENTIFIC METHOD

21. Give some examples of problems that can be approached by the scientific method.
22. What are some of the characteristics of the scientific method? What is a hypothesis? a prediction? a disconfirmation? What happens to hypotheses that are disconfirmed? What is the role of publication?

Designing a persuasive experiment
23. Be able to describe what makes a hypothesis testable.
24. Describe some of the characteristics of data collection that would make the evidence systematic. Do anecdotes count?
25. Know what the report bias is and how it might taint results.
26. What is the danger in relying on memory as the basis of data collection?

27. Be able to define a dependent and an independent variable.

28. Why is it sometimes necessary to have a panel of raters to assess the dependent variable?

29. What is a control group and how does it differ from an experimental group?

30. What is a danger of "before/after" designs?

31. Explain what one should keep in mind in designing a treatment for a control group.

32. What is a placebo, and what does it have to do with expectations?

33. How would subjects behave if they were being influenced by the demand characteristics of an experiment?

34. What is a double-blind design and how does it help assure the purity of an experimental design?

35. Be able to describe what a confound is and to give an example of a confounding variable.

An overview of an experiment's design

36. Name some quantitative measures that can be used as dependent variables.

37. What is causal ambiguity?

Evaluating evidence outside the laboratory

38. How might knowledge of good experimental design be applied outside of the laboratory?

OBSERVATIONAL STUDIES

39. What is the key difference between an experimental study and an observational one?

Correlational studies and causal ambiguity

40. Understand that the defining feature of a correlational study is understanding the relationship between an independent variable and a dependent variable.

41. Describe a case in which the direction of causality is unclear between two variables.

42. How can time-of-occurrence of a variable clear up the causality inference?

43. Explain how a third variable might cause a spurious correlation between variables A and B in which there is no direct link between A and B at all.

"Matching" the experimental and control groups

44. Understand that in principle experiments and correlational studies have a similar structure, with independent and dependent variables. So what permits experiments to escape some of the ambiguities of correlational studies?

45. What is the special property that random assignment confers on an experiment? How does this help establish causation? How does it mitigate the third-variable problem?

46. There are advantages and disadvantages to within-subject designs. Describe some. How does counterbalancing help to relieve some disadvantages?

Studies of single participants

47. Why would one ever study just a single participant when we are trying to learn about general laws of behavior?

48. What safeguards might one introduce to add rigor to the study of single cases?

TYPES OF DATA

49. What is the strength in using multiple methods to approach a problem?

GENERALIZING FROM RESEARCH

50. What is meant by external validity and how is this related to the problem of generalizing from research?

Selecting participants

51. How must participants be selected so that results from a sample can be generalized to the population of interest?

52. Describe a random sample and why a stratified sample is sometimes preferable.

53. Why is it important to gather a representative sample of responses?

External validity

54. Be aware of the issues involved in assessing the external validity of a study.

RESEARCH ETHICS

55. What are some of the protections that must be afforded to human and animal research participants?

56. What mechanisms exist for implementing these protections?

Programmed Exercises

THE SCOPE OF PSYCHOLOGY

1. Psychology involves not only the study of the mind, but also the study of _____.   behavior

2. When any part of the brain is active, more _____ flows to it.   blood

3. Many phenomena are best studied not at the _____ level but at the _____ level by focusing on the person's behavior and thinking, rather than the underlying nervous mechanisms.   biological / psychological

4. _____ questions can cause a piece of information to become implanted in a previous memory.   Leading

5. Studies of the visual _____ suggest that some perceptual knowledge of depth may not be _____, but built into us from the start.   cliff / learned

6. In animals, social interactions depend largely on _____ forms of communication.

innate

7. Many types of animal communication are based on signals called _____.

displays

8. The behavior of rioting crowds is determined not only by each individual, but also by the individual's _____ interaction.

social (group)

A SCIENCE OF MANY FACES

9. Psychology employs _____ methods and _____ types of analysis to examine its questions.

multiple, multiple

10. The feelings that are central to an emotion are laced with judgments and _____.

interpretations

11. In one study, participants were given an injection of a _____, reported feeling stirred up, and attributed this to the social situation.

epinephrine

12. Experiences we call "_____" or feeling "_____" are not simple read-outs of some internal physiological state.

happy, angry

13. The epinephrine study shows that one cannot clearly separate emotion and _____.

cognition

14. Emotional states can sometimes promote _____, so that we often end up _____ more fully or for a longer time.

memory
remembering

15. The _____, a walnut-sized structure, is central to the link between emotion and cognition.

amygdala

16. The _____ response is disrupted in animals with damage to the structure named in question 15.

fear

17. Emotion can cause _____ to be inhibited but _____ rate to increase.

digestion, heart (or breathing)

18. _____ expressions of happiness do not occur proportionally; they often are stimulated by the presence of stress.

Facial

19. _____ is an emotion that depends on knowing how we should behave.

Guilt

20. _____ is a direct emotional response to another person's circumstances.

Empathy

21. Some emotions are a result of shared biological heritage and so should be _____ across cultures.

universal

22. One emotion that appears universally is _____.

happiness

23. Emotions often vary from normality in many forms of mental illness or _____.

psychopathology

24. The various fields that have contributed to psychology include _____, _____, _____, and _____.

medicine, philosophy
physics, physiology

THE SCIENCE OF PSYCHOLOGY

25. When one conducts investigations with specific hypotheses that are subject to rigorous test, this is the _____ method.

scientific

THE SCIENTIFIC METHOD

26. Testable hypotheses allow us to make specific _____ about what we will find in an experimental test.

predictions

27. Two forms of gathering data are _____ and _____.

experimentation, observation

28. _____ data for any reason where those data did not arise directly from experimentation or observation is fraud.

concocting (inventing, fudging)

29. If facts are not consistent with a prediction, then the underlying hypothesis is _____.

disconfirmed (false)

30. Scientists often want to rerun the same study with new participants, a process called _____.

replication

31. The written public presentation of results appears in a _____.

publication

32. A _____ hypothesis is one for which you can identify the results that would confirm or disconfirm it.

testable

33. _____ evidence, often in the form of a testimonial by a single person, is often dismissed by scientists because it is not systematic.

Anecdotal

34. A _____ _____ arises when some observations are more likely to be reported than others.

report bias

35. The _____ problem is one example of report bias in which unsuccessful results are suppressed.

file-drawer

36. In an experiment, the _____ variable is the one that is a function of some other factor, the _____ variable.

dependent
independent

37. Sometimes, dependent variables cannot be measured directly, so one must enlist a panel of _____ to rate the variable.

judges

38. The extent to which a panel of judges agrees with one another constitutes the _____ reliability.

interrater

39. In an experiment, the _____ group is administered the critical manipulation (e.g., the subliminal self-help tape described in the text), while the _____ group is deprived of this manipulation.

experimental
control

40. It is important to _____ and control experimental groups in all respects except for the experimental manipulation.

match

41. Participants' expectations can have a profound influence on a study's results. This is the basis for _____ effects.

placebo

42. Sometimes there are cues in an experiment called _____ _____ that signal that one response is more desirable than another.

demand characteristics

43. _____ designs are ones in which neither the investigator nor the study participants know who is in the experimental and control groups.

Double-blind

44. A _____ is an uncontrolled factor that could influence the results and result in _____ ambiguity.

confound
causal

OBSERVATIONAL STUDIES

45. In many cases, variables can't be experimentally controlled (as in a person's height), so one must turn to an _____ study.

observational

46. One type of observational study involves an assessment of the relationship between an independent and dependent variable; this is called a _____ study.

correlational

47. The direction of causality is not always easily determined in _____ studies.

correlational

48. Sometimes, correlations arise because a _____ variable is related to each of the two variables being correlated.

third

49. Experiments escape the ambiguity about causality because the experimental and control groups start out _____ to each other.

identical

50. Often the reason that experimental and control groups are identical to each other is that participants have been _____ assigned to one or the other.

randomly

51. If you use the very same participants for experimental and control groups, this is a _____ comparison. Using different groups makes it a _____ comparison.

within-subject
between-subject

52. Within-subject designs often carry with them the problem of carryover effects from one condition to another. This can be controlled by _____.

counterbalancing

TYPES OF DATA

53. In a _____ study, psychologists investigate a single individual in great detail.

case

GENERALIZING FROM RESEARCH

54. Whether one can generalize outside the bounds of a particular study to a wider group of people depends on the external _____ of the study.

validity

55. Almost always, one wants the conclusions of a study to apply to a _____ even though the subjects in the study were drawn from a _____.

population
sample

56. Generalization to a population depends on how _____ the sample is. representative

57. A _____ sample is one in which every participant has an equal and unpredictable chance of being picked. random

58. _____ sampling involves choosing individuals based on their proportion in certain categories in a population (e.g., certain age groups). Stratified

RESEARCH ETHICS

59. Psychological research must be conducted _____, in a way that protects the rights, well-being, and confidentiality of the research participants. ethically

60. In the United States, psychological research with humans must follow the guidelines of the _____ _____ _____. American Psychological Association

61. Before a study may begin, one must obtain _____ _____ from the subjects. informed consent

Self-Test

1. Psychology is
   a. the science of the mind.
   b. the science of behavior.
   c. both of the above
   d. none of the above

2. Psychology covers a large range of topics including
   a. topics that touch on anthropology and sociology.
   b. coverage of behavior in humans.
   c. coverage of behavior in animals.
   d. all of the above

3. Studying psychological processes has been helped significantly by the development of techniques that assess which parts of the brain are active during psychological tasks. This is possible because
   a. we can measure the activity of individual neurons in the living human brain.
   b. we can measure the direct neural activity of sets of neurons when they are active in the human brain.
   c. we can measure changes in blood flow that accompany changes in regional neural activity.
   d. all of the above

4. The memories of eyewitnesses are open to question because
   a. their memories can be altered by leading questions that are presented after an event has occurred.
   b. they can be influenced to remember details of an event that never really happened.
   c. they can forget incidents that might have really happened.
   d. all of the above

5. The visual cliff results suggest that
   a. perceptual skills are learned.
   b. perceptual skills are innate.
   c. perceptual skills could be innate.
   d. all of the above

6. The displays that animals use to communicate
   a. are innate and have arisen through selection.
   b. are almost always threat signals that ward off predators.
   c. will rarely involve parts of the body other than the head.
   d. all of the above

7. Human social interactions differ from those of other animals because
   a. humans are less variable in their interactions.
   b. humans are more flexible in their interactions.
   c. human social behavior is always rational and reasoned.
   d. human behavior in groups is predictable from knowing the responses that individual humans would give in that situation.

8. One experiment on human emotions had experimenters inject a stimulant into subjects and then put them into a social situation after having told them of the stimulant or not. When subjects were not told, they often
   a. became lethargic and did not respond socially.
   b. interpreted their feelings in the situation as due to the situation itself.
   c. interpreted their feelings in the situation as due to the stimulant.
   d. none of the above

9. Is there evidence linking emotion to the quality of our memory?
   a. Yes, we tend to remember emotional events better than nonemotional ones.
   b. Yes, we tend to remember events in the past that evoked a different emotion from the one we are feeling now.
   c. Yes, we tend to remember our past as being an unhappier time than the one we are experiencing now.
   d. No, there is little evidence suggesting that emotional state has any effect on memory.

10. Being afraid is reflected physiologically in
    a. digestion, which speeds up.
    b. heart rate and breathing, which slow down.
    c. sweating, which decreases.
    d. the amygdala, which is a brain structure that responds to fear.

11. Evidence suggests that facial expressions are not merely direct reflections of the underlying emotion that they express. Rather, they
    a. frequently are not consistent with our internal emotional state.
    b. tend to be displayed in situations when we are communicating with others.
    c. are muted reflections of our internal state that are difficult to measure.
    d. all of the above

12. The evidence on the universality of emotions is mixed. Some emotions are recognized fairly universally while others are not. Which is?
    a. happiness
    b. anger
    c. surprise
    d. disgust

13. The discussion of emotion in the text indicates that this and many other psychological phenomena can be profitably studied by
    a. studying cases where they go wrong (psychopathology).
    b. studying their representations across cultures.
    c. studying their underlying neurological representation in the brain.
    d. all of the above

14. The scientific method requires
    a. collecting anecdotes about some phenomenon.
    b. creating testable hypotheses.
    c. making specific predictions that can be tested.
    d. b and c, but not a

15. Perhaps the worst sin one can commit when using the scientific method is
    a. devising a hypothesis that turns out to be incorrect.
    b. making a prediction that is later disconfirmed when tested.
    c. concocting data that have not been collected.
    d. confirming a hypothesis that is under test.

16. For a hypothesis to be testable
    a. it must be specific enough that it can be confirmed.
    b. it must be specific enough that it can be disconfirmed.
    c. it must be broad and all-inclusive so that any data collected will show that it is confirmed.
    d. a and b, but not c

17. Report bias arises when
    a. an observer reports only some of the data relevant to a situation, but not others.
    b. an observer publishes encouraging results but not ones that are inconsistent with a hypothesis.
    c. the file-drawer problem is present in some situation.
    d. all of the above

18. Imagine an experiment in which you give students in a course either an easy or a difficult examination on some topic. All students take the easy exam and the difficult exam, and you record each student's score on each exam. The purpose of your experiment is to determine whether students who score high on the easy exam are the same ones who score high on the difficult exam, and students who score low on one exam are also those who score low on the other. In this experiment,
    a. the difficulty of the exam is the dependent variable.
    b. the difficulty of the exam is the independent variable.
    c. the exam scores are the independent variable.
    d. none of the above; there are no independent and dependent variables in this experiment

19. For the experiment described in question 18, what sort of experimental design was used?
    a. a within-subject comparison
    b. a between-subject comparison

    c. a double-blind design
    d. a causally ambiguous design

20. When you use a panel of judges to rate some measure, it is important
    a. to explain to them what the independent variable is in the experiment.
    b. to get higher interrater reliability for their judgments.
    c. have them blind to what the dependent variable is.
    d. all of the above

21. Suppose you are interested in the effect of creating images of a list of words on the memorability of those words (an interesting question, as you will see in the section on "Investigating Psychological Phenomena" in chapter 7). You give one group of subjects instructions to create images of each word in a list, and you give another group of subjects instructions to repeat each word as it is presented. In this experiment,
    a. the group given the instructions to repeat the words is the experimental group.
    b. the group given the imagery instructions is the control group.
    c. the design is an observational one, not an experimental one.
    d. none of the above

22. Whenever you want to assess the effect of a placebo, you want to
    a. be sure that you have included demand characteristics in your experiment.
    b. be sure that you have included confounds in your experiment.
    c. be sure that you have designed the experiment in a double-blind way.
    d. be sure that your experiment is causally ambiguous.

23. Suppose you were interested in the effect of age on memory. You test memory by presenting participants a list of words after which they have to recall the words in any order. Your experiment includes two groups of participants, ones aged 18–25 and ones aged 65–72. As it happens the younger participants are rarely awake early in the morning, so you test them in the afternoon. Conveniently, the older participants like to awake early, so you test them in the morning. You discover that the younger participants remember more words from the lists. This experiment suffers from
    a. not having an independent variable.
    b. not having a dependent variable.
    c. having confounded age and time of testing (morning versus afternoon).
    d. being double-blind.

24. For the experiment described in question 23
    a. one could say that there is causal ambiguity if the younger participants remember more than the older participants.
    b. one could say that there is causal ambiguity if the older participants remember more than the younger participants.
    c. one could say that either time of day or age was a cause of any differences in memory performance.
    d. all of the above

25. A correlational study would be needed if
    a. you wanted to measure the effect of shoe size on intelligence.
    b. you wanted to measure the effect of age on depression.
    c. you wanted to measure the effect of alcoholism on memory.
    d. all of the above

26. Suppose you conducted a study of shoe size and its relationship to intelligence among people aged 8 to 12. To conduct this study, you measure the shoe size of each of the participants, and you give each participant an identical test of intelligence. Your results tell you that there is a positive relationship between shoe size and intelligence: the larger the shoe size, the higher the score on the intelligence test. For this study,
    a. there is a third-variable problem: larger shoe size is related to age.
    b. there is a third-variable problem: larger shoe size is related to intelligence.
    c. there is no causal ambiguity because there are no confounds in the study.
    d. none of the above

27. We are told often that a correlation by itself does not permit one to draw causal inferences. By contrast, a properly designed experiment does permit causal inferences. Why is this?
    a. because in an experiment, one randomly assigns participants to experimental and control groups
    b. because in an experiment, the experimental variable can be causally attributed to it
    c. because assigning participants to experimental and control groups randomly ensures that the two groups are matched at the beginning of the experiment
    d. all of the above

28. One problem with the design of the experiment in question 18 is that students are given both the easy exam and the difficult exam. If these exams are always given with the easy exam first and the difficult one second, or vice versa, there might be a learning effect so that students do better on the second exam they take, regardless of whether it is easy or difficult. You could solve this problem by
    a. counterbalancing the order of the easy and difficult exams.
    b. using a within-subject comparison.
    c. using a correlational study rather than an experimental one.
    d. using a double-blind procedure in which the experimenter and the participants do not know which exam is easy and which is difficult.

29. Single-case studies
    a. are typically preferred to studies with multiple participants because you simplify the testing by having fewer participants.
    b. are sometimes necessary when the object of study is precisely the case in question.
    c. are not approachable by standard experimental methods.
    d. all of the above

30. When we conduct an experiment, we typically want to generalize the results to a whole population of people. That is, we would like to draw conclusions about the entire population, but we often cannot afford to test an entire population. To solve this problem, we might
    a. test a random sample of the population.
    b. test a stratified sample of the population.
    c. either of the above would allow generalization to the entire population.
    d. None of the above would allow generalization to the entire population.

31. The concept of external validity of an experiment refers to
    a. whether the results of the experiment can be generalized to phenomena in the outside world.
    b. whether an experiment was properly controlled in its design.
    c. whether an experiment has confounds in it that prevent a proper interpretation of the results.
    d. none of the above

32. In conducting an experiment on human participants, one must assure
    a. the safety of the participants.
    b. the confidentiality of the results.
    c. that informed consent is obtained from participants before they are tested.
    d. all of the above

Answer Key for Self-Test

1.	c	17.	d
2.	d	18.	b
3.	c	19.	a
4.	d	20.	b
5.	c	21.	d
6.	a	22.	c
7.	b	23.	c
8.	b	24.	d
9.	a	25.	d
10.	d	26.	a
11.	b	27.	d
12.	a	28.	a
13.	d	29.	b
14.	d	30.	c
15.	c	31.	a
16.	d	32.	d

Investigating Psychological Phenomena

CONSISTENCY OF JUDGMENTS OF FACIAL EXPRESSION

One of the things you learned in this chapter was that there is reason to suspect that some emotions are universally expressed. For example, when people of various cultures encounter a happy face, they often perceive it as happy. This is in contrast to other expressions, for which the agreement among different observers may be as little as 30–40%. It would be quite interesting to conduct this experiment using a very wide range of emotional expressions on a very wide array of participants from multiple cultures. Of course, it is difficult for the average college student to have access to such a wide array of participants. However, the average student does have access to students of both genders, and so the question we shall ask is whether judgments of facial expressions differ as a function of gender, and further, whether the judgments of one gender are more concordant with faces of that gender than with faces of the other gender.

To conduct this experiment, you will need an array of faces that you can use as stimuli. Fortunately, in these days of widely available digital cameras and personal computers, it should be relatively easy to construct a stimulus array and organize it into a systematic set of faces about which to collect judgments. First you need to capture the images. Select a friend of each gender whose face is plain (e.g., no facial hair, no facial ornaments, no facial tattoos). Then pose each of these two "actors" in front of a digital camera set to collect images at an average resolution. In turn, ask each volunteer to pose as if he/she is

Ecstatic, Happy, Sad, Shocked, Frightened, Disgusted, Calm, Resigned, Disappointed, Angry, Resolute

Take one picture of each pose for each actor. You should now have a collection of 22 images, 11 of the male actor and 11 of the female. Import these images into a presentation program such as Microsoft Powerpoint such that each slide of the presentation has just one image and the images are in a random order (you can determine this by making up 22 slips of paper, writing a description of one slide [e.g., happy male] on each slip, and then picking them out of a bowl [without looking]. The sequence in which you pick the slips of paper is your random order). In addition, make up 20 answer sheets, each of which has the numbers 1–22 in order with a line next to each on which the participant can write his or her answer.

Next, you should choose 10 male and 10 female participants. You will be testing them one by one. When each participant is sitting in front of the computer on which the presentation is programmed (be sure that your presentation begins with a blank page so that the participant cannot see the first face), give him/her the following instruction:

"We are interested in examining how universally people are able to recognize facial expressions. So, we have prepared a set of 22 faces, each of which is posed with some expression. On the sheet in front of you there are 22 lines, and for each expression, you should enter a one-word description of that expression. If you are in doubt about some face, enter your best guess. Once you have written an answer and moved on to the next face, do not change any prior answers. Do you have any questions?"

Set the presentation program so that it presents each slide for 5 seconds cycling through all the slides. After the last slide is complete, collect the answer sheet and thank the participant.

Now you need to score the sheets. If a judgment about a face matches one of the judgments that you used to create the face originally, count that correct. If it is close to the correct label (e.g., neutral for calm or depressed for sad), you should count that correct also. Now you want to create a table for all the subjects and all the stimuli, which you can do in the following template. The template has a place to record each answer from each subject about each face. Having done this, you now want to score the correct answers by each gender group for each face. Simply count

down each column per stimulus and note (out of a maximum possible score of 11 for each gender) how many of the faces were judged correctly (of course, "correct" here is judged by definition—that is, by the instruction you gave the actor before you took his or her picture; it is not an absolute criterion).

Now you are ready to examine the data by gender. You can do this on the summary table templates that are available. First, create a total accuracy score for the female subjects and the male subjects by totaling all their respective judgments. Are males overall more or less accurate than females in judgments of facial emotion? Previous research gives little reason for this to be so, but it is possible that females and males will differ in their judgments when they are judging the emotions on female versus male faces. So, calculate the total accuracy of females on the female faces, for females on the male faces, for males on the female faces, and for males on the male faces. Once again, do a comparison to see whether there are any gender effects that might differ according to the gender of the face. There are hypotheses that might predict that people may be different in judging the expressions on faces of their own gender compared to faces from the other gender.

A final comparison is this: the popular lore suggests that males are just not as sensitive to certain emotions in women as women are in judging women. To get an informal test of this lore, examine each of the individual expressions to see whether there are any cases of large discordance between the accuracy of males and the accuracy of females (large would be, for example, a score of 7/11 by one gender but only 3/11 for the other gender).

We should note that all the comparisons you accomplished were qualitative ones. It might be that a small difference for any of them could be due to statistical fluctuation that does not reveal any true differences. The text's appendix, which concerns statistical analysis, will give you an idea about how to overcome this limitation. For now, though, you should examine your data to see whether you found any systematic differences that might be revealing about gender differences in the identification of facial expression.

	Female Subjects	Male Subjects
Total Accuracy		

	Female Subjects	Male Subjects	Total
Female Faces			
Male Faces			
Total			

	Female Subjects	Male Subjects
Female ecstatic		
Female happy		
Female sad		
Female shocked		
Female frightened		
Female disgusted		
Female calm		
Female resigned		
Female disappointed		
Female angry		
Female resolute		

	Female Subjects	Male Subjects
Male ecstatic		
Male happy		
Male sad		
Male shocked		
Male frightened		
Male disgusted		
Male calm		
Male resigned		
Male disappointed		
Male angry		
Male resolute		

CHAPTER 2

Biological Bases of Behavior

Learning Objectives

1. Offer two answers to the question: Why should psychologists be interested in the nervous system?

THE ORGANISM AS A MACHINE

Mind as mechanism
Descartes and the reflex concept
2. Be familiar with Descartes' conception of the reflex and how, in part, it still forms the basis of animal and human action.
3. Compare conceptions of the mind as machine, switchboard, and computer.

HOW THE NERVOUS SYSTEM IS STUDIED

4. What is a neuron, and approximately how many are in the human brain?

Clinical observation
5. Indicate the advantages and disadvantages of studying the human brain by clinical observations of patients with brain damage.

Invasive techniques
6. Describe the advantages and ethical limitations of using invasive techniques to study the human brain.
7. Describe the techniques of lesioning, transection, and transcranial magnetic stimulation.

Neuroimaging techniques
8. Understand the mode of operation of the neuroimaging techniques that reveal brain anatomy: CT (CAT) scan and MRI.
9. Understand how neuroimaging instruments can measure brain activity or function by using EEG, PET scan, and fMRI.
10. Be aware of the advantages and disadvantages of each of the neuroimaging and other techniques for exploring the brain. Evaluate ease of obtaining information, invasiveness, ethical concerns, and type of information (activity, structure) obtained.

THE ARCHITECTURE OF THE NERVOUS SYSTEM

Genes and the nervous system
11. Explain how a small number of genes can orchestrate the development of a nervous system with billions of neurons.

The evolution of nervous systems
12. Distinguish between ganglia and brains.
13. Describe the tendency toward increasing centralization in the evolution of the nervous system.

The developing nervous system
14. Explain how the neural tube develops into the hindbrain, midbrain, and forebrain.

The major structures of the central nervous system
15. Describe the basic anatomy of the brain: What functions do the hindbrain, midbrain, and forebrain serve? What are the functions of the cerebellum?
16. Describe the subcortical structures in the forebrain, and their function.

The central nervous system's connections with the body
17. Be able to distinguish the peripheral and the central nervous system, and the somatic and autonomic nervous system.

THE CORTEX

18. Explain the nature and functions of the convolutions of the cortex.
19. Know the structure of the cerebral cortex, including the four lobes.

Localization of function in the cortex
20. Explain localization of function.

Projection areas
21. Describe the function of projection areas of the brain, and indicate what determines how much space in these areas is devoted to different parts of the body.
22. Discuss whether the primary motor area maps body parts or locations in space.
23. Define topographic projection and contralateral control.
24. What are nonprimary (association) areas?

Disorders of the projection areas
25. What are apraxia, agnosia, and prosopagnosia? What are the symptoms of the neglect syndrome?
26. Distinguish fluent and nonfluent aphasias in terms of site of brain damage and type of symptoms. Indicate problems with this distinction.
27. Describe some of the symptoms of prefrontal lobe damage, and the history of prefrontal lobotomy.

DO WE REALLY HAVE TWO BRAINS?

28. Explain the meaning of lateralization and how the brain organization of left-handers differs from that of right-handers.

Evidence from split brains

29. What are split brain patients, and what is the function of the corpus callosum?
30. What does research on people with split brains tell us about the differences between the cerebral hemispheres?

The normal brain: two modes of mental functioning

31. What are the two modes of mental functioning that some believe are associated with the right and left hemispheres? How has this notion been distorted in the process of popularization?
32. In what sense is the central nervous system organized in a "loose" hierarchy?

BUILDING BLOCKS OF THE NERVOUS SYSTEM: NEURONS AND NERVE IMPULSES

The neuron

33. What is a neuron? What are dendrites, the axon, the myelin sheath, and the nodes of Ranvier?
34. What purposes do the sensory neurons, motoneurons, and interneurons serve?

Glial cells: Unsung heroes of the nervous system

35. Describe the nature and function of glial cells.

How the nervous system makes its own circuitry

36. Appreciate the magnitude of the problem of ensuring appropriate connections of nerve cells in the brain during development, and indicate some of the processes that bring this about.

The electrical activity of the neuron

37. Be able to describe the electrical activity of the neuron: Know the difference between resting potential and action potential.
38. Describe the events involved in the reversal of membrane polarization.
39. How is the nerve impulse propagated? What is the role of myelin?
40. What is the all-or-none law?
41. What effect does stimulus intensity have on the number of neurons stimulated and on the frequency of impulses?

INTERACTION AMONG NERVE CELLS

The synapse

42. How did Sherrington infer the existence of the synapse?
43. Describe spatial and temporal summation and reciprocal inhibition.

The synaptic mechanism

44. Know the anatomy of the synapse (pre- and postsynaptic neurons and membranes, synaptic gaps, synaptic vesicles, and neurotransmitters) and the way that neural excitation (the nerve impulse) is transmitted across the synapse.
45. Be able to explain how inhibition and excitation occur at synapses, and how the postsynaptic neuron integrates the various inhibitory and excitatory effects on it. Describe synaptic reuptake.
46. What are the basic differences between action potentials and synaptic transmission?
47. What is a neurotransmitter? Give some examples.
48. What is the lock-and-key model?
49. Distinguish primary and secondary messengers in neural function.
50. What are the effects of some major neurotransmitters (acetylcholine, serotonin, dopamine, and norepinephrine)?
51. What are drugs called agonists and antagonists, and what are the different ways in which they can exert their effects?

INTERACTIONS THROUGH THE BLOODSTREAM

Blood circulation

52. Describe the circulation of blood to the brain, and the blood–brain barrier.

The endocrine system

53. Explain the mode of action of the endocrine system, and know the similarities and differences among the types of interaction and transmission in the nervous and endocrine systems.

RECOVERY FROM BRAIN INJURY

54. Indicate some of the general determinants of whether and how much recovery of function occurs.

Finding alternative strategies

55. Explain cognitive rehabilitation.

Neural substitution of function

56. Give examples from aphasia and the split brain about how intact areas take over the function of damaged areas.

Replacing connections

57. Describe collateral sprouting and the role of neurotrophic factors, such as nerve growth factors.
58. Describe the nature and course of Alzheimer's disease and its potential treatment with nerve grafts.
59. Indicate the potential of neural stem cell grafts, and recent progress in dealing with spinal cord injury.

Programmed Exercises

THE ORGANISM AS A MACHINE

1. The conception of organisms as machines can be traced to the great French philosopher _____.

   Descartes

2. According to Descartes, excitation from the senses leads to muscle contraction in what we now call a _____.

   reflex

HOW THE NERVOUS SYSTEM IS STUDIED

3. The individual nerve cells that collectively make up the nervous system are called _____.

   neurons

4. In the method of _____ _____, the symptoms of individual patients with brain damage are assessed.

   clinical observation

5. _____ techniques involve stimulating or inactivating parts of the nervous system.

   Invasive

6. Nervous tissue is damaged in a local area with the techniques of _____ and _____.

   lesioning, transection

7. Brain tissue near the scalp can be temporarily deactivated with brief magnetic pulses, in the technique of TMS, or _____ _____ _____.

   transcranial magnetic stimulation

8. The two principal ways of imaging the structure (anatomy) of the human brain are _____ _____ and _____.

   CT (CAT) scan, MRI

9. Brain electrical activity is measured directly with the _____.

   electroencephalogram

10. Brain activity can be measured by rate of uptake of different brain areas of a radioactive substance using the _____ scan. A less invasive technique measures metabolic activity in the brain revealed by exposing the brain to a varying strong magnetic field. This technique is called _____.

    PET

    fMRI

THE ARCHITECTURE OF THE NERVOUS SYSTEM

11. The production of a nervous system by processes of cellular signaling, differentiation, migration, and proliferation is called _____.

    neurogenesis

12. Early in evolutionary history, the cell bodies of many interneurons began to clump together to form _____. This is an early stage in the evolution of _____.

    ganglia, centralization

13. The development of the vertebrate nervous system proceeds from neural _____ to neural _____, and then to the three thickenings that form the _____, _____, and _____.

    plate
    tube, hindbrain
    midbrain, forebrain

14. The brain and spinal cord together make up the _____ _____ _____.

    central nervous system

15. Excitation of the left _____ _____ _____ will lead to movements of the right side of the body. This illustrates _____ control.

    primary motor area
    contralateral

16. The portion of the hindbrain concerned with controlling some critical body processes, such as respiration and heartbeat, is called the _____.

    medulla

17. The portion of the hindbrain that controls bodily balance and motor coordination is called the _____.

    cerebellum

18. In the brain anatomy, and in the hierarchical organization of action, the part of the brain that comes between the hindbrain and forebrain is called the _____.

    midbrain

19. The _____ is a part of the forebrain involved in the control of behavior patterns that stem from basic biological urges such as feeding.

    hypothalamus

20. An older portion of the cerebral hemispheres with particular importance in the mediation of emotional and motivational activities is called the _____ _____.

    limbic system

21. The _____ _____ are subcortical structures involved in movement regulation. Movement disorders such as tremors or jerky movements follow damage to this area, as in _____ diseases.

    basal ganglia

    Parkinson's (or Huntington's)

22. _____ nerves transmit information from sense organs to the central nervous system.   Afferent

23. _____ nerves transmit information from the central nervous system to the muscles and glands.   Efferent

24. _____ nerves connect the brain and the periphery.   Cranial

THE CORTEX

25. Label the four major lobes of the human cerebral cortex.

    A. _____   C. _____   A. frontal

    B. _____   D. _____   B. parietal

C. occipital

D. temporal

26. The structure labeled E is the _____ _____ .   E. lateral fissure

27. Label the following structures on the sketch of the human brain.

    A. _____   A. hindbrain (medulla)

    B. _____   B. cerebellum

    C. _____ _____   C. cerebral cortex

    D. _____ _____   D. corpus callosum

28. The idea and demonstration that different parts of the brain have different functions is called
_____ of function.   localization

29. In humans, the greatest amount of cortical space for motor functions is assigned to the
_____ and the _____ .   fingers, tongue

30. Each portion of the body surface is represented in the _____ _____ _____ ,   primary sensory areas
located primarily in the _____ lobe.   parietal

31. The portions of the cerebral cortex that are part of neither the primary motor nor the primary sensory
areas are described as the _____ or _____ areas.   nonprimary, association

32. _____ is a serious disturbance in the organization of voluntary action. 　　　　Apraxia

33. A disorganization of aspects of the sensory world, without loss of basic sensory capacities, is termed
_____. When this type of disorder primarily involves a deficit in face recognition, it is called
_____. 　　　　agnosia
　　　　prosopagnosia

34. A disorder of attention in which a patient ignores one side of his or her world and body is
called the _____ _____. 　　　　neglect syndrome

35. A patient with a primary disorder in the expression of speech can be described as suffering from
language apraxia, or a _____ _____. This disorder is commonly caused by
lesions in _____ area, in the _____ _____ lobe. 　　　　nonfluent aphasia
　　　　Broca's, left frontal

36. In right-handed persons, aphasia usually results from lesions in the _____ hemisphere. 　　　　left

37. A language defect reflected primarily by an inability to comprehend language, or a language agnosia,
is described as a _____ _____. The lesions responsible for this disorder commonly
occur in _____ area, located in the _____ _____ lobe. 　　　　fluent aphasia
　　　　Wernicke's, left
　　　　temporal

38. _____ is the term used to describe reading deficits. 　　　　Dyslexia

39. Difficulty in applying strategies, lack of spontaneity, and deficits in response inhibition characterize
patients with damage in the _____ area. In the past, certain mental disorders were "treated"
by separation of this area from the rest of the brain, in an operation called a _____
_____. 　　　　prefrontal
　　　　prefrontal
　　　　lobotomy

DO WE REALLY HAVE TWO BRAINS?

40. The asymmetry of function in the human cerebral cortex is described as _____. 　　　　lateralization

41. In terms of differences in function between left and right cerebral hemispheres, left-handers are
generally less _____ than right-handers are. 　　　　lateralized

42. A right-hander who, following a stroke, has great difficulty with spatial representation, maps, and
interpretation of complex drawings, probably has a lesion in the _____ hemisphere. 　　　　right

43. A split-brain patient is someone whose _____ _____ has been surgically severed. 　　　　corpus callosum

44. A right-handed split-brain patient would probably not be able to name a common object placed in his
or her _____ hand. 　　　　left

45. Many psychologists believe that _____ and _____ processes represent radically
different modes of thought, which reflect different clusters of intellectual functioning. To right-
handers they assign _____ processes to the left hemisphere and _____
processes to the right hemisphere. 　　　　verbal, spatial
　　　　verbal, spatial

46. Some psychologists believe that the left hemisphere is specialized for the organization of
_____, since such a function would be relevant to both _____ and _____
skills. They believe that the right hemisphere motor is specialized for the organization of
_____. 　　　　time, language, manual
　　　　space

BUILDING BLOCKS OF THE NERVOUS SYSTEM:
NEURONS AND NERVE IMPULSES

47. The basic building block of the nervous system is the nerve cell, or _____. 　　　　neuron

48. The basic unit of nervous function is the _____ _____. 　　　　nerve impulse

49. Label the following diagram of the neuron.

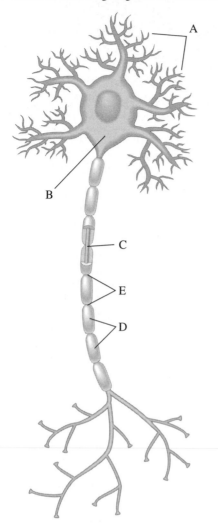

A. _____   dendrites

B. _____   cell body

C. _____   axon

D. _____ _____   myelin sheath

E. _____ _____ _____   nodes of Ranvier

50. Receptor cells _____ stimulus energy into nerve impulses.   transduce

51. The axons of _____ _____ terminate in effector cells and activate the _____ _____.   motor neurons, skeletal musculature (muscles)

52. In complex organisms, the vast majority of neurons are neither sensory nor motor, but rather , _____. Their connections form the _____ of the central nervous system.   interneurons, microcircuitry

53. The very numerous nervous system cells that form a scaffold for the system, and constitute the _____ sheath, are called _____ cells.   myelin, glial

54. The parts of the brain containing many myelinated axons are called _____ matter. The rest is called _____ matter.   white grey

55. The fine wire or tube that allows investigators to record electrical activity in neurons is called a(n) _____.   microelectrode

56. The _____ _____ of the neuron is about −70 millivolts.   resting potential

57. The reversal of polarization that passes along a nerve fiber when it is stimulated is called the _____ _____.   action potential

58. When the nerve cell membrane is depolarized past its _____ _____ by an _____ stimulus, a(n) _____ _____ results.   excitation threshold adequate, action potential

59. Ion _____ and ion _____ maintain the resting potential. The opening of the ion _____ is responsible for the sharp voltage change called the action potential.

    pumps, channels
    channels

60. The _____ speed of the nerve impulse would be relatively slow, except that _____ wrapped around the neuron allows the impulse to jump from one _____ _____ _____ to another.

    propagation, myelin
    node of
    Ranvier

61. The disease _____ _____ involves deterioration of the myelin surrounding neurons.

    multiple sclerosis

62. The _____-_____-_____ law states that the size of the action potential and its speed are independent of the intensity of the stimulus, provided the stimulus is above threshold intensity.

    all-or-none

63. The above-mentioned law does not apply to the stimulation of nerves since there is much variation in the _____ of the neurons in the nerve.

    thresholds

64. Stimulus _____ is conveyed both by increases in the number of neurons firing and by increases in individual neurons' _____ of firing.

    intensity
    frequency

INTERACTION AMONG NERVE CELLS

65. The gap between the axon terminals of one neuron and the dendritic processes of another is called the _____.

    synapse

66. The existence of the synapse was inferred from evidence at the level of _____ by the great English physiologist _____.

    behavior
    (Sir Charles)
    Sherrington

67. Sherrington studied simple _____ in the _____ animal.

    reflexes, spinal

68. Subthreshold stimulation at two adjacent points, when applied simultaneously, may lead to a response. This illustrates the phenomenon of _____ _____.

    spatial summation

69. Subthreshold stimulation, when applied a few times in rapid succession, may lead to a response. This illustrates the phenomenon of _____ _____.

    temporal summation

70. Sherrington observed that when a flexor muscle contracts, the corresponding extensor relaxes. This is an example of _____ _____.

    reciprocal inhibition

71. Electrical activity is transmitted across the synapse by neurotransmitters, from the _____ neuron to the _____ neuron.

    presynaptic,
    postsynaptic

72. The synaptic vesicles contain chemical substances called _____.

    neurotransmitters

73. Label this diagram of a synapse.

    A. presynaptic
       membrane
    B. postsynaptic
       membrane
    C. synaptic vesicle
    D. synaptic gap (or
       synapse)

74. According to Sherrington, temporal summation occurs because of integration at the _____, which is accomplished by "storage" of excitation from previous stimulation.

    synapse

75. Whether a neuron fires or not is determined by the net result of its integration of _____ and _____ stimulation.

excitatory
inhibitory

76. The activity of the postsynaptic neuron results from the summation of _____ and _____ postsynaptic potentials. These are produced by _____ liberated by firing of the presynaptic neuron.

inhibitory
excitatory,
neurotransmitters

77. While action potentials are all-or-none, synaptic potentials are _____.

graded

78. Inhibitory neurotransmitters _____ the nerve's resting potential, whereas excitatory neurotransmitters _____ it.

increase
decrease

79. Excitatory neurotransmitters open _____ channels in the postsynaptic membrane.

ion (sodium)

80. Neurotransmitters are eventually removed from the synaptic gap by deactivation or by _____ _____.

synaptic
uptake

81. The idea that neurotransmitters affect only the postsynaptic membrane if their shape fits the shape of certain receptor sites on that membrane is called the _____-_____-_____ model.

lock-and-key

82. Acetylcholine, dopamine, serotonin, and norepinephrine are all _____.

neurotransmitters

83. Neurotransmitters secreted by the presynaptic cell are called _____ messengers. Chemical processes in the postsynaptic cell that regulate its sensitivity are called _____ messengers.

primary
secondary

84. There is evidence that some neurons interact more directly than through neurotransmitters, by transmission across very narrow _____ synapses.

electrical

85. Drugs that enhance a transmitter's activity are called _____. Drugs that impede a transmitter's activity are called _____.

agonists
antagonists

86. Some drugs enhance synaptic function by interfering with _____ by the presynaptic cell. Some drugs act by altering the levels of substances called _____, which are required for the synthesis of particular neurotransmitters.

reuptake
precursors

87. Drugs of "abuse" may act by their involvement with brain neurotransmitter systems. Thus, heroin is an agonist for the brain _____ system, and marijuana activates _____ receptors.

endorphin, cannabinoid

INTERACTIONS THROUGH THE BLOODSTREAM

88. The brain gets special protection from potential toxins in the blood through the action of the _____-_____ _____.

blood-brain barrier

89. The _____ glands secrete _____ into the bloodstream.

endocrine, hormones

90. _____ are chemical messengers that are distributed indiscriminately throughout the body, whereas _____ exert their effects in a very limited area.

Hormones
neurotransmitters

RECOVERY FROM BRAIN INJURY

91. Recovery, within the nervous system, from loss of cerebral nerve cells can occur by the processes of recovery of _____ _____, _____ _____, and _____ _____ _____.

damaged neurons,
collateral sprouting
substitution of function

92. The brain's capacity to recover, generally greater in younger people, is called its _____..

plasticity

93. Three new methods for producing repair in the damaged nervous system are _____ . transplants, administration of _____ factors, or injection of neural _____ cells.

fetal
neurotrophic, stem

94. Three modes of recovery from cerebral brain damage are _____, _____, _____.

finding alternative
strategies (cognitive
rehabilitation), neural
substitution of
functions, replacing
connections (or
neurons)

95. A rather common disease of the elderly involving a general decline in intellectual functioning is _____ disease. One of the pathological features of brain anatomy in these patients is _____ _____ .

Alzheimer's

neurofibrillary tangles (or amyloid plaques)

96. Brain _____ involving fetal brain tissue of rats have had some success and hold the promise of replacing cells lost in _____ disease.

transplants
Alzheimer's

Self-Test

1. Which of the following commonly observed characteristics of human or animal behavior goes counter to Descartes' reflex notion?
   a. the withdrawal response upon touching a hot object
   b. the appearance of a behavior (e.g., running) in the absence of any obvious stimulus
   c. the existence of nerves connecting receptors and effectors to the brain
   d. the repeatability of reflexes
   e. none of the above

2. By viewing animal behavior as the result of a machine's responding to external stimuli, Descartes made the claim that
   a. animal behavior is governed by physical laws and is therefore predictable.
   b. animal behavior can be understood only in terms of the hierarchical organization of the nervous system.
   c. animals must have rich mental lives.
   d. neither humans nor animals have free will.
   e. introductory psychology is *the* fundamental science.

3. Clinical observation has the following advantage(s) over other techniques for investigating the human brain:
   a. It is replicable.
   b. It can measure the activity of the brain.
   c. It can control precisely the area of the brain that is damaged.
   d. It allows for detailed analysis of symptoms produced by specific brain damage in an individual.
   e. It is more invasive.

4. Which of the following brain exploration techniques can be described as destroying nervous tissue?
   a. transection
   b. TMS
   c. MRI
   d. EEG
   e. CT (CAT) scan

5. In terms of providing information about structure versus activity, EEG is to CAT scan as
   a. PET scan is to fMRI.
   b. EEG is to PET scan.
   c. lesioning is to MRI.
   d. transection is to PET scan.
   e. fMRI is to MRI.

6. Which of the following procedures would you most prefer to experience, assuming your brain was normal and your aim was to keep it that way?
   a. transection
   b. lesioning
   c. EEG
   d. PET scan
   e. c or d

7. Assume a patient is suspected of having brain seizures (uncontrollable activity in some part of the brain). Which brain exploration technique(s) would be most likely to reveal the affected brain area?
   a. EEG
   b. CAT scan
   c. fMRI
   d. a and b
   e. a and c

8. Thousands of genes program the development of the human nervous system containing billions of neurons. Which of the following help to make this possible?
   a. interactions between genes
   b. genes turning on and off
   c. Genes only set up guidelines for the structures.
   d. all of the above
   e. none of the above

9. Neuron is to ganglion as
   a. brain is to hierarchical organization.
   b. ganglion is to brain.
   c. excitation is to inhibition.
   d. synapse is to neurotransmitter.
   e. dentist is to pain.

10. Match the structure on the left with its associated function on the right
    i. medulla   a. respiration and heartbeat
    ii. cerebellum   b. basic biological urges
    iii. hypothalamus   c. balance and motor coordination

    i. _____
    ii. _____
    iii. _____

11. Which of the following statements is *not* true of the limbic system?
    a. It is a subcortical structure.
    b. It is anatomically associated with the hypothalamus.
    c. It is present on both sides of the brain.
    d. It is involved in the control of emotional and motivational activities.
    e. It integrates the functions of the cerebral hemispheres.

12. In which of the following sequences are the main divisions of the central nervous system arranged in ascending order?
    a. peripheral, somatic, autonomic
    b. cerebellum, integration centers, transmission tracts
    c. spinal cord, autonomic system, brain
    d. spinal cord, basal ganglia, hypothalamus
    e. spinal cord, brain stem, cerebral hemispheres

13. The lobes of the cerebral hemisphere are
    a. frontal, parietal, occipital, temporal.
    b. hindbrain, midbrain, forebrain.
    c. limbic system, corpus callosum, cerebral cortex.
    d. Each cerebral hemisphere is a single lobe of the cerebral cortex.
    e. none of the above

14. What part of an elephant might you expect to have a particularly large representation in the motor homunculus?
    a. the ears
    b. the front legs
    c. the back legs
    d. the trunk
    e. the eyes

15. Following a stroke, a patient shows grossly diminishing sensitivity to touch and other stimulation in the right hand and arm. The probable site of the lesion is
    a. the motor homunculus.
    b. the left somatosensory area.
    c. the right somatosensory area.
    d. the left frontal area.
    e. the right frontal area.

16. A disorder in the organization of voluntary movement is called
    a. agnosia.
    b. aphasia.
    c. apraxia.
    d. amenorrhea.
    e. none of the above

17. A person exhibiting an inability to coordinate the separate details of the visual world into a whole suffers from
    a. visual agnosia.
    b. receptive aphasia.
    c. a lesion in Broca's area.
    d. a lesion in Wernicke's area.
    e. visual apraxia.

18. A patient with the neglect syndrome and damage to her right parietal area looks straight at the X in the figure below. She is asked how many dots she sees. The answer we would expect is

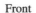

    a. 1.
    b. 2.
    c. 3.
    d. 4.
    e. 5.

19. Just as a fluent aphasia can be described as a language agnosia, a nonfluent aphasia can be described as
    a. a fluent dyslexia.
    b. a language neglect.
    c. a language apraxia.
    d. a language deficit.
    e. none of the above

20. Apraxia, neglect syndrome, and nonfluent and fluent aphasia have in common
    a. lesions in the same brain area.
    b. basic sensory and motor functions that are intact.
    c. some deficit in voluntary motor function.
    d. a and b
    e. a and c

21. Damage in a left-handed person in the language center often has less drastic consequences than in a right-handed person because
    a. left-handers are slower to develop language functions.
    b. recovery is more rapid in the left hemisphere in left-handers.
    c. the hemispheres are not as functionally lateralized in left-handers.
    d. highly developed visual-spatial abilities compensate for language loss.
    e. a and d

22. Afferent input from the right hand projects primarily to the left hemisphere whereas the left hand projects primarily to the right hemisphere. In an average right-handed, split-brain patient, which hand would the patient have to use to handle an unseen object in order to name it?
    a. the left hand
    b. the right hand
    c. Neither hand could do it.
    d. Both hands could do it equally well.
    e. A split-brian patient cannot name any objects.

23. A right-handed person has lost the entire projection area of his left occipital cortex, as shown below, but is otherwise normal. Which of the following deficits would you expect?

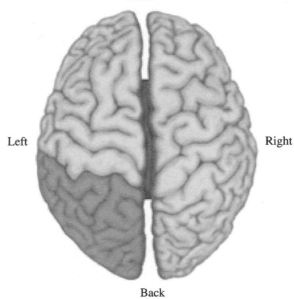

    a. loss of the right side of his visual field
    b. loss of the left side of his visual field
    c. inability to produce speech despite ability to understand it
    d. inability to understand speech despite the ability to produce it
    e. inability to read

24. The same person referred to in the previous question suffers an additional defect: his corpus callosum is completely cut. What is the extent of his deficit?
    a. inability to produce or understand speech
    b. inability to produce speech despite understanding it
    c. inability to understand speech despite the ability to produce it
    d. inability to read
    e. visual agnosia

25. In which of the following tasks would you expect superior performance from the left hemisphere of a right-hander?
    a. matching paint colors
    b. recognizing faces
    c. remembering a series of movements to be performed in a specific order
    d. drawing the floor plan of a familiar house
    e. all of the above

26. Theories of lateralization hold that for right-handers, the left hemisphere is more involved with _____, and the right hemisphere is more involved with _____.
    a. spatial material, verbal material
    b. organization in time, organization in space
    c. PET scans, CAT scans
    d. visual perception, auditory perception
    e. a and d

27. Which of the following is *not* part of an individual neuron?
    a. axon
    b. myelin sheath
    c. synapse
    d. dendrite
    e. cell body

28. Receptor cells
    a. are always a specialized part of sensory neurons.
    b. transduce physical stimuli into neural impulses.
    c. are responsible for the conduction of optic stimuli.
    d. a and b
    e. b and c

29. Which of the following properties is (are) characteristic of interneurons?
    a. They usually show much branching of dendrites.
    b. They form the microcircuitry of the central nervous system.
    c. They comprise the majority of neurons.
    d. all of the above
    e. none of the above

30. When graphed over time, the complex electrical event known as the action potential looks something like which of these diagrams?

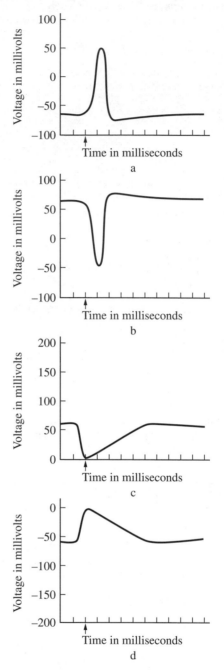

e.   none of the above

31. The all-or-none law states that
    a. the threshold of a single neuron is a property that alternates between two extreme values but never has any of the values in between.
    b. reflexes cannot involve just the spinal cord; the entire nervous system must respond by generating a central excitatory state.
    c. an axon terminal releases a chemical substance, called a neurotransmitter, when an action potential arrives.
    d. the frequency of spikes in an individual nerve fiber increases with the number of action potentials per unit of time.
    e. once a stimulus exceeds the threshold of an individual neuron, further increases in stimulation intensity make no difference in the height and form of the action potential generated.

32. The all-or-none action potential is
    a. accompanied by depolarization of the nerve membrane.
    b. accompanied by opening of the sodium channels in the membrane.
    c. propagated from one part of the membrane to another.
    d. all of the above
    e. none of the above

33. How can the nervous system represent increase in the intensity of a *stimulus*?
    a. by an increase in the size of the action potential in every neuron fired by the stimulus
    b. by an increase in the number of neurons being fired by the stimulus
    c. by an increase in the frequency of firing in the neurons fired by the stimulus
    d. b and c
    e. a and c

34. Sherrington used a spinal animal in order to
    a. eliminate inhibition.
    b. simplify the system he was studying.
    c. take advantage of brain modulation in neural activity in the spinal cord.
    d. study the irreversibility of conduction.
    e. cut expenses.

35. From his observations of temporal and spatial summation in reflexes, Sherrington inferred the existence of
    a. receptors.
    b. inhibition.
    c. the synapse.
    d. disinhibition.
    e. the simple reflex.

36. Consider this example: brief strong stimulation of a receptor produces no movement, but a longer period of stimulation causes a particular muscle to stop contracting. These results could most easily be explained by the principles of
    a. excitation and inhibition.
    b. inhibition and spatial summation.
    c. all-or-none law and inhibition.
    d. temporal summation, spatial summation, and the all-or-none law.
    e. inhibition and temporal summation.

37. Sherrington reported that the time (reflex latency) between stimulation of a reflex and the reflex response was much longer than the time it would take for an action potential to go from the receptor to the muscle. This "delay" could be accounted for in terms of
    a. inhibition.
    b. excitation.
    c. spatial summation.
    d. the time for depolarization of the axon membrane.
    e. the time for the neurotransmitter to cross the synaptic gap and stimulate the postsynaptic neuron.

38. Axon conduction resembles synaptic transmission in that
    a. both involve neurotransmitters.
    b. both are about the same speed.
    c. both are all-or-none.
    d. all of the above
    e. none of the above

39. Many neurons fire action potentials at a moderate rate even when they are not receiving synaptic excitation from presynaptic neurons. This is called spontaneous activity. Which plot indicates what would happen to the firing rate of such a neuron if it was first exposed to synaptic inhibition and then synaptic excitation?

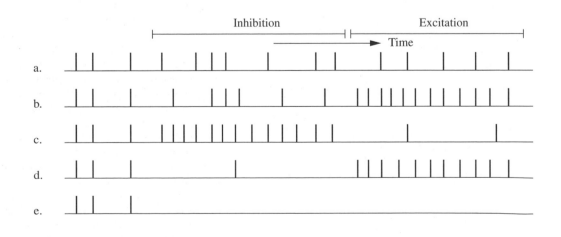

40. Both excitatory neurotransmitters and above-threshold depolarization of axons
    a. open ion channels.
    b. produce synaptic delay.
    c. explain temporal summation.
    d. all of the above
    e. none of the above

41. The lock-and-key model accounts for
    a. the existence of neurotransmitters.
    b. the summation of excitation and inhibition in postsynaptic neurons.
    c. the fact that specific neurotransmitters stimulate specific postsynaptic neurons.
    d. the release of neurotransmitters from synaptic vesicles.
    e. the all-or-none law

42. A new drug is found to increase arousal. All but one of the following are possible modes of action of that drug. Which is *not*?
    a. blocks reuptake of dopamine
    b. increases availability of norepinephrine
    c. blocks the enzyme that breaks down dopamine at the synapse
    d. mimics the effect of norepinephrine
    e. blocks the postsynaptic receptor for norepinephrine

43. Hormones and neurotransmitters are both
    a. secreted only by endocrine glands.
    b. secreted into the bloodstream.
    c. chemical messengers.
    d. all of the above
    e. none of the above

44. Recovery from cerebral damage occurs in a number of ways. Which of the following actually involves addition of new nerve cells to the damaged brain?
    a. transplantation of fetal nerve tissue
    b. rehabilitation
    c. collateral sprouting
    d. substitution of function
    e. all of the above

45. A person has a stroke that results in paralysis of the left side of his body. With no treatment except for rest, he makes a complete recovery. Possible accounts for this recovery are
    a. cognitive rehabilitation.
    b. collateral sprouting.
    c. fetal brain transplant.
    d. injection of nerve stem cells.
    e. none of the above

46. Which of the following is *not* a feature of Alzheimer's disease?
    a. decline in cognitive function
    b. neurofibrillary tangles
    c. amyloid plaques
    d. absence of brain neurotrophic factor
    e. onset typically after age 65

Answer Key for Self-Test

1.	b	24.	d
2.	a	25.	c
3.	d	26.	b
4.	a	27.	c
5.	e	28.	b
6.	c	29.	d
7.	e	30.	a
8.	d	31.	e
9.	b	32.	d
10.	i. a, ii. c, iii. b	33.	d
11.	e	34.	b
12.	e	35.	c
13.	a	36.	e
14.	d	37.	e
15.	b	38.	e
16.	c	39.	d
17.	a	40.	a
18.	c	41.	c
19.	c	42.	e
20.	b	43.	c
21.	c	44.	a
22.	b	45.	b
23.	a	46.	d

Investigating Psychological Phenomena

SPEED OF THE NERVE IMPULSE: THE USE OF REACTION TIME IN THE MEASUREMENT OF A PSYCHOLOGICAL PROCESS

Equipment: A stopwatch that indicates seconds
Number of participants: Five
Time per participant: Fifteen minutes (all participants are involved at the same time)
Time for experimenter: Twenty-five minutes

One of the great stumbling blocks to advances in theory about psychological processes was the belief that thought, and hence nervous impulses, occurred instantaneously or nearly so. In fact, the German physiologist Johannes P. Müller (1801–1858) once estimated that the speed of the nerve impulse was eleven million miles per second. Naturally, this claim that nerve impulses travel at an immeasurably fast rate discouraged scientific research on the physiology of the nervous system and encouraged mystical or dualistic interpretations of mind. It also discouraged study of the speed of various mental activities, research that is today an important cornerstone of the field of cognitive psychology.

In 1850, Herman Ludwig Ferdinand von Helmholtz (1821–1894) succeeded in measuring the speed of the nerve impulse and found it to be much slower than previously believed, between fifty and one hundred meters per second in humans. This finding was followed by intensive investigation of the nervous system within the framework of the physical and biological sciences. It also opened the door to the use of reaction time as a tool in the study of thought processes. This experiment is an attempt to familiarize you with the general logic used by a psychologist who is interested in measuring the speed of a psychological event that cannot be directly observed. To accomplish this, you must first understand the experiment that Helmholtz performed and also how his experimental technique can be applied to the measurement of the speed of the nerve impulse in humans.

Helmholtz's technique was quite simple. He first dissected out a muscle and an attached nerve fiber from a frog's leg. The experiment then consisted of stimulating the nerve at various distances from the muscle and measuring the length of time between nerve stimulation and muscle contraction. First, he electrically stimulated the nerve close to the point at which it was attached to the muscle, then he stimulated the nerve farther from this point of attachment. He found that the second reaction time (i.e., the time between stimulation and contraction) was longer than the first. To obtain an estimate of nerve impulse speed, he used a simple bit of reasoning: the difference in time between the two measurements must correspond to the time it takes the impulse to travel the distance between the two points of stimulation (see figure). Hence, the distance between the points of stimulation divided by the time *difference* between the conditions of stimulating close to the muscle versus stimulating farther away should yield an estimate of nerve impulse speed. This is how he obtained his estimate of fifty to one hundred meters per second. Let A and B be two points of stimulation, M be the point at which the nerve connects to the muscle, t_A be the time to contraction from stimulation at A, and t_B, the time to contraction from stimulation at B.

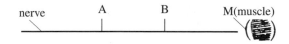

Then $\frac{(A \text{ to } M) - (B \text{ to } M)}{t_A - t_B}$ = speed of nerve impulse.

Happily, Helmholtz's estimate can be demonstrated in humans without resorting to dissection. You might suppose that the simplest way to do this would be to perform the following sort of experiment: stimulate someone on the ankle (e.g., by pinching) and have the participant respond by pushing a button as soon as he or she feels the stimulation. With a good timer, you could then measure the time between stimulation and depression of the button. To estimate nerve conduction time, you would then measure the total distance between ankle and brain, and between brain and finger, add the two together, and divide this number by the participant's reaction time. But there are complications that make this procedure unsuitable. Part of the reaction time, for example, would be due to the length of time it took the participant to decide to press the button, a figure that is obviously more than simply nerve impulse time. From the point of view of processes in the nervous system, the reaction time includes the time to cross synapses as well as axon conduction time. In short, total reaction time is a confounded measure.

Thus, the experiment must be made more complicated. Using Helmholtz's logic, one could measure not only the time between ankle stimulation and response, but also between, say, upper arm stimulation and response. The ankle condition should result in a longer reaction time than the upper arm condition. The difference between these reaction times corresponds to the time it takes for the nerve impulse to travel a distance equal to the difference between the ankle and the finger, and the upper arm and the finger. Notice that this difference excludes any time due to such things as decision-making processes. So the nerve conduction time can be estimated by subtracting the distance of the upper arm to the brain from the distance of the ankle to the brain (the distance from the brain to the finger is constant) and dividing by the reaction time difference.

In practice, the reaction time for either stimulating the ankle or stimulating the upper arm is quite small, and hence a clock that measures time in hundredths of a second would be needed to measure it. This problem can be solved by adding together the reaction time of several people; after obtaining the total time, simply dividing this by the number of people would give the average individual time. This general mass reaction time technique will be used to measure the speed of the nerve impulse. Perform the nerve impulse speed experiment in the following way:

Get five people to participate. Have them form a circle with each person very loosely clasping the ankle of his or her neighbor to the right. Tell participants to squeeze the ankle they are holding when they feel their ankle squeezed. Be sure the participants' eyes are closed during all trials. You can then start the experiment by squeezing one person's ankle and simultaneously noting the time on a second hand of a watch. Now watch the ankle that you squeezed. When you see it squeezed for the fifth time (excluding your initial squeeze) note the time that elapsed. Repeat this procedure for a total of five times, each time recording the time in the spaces provided in Part I of the answer sheet (record results to an accuracy of .1 second).

Next have everyone in the circle release the ankle he or she is holding and grasp the upper arm, *just below the shoulder* of the person to the right. You run another five trials exactly as you did for the ankle trials, each time recording the time in Part II of the answer sheet.

You will probably note that the total reaction time dropped within each set of five trials. Why? The last two to three trials probably yielded about the same values.

These ten trials serve as practice: The group of five participants and the measurer "learn" in some general way to do this task efficiently. Having completed practice, you are now ready to begin the measurement of the speed of the nerve impulse. Run four more trials as before, the first and fourth with ankle stimulation, the second and third with upper arm. This will generate two ankle and two upper arm mass reaction times (record these in Part III of the data sheet).

Each reaction time represents the sum of twenty-five reaction times (five participants, five times each). Obtain the average individual reaction time by dividing the total reaction times by twenty-five. Now average the two ankle reaction times and separately, the two upper arm reaction times. Subtract the average arm time from the average ankle time. This is the amount of time it takes the impulse to go the extra distance from the ankle to the level of the shoulder. To calculate the speed of the nerve impulse, you must estimate the magnitude of this distance (in meters).

Measure the distance for the third tallest person in your group of five participants. Measure the distance from the ankle to the base of the neck and from the upper arm to the base of the neck. Take the difference between the numbers, divide by the time difference, and you will have an estimate of the speed of the nerve impulse. How does it compare with Helmholtz's estimate? (Helmholtz estimated a speed of from 50 to 100 meters per second. Modern measurements range from 6 to 122 meters per second, depending on the type of nerve fiber.) *(If your instructor collects the data, fill out the report sheet in Appendix 2.)*

FURTHER EXPERIMENTS

Now that you have calculated an estimate of the speed of the nerve impulse, you might want to test whether some fairly common variables will affect this speed. Consider fatigue, for instance. If a person is tired, does his or her nerve impulse speed slow down? To test this, design your own experiment, using the same measurement technique you used to get your main estimate of nerve impulse speed. To test whether fatigue has an effect, measure the speed both at a time when participants are well rested and at a time when the same participants are tired (e.g., in the morning and at night, or before and after exercise). Does fatigue affect nerve impulse speed? Note that given the way the estimate is obtained, it is possible to find that fatigue may well slow down reaction time in general, yet have no effect on the speed of the nerve impulse.

Can you think of other variables that might affect (speed up or slow down) nerve impulse speed? If so, design experiments to test your hypotheses.

REPORT SHEET

Practice   Time in seconds*

Part I   Trial 1 ankle = _____

               Trial 2 ankle = _____

               Trial 3 ankle = _____

               Trial 4 ankle = _____

               Trial 5 ankle = _____

Part II   Trial 1 upper arm = _____

               Trial 2 upper arm = _____

               Trial 3 upper arm = _____

               Trial 4 upper arm = _____

               Trial 5 upper arm = _____

Test

Part III   Trial 1 ankle time = _____

$\div 25 =$ _____ (a)

               Trial 2 upper arm time = _____

$\div 25 =$ _____ (b)

               Trial 3 upper arm time = _____

$\div 25 =$ _____ (c)

               Trial 4 ankle time = _____

$\div 25 =$ _____ (d)

$\dfrac{a + d}{2} =$ _____ (average ankle time)

$\dfrac{b + c}{2} =$ _____ (average upper arm time)

Average ankle time – average upper arm time = _____ (difference 1)

(1) Distance of ankle to base of neck

     (for third tallest person) = _____

(2) Distance of upper arm to base of neck

     (for third tallest person) = _____

     Distance 1 – distance 2 = _____ (difference 2)

$\dfrac{\text{difference 2}}{\text{difference 1}} =$ (speed of nerve impulse)

*Record time accurate to .1 second.

CHAPTER 3

Motivation

Learning Objectives

1. Describe the organization of individual motives into those that are biological or social, or those that serve self-regulation, self-preservation, and self-restoration.
2. Indicate the relation between potentiation and motivation.

MOTIVATION AS DIRECTED ACTION

3. Can directed action be reconciled with Descartes' notion of humans and animals as reflex machines?

Control systems

4. Describe the action of negative and positive feedback systems. Give examples of negative and positive feedback systems from modern technology.

Homeostasis

5. What is homeostasis?

TEMPERATURE REGULATION

6. Distinguish endotherms and ectotherms.

Temperature control by internal adjustment

7. Know how reflexes and behavior function to maintain body temperature. Define setpoint.

Temperature control by externally directed behavior

8. Provide examples of how behavior affects body temperature.

The autonomic nervous system and temperature control

9. Describe the way the two branches of the autonomic nervous system function in temperature regulation.

Sensing the internal environment: the hypothalamus

10. Describe how the hypothalamus is involved in thermoregulation.
11. Describe parallels between thermoregulation and water regulation.

HUNGER

Body weight, nutrition, and energy

12. What is the evidence indicating that animals regulate calorie (energy) intake? What is basal metabolic rate?

The signals for feeding

13. Indicate the internal and external signals that influence hunger and satiety.

14. Contrast signals that indicate short-term (e.g., stomach) and long-term (e.g., adipose tissue) needs for food.
15. What evidence makes it likely that animals and humans stop eating in anticipation of the arrival of sufficient nutrients in the cells?

Hypothalamic control centers

16. Describe the role of the hypothalamus in feeding.
17. What is the dual-center theory? What are the main lines of evidence for and against it?
18. Review evidence that the hypothalamus is involved in the control of feeding (e.g., orexins) but that other brain areas are also involved (e.g., neuropeptide Y studies).

Obesity

19. Discuss the definition, incidence, and disadvantages of obesity.
20. Indicate bodily factors that may contribute to obesity, and review genetic evidence that establishes a role for bodily factors.
21. What aspects of obesity can the setpoint hypothesis explain?
22. What are the major modes of treatment of obesity?
23. Review the success of treatments for obesity. What are some factors that interfere with treatment success?
24. Is being overweight a disorder? What are its health and social consequences?

Anorexia nervosa

25. Describe the symptoms and possible causes of anorexia nervosa.
26. Describe and evaluate possible biological and psychological causes of anorexia nervosa.
27. Why do some think there is a relation between anorexia and obsessive-compulsive disorder?

Bulimia nervosa

28. Describe the symptoms of bulimia nervosa, and contrast it with anorexia nervosa.

THREAT

29. Evaluate the relevance of homeostasis and potentiation to fear and rage.

Threat and the autonomic nervous system

30. What are the functions of the parasympathetic and sympathetic systems?

The emergency reaction
31. Describe the emergency reaction. What role does the sympathetic arousal system play in the flight-or-fight response? Understand the biological survival value of the emergency reaction.

Disruptive effects of autonomic arousal
32. Describe the immediate disruptive effects of sympathetic arousal, and possible long-term effects on health.

PAIN

Pain as an aid to survival
33. Describe the adaptive value of pain. What are the consequences of inability to feel pain?

Pain relief through endorphins
34. What is the role of the endorphins in producing analgesia?

SEX
35. Explain the fundamental motivational difference between sex and hunger, thirst or thermoregulation.

Hormones and animal sexuality
36. Describe the mammalian female hormonal cycle.
37. Indicate how sex hormones affect behavior, and the role of the hypothalamus.
38. Illustrate how behavior affects hormones.

Hormone and human sexuality
39. Indicate how sex hormone effects are different in humans.

The phases of the human sexual response
40. Describe the phases of the human sexual response.
41. Describe orgasm or the role of oxytocin

The function of the orgasm
42. What is the function of the orgasm for males and for females?

SLEEP AND WAKING

Waking
43. Describe the role of subcortical and cortical areas in wakefulness.

Sleep and physiological activity
44. Describe the EEG and its relation to sleep.

The stages of sleep
45. Be able to describe the stages of sleep and the two kinds of sleep.

Sleep and biological rhythms
46. Indicate the evidence for circadian rhythms and melatonin in the sleep-waking cycle.

The functions of sleep
47. What are the effects of sleep deprivation? What is known about the functions of sleep and the determinants of the sleep cycle?

Dreams
48. What is the relation between REM sleep and dreaming?
49. Discuss whether dreaming has a function, and if so, what it might be. What is the activation-synthesis hypothesis?

WHAT DIFFERENT MOTIVES HAVE IN COMMON

Arousal and the psychology of reward
50. Describe Hull's theory of drive reduction. Be able to criticize this theory and present evidence that people prefer an arousal level above zero.
51. Explain how drugs can be used to manipulate arousal. Give examples of depressant and stimulant drugs, and contrast the effects of these two types of drugs.
52. Describe drug addiction and the phenomena of tolerance withdrawal and lack of control.

The biology of reward
53. Describe the phenomenon of electrical stimulation of the brain, and its relation to the idea of pleasure centers in the brain.

The dopamine hypothesis of reward and drug effects
54. Explain the dopamine hypothesis of reward, and indicate how it may account for the rewarding effects of stimulant drugs.

Programmed Exercises

1. Hunger is a _____ motive in contrast to the need for friendship, which is a _____ motive. — biological / social

2. Temperature maintenance, hunger, and thirst involve motives aimed at self-_____. Fear and rage are associated with motives of self-_____, whereas sleep is directed at self-_____. — regulation / preservation, restoration

3. Motives increase the tendency to perform specific groups of behaviors. This tendency is sometimes called _____. — potentiation

MOTIVATION AS DIRECTED ACTION

4. In _____ _____ systems, the feedback strengthens the initial behavior. — positive feedback

5. In a _____ _____ system, the feedback stops, or even reverses, the original behavior. — negative feedback

6. The maintenance of a stable equilibrium in the body is called _____. — homeostasis

TEMPERATURE REGULATION

7. As opposed to _____, _____ can control their temperature internally.   ectotherms, endotherms

8. Vasoconstriction and piloerection are two forms of _____ responses to _____ in body temperature.   reflexive, decreases

9. Voluntary and reflexive heat-loss responses are brought into play when the body temperature drops below a temperature standard determined internally, which is called the _____.   setpoint

10. The autonomic nervous system sends its commands to _____ and _____ _____.   glands, smooth muscles

11. The _____ and _____ divisions of the autonomic nervous system work in opposite directions to control temperature. The _____ division acts to generate heat, to counteract low temperatures.   sympathetic, parasympathetic, sympathetic

12. The control of body temperature is called _____.   thermoregulation

13. The part of the brain that is most involved in thermoregulation is called the _____.   hypothalamus

HUNGER

14. The fact that animals increase intake of foods that are diluted with nonnutritive substances suggests that they regulate _____.   calories (energy)

15. Basal _____ _____ refers to the body's expenditure of energy to maintain basic body and cell functions.   metabolic rate

16. Receptors sensitive to the metabolic state (energy need) of the organism have been postulated to exist in the _____ and _____.   liver, brain

17. These receptors respond to blood levels of the basic source of short-term energy, which is _____. The liver controls the level of blood_____ by reversibly converting it to the stored animal starch, _____.   glucose, glucose glucogen

18. Satiety signals also originate in the gastrointestinal system, from nutrient receptors in the _____, and as a result of release of _____ when food passes into the duodenum.   stomach, CCK

19. The brain may also be informed about the state of long-term energy stores (fat) in the body, by detecting the level of _____, secretion of _____ cells, in the blood.   leptin, adipose

20. _____ stimuli, like the attractiveness of food, can influence the amount ingested, but their effectiveness depends in part on the _____ state of the organism.   External internal (metabolic)

21. The dual-center theory is supported by the fact that lesions in the lateral hypothalamus produce _____ eating, while lesions in the ventromedial hypothalamus produce _____ eating.   less, more

22. The ventromedial hypothalamus affects eating directly, but also indirectly by affecting _____ storage.   fat

23. In favor of hypothalamic control of eating, neurochemicals called _____ are secreted by the lateral hypothalamus and initiate eating.   orexins

24. However, the potent appetite stimulant _____ _____ seems to act outside of the hypothalamus.   neuropeptide Y (NPY)

25. One nonpsychological difference among people that can affect obesity involves _____ "efficiency."   metabolic (digestive)

26. The high resemblance in obesity and body distribution of fat in _____ _____ argues for a _____ determinant of obesity.   identical twins genetic

27. Obese people may have, on the average, higher _____ than the rest of the population.   setpoints

28. A justification of getting treatment for obesity is that thinner people are more attractive, and hence are more _____ successful. There are also _____ benefits for not being very obese.   socially, health (medical)

29. Treatments for obesity include _____, _____, and _____.   psychotherapy, drugs, surgery

30. _____ _____ is an eating disorder characterized by extreme and self-imposed underweight.　Anorexia nervosa

31. Genetic evidence and some resemblance in symptoms suggests a relation between anorexia nervosa and _____-_____ disorder.　obsessive-compulsive

32. _____ _____ is an eating disorder characterized by repeated binge and purge bouts, but with roughly normal weight.　Bulimia nervosa

THREAT

33. The parasympathetic system handles the _____ functions of the body.　vegetative

34. The sympathetic system has an _____ function.　activating

35. Sympathetic action is supported or amplified by the secretion of the hormone _____ (or _____).　adrenaline epinephrine

36. The emergency reaction results from activation of the _____ nervous system.　sympathetic

37. _____ arousal can have disruptive effects, which, if maintained, can compromise health.　Autonomic (or Sympathetic)

PAIN

38. _____ can trigger fear and rage, and serves as an indicator that something is wrong or damaged.　Pain

39. Reduced feeling of pain, or _____, is produced by secretion of opiatelike substances in the brain called _____.　analgesia endorphins

SEX

40. Except for primates, mammals mate only when the female is in "heat" or _____.　estrus

41. The most important hormones involved in the mammalian female reproductive cycle are _____ and _____.　estrogen progesterone

42. Implantations of male hormone, that is, _____, into the part of the brain called the _____, can cause a castrated male animal to show male sexual behavior.　testosterone hypothalamus

43. Although the biological aspects of the human female reproductive cycle are controlled by hormones, in the human female, _____ _____ is relatively independent of hormones.　sexual activity (sexual behavior)

44. The first phase of the human sexual response is the _____ stage.　excitement

45. At this stage, both male and female have _____ of the body's _____ tissues.　vasocongestion, erectile

46. The second phase of the human sexual response is the _____ stage.　plateau

47. The third phase of the human sexual response is the _____.　orgasm

48. The hormone, _____, triggers the contractions in orgasms.　oxytocin

49. The fourth and final phase of the human sexual response is the _____ stage.　resolution

SLEEP AND WAKING

50. The record of the voltage changes occurring in the brain over time is called the _____ (_____).　electroencephalogram (EEG)

51. An EEG associated with waking relaxation shows _____ waves. The lower voltage, higher frequency EEG associated with alertness is called _____ waves.　alpha beta

52. Rapid eye movements (REM), a waking EEG, relaxed muscles, and low sensitivity to external stimulation all characterize _____ sleep.　REM

53. In contrast, a more restful type of sleep occurs for most of the night; this _____-_____ sleep goes through a number of _____.　slow-wave stages

54. The tendency to sleep varies across any 24-hour period, suggesting that sleep is _____-_____ or _____. This may be mediated by the hormone _____.　clock-driven, circadian, melatonin

55. The 90- to 100-minute intervals between REM episodes are described as an _____ rhythm.　ultradian

56. Dreaming occurs more frequently during _____ sleep.   REM

57. Dreams do not occur instantaneously, as suggested by the notion of dream _____.   condensation

58. The specific need for both REM and non-REM sleep has been shown through experiments in
    selective _____ _____. These results suggest that sleep of both types is a   sleep deprivation
    _____ process.   restorative

59. According to _____, dreams have a function of allowing expression of unacceptable wishes   Freud
    in a disguised form.

60. According to the _____- _____ hypothesis, the dream is simply a reflection of the   activation-synthesis
    brain's aroused state during active sleep.

WHAT DIFFERENT MOTIVES HAVE IN COMMON

61. Hull believed that all built-in rewards produce some decrease in tension, or _____   drive
    _____.   reduction

62. The fact that animals will learn to press a lever to engage in sexually arousing behavior argues for a
    preferred level of _____ that is greater than zero.   arousal

63. Alcohol, barbiturates, and opiates are examples of _____ drugs.   depressant

64. Amphetamines and cocaine are examples of _____ drugs.   stimulant

65. Addiction is associated with decreased sensitivity to a drug. This effect is called _____.   tolerance

66. Addiction is also characterized by effects opposite to a drug's effects when the drug is discontinued.
    This is called _____.   withdrawal

67. Another feature of addiction is loss of _____.   control

68. Rats will learn to press a lever if doing so is followed by _____ _____ of certain   electrical stimulation
    _____ centers in the brain.   pleasure

69. According to the _____ hypothesis, _____ release in the nucleus accumbens may   dopamine, dopamine
    account for reward in general, including the effects of _____ drugs.   stimulant

Self-Test

1. In the context of motivation, potentiation is
   a. electrical in nature.
   b. selective facilitation of certain responses.
   c. hunger and thirst.
   d. self-restorative.
   e. the shift from one motive-state to another.

2. Motivated behavior presents a serious problem to some
   machine models of behavior because
   a. motivated behavior involves a whole set of different
      reactions, any of which may lead toward the same goal.
   b. motivated behavior involves direction, and this assumes a
      type of feedback that cannot be incorporated into
      machines.
   c. motivated behavior assumes the operation of at least one
      type of feedback.
   d. all of the above
   e. none of the above

3. In human sexual behavior, sexual foreplay seems gradually
   to increase sexual arousal of the partners. This would be an
   example of
   a. homeostasis.
   b. negative feedback.
   c. a reflex.
   d. positive feedback.
   e. none of the above

4. Which of the following is a reflexive thermoregulatory
   response to high temperature?
   a. shivering
   b. constriction of the blood vessels in the skin
   c. sweating
   d. piloerection (ruffling of fur)
   e. moving to a colder place

5. The word pair *reflexive-voluntary* represents a relationship
   paralleled by which of the following pairs?
   a. homeostasis-whole organism
   b. vasoconstriction-vasodilation
   c. sweating-panting
   d. vasoconstriction-building a shelter
   e. none of the above

6. A dog is in a room comfortably heated to 75°F. His
   hypothalamus is cooled experimentally. As a result,
   a. he will shiver and his body temperature will go up.
   b. he will shiver and his body temperature will go down.
   c. he will pant and his body temperature will go up.
   d. he will pant and his body temperature will go down.
   e. he will have no change in temperature, because his skin
      temperature remains unchanged.

7. A rat's hypothalamus is cooled, and it learns to settle down over a warm air current in one part of its cage. This behavior illustrates
   a. reflexive behavior.
   b. the mobilization of voluntary behavior by the hypothalamic thermoregulatory system.
   c. that directly manipulating hypothalamic temperature can cause an animal to make a response that is inappropriate to its actual body temperature.
   d. b and c
   e. all of the above

8. In both thermoregulation and thirst
   a. there is voluntary control.
   b. homeostasis occurs.
   c. there is reflexive control.
   d. all of the above
   e. none of the above

9. When rats are given a great deal of exercise, their intake of food increases; that is, they eat a larger amount of food. Rats also decrease their intake of a food if it is enriched, so that it contains more calories per gram. These findings suggest that
   a. stomach fullness must be critical in regulating the rat's food intake.
   b. the rat is regulating the volume of food consumed.
   c. the rat is regulating the caloric or energy value of the food consumed.
   d. all of the above
   e. a and c

10. Which of the following statements best summarizes the way that internal and external signals influence food intake?
    a. Signals from various internal structures (brain receptors, liver, etc.) determine the amount eaten; external factors have almost no effect.
    b. Metabolic information from receptors in the brain controls about half of food intake, and external stimulation the other half.
    c. Metabolic information from receptors in the liver, brain, and possibly other locations interacts with external stimulation to determine the amount eaten.
    d. Internal signals determine levels of leptin and glucose; external signals determine levels of glycogen.
    e. Hypothalamic receptors for internal and external events have a dual role in maintaining caloric intake.

11. Leptin, blood glucose, and CCK have the following in common:
    a. They are all produced by the liver.
    b. They can all be converted to glycogen.
    c. When levels are high in the blood, they promote satiety.
    d. a and b
    e. all of the above

12. Food intake usually ceases before significant amounts of food have been absorbed from the bloodstream. This suggests that
    a. the stomach may play an important role in satiety.
    b. learning may play an important role in satiety.
    c. oral factors (e.g., monitoring how much has gone into the mouth) may play a role in satiety.
    d. a and c
    e. all of the above

13. Initiation of eating is most likely to be associated with
    a. high blood glucose.
    b. excitation of the lateral hypothalamus.
    c. inhibition of the lateral hypothalamus.
    d. high liver glycogen.
    e. excitation of the ventromedial hypothalamus.

14. Dual-center theory makes all but one of the following assumptions or predictions. Which assumption is not a necessary part of the theory?
    a. Information from internal and external receptors is integrated in the hypothalamus.
    b. The two hypothalamic feeding centers perform opposite functions.
    c. The liver is the primary source of information concerning the metabolic state of the organism.
    d. Damage to the "on" center should produce reduced eating.
    e. Damage to the "off" center should produce overeating.

15. Evidence suggests that hypothalamic control of eating operates
    a. directly.
    b. indirectly via control of metabolism.
    c. exclusively through the process of inhibition.
    d. primarily to control the type of food eaten.
    e. a and b

16. Two rats (or people) differ greatly in weight and fatness, but each of them holds its weight rather constant over a period of months. These results suggest that the two differ in
    a. setpoint.
    b. stomach size.
    c. ability to regulate body weight.
    d. ability to regulate food intake.
    e. size of hypothalamus.

17. Which one of the following has *not* been suggested as a cause of obesity in humans?
    a. damage to the lateral region of the hypothalamus
    b. high digestive efficiency
    c. a high setpoint
    d. genetic predisposition
    e. low metabolic rate

18. Which of the following findings supports a setpoint account of obesity?
    a. Obese people eat relatively more of highly palatable foods.
    b. Obese people tend to maintain a steady weight.
    c. Obese individuals who lose weight on diets tend to return to their previous obese weight.
    d. b and c
    e. all of the above

19. Effective therapy (including better adjustment) for obese individuals might be accomplished by
    a. drugs that effectively reduce setpoint.
    b. a consistent pattern of dieting.
    c. curbing the ideal of thinness in Western society.
    d. b and c
    e. all of the above

20. A major distinction between anorexia nervosa and bulimia is that
    a. females predominate only in anorexia nervosa.
    b. only anorexics are well below normal weight.
    c. only bulimia is commonly found in people in the 15- to 25-year age range.
    d. all of the above
    e. none of the above

21. The sympathetic branch of the autonomic nervous system is responsible for which of the following?
    a. decreased heart rate
    b. crying after a sad movie
    c. vegetative functions, such as digestion
    d. emptying of the colon and bladder
    e. none of the above

22. The responses of a cat about to do battle with a dog are mediated by
    a. the parasympathetic system.
    b. the sympathetic system.
    c. vegetative functions.
    d. the digestive system.
    e. b and c

23. Which of the following is *not* associated with activity of the sympathetic system?
    a. the emergency reaction
    b. epinephrine
    c. secretion by the adrenal medulla
    d. increased heart rate
    e. secretion of digestive enzymes

24. Imagine a person who has an unusual amount of voluntary control over her autonomic nervous system. Such a person should be able to
    a. markedly reduce her weight.
    b. successfully control her heart rate.
    c. never experience fear.
    d. get along without sleeping.
    e. a and d

25. Which of the following statements about pain is false?
    a. Experience of chronic pain is adaptive.
    b. Experience of acute pain is adaptive.
    c. Endorphins often reduce pain.
    d. Endorphins and opiate drugs both produce analgesia.
    e. a and b

26. In terms of motivation, sex differs from hunger, thirst, and thermoregulation, in that
    a. chemicals in the blood affect only sex.
    b. sex is not involved in self-preservation.
    c. sex is inherently social.
    d. a and b
    e. b and c

27. During estrus, the female (nonprimate) mammal is
    a. secreting estrogen.
    b. most receptive to sexual approach of males.
    c. fertile.
    d. all of the above
    e. none of the above

28. In some species in which the female has a clearly defined estrus cycle, the male is always ready for sexual activity. This would make sense if in these species
    a. all females come into estrus at the same time.
    b. estrus is dependent on the season.
    c. estrus occurs throughout the year and females are not synchronized in their cycles.
    d. hormonal factors are especially important in determining the receptivity of the female.
    e. a and b

29. Unlike other mammals, for humans
    a. hormones have no effect on sexual behavior.
    b. hormones have effects on only male sexual behavior.
    c. sexual receptivity in females is relatively independent of the fertile period in the sexual cycle.
    d. sex is a social activity.
    e. b and c

30. Vasocongestion
    a. is linked to secretion of oxytocin.
    b. occurs only in male erectile tissue.
    c. occurs only in female erectile tissue.
    d. occurs primarily in the excitement stage.
    e. occurs only in nonhuman animals.

31. What is usually the shortest phase in the human sexual response cycle?
    a. excitement
    b. plateau
    c. orgasm
    d. resolution
    e. a or b

32. REM sleep is sometimes called paradoxical sleep because
    a. behaviorally the person seems to be sleeping, but his or her brain waves show a pattern of activity usually associated with a waking EEG.
    b. it occurs at unexpected times (e.g., in a noisy environment or during the day).
    c. the person is easily roused, yet his or her EEG consists of slow, large amplitude, synchronous waves.
    d. all of the above
    e. a and b

33. Which of the following pairings represents a contrast between REM sleep and slow-wave sleep?
    a. rapid eye movements—no rapid eye movements
    b. dreaming—lack of dreaming
    c. EEG waking activity—EEG slow waves
    d. all of the above
    e. a and c

34. Restorative functions for slow-wave sleep are suggested by
    a. increased duration of quiet sleep after quiet sleep deprivation.
    b. linkage of quiet sleep to subcortical centers.
    c. increased duration of quiet sleep after bodily exhaustion.
    d. the existence of active sleep.
    e. a and c

35. When research participants are awakened after fifteen minutes of REM they relate longer dreams than when they are awakened after five minutes of REM. This result is evidence that
    a. dreams are not only better remembered during REM, but actually unfold during REM.
    b. dreams are rarely influenced by external sensory stimulation.
    c. as dreams progress, they are related to memories of waking life.
    d. dreams are mediated by the cerebral cortex and subcortical centers.
    e. all of the above

36. The activation-synthesis hypothesis of dreaming differs from the Freudian theory as
    a. it holds that dreams are always meaningless.
    b. it considers memories important as the raw materials of dreams.
    c. it does not focus on dreams as unconsciously motivated ways of solving problems.
    d. it links dreaming to REM sleep.
    e. c and d

37. Nonnutritive saccharin serves as a reward for rats, and solving a puzzle seems to be its own reward for monkeys and humans, suggesting that
    a. drive reduction is not the only mechanism of reward.
    b. Hull's conception of reward was correct.
    c. drive reduction does not depend on electrical stimulation of the brain.
    d. organisms seek to diminish their arousal levels.
    e. a and d

38. The mechanical puzzle is used to demonstrate that monkeys
    a. will be motivated by drive reduction.
    b. will perform some acts as ends in themselves.
    c. will work only for drive reduction.
    d. can be stimulated
    e. none of the above

39. Suppose a person is drowsy and inactive much of the time. Which of the following drugs is most likely to reverse these effects?
    a. alcohol
    b. barbiturates
    c. opiates
    d. cocaine
    e. heroin

40. A person addicted to a specific euphoria-producing drug suddenly stops using this drug. He goes into a deep depression. This reaction is an example of
    a. the effects of tolerance.
    b. the effects of addiction.
    c. a withdrawal symptom.
    d. drive reduction.
    e. a and c

41. Imagine a drug that excites neurons, but the neurons that it excites are inhibitory neurons. The effects of this drug would be like
    a. depressant drugs.
    b. stimulant drugs.
    c. cocaine.
    d. all drugs.
    e. a and c

42. Studies on electrical stimulation of the brain have indicated
    a. the existence of "pleasure centers" in the brain.
    b. the relation of tolerance to withdrawal.
    c. the importance of the medial forebrain pathway in reward.
    d. a and c
    e. all of the above

43. According to the dopamine hypothesis of reward,
    a. stimulant drugs directly cause reward by initiating dopamine activity in the nucleus accumbens.
    b. dopamine is responsible for inhibition.
    c. there is a common neurotransmitter basis for all rewards.
    d. a and c
    e. all of the above

Answer Key for Self-Test

1.	b	23.	e
2.	a	24.	b
3.	d	25.	a
4.	c	26.	e
5.	d	27.	d
6.	a	28.	c
7.	d	29.	c
8.	d	30.	a
9.	c	31.	c
10.	c	32.	a
11.	c	33.	d
12.	e	34.	e
13.	b	35.	a
14.	c	36.	e
15.	e	37.	a
16.	a	38.	b
17.	a	39.	d
18.	d	40.	c
19.	e	41.	a
20.	b	42.	d
21.	e	43.	d
22.	b		

Investigating Psychological Phenomena

EFFECTS OF MENTAL PROCESSES ON AUTONOMIC ACTIVITY

Equipment: Stopwatch or watch with second indicator
Number of participants: Three
Time per participant: Ten minutes
Time for experimenter: Forty minutes

As part of its role in the control of bodily functions, the autonomic nervous system (ANS) controls heart rate. In this way it can influence the rate of delivery of oxygen and nutrients to the cells of the body. In times when the body is stressed, increased heart rate (and other changes) increases the delivery of nutrients to cells, as well as increasing the rate of disposal of waste products. The changes in heart rate are produced directly by nerve impulses sent to the heart. They are also produced indirectly by stimulation, through autonomic pathways, of the release of epinephrine (adrenaline) and related substances from the adrenal glands.

Arousal of the sympathetic system, and hence increased heart rate, occurs when the organism is undergoing physical exertion. But it can also be produced by mental events. Such a pathway would allow an organism to mobilize its physiological resources in anticipation of a physical stress. On the other hand, it also allows for high and ultimately damaging levels of sympathetic arousal based on chronic anxiety or mental tension.

In this study we will demonstrate the effectiveness of the sympathetic nervous system link between mental activity and heart rate. Participants will be asked to increase their heart rate by thinking about either a strenuous physical activity or something that is mentally exciting.

Make sure that your participant is seated comfortably, has been relaxing for at least ten minutes, and did not engage in any strenuous activity in the last half hour. Before reading the instructions make sure you can find the participant's pulse on his or her wrist. The unit of recording for heart rate will be a thirty-second interval. You will record the number of beats every thirty seconds on the data sheet on the next page. Allow fifteen seconds to pass between each thirty-second interval or recording so that you will have enough time to record the pulse and give the instruction. If you have an instruction to give the participant (e.g., "Relax," "Increase Mental"), give the instruction as soon as you have recorded the pulse rate, but wait the full fifteen seconds before counting heartbeats.

Instructions to read to the participant:

This is a short, ten-minute experiment to determine whether you can control the rate of beating of your heart. When I say "Begin," you should close your eyes and relax while I take your pulse. After a minute I will say "Increase physical activity," and you should try to increase your heart rate by thinking about some physical activity in which you are personally engaged and which requires a lot of exertion. After I record your pulse I will say, "Relax," and you should stop trying to increase your heart rate and relax again. I will take your pulse for another minute and then I will say "Increase mental activity." This time you should try to increase your heart rate by thinking of something that is exciting but that does not involve a lot of physical activity. This could be a fearful experience that you have had, the excitement from watching a sports event, preexamination anxiety, and so on. Following this one-minute episode I will say, "Relax," and you should stop trying to increase your heart rate and relax. I will take your pulse for one final minute. Before you begin the experiment decide on each image you will think about for the physical activity and the mental activity. After you have decided, stop thinking about the images until I give you the instruction during the actual experiment.

Give the participant a few minutes to decide on images and then to stop thinking about them before you begin the experiment. Wait one minute after the participant has selected the two images, to allow any excitation that this may have produced to go away.

DATA FROM THREE PARTICIPANTS (A, B, AND C)

Instruction and time	A	B	C
"Begin and relax"			
00:00–0:30			
0:45–1:15			
"Increase physical activity"			
1:30–2:00			
2:15–2:45			
"Relax"			
3:00–3:30			
3:45–4:15			
"Increase mental activity"			
4:30–5:00			
5:15–5:45			
"Relax"			
6:00–6:30			
6:45–7:15			

List for each participant the basic situation that he or she imagined in the "increase" minutes.

	Physical	Mental
A	_____	_____
B	_____	_____
C	_____	_____

Plot the data for each participant on the graph below. Use a different symbol for each participant, and connect the symbols for each participant by lines. Since heart rate is usually expressed as beats per minute, double each of the numbers you have recorded (since you recorded beats per thirty seconds) before plotting. We have plotted the results from ten undergraduates (mean). In our study, nine of the ten undergraduates showed the increased heart rate effect.

Do all of your participants show an ability to increase heart rate by mental activity? Which procedure, thinking of physical activity or something mentally exciting, is more effective? *(If your instructor collects the data, fill out the report sheet in Appendix 2.)*

FURTHER PROJECTS

Lowering heart rate is much more difficult than raising it. You might see if you can get some participants to do that.

Some people have great difficulty in raising their heart rate. If one of your participants is such a person, you could try to get an increase by having the participant talk about physical activity or something exciting during a one-minute period.

You could also explore whether certain kinds of "exciting thoughts" (e.g., fear, excitement of a spectator at a sports event) are more effective in raising heart rate.

CHAPTER 4

Learning

Learning Objectives

1. Describe the point of view of learning theorists, their fit with American values, and the reason that most of their work focused on nonhuman animals.

HABITUATION

2. Define habituation and discuss its adaptive significance.

CLASSICAL CONDITIONING

Pavlov and the conditioned reflex
3. Explain the basic procedure (paradigm) of classical conditioning, and define conditioned and unconditioned stimuli and responses.
4. Distinguish between classical conditioning and habituation.

The major phenomena of classical conditioning
5. Describe the two measures of conditioned response strength: response amplitude and probability of response latency.
6. Draw a curve to represent the acquisition and extinction of a conditioned response.
7. Be able to define second-order conditioning, extinction, spontaneous recovery, and reconditioning.
8. Describe generalization and discrimination, and contrast the two processes.
9. Explain generalization gradients and the role of inhibition in discrimination.

Extensions of classical conditioning
10. Indicate how classical conditioning can account for acquired fears and phobias, and describe how conditioned fear is measured.
11. Show that the conditioned response often functions to prepare the organism for the unconditioned stimulus, and hence that the CR and UR often differ.
12. Indicate the CR can be the opposite of the UR, as for example in cases of repeated drug administration.

INSTRUMENTAL CONDITIONING

13. Review the major similarities and differences between classical conditioning and instrumental conditioning.

Thorndike and the law of effect
14. Explain the law of effect and indicate the evidence that supports it.
15. What is the relation between the law of effect and the evolutionary principle of survival of the fittest?

Skinner and operant behavior
16. What additions and modifications did Skinner propose to Thorndike's view of instrumental conditioning? How did Skinner change the way instrumental learning was studied in the laboratory?

The major phenomena of instrumental conditioning
17. How do the phenomena of instrumental conditioning parallel those of classical conditioning?
18. Describe the processes of generalization, discrimination, and shaping in instrumental conditioning.
19. Give examples of conditioned and primary reinforcers, and describe how a conditioned reinforcer can be produced or eliminated.
20. Evaluate the importance of information, behavioral contrast, and intrinsic motivation as extensions or modifiers of the concept of reinforcement.
21. Define and describe schedules of reinforcement and their properties, and indicate the effect of the schedules on resistance to extinction.
22. Indicate the ways in which aversive stimuli influence learning, by describing punishment, escape, and avoidance learning.
23. Why does avoidance learning present a problem for learning theory?

COGNITIVE LEARNING

24. Compare learning theory with cognitive learning theory, contrasting learning of responses to learning of cognitions (representations).

A cognitive view of classical conditioning
25. Discuss the effects of different times of onset of the conditioned and unconditioned stimulus. What is the most effective CS–US interval, and why is this adaptive?
26. Distinguish contiguity and contingency, and explain the studies that indicate that contingency is a critical factor in the formation of conditioned responses.

27. Explain the role of surprise in learning, and show how blocking demonstrates this.

A cognitive view of instrumental conditioning
28. Review the evidence supporting the position that what is learned in instrumental conditioning is act-outcome associations, as opposed to the strengthening of specific responses. Describe latent learning.
29. Explain the role of contingency in instrumental conditioning, and its relation to learned helplessness.
30. How has learned helplessness been used to explain some types of depression in humans?

VARIETIES OF LEARNING

Biological constraints on learning: belongingness
31. What is the equipotentiality principle, and what is the evidence against it? Describe belongingness or preparedness.
32. Describe the phenomenon of taste aversion learning, and indicate why it illustrates biological constraints. Describe acquired taste aversions in humans.
33. Discuss belongingness in response–outcome relations in instrumental conditioning.
34. In what sense is key-pecking by pigeons not an arbitrary operant? In what sense is key-pecking classically conditioned?

Adaptive specializations of learning
35. Summarize the argument that there are specialized types of learning in particular species and ecological niches. Provide an illustration.
36. Indicate some similarities across situations and species in properties of learning. How do these relate to environmental "universals"?

THE NEURAL BASIS FOR LEARNING

Changes in synaptic efficiency: presynaptic facilitation
37. What is presynaptic facilitation, and how might it account for learning?

Long-term potentiation
38. What is long-term potentiation, and how might it account for learning?

Structural changes produced by learning
39. Contrast presynatpic facilitation and long-term potentiation with structural changes, such as growth of dendritic spines.

COMPLEX COGNITION IN ANIMALS

Cognitive maps
40. What are cognitive maps and what is the evidence that animals have them?

Insightful behavior
41. Describe the phenomenon of insight in animals, andindicate why it presents problems for traditional learning theory.
42. How do we determine whether insight or trial and error is a better way of describing a particular learned behavior? What is the role of transfer of training in making this distinction?
43. Distinguish between generalization and transfer.

Complex perceptual concepts in animals
44. Describe complex perceptual concepts, like the concept of "water" in pigeons.

Programmed Exercises

1. _____ _____ believe that a few simple laws of learning can account for most of human and animal behavior.   Learning theorists

HABITUATION

2. _____ is a decline in the tendency to respond to stimuli that have become familiar through repeated exposure.   Habituation

CLASSICAL CONDITIONING

3. Unlike habituation, classical conditioning involves the formation of _____ between events.   associations

4. _____ _____ was first demonstrated in the laboratory by Ivan Pavlov.   Classical conditioning

5. After classical conditioning, the salivation of a dog upon presentation of a previously neutral bell would be called a(n) _____ _____. The previously neutral bell is now called a(n) _____ _____.   conditioned response conditioned stimulus

6. In Pavlov's laboratory, food in the mouth was a(n) _____ _____, and the salivation it produced was a(n) _____ _____.   unconditioned stimulus unconditioned response

7. Salivation to meat powder in the mouth is a(n) _____ _____. Salivation to a tone paired with meat powder in the mouth is a(n) _____ _____.   unconditioned reflex (response), conditioned reflex (response)

8. Response strength in classical conditioning can be measured as the *amount* of response, that is, the response _____, the time from onset of CS to the onset of the CR, called the _____, or the proportion of trials on which the CR is made when the CS is presented, the _____ of response.

amplitude, latency
probability

9.

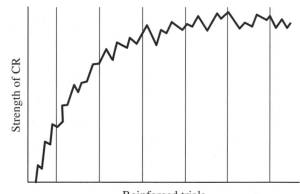

Reinforced trials

This graph is an example of an idealized _____ _____.

learning curve

10. A light is paired with shock. Subsequently, a tone paired with the light comes to elicit fear. This is an example of _____-_____ _____.

second-order
conditioning

11. If after a CR has been established, the CS is presented but is not followed by the US, the result will be _____ of the CR.

extinction

12. If time is allowed to pass, the CR will reappear when the CS is presented. This is the phenomenon of _____ _____.

spontaneous recovery

13. Extinction can be reversed with further training, resulting in _____.

reconditioning

14. Horizontal stripes on a card (CS) are paired with a puff of air to the eye (US), resulting in a conditioned eye blink response. Now, the first time vertical stripes are presented, a conditioned eye blink is observed. This is an example of _____ _____.

stimulus generalization

15. The greater the difference between a CS and another test stimulus, the weaker the CR to this test stimulus. This relationship is described as a _____ _____.

generalization gradient

16. US presentation after CS^+, and no US after CS^-, leads to _____.

discrimination

17. Because the CS^- acts to suppress the conditioned response, it is said to take on the role of _____.

inhibitor

18. Animals show _____ _____ when a stimulus paired with shock is presented to them. This is called the _____ _____ _____.

response suppression
conditioned emotional
response

19. According to a classical conditioning analysis, the object of a phobia or fetish can be considered a _____ _____.

conditioned stimulus

20. In many instances, the CR does not duplicate the UR, but rather _____ the animal to deal with the UR.

prepares

21. Sometimes the CR has the opposite effect from the UR, as when the CS signals drug arrival (US). This is accounted for by the _____-_____ hypothesis.

compensatory-reaction

INSTRUMENTAL CONDITIONING

22. In classical conditioning, a relation between two stimuli is learned. In instrumental conditioning, however, the relation that is learned exists between a _____ and a _____.

response, reward

23. The experimental study of instrumental learning was begun by _____ in the context of a debate over the mental continuity of humans and animals, which was stimulated by the evolutionary theories of _____.

(Edward L.) Thorndike

(Charles) Darwin

24. Thorndike's _____ _____ _____ states that the consequences of a response determine whether it becomes strengthened or weakened.

law of effect

25. The most prominent figure in modern learning theory was _____.

(B. F.) Skinner

26. Skinner emphasized distinctions between classical conditioning and instrumental learning. In the former, responses are _____; in instrumental learning they are _____.

elicited, emitted

27. Skinner used the term "_____" to describe the "voluntary" or "emitted" responses that are studied in instrumental learning. He preferred to measure _____ _____ as a measure of response strength.

operants
response rate

28. Although operants are not elicited by external stimuli, the stimuli can control behavior as _____ _____.

discriminative stimuli

29. Animals can be trained to perform difficult responses by the process of _____, using the method of _____ _____.

shaping
successive
approximation

30. After a neutral stimulus is paired with a reinforcer such as food, the neutral stimulus acquires reinforcement properties. This is called _____ _____.

conditioned
reinforcement

31. Conditioned reinforcement is established by a procedure that seems to be the same as _____ conditioning.

classical

32. Animals and humans can be reinforced not only by events that reduce biological needs, but also by _____ from the environment.

information

33. The effectiveness of a reinforcement depends on the context of reinforcement; whether prior reinforcements were larger or smaller than the current one. This is called _____ _____.

behavioral contrast

34. Behaviors performed for their own sake, providing their own reward, are described as cases of _____ motivation.

instrinsic

35. The rule set up by the experimenter (or society) that determines the occasions on which a response is reinforced is called a _____ _____ _____.

schedule of
reinforcement

36. An animal that is reinforced for every five responses is on a _____ _____ schedule.

fixed ratio

37. Responses acquired with intermittent reinforcement exhibit greater resistance to extinction. This is termed the _____ _____ _____.

partial reinforcement
effect

38. Loud noises, painful stimuli, bitter tastes, and social rejection are examples of _____ stimuli.

aversive

39. In _____ training, an aversive stimulus follows a particular response.

punishment

40. _____ learning is a type of instrumental learning in which the organism is required to perform a response that terminates or reduces an aversive stimulus.

Escape

41. Avoidance learning presents problems for behavior theory because it is not easy to identify the _____ for the avoidance response.

reinforcer

42.

This graph illustrates the transition from _____ to _____ learning.

escape, avoidance

COGNITIVE LEARNING

43. Learning theorists emphasize that learning modifies _____. In contrast, cognitive theorists argue that learning involves acquisition of _____.

responses (action) knowledge (cognitions, representations)

44. Learning of a conditioned response (CR) occurs most efficiently when the _____ precedes the _____ by a small time interval. This is called _____ pairing.

CS, US, forward

45. Pavlov and others claimed that togetherness in time, pairing, or _____ forms the basis for classical conditioning.

(temporal) contiguity

46. Later research suggests that what is critical for conditioning is that the CS predict the US, so that there is a _____ between CS and US.

contingency

47.

The pattern of shock and signals shown in A above is most likely to give rise, in the presence of the tone, to the state of _____, whereas the _____ shock shown in B is likely to give rise to the state of _____.

fear, unsignaled (uncontingent), anxiety

48. According to several theorists, the greater the _____ at the onset of the US, the more learning will occur.

surprise (unexpectedness)

49. A stimulus (CS-1) is presented contingently with a US. Then, a second stimulus (CS-2) is also presented at the same time as CS-1, and both are followed by the US. Often, only CS-1 will show classical conditioning. This phenomenon is called _____.

blocking

50. Two conditions that seem necessary for classical conditioning to occur are that the CS must show a _____ relation to the US, and the CS must provide _____ that the organism did not have before.

contingent, information

51. Evidence indicates that rather than strengthening specific responses, instrumental reinforcement creates _____-_____ associations.

act-outcome

52. Learning in the absence of reward indicates that responses need not occur for learning to occur. This is called _____ learning.

latent

53. Just as is the case with classical conditioning, what is learned in instrumental learning is a _____.

contingency

54. Dogs given inescapable shocks are then placed in an avoidance situation shuttlebox where they could learn a jumping response to escape and avoid shock. Instead, they lie quietly and take the shocks. Their behavior has been interpreted as learning that the presence or absence of shocks is not contingent on their behavior, a state called _____ _____.

learned helplessness

55. The symptoms shown by helpless dogs resemble those seen in the human disorder of _____.

depression

VARIETIES OF LEARNING

56. Traditional learning theory assumes that the relation between stimuli in classical conditioning, or between response and outcome in instrumental learning, is arbitrary. This assumption is known as the _____ principle.

equipotentiality

57. One criticism of traditional learning theory holds that there are certain built-in limitations called _____ _____ that determine what a given animal can easily learn.

biological constraints

58. _____ _____ aversions are an example of belongingness, and their rapid acquisition makes them an example of _____-_____ learning.

Learned taste
one-trial

59. Belongingness in animal learning, as illustrated by taste aversion learning, seems to fit well with the survival needs of animals. Thus, rats, who rely heavily on _____ in feeding, tend to associate that with the aftereffects of eating, while birds, which rely on _____ in feeding, tend to associate this type of stimulus with the aftereffects of eating.

taste
vision (sight)

60. The fact that it is easier to train a pigeon to flap its wings to escape shock than to receive food is an instance of _____ in _____-_____ relations in instrumental learning.

belongingness (preparedness), response (act)-outcome

61. Acquisition of bird song, navigational abilities, and memories for sites where food has been stored all represent _____ _____ of learning.

adaptive specializations

62. Similarities in properties of learning across species and situations suggest _____ features of the world across environments.

common (universal)

THE NEURAL BASIS FOR LEARNING

63. The capacity for neurons to change the way they function as a consequence of experience is called _____ _____.

neural plasticity

64. The study of the marine mollusk, *Aplysia,* is advantageous for research on the neural basis of learning because the nervous system of *Aplysia* is a relatively _____ system.

simple

65. One form of neural plasticity, as demonstrated in Aplysia, involves activation of neurons that increases the transmitter release at their synapses of another pathway. This is called _____ _____.

presynaptic
facilitation

66. In the process of _____-_____ _____, activation of a synapse makes that synapse more sensitive for periods lasting for days or weeks.

long-term potentiation

67. Learning in mammals produces structural changes, such as the growth of _____ spines.

dendritic

COMPLEX COGNITION IN ANIMALS

68. Tolman's original work, later work on the radial-arm maze with rats, and food retrieval by chimpanzees suggest that animals have _____ _____.

cognitive maps

69. Köhler claimed that animals can acquire _____, as well as responses.

cognitions

70. The photograph below represents a situation studied by Köhler in which he demonstrated the phenomenon of _____.

insight

71. A chimpanzee solves the problem of knocking down a piece of fruit hung above the cage by throwing a ball at it. When the ball is taken away, it throws a piece of fruit. This demonstrates _____ _____ _____.

transfer of training

72. Traditional learning theory interprets transfer effects as instances of _____ _____, but transfer often seems to be based on abstract _____ relationships.

stimulus generalization, conceptual (meaningful)

73. The concepts of water or tree in pigeons are examples of _____ _____ concepts.

complex perceptual

Self-Test

1. Learning theorists share with Descartes the conviction that
   a. one must study the nervous system to understand behavior.
   b. learning is the most important aspect of animal behavior.
   c. complex behavior can be analyzed into simpler, more elementary processes.
   d. almost all behavior can be described as hardwired (innate).
   e. c and d

2. An animal startles when it is exposed to the sound of either a door slamming or a gong ringing. It is then exposed, about ten times, to the gong ringing followed by the door slamming. Now, when the gong rings, the animal does *not* startle. This is an example of
   a. habitation.
   b. classical conditioning.
   c. extinction.
   d. associations.
   e. a learning curve.

3. Both classical conditioning and habituation
   a. involve associations.
   b. require a conditioned stimulus.
   c. are built-in responses that animals show in laboratory situations.
   d. involve a change in response to a stimulus.
   e. occur primarily in dogs, though they may occur in some other species.

4. In a classical conditioning experiment in which a tone is paired with meat in the mouth, a dog comes to salivate to the sound of the tone. The tone is called the
   a. conditioned stimulus.
   b. unconditioned stimulus.
   c. unconditioned response.
   d. stimulus generalization.
   e. reinforcer.

5. Ivan Pilaff developed a fear of German shepherds because, on a few occasions, he was bitten by them. Some weeks later, he became friendly with someone who had a German shepherd as a pet. After a few visits to this friend when the shepherd was present, he became fearful of the friend, even though this particular German shepherd never bit him. This is an example of
   a. discrimination.
   b. extinction.
   c. reinforcement.
   d. learning with a long delay.
   e. second-order conditioning.

6. A dog is first classically conditioned to seven stimuli (A–G) until he responds equally to all. He then gets some further training. At the end he produces the unusual generalization curve shown below. What was the further training the dog received?

   a. extinguished stimuli A, B, D, F, and G
   b. extinguish B, D, and F; further condition A and G
   c. extinguish C and E
   d. extinguish C, D, and E
   e. further condition A and G

7. This figure illustrates the phenomenon of

   a. conditioning.
   b. generalization.
   c. extinction.
   d. reconditioning.
   e. spontaneous recovery.

8. Classical conditioning has been
   a. shown to occur only with salivation.
   b. used to explain responses to music, in conjunction with Romantic conditioning.
   c. demonstrated only in vertebrates.
   d. suggested as an explanation for phobias.
   e. a and c

9. During World War II, air raid sirens preceded bombing raids. A person who, as a result of fear, stopped her ongoing activity (e.g., eating, working) when sirens sounded showed
   a. response suppression.
   b. a siren phobia.
   c. extinction.
   d. spontaneous recovery.
   e. a generalization gradient.

10. An experienced skydiver does not show nearly as much arousal, on entering the plane from which he will jump, as does a novice skydiver. Consider an experienced skydiver who is just about to enter the plane, but is called back at the last minute. If he shows a conditioned compensatory response, we would expect that
    a. his arousal would be about the same as that of the novice.
    b. he would show a bigger increase in arousal than the novice.
    c. he would show the same decrease in arousal as the novice.
    d. he would show the same increase in arousal as the novice.
    e. he would become less aroused than he normally is in daily life.

11. The relation between a UR and a conditioned compensatory response is like the relation between excitation and
    a. conditioning.
    b. reconditioning.
    c. extinction.
    d. response suppression.
    e. inhibition.

12. Instrumental learning differs from classical conditioning in that
    a. in instrumental learning, a response-reward association is learned, whereas in classical conditioning, a relation between stimuli is learned.
    b. associations are formed only in classical conditioning.
    c. responses are never involved in classical conditioning.
    d. instrumental learning always occurs gradually, in trial-and-error fashion, whereas classical conditioning occurs very rapidly.
    e. a and c

13. According to the law of effect, responses followed by reward
    a. increase in latency.
    b. are not always reinforced.
    c. become trials or errors.
    d. are strengthened.
    e. all of the above

14. The parallel between Darwin's theory of evolution and instrumental conditioning is between
    a. mental continuity and trial-and-error learning.
    b. learning and extinction.
    c. survival of the fittest and the law of effect.
    d. a and b
    e. all of the above

15. As described by Thorndike, instrumental learning
    a. is gradual.
    b. involves no complex, uniquely human processes.
    c. is accomplished on a trial-and-error basis.
    d. is a means of strengthening particular responses.
    e. all of the above

16. Skinner added to Thorndike's conception(s) the idea that the responses conditioned in instrumental learning were
    a. emitted or voluntary, as opposed to elicited as in classical conditioning.
    b. increased in strength by the process of reinforcement.

    c. selected from all responses emitted on the basis of the law of effect.
    d. a and c
    e. all of the above

17. Skinner and Thorndike share in common a belief in
    a. the importance of schedules of reinforcement.
    b. the law of effect.
    c. the idea that instrumental behavior is emitted.
    d. the superiority of instrumental training with discrete trials.
    e. all of the above

18. A rat is placed in a chamber and is given a number of pellets of food, each preceded by a clicking sound. It is later trained to lever press, with the reinforcement only the sounding of the click, but no food. Every other day the rat receives pairings of click and food, and on the alternate days, it presses only for the click. Eventually, it stops pressing the lever on the "click" days. This cessation could be explained as
    a. generalization.
    b. loss of conditioned reinforcement properties by the click.
    c. discrimination between clicks in two different situations.
    d. an illustration of the importance of extinction.
    e. spontaneous recovery.

19. To shape an animal to perform a difficult response, all but one of the following procedures should be followed. Which procedure is *not* appropriate?
    a. Provide a clear signal for the arrival of reinforcement.
    b. Present the reinforcement immediately after the response is performed.
    c. Initially reinforce approximations to the desired response.
    d. At first, reinforce those parts of the desired response sequence that come at the end of the sequence.
    e. Work with the most difficult component in the response sequence first.

20. The desire for good grades illustrates the phenomenon of
    a. stimulus generalization.
    b. simultaneous discrimination.
    c. conditioned reinforcement.
    d. successive approximation.
    e. a and d

21. The idea that reinforcement can be understood completely by reduction of biological need is challenged by
    a. intrinsic motivation.
    b. behavioral contrast.
    c. schedules of reinforcement.
    d. a and b
    e. all of the above

22. Consider each swing by a baseball player as an operant response, and every successful hit (single, double, etc.) as a reinforced swing. What schedule of reinforcement is a baseball batter on?
    a. continuous reinforcement (fixed ratio 1)
    b. fixed ratio
    c. variable ratio
    d. extinction
    e. variable interval

23. Paradoxically, when an operant is reinforced on a schedule (e.g., every third response is reinforced), the response shows a greater resistance to extinction than when it received an equal number of reinforced responses on *every trial*. This effect (partial reinforcement effect) is paradoxical because
    a. the nonreinforced trials in partial reinforcement training are extinction trials and should weaken the response.
    b. CS-US contingencies must be precisely controlled for good conditioning to occur.
    c. the animal on partial reinforcement performs more responses in training.
    d. the organism is learning a discrimination during training.
    e. all of the above

24. Avoidance learning typically
    a. involves extinction.
    b. is preceded by escape learning.
    c. involves aversive stimuli.
    d. b and c
    e. all of the above

25. A classic experiment (appropriately) on classical conditioning showed that classical conditioning could occur when animals were temporarily paralyzed with a drug, so that they could not respond. (Of course, when testing for conditioning with a CS, the animals were no longer paralyzed.) Which position does this result support?
    a. the cognitive learning view
    b. the learning theory view
    c. Pavlov's position
    d. Skinner's position
    e. b and c

26. This figure demonstrates that it is very difficult to produce conditioning with

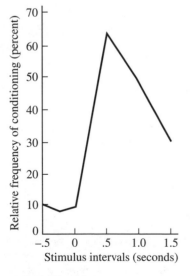

    a. forward pairing.
    b. second-order conditioning.
    c. extinction.
    d. simultaneous pairing.
    e. all of the above

27. Consider the following table of occurrences of CS and US. What predictions would the contiguity and contingency accounts make of whether conditioning would occur in this case?

	US	No US
CS	9	1
No CS	9	1

    a. both predict conditioning
    b. both predict no conditioning
    c. only contingency predicts conditioning
    d. only contiguity predicts conditioning
    e. neither predicts conditioning

28. Consider the following table of occurrences of CS and US. What predictions would the contiguity and contingency accounts make of whether conditioning would occur in this case?

	US	No US
CS	7	3
No CS	3	7

    a. both predict conditioning
    b. both predict no conditioning
    c. only contingency predicts conditioning
    d. only contiguity predicts conditioning
    e. neither predicts conditioning

29. In the case of unsignaled shock (a random relation between a signal and shock), the relation between a signal and the shock is one of
    a. anxiety.
    b. absence of contingency.
    c. contingency.
    d. contiguity.
    e. blocking.

30. Some properties of classical conditioning suggest that it functions to make predictions about events in the world, somewhat like a scientist makes. Which feature(s) of classical conditioning suggests(s) this property?
    a. sensitivity to contingency
    b. forward pairing
    c. blocking
    d. all of the above
    e. b and c

31. Harriet gets very excited whenever she approaches the house of her boyfriend, Milton. She notices that her heart starts beating when she turns his corner and sees the name of his street on the corner sign. But she is surprised one day to note that the sign is down, and that she does not get excited on turning the corner, nor on passing Milton's street mailbox, just twenty feet from the corner. Why doesn't the mailbox cause her heart to increase beating?
    a. blocking
    b. backward pairing
    c. Harriet is in extinction.
    d. The mailbox doesn't have a contingent relation with Milton.
    e. Fear suppresses her response.

32. A rat learns to run down a runway when reinforced with a sugar solution in the end box. After learning this, it is then fed a bitter (negatively reinforcing) solution in this same end box. When put back in the start box of the runway, it runs to the end less quickly than before. This illustrates
    a. second-order conditioning.
    b. blocking.
    c. learned helplessness.
    d. the law of effect.
    e. cognitive learning.

33. Studies on learned helplessness in dogs' and infants' responses to mobiles that they could or could not control are evidence for the importance of
    a. the law of effect.
    b. contiguity.
    c. contingency.
    d. belongingness.
    e. none of the above

34. Animals exposed to lights randomly paired with shock (hence, unsignaled shock) sometimes develop pathologies related to stress. The relation of this finding to learned helplessness is the same as the relationship of
    a. conditioning to extinction.
    b. the optimum CS-US interval to contingency.
    c. generalization in classical conditioning to generalization in instrumental conditioning.
    d. extinction to the partial reinforcement effect.
    e. extinction of instrumental conditioning to establishment of classical conditioning.

35. A simplified version of John Garcia's belongingness experiment would present bright-noisy tasty water to rats, followed by X-ray produced illness. The rats would show an aversion only to the taste (one of the groups in the experiment described in the text). However, without the use of a second group in which shock is the US, this experiment could be criticized by a learning theorist, because
    a. bright-noisy types of stimuli do not associate well with USs like those induced by X-rays.
    b. the bright-noisy stimuli might have been generally less effective as CSs than the taste stimulus.
    c. this result would contradict the bird studies, showing selective association of visual stimuli and gastrointestinal effects.
    d. the selective association could have been previously learned by the rats.
    e. all of the above

36. Rats have a special ability to associate tastes with illness. Pigeons learn to peck a key for food but have difficulty learning to peck a key to avoid shock. Both of these phenomena demonstrate belongingness. However, they differ in that the belongingness in the case of learned taste aversions occurs between _____ while in the pigeon example it occurs between _____ .
    a. species-specific stimuli, general stimuli
    b. stimuli, responses
    c. responses, stimuli
    d. stimuli, responses and outcomes
    e. stimulus and response, responses

37. Which of the following instances of human learning most clearly represents arbitrary, as opposed to biologically specialized or prepared, learning?
    a. acquisition of grammar
    b. learning to catch a ball
    c. learning the rules of chess
    d. learning to judge distance
    e. a and b

38. Differences in types of learning in different species or situations are referred to as
    a. convergent evolution.
    b. insight learning.
    c. adaptive specializations of learning.
    d. a and b
    e. all of the above

39. Some similarities in the properties of learning across species and situations result from
    a. universal properties of environments.
    b. the equipotentiality principle.
    c. adaptive specializations of learning.
    d. a and b
    e. all of the above

40. Both presynaptic facilitation and long-term potentiation are possible neural bases of learning because
    a. both are examples of neural plasticity.
    b. both involve changes in the presynaptic neuron.
    c. both have shown some contingency sensitivity.
    d. a and c
    e. all of the above

41. Presynaptic facilitation and long-term potentiation
    a. have been demonstrated only in the marine mollusk, *Aplysia.*
    b. involve changes in sensitivity of the presynaptic neuron.
    c. do not show activity dependence.
    d. produce a net increase in sensitivity by acting at different sites.
    e. a and b

42. Growth of dendritic spines differs from presynaptic facilitation or long-term potentiation in that
    a. it is the only change that really explains learning.
    b. it has nothing to do with snapses.
    c. it is a structural change.
    d. it is not activity dependent.
    e. a and b

43. Which of the following phenomena presents a serious problem to traditional learning theory?
    a. learning without performing a response or without getting a reward
    b. taste aversion learning
    c. insight learning
    d. cognitive maps
    e. all of the above

44. Which of the following statements describes a fundamental difference between learning and cognitive theorists?
    a. Learning theorists think a response is necessary for learning, whereas cognitive theorists think responses may be merely an index of learning.
    b. Learning theorists believe in reinforcement, and cognitive theorists believe in belongingness.
    c. Only learning theorists believe in belongingness.
    d. all of the above
    e. none of the above

45. In his attempts to demonstrate higher mental processes in animals, Köhler's experiments differed from those of Thorndike in that
    a. Köhler used an animal that might have greater reasoning power.
    b. Köhler used situations in which it was possible to "reason" a solution.
    c. Köhler used problems that could be gradually understood
    d. a and c
    e. a and b

46. Köhler suggested that a way to distinguish insightful from trial-and-error learning is that only insightful learning would
    a. generalize.
    b. show transfer of training.
    c. be arbitrary.
    d. be accomplished by apes.
    e. show belongingness.

47. Which of the following pairs best expresses a distinction between learning theory and cognitive theory?
    a. discrimination versus generalization
    b. same versus different
    c. biological constraints versus abstract concepts
    d. insight versus out of sight
    e. doing versus knowing

48. Cognitive theorists criticize learning theorists on the grounds that learning theorists
    a. assume animals are able to learn any arbitrary relationship.
    b. underestimate the ability of some animals to show sophisticated learning in some specific situations.
    c. rely too much on the response as a necessary part of learning.
    d. a and c
    e. all of the above

49–51. For the following three questions, the same set of answer alternatives is relevant.

Each question describes a major principle of traditional learning theory. For each one, choose the answer that describes a finding that casts doubt on this principle. The possible answers are listed below.
    a. learning sets
    b. Random pairing of CS and US leads to no conditioning.
    c. insight learning
    d. learned helplessness
    e. taste-aversion learning

49. Contiguity in time of two stimuli is sufficient grounds for conditioning.

50. Any CS can be associated equally well with any US.

51. Learning occurs gradually.

Answer Key for Self-Test

1.	c	27.	d
2.	a	28.	a
3.	d	29.	b
4.	a	30.	d
5.	e	31.	a
6.	c	32.	e
7.	c	33.	c
8.	d	34.	c
9.	a	35.	b
10.	e	36.	d
11.	e	37.	c
12.	a	38.	c
13.	d	39.	a
14.	c	40.	d
15.	e	41.	d
16.	a	42.	c
17.	b	43.	e
18.	c	44.	a
19.	e	45.	e
20.	c	46.	b
21.	d	47.	e
22.	c	48.	e
23.	a	49.	b
24.	d	50.	e
25.	a	51.	c
26.	d		

Investigating Psychological Phenomena

MAZE LEARNING

Equipment: Stopwatch or watch with second indicator
Number of participants: One (yourself)
Time per participant: Twenty to thirty-five minutes
Time for experimenter: Twenty to thirty-five minutes

This experiment illustrates a basic feature of learning: the acquisition curve, or the gradual acquisition of a skill or task. It employs a technique that was commonly used with animals in the earlier part of this century. The task is to find a way through a maze, presumably through learning a series of correct choices at the various choice-points. In the experiment you will proceed through the same maze four times: each time, a record will be kept of both your total time to completion and the number of errors (false entries). Learning would be demonstrated by a drop in either time to completion or the number of errors, as the number of trials increases.

Beginning on page 48, a maze is reprinted four times. In each case, using the second indicator on a wrist watch or a stopwatch, time yourself from the time you begin with a pencil at the starting point to the time you leave the maze. You should never pick your pencil off the paper until the maze is completed. If you make an error, simply retrace your steps with the pencil. Upon completion of the maze, record the total time taken at the bottom of the page. Do not record the number of errors until you have finished all the mazes, since calculation of errors would be like another trial (you would have to work through the maze again).

Finish all four trials and then calculate errors for each trial. An error is defined as the crossing of the imaginary line at the mouth of an "alley" that leads to a dead end. One such entry can only count for one error, no matter how far you go up the blind alley before realizing that it is blind. In other words, once you have entered an alley that will ultimately be blind, you can only score one error, even if there is a further choice-point along this path (both of these choices would of course have to be blind alleys). The only way you can score two errors for the same blind alley is to enter it twice.

Plot the time/trial and errors/trial on the two graphs provided below. Do you show evidence for gradual mastery of the maze? Compare your results with those from a group of undergraduate students that we have plotted on the same graph. We have plotted the mean (the average) scores. Individuals vary a lot; not all individuals show smooth curves like these averaged curves. In the graph, •——• represents the mean for eight participants. H and L represent the range. H is the highest value of eight participants; L is the lowest score of eight participants.

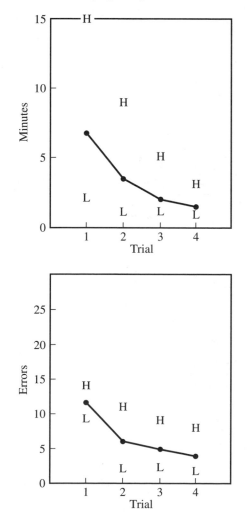

In the earlier part of this century, psychologists speculated about what exactly is learned when a rat or human learns a maze. Some, like John B. Watson, took a "molecular" position and claimed that a sequence of responses is learned. The most critical responses would be those at the choice-points: from this point of view, the learning would be represented as a series of turning instructions (e.g., left, right, right), one for each successive choice-point. Others, such as Edward Chace Tolman, argued that the participant, rat or human, developed a spatial representation of the maze in his or her head, a "cognitive map," rather than a sequence of responses. What do you think you actually learned in this task?

You should realize that this type of maze differs markedly from the mazes used for rats, or the life-size mazes for humans. In these cases, the participant does not get a direct picture of the whole layout; rather, the participant can only see the part of the maze in the immediate vicinity of the choice-point. This, of course, would make it much harder for the participant to build up a map of the maze. To get a feeling for the difference, cut out a hole about 1/2" square from the center of a full-sized piece of paper. Place it at the beginning of the fifth duplication of the maze, and attempt to move through the maze with the pencil again, moving the hole along as you move the pencil. If you had learned a series of turns or choices, this procedure should not seriously affect your performance. On the other hand, insofar as you used a "map," or some sort of larger view of the shape of the maze and your path through it, this procedure would seriously affect your performance.

(If your instructor collects the data, fill out the report sheet in Appendix 2.)

FURTHER ACTIVITIES

We have included one extra copy of the maze. You can use this copy for further experiments. If you need more than one maze, you can make a copy of this unused maze.

You might wish to test the idea of a map of the maze versus a set of turning responses by trying to run the maze backward (start at finish and end at start). What predictions would you make? A cognitive map view would hold that the backward run would be a lot easier than the first run in the "proper" direction, since the same maze map would work in both directions. But a response-learning view would not predict that having learned the maze in the original order would aid in the learning of the reversed maze. The sequence of turns (e.g., left, left, right, left, etc.) would be entirely different when running the maze backward.

Of course, there is a problem here. How do you know how long it would have taken to run the maze backward if you did that on your first trial? You don't. One possibility would be to run a few people on one trial forward and a few others on one trial backward. You could then see if one direction was harder than the other. Another possibility, not as satisfying, is just to assume that it should be about as easy forward as backward, since it wasn't designed to be more difficult one way than the other.

Another activity would be to look at forgetting. Do the final maze in a few days or a week and compare your time and errors to your performance today. Would you expect your performance to be about the same as Trial 4? Better than Trial 1?

On the following three pages, cover the top (completed) maze while doing the bottom one.

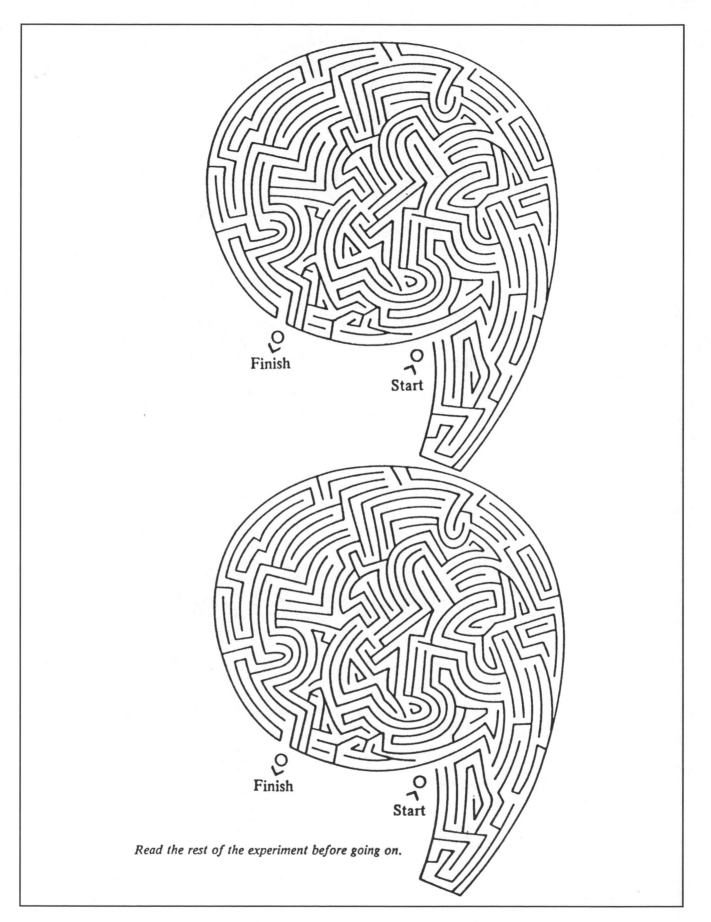

Finish

Start

Finish

Start

Read the rest of the experiment before going on.

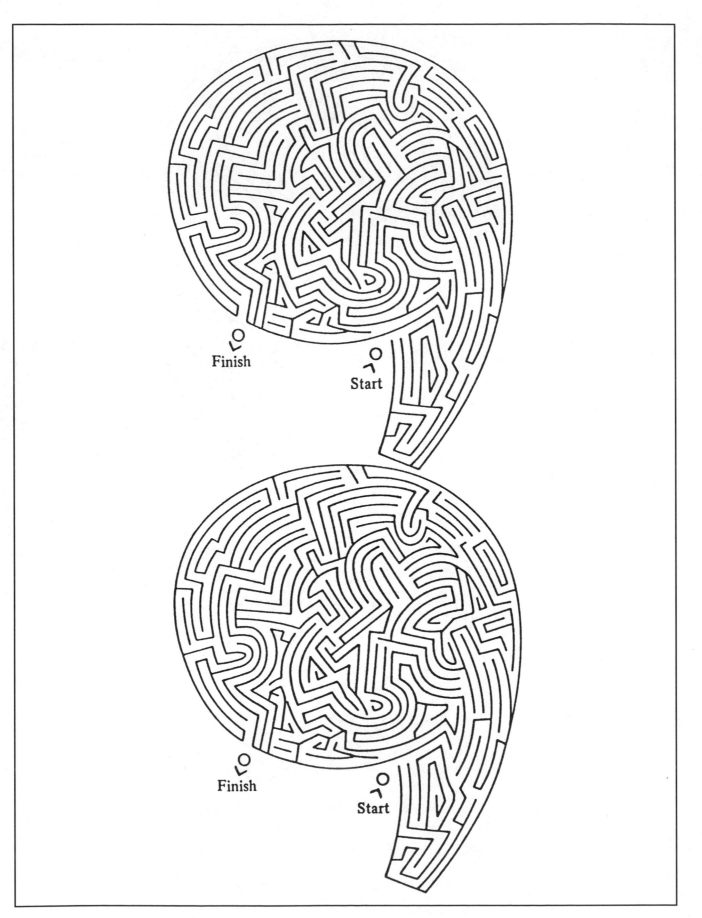

LEARNED TASTE AVERSIONS

Equipment: None
Number of participants: Five to eight
Time per participant: Five minutes
Time for experimenter: Sixty minutes

One of the basic assumptions of behavior theory is that any conditioned stimulus (CS) could become associated with any unconditioned stimulus (US). That is, it is assumed that the relation of the CS to the US is arbitrary. This assumption has been seriously challenged by the discovery of the phenomenon of learned taste aversions in rats. As first documented by John Garcia and his colleagues, rats can learn in one trial to associate a taste (CS) with illness (US). They will subsequently avoid the taste. This learned taste aversion was of particular importance because Garcia and his colleagues showed that this rapid learning would occur only with tastes as the CS and certain types of illness as the US. This specificity of association between tastes and illness is an illustration of belongingness, the nonarbitrariness of associations.

Because learned taste aversions differ from most of the frequently studied types of learning, they were investigated in some detail. We now know that

1. The specificity (belongingness) is between tastes and specific types of illness: symptoms from the upper gastrointestinal system, especially nausea, seem by far the most effective.

2. The learning typically occurs in one trial (thus allowing rats to avoid poisons without too many life-threatening trials).

3. The rat can accomplish this learning even if the illness follows the taste by more than one hour. This challenges the view that two stimuli must occur close together in time to be associated. CS-US intervals of more than an hour rarely, if ever, support conditioning in traditional classical conditioning, using salivation or startle responses, and tones, bells, and lights.

4. Novel tastes show much more conditioning than familiar ones. This makes sense: if eating the familiar food has not been followed by illness, it is reasonable to associate the illness with the new food. This is true in other types of classical conditioning as well: there is generally more conditioning to novel stimuli.

Often after a new phenomenon is described, it is found to be common, and one wonders how it could have escaped notice before. So it was with learned taste aversions. A phenomenon similar to that described by Garcia in the rat seems to occur in humans. Most commonly, someone eats a (usually new) food and gets ill within a few hours. Nausea and vomiting are particularly common symptoms. After this one experience, a person finds the food distasteful. Garb and Stunkard (1974) distributed a questionnaire about such experiences to about 700 people. They found that somewhat over one-third of people have had at least one such experience. The analysis of the results of their questionnaire confirmed the presence of the basic properties of learned taste aversions in humans:

1. Belongingness. Aversions were almost always limited to the food and its taste. Rarely were there reports of aversion to the restaurant, tablecloth, accompanying people, or other stimuli that were also associated, in time, with the illness. Furthermore, the illness in question almost always (87 percent of the time) involved the gastrointestinal system.

2. One-trial learning. The aversions usually occurred after one food-illness pairing.

3. Long CS-US intervals. There was often an interval measured in hours between food ingestion and illness.

4. Novelty. Novel foods (tastes) seem more effective. Although almost everything eaten on any given day would be familiar, 45 percent of the aversions involved foods that had been eaten no more than twice before the pairing with illness.

5. "Irrationality." In many cases, a participant knew that the food did not cause the illness (e.g., other people eating the same food did not get ill, and/or other friends not at the meal came down with the same viral illness at about the same time). Yet, this knowledge that the food did not cause the illness did not weaken the aversion.

We will attempt to confirm the phenomenon of learned taste aversion in humans and highlight its unusual properties. Since, according to Garb and Stunkard, about one-third of people show this phenomenon, we will ask you to interview five to eight people, in the hope that you will find one to four participants with aversions. We will use an interview protocol that asks many of the same questions covered in Garb and Stunkard's questionnaire. Read the introduction below to each participant. If the participant has an aversion, ask each of the questions indicated and record the answers.

LEARNED TASTE AVERSIONS: INTERVIEW PROTOCOL

If a person becomes sick after eating a particular food, he or she may develop an intense dislike, called an aversion, for that food, whether or not it was responsible for the illness. For example, one person developed a high fever after eating pizza in a restaurant and found that he did not like pizza any more. Another person became very nauseous after eating a breakfast with hash-brown potatoes and found the potatoes distasteful after this experience. She also found she did not want to eat from the plate that the potatoes were on. Have you ever come to dislike a food because you became ill after eating it? If so, please answer the following questions:

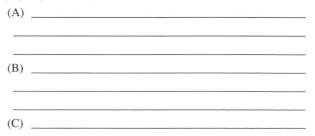

1. Your current age.
   (Participant A) _____ (B) _____
   (C) _____ (D) _____

2. Age when the aversion experience occurred.
   (A) _____ (B) _____ (C) _____ (D) _____

3. What is the food? (A) _____ (B) _____
   (C) _____ (D) _____

4. Describe the experience in terms of what and where you were eating, and the symptoms of the illness. (*Use extra sheet of paper if necessary.*)
   (A) _____
   _____
   _____
   (B) _____
   _____
   _____
   (C) _____

_____

_____

_____

(D) _____

_____

_____

5. Did this happen only once? If more than once, how many times? (A) _____, _____ (B) _____, _____ (C) _____, _____ (D) _____, _____

6. What was the most important symptom you had?

    (A) _____ (B) _____

    (C) _____ (D) _____

7. Were you nauseous? Did you vomit (if not mentioned in answer above)? (A) _____, _____

    (B) _____, _____ (C) _____, _____

    (D) _____, _____

8. About how long after you ate the food did the symptoms appear? (A) _____ (B) _____

    (C) _____ (D) _____

9. Do you believe that the food actually caused your illness?

    (A) _____ (B) _____

    (C) _____ (D) _____

10. List all the foods that you can remember at the meal before you got sick. Indicate for each food whether it was relatively unfamiliar (you ate it no more than three times in your life). Indicate whether you developed an aversion to any of these foods:

Food	Unfamiliar	Aversion
(A)		
_____	_____	___
_____	_____	___
_____	_____	___
_____	_____	___
(B)		
_____	_____	___
_____	_____	___
_____	_____	___
_____	_____	___
(C)		
_____	_____	___
_____	_____	___
_____	_____	___
_____	_____	___
(D)		
_____	_____	___
_____	_____	___
_____	_____	___
_____	_____	___

11. List all the other things or events that you can remember at this same meal and in the time after the meal and before the illness (e.g., the restaurant, table settings, people with you, books read, and so on). Indicate whether you acquired an aversion to any of these items.

(A) _____

_____

_____

(B) _____

_____

(C) _____

_____

_____

(D) _____

_____

12. Do you still have this aversion? (A) _____ (B) _____

    (C) _____ (D) _____

13. Was (Is) the aversion to the taste, smell, and/or sight of the food?

Taste	Smell	Sight
(A) _____	(A) _____	(A) _____
(B) _____	(B) _____	(B) _____
(C) _____	(C) _____	(C) _____
(D) _____	(D) _____	(D) _____

Summarize the results from all of your participants below. You decide which questions are relevant to each feature of learned taste aversion and summarize your results with respect to each of the features listed below.

BELONGINGNESS Relevant questions (Nos.)

_____

_____

_____

ONE-TRIAL LEARNING Relevant questions (Nos.)

_____

_____

_____

LONG CS-US INTERVAL Relevant questions (Nos.)

_____

_____

_____

NOVELTY EFFECT Relevant questions (Nos.)

_____

_____

_____

"IRRATIONALITY" Relevant questions (Nos.)

_____

_____

_____

OTHER INTERESTING RESULTS

_____

_____

_____

Do your data confirm the basic properties of learned taste aversion?

Comment: Interview protocols like this are quite common in psychological research. They are essentially questionnaires, but they are administered by a researcher or someone on his or her staff. In a way they are more subjective than questionnaires because the interviewer could influence the answers of the participant, especially if there is embarrassing material in the protocol. On the other hand, the interview allows for an interaction between the researcher and the participant: if a participant misunderstands a question, he or she can be corrected. If the participant says something that is ambiguous, it can be expanded. Similarly, if the participant says something of unusual interest, it can be followed up.

The introductory statement in the interview is critical. We tried to write it so as not to guarantee that participants would only describe specific food aversions based on gastrointestinal illness. Note that we gave one example of another sort of illness and also suggested the possibility of an aversion to items other than tastes. This certainly does not guarantee an "unbiased" sample of aversions, but it allows for exceptions to the phenomena as described by Garcia and later by Garb and Stunkard. Garb and Stunkard's introductory paragraph was more suggestive of gastrointestinal illness than is the paragraph we use here. *(If your instructor collects the data, fill out the report sheet in Appendix 2.)*

PROBLEMS AND FURTHER ACTIVITIES

Garb and Stunkard's questionnaire and our interview are not experiments. They can demonstrate that one-trial taste-illness aversions occur in humans. But by themselves they cannot demonstrate belongingness. Remember that Garcia's experiments with rats showed that although lights and tastes were equally paired with both illness and electric shock, the taste was much more strongly associated with illness and the lights with shock. Our introduction for the participants (and more so Garb and Stunkard's) pointed the participant toward taste-illness associations. We did not ask the participants if they ever came to dislike a restaurant or a person because either was "followed by" illness or whether they ever came to dislike a food because it was followed by pain or a variety of other unpleasant events. On the contrary, we could ask whether, as a consequence of a very unpleasant event such as a death in the family or painful injury, a participant developed an aversion to any object, event, or food. Such questions have not been asked systematically. Do you have any such aversion? Do any of your friends? If there are many aversions linking food with unpleasant events "outside of the body" or outside of the gastrointestinal system, or if there are aversions to visual or other objects paired with illness, then there is little evidence for the belongingness effects in humans. We don't think there *are* many such effects, but we are not sure at this time.

We have suggested that nausea and vomiting are especially important in generating taste aversion. See whether you can find evidence for this. If you know anyone (including yourself) with a food allergy, interview that person, using a protocol like the one we have used for aversions. (You will have to make a few modifications.) The critical question is whether people with food allergies develop aversions to these foods. In particular, if the allergy produces no symptoms in the gastrointestinal system, is there an aversion? There are some data (Pelchat and Rozin, 1982) that suggest that people with food allergies outside of the gastrointestinal system do not have aversions to these foods—that is, they don't dislike these allergenic foods.

References

Garb, F., & Stunkard, A. (1974). Taste aversions in man. *American Journal of Psychiatry, 131,* 1204–1207.

Logue, A. W., Ophir, I., & Strauss, K. E. (1981). The acquisition of taste aversion in humans. *Behavior Research and Therapy, 19,* 319–333.

Pelchat, M. L., & Rozin, P. (1982). The special role of nausea in the acquisition of food dislikes by humans. *Appetite, 3,* 341–351.

CHAPTER 5

Sensory Processes

Learning Objectives

THE ORIGINS OF KNOWLEDGE

An early view—the empiricists
1. Be familiar with the viewpoint of the British empiricists.
2. What is the distinction between proximal and distal stimuli?
3. What are sensations?
4. Understand the role of association in the empiricists' view of perception.
5. What is the relevance of linear perspective in a discussion of association?

The active perceiver
6. How does nativism differ from empiricism?
7. What is the psychophysical approach to this problem?

Measuring sensory intensity
8. Why is the just-noticeable difference (jnd) important in measuring sensory intensity?
9. What is Weber's law? How is Weber's fraction used to compare the sensitivities of different sensory modalities?
10. Why is Fechner's law biologically plausible?

Detection and decision
11. What is the role of expectations in signal detection?
12. What sorts of errors might result from setting a criterion? How do payoff manipulations affect response bias?
13. How can an analysis of the proportions of "yes" and "no" responses measure the separate effects of sensitivity and response bias?
14. How is signal-detection theory applicable to problems other than the detection of weak stimuli?
15. Why are false alarms and misses nearly inevitable in decision situations?

Sensory coding
16. How is stimulus intensity coded?
17. Explain the doctrine of specific nerve energies as it applies both within and between sensory modalities. Explain how specificity and pattern theories account for sensory coding.

THE FUNCTIONING OF THE SENSES

18. What are the various senses that humans have?

HEARING

Sound
19. What is the stimulus for hearing? How do sound waves vary?
20. Know how the amplitude and frequency of sound stimuli are measured.
21. What is the difference between simple and complex auditory stimuli? How does the brain treat complex stimuli?

From sound waves to hearing
22. Describe the structure of the ear as it collects the auditory stimulus. How does this structure permit the perception of sounds?
23. How is the cochlea designed?
24. Describe the place and firing frequency theories of pitch perception. Why does each seem important to perception, and what triggers each?

VISION

The stimulus: light
25. What are the characteristics of light, and what are their visual consequences?

Gathering the stimulus: the eye
26. How is the eye like a camera?

The visual receptors
27. Describe the retina.
28. Be familiar with the following terms: rods, cones, bipolar cells, ganglion cells, optic nerve, and blind spot.
29. Where is visual acuity greatest, and why?
30. Understand the duplex theory of vision. What is the evidence for two types of receptors, and why are they needed?
31. How does spectral sensitivity help to distinguish rods from cones?
32. What is a visual pigment and how does it result in a neural signal from a light stimulus?

The importance of change: adaptation
33. What is sensory adaptation? What does the organism gain by sensory adaptation?
34. Explain the technique used to show that stabilization of the retinal image leads to visual adaptation.
35. What is the biological significance of involuntary eye movements?

Interaction in space: contrast

36. Recall that brightness contrast increases with progressive intensity difference between two regions and with decreasing distance between them. How is this phenomenon important to visual perception? How do Mach bands illustrate this?
37. What is the physiological mechanism that underlies Mach bands?
38. Be familiar with the effects of lateral inhibition. What is its effect on vision?

Color

39. What are the dimensions of color?
40. Describe the "unique" colors.
41. Are differences in brightness best observed in chromatic or in achromatic colors?
42. How can colors be varied in saturation?
43. Describe the color solid. How are different dimensions of color represented in it? What is its relationship to the color circle?

The physiological basis of color vision

44. Explain the differences among the three cone types in human color vision.

45. What are complementary colors? How do their complementary characters account for simultaneous color contrast and negative afterimages?
46. It is important to understand the opponent-process theory thoroughly. Be aware of the relevance of primary colors, color antagonists, and inhibition in the perception of hue and brightness.
47. What is the physiological evidence for the opponent-process theory?
48. Describe different types of color blindness.

Perceiving shapes

49. How do electrophysiological studies of the action of single neural cells tell us about the perception of contours?
50. Define a receptive field.
51. What is the significance of studies of "bug detectors"?
52. Understand how the perception of complex forms such as faces might be related to the use of feature detectors.

Programmed Exercises

THE ORIGINS OF KNOWLEDGE

1. John Locke postulated that all knowledge comes by way of experience. This school of thought is known as _____.

   empiricism

2. Locke used the metaphor of a _____ _____ in describing the human mind at birth.

   tabula rasa (blank slate)

3. An object in the real world is known as a _____ stimulus.

   distal

4. When the energy from an object impinges on a sensory surface, we say that this pattern of energy has become a _____ stimulus.

   proximal

5. Empiricists assumed that the raw materials of knowledge are _____.

   sensations

6. According to the empiricists, complex ideas are perceived by the linking together, or _____, of two or more sensations.

   association

7. Two identical objects have different retinal sizes. This clue that one object is closer than the other is known as _____ _____.

   linear perspective

8. Kant believed that a number of aspects of perception are innate. This view has since been labeled _____.

   nativism

9. The study of the relationship between properties of the stimulus and sensory experience is known as _____.

   psychophysics

10. You find that you are unable to tell the difference between a 25-lb. weight and a 28-lb. weight, but you can differentiate the 25-lb. weight from any other weight over 28 lbs. Something slightly over 3 lbs. is your _____ _____. It will produce a _____-_____ _____ in this weight range.

    difference threshold, just-noticeable difference (jnd)

11. A difference threshold is 2 lbs. when the standard is 40 lbs. _____ law predicts that the difference threshold with a 20-lb. standard would be _____ lb(s).

    Weber's
    1

12. The jnd divided by the standard stimulus is known as _____ _____ and, in general, seems to be constant.

    Weber's fraction

13. Imagine that for a certain psychophysical task we found that sensation grew as a function of the logarithm of the physical stimulus intensity. This would be support for _____ law.

    Fechner's

14. One duty of air traffic controllers is to watch a radar screen and determine what planes are in the area. There are two kinds of errors they might make in this task. First, they may not see a small dot on the screen, thus committing a _____, as it is often called in signal-detection theory. On the other hand, they may report a plane when there is none there. This is called a _____ _____. Considering the costs of these two errors, the _____ _____ error is probably more common than the _____.

    miss
    false alarm
    false alarm
    miss

15. Corresponding to the two types of errors, there are also two kinds of correct responses. When an event occurs in the world and we say that the event occurred, that is known as a _____. When an event hasn't occurred in the world and we say that it hasn't, we have given a _____ _____.

    hit
    correct negative

16. If you make a selection error during the admission of a student to medical school that results in admitting a student who cannot complete the degree requirements, you have made a _____ _____ error .

    false
    alarm

17. The theory that accounts for performance when participants are trying to determine whether a weak stimulus was presented is called _____-_____ theory.

    signal-detection

18. When a weak stimulus is presented, participants must set a _____ to determine whether the level of activity within their sensory system warrants saying that the stimulus was present.

    cutoff

19. There clearly are qualitative differences in sensations (e.g., smells are different from sounds). These differences are due to differences in sensory _____.

    quality

20. According to the doctrine of _____ _____ _____, differences in subjective quality are caused by differences in associated nervous structures rather than by differences inherent in the stimuli.

    specific nerve energies

21. There are two theoretical approaches that explain the neural processes that underlie sensations. The _____ theory states that different sensory qualities are signaled by different quality-specific neurons. The other theory, the across-fiber _____ theory, asserts that substances produce a pattern of activation across a set of fibers, and that this pattern is the neural code that gives rise to sensory quality.

    specificity
    pattern

THE FUNCTIONING OF THE SENSES

22. In addition to the senses of vision, hearing, touch, taste, and smell, humans also have the sense of _____ (sensitivity to body position) and the _____ sense (signaling movements of the head).

    kinesthesis, vestibular

23. The sense of touch can be subdivided into the four sensations of _____, _____, _____, and _____.

    pressure, warmth
    cold, pain

HEARING

24. The _____ canals indicate rotation of the head. They are located in the _____ _____.

    semicircular, inner
    ear

25. Light intensity is to vision as _____ is to hearing.

    amplitude

26. Hue is to vision as _____ is to audition.

    pitch

27. Many different _____ _____, differing in both frequency and amplitude, combine to form a _____ _____.

    sine waves
    complex wave

28. The purpose of the middle ear, oval window, and inner ear is to _____ and _____ sound waves.

    conduct, amplify

29. The structure that actually contains the auditory receptors is known as the _____.

    cochlea

30. The actual auditory receptors are the _____ _____, which are stimulated by deformation of the _____ _____.

    hair cells
    basilar membrane

31. Pitch perception seems to be based on two mechanisms. High frequencies are coded using _____ of excitation, whereas lower frequencies are coded by _____ firing rate.

    place, neural

32. For all modalities, stimulus energy must be converted into a form that can be used by the senses. The translation is termed _____.

    transduction

VISION

33. Objects can either _____ or _____ light.

emit, reflect

34. Light energy can vary in _____, thus giving rise to perceived brightness, and in _____, which determines perceived hue.

intensity, wavelength

35. The visible spectrum extends from roughly _____ to roughly _____ nanometers.

360, 750

36. The first place at which light energy from the world interacts with the senses is at the _____.

retina

37. The focusing of the eye is affected by _____ of the lens.

accommodation

38. _____ are most densely packed in the fovea, while _____ are most frequent in the periphery.

Cones, rods

39. The first cells to be stimulated by light are the _____, which activate the _____ cells, which in turn stimulate the _____ cells.

receptors, bipolar ganglion

40. The axons of the ganglion cells form a bundle, which is known as the _____ _____; this exits the eyeball at the _____ _____.

optic nerve
blind spot

41. The fact that primarily nocturnal animals have no cones and many rods, whereas animals that operate in daylight have many cones and few rods, is evidence for a _____ theory of vision.

duplex

42. The fact that sensitivity to dim light is greater in the periphery of the visual field (where rods are) than in the fovea (where cones are) supports the _____ theory of vision.

duplex

43. The chemical reaction in which the visual pigment rhodopsin breaks down and then reforms into rhodopsin takes place in the _____ .

rods

44. _____ _____, as examples of visual adaptation, illustrate the role of temporal interaction in vision.

Stabilized images

45. _____ _____, a phenomenon of brightness contrast, are examples of spatial interaction.

Mach bands

46. The physical resolution of the eye is not very good. In terms of physics, we shouldn't be able to see as clearly as we do. However, the exaggeration of contrast through _____ _____ enhances the visual message.

lateral inhibition

47. The three attributes used to describe color are _____, _____, and _____.

hue, brightness, saturation

48. _____ colors cannot be distinguished on the basis of hue.

Achromatic

49. Unique red is the red that appears to have neither any _____ nor any _____ in it.

blue, yellow

50. Only _____ colors can differ in saturation.

chromatic

51. The _____ _____ equates spatial relationships along three dimensions with the three dimensions of color.

color solid

52. A _____ hue is one that, when mixed with another hue in the correct proportion, will produce the color gray.

complementary

53. A gray color, when surrounded by green, appears reddish. This is known as _____ _____ _____ and is evidence for antagonistic pairing of colors.

simultaneous
color contrast

54. _____ _____ have the complementary hue and the opposite brightness of the original stimulus.

Negative afterimages

55. Human vision is termed _____, since there are three cone types.

trichromatic

56. According to the opponent-process theory of color vision, it should never be possible to see a red hue with a trace of _____ in it.

green

57. Color blindness is most common in _____ and could entail the _____ of one of the opponent-process pairs.

males, absence

58. _____ have contributed significantly to the study of form perception by studying the behavior of single nerve cells in the visual system.

Electrophysiologists

59. In recording from a single nerve cell, you discover that its firing rate varies when a stimulus is presented at a certain place in the visual field. This is the cell's _____ field.

receptive

60. A nerve cell that selectively responds to some characteristics of a stimulus but not to others is often called a _____ _____.

feature detector

61. One of the characteristics that visual nerve cells respond to selectively is _____.

orientation

62. It has been shown that monkeys have feature detectors that are selectively sensitive to very complex stimuli, such as _____.

faces (or hands)

Self-Test

1. John Locke, the British empiricist, would most likely agree with which of the following statements?
   a. "All knowledge is determined by innate mechanisms."
   b. "We are born with a fair amount of innate knowledge, with experience playing a small role."
   c. "Knowledge arrives through the senses."
   d. John Locke was not an empiricist and would not have agreed with any of the above statements.

2. The metaphor that best describes the empiricists' view of the human mind at birth is
   a. a camera.
   b. an encyclopedia.
   c. a pad and pencil.
   d. a blank slate.

3. An example of a distal stimulus would be
   a. the pattern of light energy hitting the retina.
   b. a Chevrolet.
   c. the sensation produced by a distant mountain.
   d. a hallucination.

4. An example of a proximal visual stimulus is
   a. the activity of the retina hit by an array of photons.
   b. an object situated very close to the retina.
   c. a distant object that appears closer than it really is.
   d. all of the above

5. According to the empiricists, linear perspective serves as a depth cue because
   a. it produces a memory of an associated movement and an experience of depth.
   b. it mitigates the effect of convergence.
   c. its use by painters has familiarized us with its symbolic representation of depth.
   d. we are classically conditioned to accept it as such.

6. Immanuel Kant believed
   a. in innately determined categories of perception.
   b. that all knowledge came through the senses.
   c. that associations of sensations determined perception.
   d. in none of the above

7. Psychophysics studies the relationship between
   a. the distal and proximal stimulus.
   b. the distal stimulus and sensory experience.
   c. nativism and empiricism.
   d. the proximal stimulus and sensory experience.

8. It can be argued that sensations cannot be measured directly. It should be possible, though, to compare sensations. For instance, we should be able to determine whether one sensation is the same as or different from another. This viewpoint would most likely be expressed by
   a. Kant.
   b. Locke.
   c. Fechner.
   d. Berkeley.

9. You are shopping for a new car. You have test-driven a number of cars to determine which models have the best performance. You discover that you cannot tell the difference between models A and C. The difference (however measured) between cars A and C is below your
   a. difference threshold.
   b. response bias.
   c. criterion.
   d. sensitivity.

10. Which of the following agrees with Weber's law? (In each case, the first number represents the weight difference needed to produce a jnd, and the absolute stimulus energy is specified by the second number. Two pairs are provided for each possible answer.)
    a. 1, 10/2, 100
    b. 20, 50/1, 2.5
    c. 5, 100/5, 50
    d. All of the above are in agreement with Weber's law.

11. As in 10 above, each of the pairs of numbers below represents a hypothetical difference threshold with its associated stimulus energy value. Which of the Weber fractions that results from these values represents the greatest sensitivity?
    a. 1, 100
    b. 1, 10
    c. 100, 1000
    d. 50, 1000

12. Fechner's law states that the strength of the sensation increases _____ with stimulus intensity.
    a. inversely
    b. minimally
    c. logarithmically
    d. linearly

13. A doctor is scanning a lung X-ray. She sees something that may be either the beginnings of a tumor or harmless scar tissue. It is likely that some factors will come into play when the doctor decides whether to operate or not. Which are some of these factors?
    a. probability that it is a tumor
    b. risks associated with surgery
    c. risks associated with an untreated tumor
    d. all of the above
    e. none of the above; response bias is fixed and cannot be easily changed

14. In the example in question 13, what type of error is worse to make?
    a. false alarm
    b. miss
    c. a and b are equally important
    d. cannot be determined without knowing associated costs and benefits

15. Still considering the example in question 13, imagine that there are five different types of tumors such that each is associated with a different death rate when left untreated. Type I has the highest death rate, and Type V has the lowest rate (with the others falling between I and V, in order). Imagine further that these five tumors can be distinguished from each other with X-rays, but none of them can be distinguished from scar tissue (which is harmless). Assuming that everything else is constant from one tumor type to another, under which condition would the doctor be most likely to operate and risk putting the patient under the dangers of surgery?
    a. The patient has either scar tissue or Type III tumor.
    b. The patient has either scar tissue or Type V tumor.
    c. The patient has either scar tissue or Type I tumor.
    d. If the doctor were competent, the probability of her operating would be constant, despite the type of tumor.

16. If, under certain circumstances, a participant's hit rate went up while his false alarm rate stayed the same, we could conclude that his
    a. bias to say "yes" went up.
    b. accuracy decreased.
    c. sensitivity increased.
    d. accuracy and bias both changed.

17. Which of the following is an example of transduction?
    a. sound waves in the air being translated into electrical energy by a microphone
    b. electrical waves being translated into sound waves by a loudspeaker
    c. light energy being converted into nerve energy by the retina
    d. all of the above

18. Differences among the taste of a cold beer, the sound of a Mozart quartet, and the sight of a fireworks display are due to
    a. our past experiences with these stimuli.
    b. differences in the sense organs that respond to the stimuli.
    c. physiological differences in the conduction velocities of the neurons attached to the various sense organs.
    d. all of the above

19. If, by some freak of nature, the optic and olfactory nerves were crossed and led to the opposite sense organ, the law of specific nerve energies would predict the following result:
    a. smelling red
    b. normal sensations
    c. The law of specific nerve energies makes no predictions in such a case.
    d. any of the above

20. Kinesthesis is
    a. information from the muscles, tendons, and joints.
    b. a function of the ossicles in the inner ear.
    c. the movement of hair cells in the cochlea.
    d. the crystallization of the viscous liquid in the semicircular canals.

21. The physical stimulus for hearing is described in terms of amplitude and frequency. The corresponding psychological dimensions are
    a. loudness and tone.
    b. amplitude and pitch.
    c. loudness and timbre.
    d. loudness and pitch.

22. Which pair of the following representative sound waves includes both a simple and a complex wave?
    a. 1 and 3
    b. 2 and 4
    c. 2 and either 3 or 4
    d. either 1 or 2 and 3

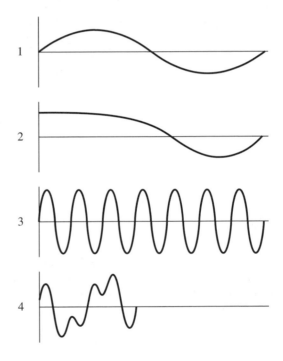

23. The correct ordering of anatomical structures in the ear (from outside in) is
    a. eardrum, middle ear, oval window, cochlea.
    b. oval window, middle ear, eardrum, cochlea.
    c. eardrum, oval window, middle ear, cochlea.
    d. none of the above

24. For low frequency tones (below 400 hz), pitch is detected by
    a. the eardrum.
    b. localization on the basilar membrane.
    c. firing frequency of the auditory nerve.
    d. none of the above

25. For frequencies above 5000, pitch is detected by
    a. the eardrum.
    b. localization on the basilar membrane.
    c. firing frequency of the auditory nerve.
    d. none of the above

26. One light source appears bluish and another appears greenish. This difference in appearance is due to differences in
    a. intensity.
    b. wavelength.
    c. opponent processes.
    d. none of the above

27. Intensity is to brightness as wavelength is to
    a. sensitivity.
    b. darkness.
    c. wattage.
    d. hue.

28. Which of the following wavelengths is not considered to be part of the visible spectrum?
    a. 650
    b. 400
    c. 300
    d. 575

29. The structure that bends light rays so that they are projected onto a light-sensitive surface is the
    a. retina.
    b. iris.
    c. lens.
    d. all of the above

30. During the process of accommodation, a close object will result in _____ of the lens.
    a. thickening
    b. flattening
    c. no change
    d. increased transparency

31. You arrive late to a movie theater and are forced to sit in the far right-hand seat of the first row. You must then look to your left to see the rectangular screen. What is the image of the screen that is projected onto your retina?

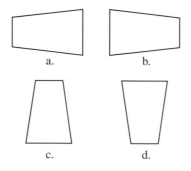

32. The two types of receptors in the human eye are known as _____ and _____.
    a. bipolars, horizontals
    b. ganglions, bipolars
    c. rods, cones
    d. bipolars, cones

33. An area near the center of the retina has virtually no rods, consisting entirely of cones. It is approximately two degrees in diameter and is known as the
    a. periphery.
    b. optic nerve.
    c. optic chiasm.
    d. fovea.

34. Which of the following is not in agreement with the duplex theory of vision?
    a. The rods are the receptors for night vision, whereas cones serve day vision.
    b. Rods respond to low light levels, cones to high levels.
    c. Rod vision provides good acuity; cones provide poor acuity.
    d. Rods result in achromatic vision; cones provide color vision.

35. In a psychophysical task, we ask a participant to tell us when she can see a dim light. We vary the intensity until she reports that she sees it. We then record the luminance level. Now we change the wavelength and plot sensitivity again. This figure is known as the
    a. dark adaptation curve.
    b. spectral sensitivity curve.
    c. receiver operating characteristic (ROC).
    d. sensory adaptation curve.

36. What happens when light hits a visual receptor?
    a. Silver bromide molecules combine with light to release silver.
    b. Light strikes the retina and generates rhodopsin.
    c. Energy is converted to nervous impulses via a photochemical process that bleaches rhodopsin.
    d. The reflected light from the receptor causes a photochemical alteration leading to neural excitation.

37. Which of the following is an example of sensory adaptation?
    a. The cold ocean feels warmer after we've been in it for a while.
    b. being able to see in a dark room after a period of adjustment
    c. increasing sensitivity to salt with continued exposure
    d. all of the above
    e. a and b

38. The first time you see a friend's new car, it is parked against a black wall. Later you see that same car parked against a white backdrop (at the same time of day) and comment that you remember the car as being much brighter. This is an example of
    a. brightness contrast.
    b. adaptation.
    c. temporal interaction.
    d. none of the above

39. Lateral inhibition is responsible for which phenomenon?
    a. color vision
    b. Mach bands
    c. stabilized image
    d. all of the above

40. Which of the following is not used to classify colors?
    a. brightness
    b. hue
    c. amplitude
    d. saturation

41. White and black can be distinguished only on the basis of which dimensions?
    a. brightness
    b. hue
    c. wavelength
    d. saturation

42. Red and green must differ on which dimension (at least)?
    a. brightness
    b. hue
    c. amplitude
    d. saturation

43. White and black cannot possibly differ on which dimension?
    a. hue
    b. saturation
    c. both of the above
    d. none of the above

44. The extent to which a color of some fixed hue is mixed with an achromatic color is represented by a value on the _____ dimension.
    a. brightness
    b. hue
    c. intensity
    d. saturation

45. Any wavelength will stimulate
    a. all three receptor types, but unequally.
    b. all three receptor types, and equally.
    c. only one or two receptor types.
    d. from one to three receptors, depending on the intensity and wavelength.

46. In the opponent-process theory, the three pairs of receptors are
    a. red-blue, green-yellow, black-white.
    b. red-yellow, blue-green, black-white.
    c. red-green, blue-yellow, black-white.
    d. never specified.

47. An achromatic color results when which system(s) is(are) in balance?
    a. red-green
    b. blue-yellow
    c. red-green and blue-yellow
    d. black-white

48. Which of the following would be predicted by the opponent-process theory?
    a. The dark gray appearance of black pepper placed against a gray background.
    b. chromatic contrast
    c. negative afterimages
    d. all of the above

49. A person who is color-blind will probably
    a. use color names appropriately.
    b. be female.
    c. be unable to distinguish any hues at all.
    d. be unable to imagine how ultraviolet looks to a bee.

50. The presence of "bug detectors" in frogs indicates that feature detectors
    a. can be responsive to quite complex objects.
    b. cannot be wired to detect anything but simple attributes of shapes.
    c. cannot be shaped by evolutionary pressure.
    d. are a minor part of the visual response to objects.

Answer Key for Self-Test

1. c		26. b	
2. d		27. d	
3. b		28. c	
4. a		29. c	
5. a		30. a	
6. a		31. a	
7. b		32. c	
8. c		33. d	
9. a		34. c	
10. b		35. b	
11. a		36. c	
12. c		37. e	
13. d		38. a	
14. d		39. b	
15. c		40. c	
16. c		41. a	
17. b		42. b	
18. b		43. c	
19. a		44. d	
20. a		45. a	
21. d		46. c	
22. b		47. c	
23. a		48. d	
24. c		49. a	
25. b		50. a	

Investigating Psychological Phenomena

MEASURING BRIGHTNESS CONTRAST

*Equipment: Stimuli are included; one sheet of black construction
    paper needed*
Number of participants: One or more
Time per participant: Ten minutes
Time for experimenter: Twenty minutes

In this "Sensory Processes" chapter, the authors describe a phenomenon that clearly illustrates the effect of context on perception. The phenomenon is brightness contrast. Examine Figure 5.14 in the text once again. Note how sharply different in brightness the four central gray squares appear to be; yet they are identical. (You can prove this to yourself by laying a sheet of paper over the figure with holes cut out where the squares are located.) The difference in brightness is apparently a result of interaction between each central square and its surrounding light or dark border. As the text explains, the surrounding border induces a contrast effect such that a patch will appear lighter when surrounded by a dark border, and darker when surrounded by a light border. The greater the difference in lightness between the center and its surroundings, the greater the illusion.

Of course, as you have probably already suspected, brightness contrast has limits. That is, there is just so much illusion that can be produced by a surrounding context, no matter how great the difference between the center and its surroundings. The present experiment provides an opportunity to examine the extent to which the visual system can be fooled by context. More important, however, in this exercise you will have a chance to conduct an actual psychophysical experiment to measure quantitatively the relationship between physical stimuli and psychological experience.

The purpose of the experiment is to measure the magnitude of brightness contrast for a particular test patch of a given, fixed lightness. This test patch will be surrounded by several borders that differ in their lightness, one from another. With this arrangement, we should be able to produce different degrees of brightness contrast. But how do we measure the extent of the effect? One way would be to ask a participant to assign numbers to the test patch corresponding to how bright she thought it was. But we shall use a more accurate technique: each time we present a border around the test patch, we shall ask the participant to match the apparent brightness of the test patch by choosing another patch that seems to match it. The matching patch that is chosen, having been carefully measured for its lightness, will then serve as an index of how light the participant perceived the test patch to be.

First, cut out the matching patches and the borders on the insert for Chapter 5. The matching patches are the ten squares on the left. Note that there is a number on the back of each that corresponds to its lightness. (The units for these numbers have to do with how various lightnesses are actually created by printers,

and it is not necessary to know them for this exercise. It is sufficient that the patches are ordered correctly.) Now cut out the six borders on the right side of the insert, and cut out the central square area of each. Note that the borders are also marked with a lightness code on the back. Be very careful with both matching patches and borders to trim away any gray from the adjoining figures so that each cutout is an even gray. On the bottom of the insert is the test patch that has already been placed on a white surrounding region. The test patch has a lightness value of 6. *Do not cut out the test figure!* Leave it on its background and place this in turn on a sheet of black construction paper.

Now you are ready to run the experiment. The procedure is to select one background, place it over the test patch, and ask your participant to select a matching patch from among her ten choices that appears to match the test patch in brightness. (Be sure that she lays down the matching patch on the black area to the right of the background to be certain of her choice.) Be careful to tell the participant not to hesitate to select different matching patches with different backgrounds if she feels this is appropriate. Participants may think that because the test patch remains the same, they should always select the same matching patch. Do not let the participant see the test patch without a border between trials as this may also cause a bias toward a particular matching patch.

Place the matching patches at the top of the black construction paper haphazardly. Run the participant through eighteen trials of the experiment, three trials with each background. To have the backgrounds presented in a random order in each set of six, here are three random orders that you may use to determine the sequence in which the backgrounds are presented: 5, 10, 3, 1, 4, 7; 4, 3, 10, 7, 1, 5; 10, 4, 1, 5, 7, 3 (the numbers refer to the lightness codes on the back of each background).

After you have presented a background over the test patch and the participant has chosen her matching patch, place the value of the matching patch in the appropriate space in the table that follows. After the experiment is complete, add up the values in each column and divide by three to get an average matching patch value for each background.

Now you can plot these data in the graph provided. Along the x-axis are the six values of background that you used. Above each find the average value of matching patch that you calculated from the table, and place a dot at the value (as determined from the y-axis). Now connect the dots and note the shape of the function.

Recall that the test patch has a lightness value of 6. Given this, what shape should the function have? How much of a brightness contrast were you able to obtain? How could you improve the experiment to get an even larger effect?

Reference

Heinemann, E. G. (1955). Simultaneous brightness induction as a function of inducing- and test-field luminance. *Journal of Experimental Psychology, 50,* 89–96.

Background values:	1	3	4	5	7	10
Matching value 1:	_____	_____	_____	_____	_____	_____
Matching value 2:	_____	_____	_____	_____	_____	_____
Matching value 3:	_____	_____	_____	_____	_____	_____
Total matching value:	_____	_____	_____	_____	_____	_____
Average matching value:	_____	_____	_____	_____	_____	_____

Test patch lightness value = 6

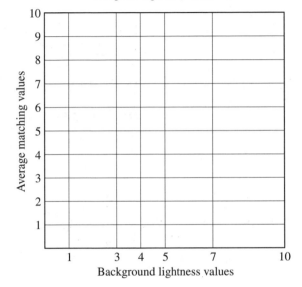

CHAPTER 6

Perception

Learning Objectives

THE COMPLEXITY OF PERCEPTION

1. Know that the central issue of perception is not why a stimulus is recognized as an object, but why it is even seen as an object.
2. Keep in mind the characteristics of the proximal stimulus in comparison with the distal stimulus.
3. Understand that to organize the sensory world, three questions must be asked of any given stimulus: Where is it? Where is it going? What is it?

THE PERCEPTION OF DEPTH: WHERE IS IT?

Binocular cues
4. Be aware of the significance of binocular disparity in depth perception.

Monocular cues
5. What are the monocular cues to depth perception? How is texture important?

The perception of depth through motion
6. How do motion parallax and optic flow contribute to our perception of depth? How do they differ?

The role of redundancy
7. Why do we have multiple mechanisms for perceiving depth?

THE PERCEPTION OF MOVEMENT: WHAT IS IT DOING?

Retinal motion
8. Be familiar with motion detector cells.

Apparent movement
9. Be familiar with the phenomena of apparent and induced movement, and the relevance of these phenomena to the study of real movement.

Eye movements
10. How are we able to distinguish between a moving world with a stationary self (e.g., watching a car go by) and a stationary world with a moving self (e.g., looking out the window of a moving train)?

11. Understand that there is a mechanism that compensates for retinal displacement of objects when the eyes move.

Illusions of motion
12. Describe some motion illusions.

FORM PERCEPTION: WHAT IS IT?

13. Why is form perception not simply a matter of accumulating a checklist?
14. What is transposition and how is it important to the study of form perception?
15. Be aware of the central assumption of Gestalt psychology as it applies to perception.
16. Why does one need to understand both the perception of parts and the relationships among the parts to account for form perception?

The elements of form
17. Review the evidence for mechanisms in the physiology of the brain that underlie the perception of features.
18. Describe some behavioral evidence for the existence of elementary feature detectors in the visual system.
19. Be aware of the later stage of processing at which features are assumed to be conjoined. How does the study of illusory conjunctions pinpoint the stage of processing that is at work in pattern recognition?

Perceptual segregation
20. What is the role of perceptual segregation in scene perception? Why is it important?
21. Give examples of how perceptual segregation occurs in vision and audition.
22. How is the segregation of figure and ground an example of perceptual segregation?
23. Be familiar with reversible figures and how they contribute to our understanding of perceptual segregation. What proposal has been made about the perception of reversible figures?
24. What are the laws of perceptual grouping and how do they relate to each other?

Pattern recognition
25. Describe the feature net model as an approach to pattern recognition. Be familiar with its elements of activation and deactivation.

26. What phenomena show that context affects pattern recognition? What is priming?
27. How does bidirectional activation combine to yield pattern recognition?
28. Why is an intermediate step corresponding to the use of geons necessary in some perception? What are geons?
29. How do patients with visual agnosias inform us about the creation of structural descriptions and the interpretation of them in perception?

The processing sequence in form perception

30. Review the major steps in form perception. Be prepared to discuss how these may be arranged in sequence or in parallel in actual perception.

The perceiver's active role

31. What examples illustrate that the perceiver has an active role in perception?
32. Describe a study of apparent movement that illustrates the constructive nature of perception.

FORM PERCEPTION AND THE NERVOUS SYSTEM

Early stages of visual processing

33. Know the difference between magno and parvo cells. How do they function differently in perception?

Visual processing in the brain

34. Be able to distinguish between the "what" and "where" pathways in the brain. How are they different anatomically and in function? What evidence supports these differences?

The binding problem

35. Be aware of the binding problem and how it is created by a visual system that is based on component analyses of scenes.
36. How does firing synchrony among neurons figure into a solution to the binding problem?

PERCEPTUAL SELECTION: ATTENTION

37. What is attention?

Selection through orientation

38. How can the study of orienting movements inform us about attention?

Central selection

39. Be familiar with the concept of central selection and its manifestations in the auditory and visual modes. What is visual search?
40. What are the conditions that permit parallel visual search, and what are those that require serial search?
41. Be familiar with studies showing that even in vision, attention can be moved internally without moving the eyes.
42. What role does attention play in solving the binding problem?
43. How is priming relevant to attention?
44. What happens to perception when an object is not in the focus of attention? Is it processed duply?
45. How does the study of shadowing inform us about attention?

PERCEIVING CONSTANCY

46. What is the relationship between distal objects and the proximal stimuli they cause that gives rise to the problem of constancy?

Size and shape constancy

47. Be able to describe the phenomena of size and shape constancy.
48. What is meant by higher-order invariants, and how can these be used to solve the problem of size constancy?
49. What role is played by distance cues such as motion parallax in the perception of constant size?
50. Helmholtz's principle of unconscious inference is a powerful explanation of size constancy. Describe it and give an example.
51. How important are distance cues to the perception of size constancy?

Programmed Exercises

THE COMPLEXITY OF PERCEPTION

1. The properties of a three-dimensional distal stimulus are perceived as constant despite continuing variation of the _____ stimulus.

    proximal

2. To perceive an object, the observer must _____ the sensory world into a coherent, meaningful scene.

    organize

THE PERCEPTION OF DEPTH: WHERE IS IT?

3. The two eyes look out on the world from slightly different positions and thus obtain a somewhat different view of any solid object on which they converge. This is called _____ _____.

    binocular disparity

4. Relative size is an example of a _____ depth cue.

    monocular

5. Abrupt change in a _____ _____ produces the impression of a sharp drop, a "visual cliff."

    texture gradient

6. Far-off objects are blocked from view by other opaque objects that obstruct their optical path to the eye. This is a depth cue called _____.

    interposition

7. As we move our head or body from right to left, the images projected by the objects outside will move across the retina. The direction and speed of this motion is an effective monocular depth cue called _____ _____.

    motion parallax

8. The phenomenon that causes an apparent change in the size of objects as we move toward or away from them is known as _____ _____.   optic flow

THE PERCEPTION OF MOVEMENT: WHAT IS IT DOING?

9. Suppose we briefly turn on a light in one location in the visual field, then turn it off, and after an appropriate period of time (somewhere between 30 and 200 msec), turn on a second light in a different location. The resulting phenomenon is called _____ movement.   apparent

10. If the ground is moving and a figure is stationary in the visual field, the figure is seen as moving. This phenomenon of illusory movement is called _____ movement.   induced

11. The perception of movement in one of two stimuli depends on which is seen as a stationary _____ of reference.   frame

12. Perceived _____ seems to be a result of the brain's compensation for the retinal displacement caused by voluntary eye movements.   stability

13. To perceive movement, the perceptual system must solve the _____ problem, matching current elements in the field of view to elements in the immediate past.   correspondence

FORM PERCEPTION: WHAT IS IT?

14. One theory of form perception is that observers consult a mental _____ to see if an object has certain properties.   checklist

15. The fact that a triangle appears as such regardless of the elements that make it up is called _____ of form.   transposition

16. A form is perceived as a _____, a whole that is different from the sum of its parts.   Gestalt

17. A task used frequently to study form perception requires a research participant to indicate whether a certain target appears in a briefly presented array. This is called a _____ _____ task.   visual search

18. Examples of features that are processed automatically are _____, _____, and _____.   color, curvature orientation

19. An _____ _____ occurs when a participant mistakenly ties together two features in an object that did not occur together.   illusory conjunction

20. The process known as _____ _____ enables us to separate figure from ground.   visual segregation (or perceptual parsing)

21. _____ figures are ones in which either of two figure-ground organizations is possible.   Reversible (ambiguous)

22. Proximity, similarity, and good continuation are examples of the laws of _____ _____.   perceptual grouping

23. Contours that continue smoothly along their original course follow the law of _____ _____, a principle that is illustrated by _____ contours (perceiving contours when they don't exist).   good continuation, subjective

24. The model of feature analysis that uses activation and deactivation to recognize stimulus patterns is known as the _____ _____ model.   feature net

25. A feature net model is an example of _____-_____ processing, an approach to pattern recognition that begins with component features and builds up to larger units.   bottom-up

26. The _____-_____ process of pattern recognition begins with higher units, because it is often affected by higher-level knowledge and expectations.   top-down

27. _____ effects demonstrate that there is some top-down processing in the perceptual process.   Priming

28. Perceptual processing is necessarily _____: it is affected by the stimulus and also by prior knowledge.   bidirectional

29. One model by Biederman uses approximately 30 geometric primitives called _____ as the basis for recognizing all objects.   geons

30. The total of the primitives plus the relationships among the primitives for an object is called its _____ _____.   structural description

31. If a patient is able to perceive an object but not recognize it, her or she has a visual _____. agnosia

32. The processing steps that occur during the course of object recognition may occur all at once or sequentially, demonstrating _____ and _____ processing, respectively. parallel, serial

33. The stimulus information we receive is often _____. It is not sufficient to permit a clear perception of what the distal stimulus is. ambiguous

34. We rarely encounter perceptual _____ in daily life because there are multiple sources of information about each object we encounter. illusions

FORM PERCEPTION AND THE NERVOUS SYSTEM

35. There are two sorts of ganglion cells that exit the retina. One is responsible for detecting movement in the periphery and is composed of _____ cells, and the other is responsible for carrying pattern and form information from the fovea and is composed of _____ cells. magno / parvo

36. The _____ system, located in temporal cortex, codes for object identity, while the _____ system, located in parietal cortex, is responsible for detecting object location. what / where

37. The _____ problem is caused by the visual system's analysis of scenes by breaking them up into parts; the consequence is that there must be a mechanism that puts the parts back together again. binding

38. The _____-_____ oscillation refers to the 40 times-per-second rate at which neurons fire. gamma-band

PERCEPTUAL SELECTION: ATTENTION

39. The ways by which we perceive selectively are grouped under the label "_____." attention

40. On the average, our eyes move three or four times per second to fixate objects. These fixations are purposeful, not random. Our eye movements serve the purpose of _____ us to salient stimuli. orienting

41. During _____ _____, the mind's eye moves although there is no physical movement of the eyes. central selection

42. Visual search for _____ features can be accomplished by examining all the objects in an array of the same time; when searching for a _____ object, though, search proceeds one object at a time. simple / complex

43. Injury to the _____ cortex impairs a patient on tasks with conjoined features. parietal

44. _____ can bias perceivers to process information at a particular spatial location if that location is cued in advance of the information that is presented to them. Priming

45. In the absence of _____ it is remarkable how little of a visual display is processed even if an observer is looking right at the objects he or she fails to process. attention

46. When stimuli are presented over earphones so that each ear receives a different message, this is called a _____ presentation. dichotic

47. When participants are asked to _____ a message, they are repeating it aloud, word for word, as it comes over one of their earphones. shadow

PERCEIVING CONSTANCY

48. The perceptual system responds to real objects outside regardless of variations in their proximal images. This is best illustrated by the perceptual _____: lightness, size, and shape. constancies

49. Gibson has stressed the importance of _____ relationships within a stimulus pattern in explaining perceptual organization. invariant (higher-order)

50. A Boeing 747 at a distance of 1,000 feet will look larger than a single-engine two-seater at a distance of 50 feet even though the retinal image of the latter will be greater than that of the former. This is called _____ _____. An analogous phenomenon occurs in the perception of _____. size constancy / shape

51. According to Gibson, an important influence on size constancy is the proportion of _____ elements that are occluded by an object. This remains constant regardless of the distance of the observer from the object. texture

52. An alternative view of Gibson's is that of Helmholtz, who argued that size constancy is achieved by a process of unconscious _____, making a sort of internal calculation of the relationship of distance and image size.   inference

53. _____ information appears to be a critical component of size constancy.   Existence

Self-Test

1. Which of the following is not true of the proximal stimulus?
   a. It is two-dimensional in vision.
   b. It can vary in size and shape.
   c. It alone enables us to perceive the constant properties of objects.
   d. It is the retinal image of the distal stimulus in vision.

2. Binocular disparity is caused by
   a. a slight difference in the size of the two eyes.
   b. small imperfections in the lens and/or cornea.
   c. the slightly different position of each eye.
   d. the favoring of one eye over the other.

3. Binocular disparity
   a. is an effective cue to depth for long distances.
   b. occurs because our eyes receive virtually the same image.
   c. is not by itself a sufficient cue to depth.
   d. can be simulated by viewing specially designed two-dimensional drawings.
   e. is effective only for familiar objects.

4. The figure below illustrates all of the following monocular cues to depth except
   a. linear perspective.
   b. relative size.
   c. binocular disparity.
   d. texture gradients.
   e. interposition.

5. The impression of a "visual cliff" is accounted for by which depth cue?
   a. linear perspective
   b. relative size
   c. texture gradients
   d. interposition

6. Which of the following is not true of motion parallax?
   a. Nearby objects move in a direction opposite our own as we move through space.
   b. Objects farther away move in a direction similar to our own as we move through space.
   c. Objects farther away move at a lesser velocity.
   d. Objects closer to us move at a greater velocity.

7. The change in the size of objects as we move closer or farther away from them is known as
   a. optic flow.
   b. motion parallax.
   c. linear perspective.
   d. apparent movement.

8. One of the most effective monocular depth cues is _____, which is absent in pictorial representations but present in real life.
   a. linear perspective
   b. relative size
   c. interposition
   d. motion parallax

9. The results of the visual cliff experiment (illustrated on the previous page) suggest that
   a. infants cannot use motion parallax as a cue to depth.
   b. infants' eye fixations tend to be directed to edges and vertices.
   c. depth perception is largely innate.
   d. texture gradients are not useful cues to distance.
   e. none of the above

10. Apparent movement refers to
    a. the perception of movement when two stimuli are presented in alternation at the proper temporal and spatial intervals.
    b. the perception of movement of a target when in fact it is stationary but the background is moving.
    c. the perception of self-movement when you are stationary but the scene that you are watching is moving.
    d. none of the above

11. Induced movement differs from apparent movement in that
    a. in the former case it is the figure that moves, whereas in the latter case it is the ground that moves.
    b. the former is a physical phenomenon; the latter is a retinal phenomenon.
    c. induced movement is based on relative displacement, whereas apparent movement is based on absolute displacement.
    d. none of the above

12. Which two of the following are examples of induced movement?
    a. the moon moving through the clouds
    b. perceiving movement of a stationary spot of light in darkness
    c. perceiving movement of a stationary spot of light when the rectangular frame around it moves
    d. perceiving that the moon moves when you move with respect to it
    e. perceiving movement in the successive frames in a movie

13. When several investigators temporarily paralyzed their eye muscles and then tried to move their eyes, they saw objects move in their visual field even though their eyes did not actually move (nor did the objects). This suggests that
    a. paralyzing the eye muscles doesn't affect motion perception.
    b. perceived stability is produced by compensating for motor movement.
    c. perceived motion is produced by compensating for motor movement.
    d. none of the above

14. One of the most interesting features of form recognition is that forms are recognized in spite of
    a. transpositions of pattern.
    b. the fact that their apparent lightnesses change with changes in illumination.
    c. the change in perceived shape that occurs when the angle of regard of an object is changed.
    d. none of the above

15. According to the Gestalt point of view, the perception of an object depends on
    a. the perception of the relations among parts of the object.
    b. the perception of the elementary features of the object.
    c. the perception of the object's geons.
    d. the flow of information as an object is transformed with successive process steps.

16. Object recognition begins with
    a. recognition of Gestalt properties.
    b. visual search.
    c. selective attention.
    d. conjunction of features.
    e. feature detection.

17. If a target in a visual search task differs from the background items on a feature such as color or curvature, participants will
    a. struggle to detect the target.
    b. engage in a conjunctive search for the target.
    c. perceive the target quickly with little search required.
    d. none of the above

18. If a participant were presented with a display of letters printed in colored inks that included a blue G, a red M, and a yellow B, and if this display were presented briefly, he or she might see
    a. a blue D.
    b. a red T.
    c. a yellow R.
    d. a blue M.

19. Which of the following statements about perceptual parsing is *not* true?
    a. It is also called visual segregation.
    b. It is contributed by the individual and is not a part of the stimulus.
    c. It is the first stage of perceptual organization and separates the stimuli into various subcomponents.
    d. It occurs only in the realm of visual perception.

20. Segregating figure from ground (as in a reversible figure)
    a. is a high-level perceptual process that requires a good deal of preliminary analysis.
    b. can be done only with reversible figures.
    c. is accomplished by perceiving the contour separating two regions as belonging to the ground.
    d. is too elementary a perceptual process to be used effectively by artists.
    e. none of the above

Reversible figure that can be perceived either as two faces in profile or as a white vase.

21. For reversible figures such as the one above, which of the following is false?
    a. The figure is generally seen in front of the ground.
    b. A reversible figure-ground display is characterized by two adjoining regions alternately acting as figures.
    c. A contour can be seen as simultaneously belonging to figure and ground.
    d. none of the above

22. All of the following are "laws of perceptual organization" *except*
    a. proximity.
    b. similarity.
    c. good continuation.
    d. simplicity.

23. The law of proximity states that
    a. the closer an object is to an observer, the easier it is to identify it.
    b. the closer two objects are to each other, the greater the chance that they will be grouped together perceptually.
    c. given any two objects, one is always nearer (perceptually) to an arbitrary third object than the other.
    d. none of the above

24. Feature net and other similar theories of pattern recognition are based on the principle that
    a. feature detectors can be in competition and the correct one can win out.
    b. feature detectors are all independent of one another in their analysis of a pattern.
    c. feature detectors work on an object only after the relationships among the parts have been determined.
    d. top-down and bottom-up processes cannot work together in object recognition.

25. Pattern recognition is a
    a. top-down process.
    b. horizontal process.
    c. bottom-up process.
    d. a and c
    e. a and b

26. A professor is giving a lecture on the state of the U.S. economy. His lecture is suddenly broken up by several coughs, which interrupt but do not stop his speech stream. Although there are physical gaps in the utterance, the students hear and understand the presentation. This is an example of
    a. feature analysis.
    b. context effect.
    c. bottom-up processing.
    d. attention.

27. Which of the following statements about geons is (are) not true?
    a. About 70 geons serve as the geometric primitives of the perceptual system.
    b. Geons can be combined with other geons to make up many different objects.
    c. The recognition of geons is accomplished by an early stage of pattern recognition.
    d. The relationships among geons are an important part of perceptual recognition.

28. A person with an agnosia would
    a. be able to recognize an object but not perceive its parts.
    b. be unable to recognize an object even though he or she could perceive its shape.
    c. be unable to recognize the color or shape of an object.
    d. be able to write a structural description of an object but be unable to copy the object.

29. Which of the following does not illustrate the active role that perceivers play in perception?
    a. the segregation of figure from ground
    b. the perception of an ambiguous figure
    c. priming
    d. visual search for a single feature that can proceed by simultaneous examination of several objects in a display

30. Given the properties of magno and parvo cells, and given the two flows of information in the visual system into the "what" and "where" streams, it seems likely that
    a. magno cells feed into the "where" system.
    b. parvo cells feed into the "what" system.
    c. magno cells feed into the "what" system.
    d. parvo cells feed into the "where" system.
    e. magno and parvo cells feed into both systems.
    f. a and b
    g. c and d

31. The binding problem is caused by the visual system's breaking up of
    a. proximity and similarity information.
    b. form and location information.
    c. size and shape information.
    d. location and movement information.
    e. information about large and small objects.

32. Orienting movements, like turning of the head, are external manifestations of
    a. differentiation.
    b. attention.
    c. recalibration.
    d. adaptation.

33. During a visual search procedure
    a. a participant is asked to pick out the most relevant component of a stimulus pattern as quickly as possible.
    b. participants may employ methods of physical orientation and central selection to locate the target.
    c. the orienting movements that a participant makes show little relation to the features of objects that are attended to during scanning.
    d. the internal selection process often hinders accurate scanning and location of the correct target.

34. In a visual search task, if the target is a blue T that is embedded among green Rs, blue Gs, and red Ts, participants would have to engage in
    a. a serial search for the target.
    b. a parallel search for the target.
    c. either a serial or a parallel search for the target, depending on their choice.
    d. none of the above

35. Imagine the following study: Subjects are presented with a sequence of visual displays each of which is composed of a line drawing of one object superimposed on a line drawing of another object. One of the drawings is in red and the other in blue. We ask subjects to monitor the red line drawing and respond when they see any object that is man made (e.g., a wrench). Suppose we surprise the subjects after they see the entire sequence by asking them about the blue objects. Based on what you know about the effect of attention on perception, they should be able to
    a. name quite a number of objects
    b. accurately judge whether there were many man-made objects drawn in blue.
    c. both of the above
    d. none of the above

36. Which of the following is not true of the effects of selective attention?
    a. Some information gets in from an unattended message.
    b. It primes certain feature analyzers.
    c. It helps prepare us for an upcoming stimulus.
    d. It is restricted to vision only.
    e. all of the above

37. Two proposals have been made about the perception of constancies. One is based on the idea that
    a. there are invariant relationships among elements of the distal stimulus.
    b. there are invariant relationships among elements of the proximal stimulus.
    c. there is an unconscious inference made about the relationships between elements of a proximal stimulus.
    d. there is an unconscious inference made about the relationships between invariant features of a distal stimulus.

38. The other proposal about the perception of constancy is based on the idea that
    a. we perceive constancy in shape by making an unconscious inference about orientation of a retinal image and texture elements from the background.
    b. we perceive size constancy by making an unconscious inference about the size of a retinal image and the distance we are from an object.

c. we perceive lightness constancy by making an unconscious inference about the size of a retinal image and the reflectance of that image.
    d. none of the above

39. Size constancy appears to depend on
    a. the fact that although the retinal image of an object changes as we move away from it, its size relative to other objects in a display does not.
    b. the perceived distance that an object is from an observer.
    c. various cues such as linear perspective, binocular disparity, and motion parallax.
    d. all of the above

Answer Key for Self-Test

1.	c	21.	c
2.	c	22.	d
3.	d	23.	b
4.	c	24.	a
5.	c	25.	d
6.	b	26.	b
7.	a	27.	a
8.	d	28.	b
9.	c	29.	c
10.	a	30.	f
11.	c	31.	b
12.	a, c	32.	b
13.	b	33.	b
14.	a	34.	a
15.	a	35.	d
16.	e	36.	d
17.	c	37.	a
18.	d	38.	b
19.	d	39.	d
20.	e		

Investigating Psychological Phenomena

THE EFFECT OF MENTAL SET

Equipment: Stimuli are included
Number of participants: One
Time per participant: Twenty minutes
Time for experimenter: Twenty minutes

The issue of how past experience influences perception (an example of top-down processing) is an important one in psychology and has generated quite a bit of research. This is a difficult issue to resolve because there are many ways in which past experience might influence perceptual processes. In this problem you are asked to consider a series of hypothetical experiments (modeled after a study by Epstein and Rock, 1960) and to provide alternative interpretations of the hypothetical results. As you move through the experiments, try to develop one hypothesis that will account for all of the results described. The stimuli for all the experiments are the ambiguous and unambiguous versions of Leeper's old woman-young woman figure shown below.

A   Y   O

Notice that the first picture (A) can be seen either as a young woman or as an old woman—that is, it is ambiguous. The second picture (Y) is quite similar to the first (A) except that some detail has been changed so that it has become a fairly unambiguous picture of a young woman. Likewise, the third picture (O) is a fairly unambiguous version of an old woman. The purpose of all the experiments is to determine how prior exposure to the unambiguous versions of the figure influences whether participants call the ambiguous version an old woman or a young woman. Imagine that twenty participants are run in each hypothetical experiment.

EXPERIMENT 1

Each participant is shown the following series of slides (at a rate of one slide every eight seconds) and asked to name each picture as "young" or "old" as it is presented: YYOOOOOOOOA (Y refers to a presentation of the unambiguous young woman, O

refers to a presentation of the unambiguous old woman, and A refers to the presentation of the ambiguous image.) All participants name the Y and O versions of the figure correctly. On the critical trial, the ambiguous picture A, the results are as follows: Twenty participants call it "old," no participants call it "young." One interpretation of this result is that the more frequently presented unambiguous version determined the perception of the ambiguous picture. This is listed as Hypothesis 1 on the answer sheet. What alternative explanations can you propose to explain the responses of participants in this hypothetical experiment? Write them on the answer sheet. There are at least three other plausible possibilities.

Before you go on to experiments 2 through 4, check to see whether the hypotheses you have developed coincide with those given in the answers to the problem. If not, use the given hypotheses as the basis for your answers to the questions posed in Experiments 2 through 4.

EXPERIMENT 2

A new set of twenty participants receives the following series: YYYYYOOOOOA. Again the responses to all the Y and O stimuli are correct, and the responses to the A stimulus are as follows: Twenty participants respond "old woman," none respond "young woman." Consider each of the four hypotheses raised to account for the results of Experiment 1 and evaluate how each fares with the results of the experiment. Record your responses under Experiment 2 on the answer sheet.

EXPERIMENT 3

Twenty participants each receive the series OOOOOOOYYYA. All respond correctly to the Y and O stimuli; the responses to A are these: twenty participants call it "young woman," none call it "old woman." Again evaluate the success of each of the four hypotheses at accounting for these results.*

EXPERIMENT 4

Twenty new participants are shown the series YYOYYOYYOA. All Os and Ys are identified correctly; the data on the A presentations are these: eighteen participants respond "old woman," two participants respond "young woman" (a reliable difference). Which of the four hypotheses can explain these results? Is one of the four hypotheses confirmed by the results of all four experiments?

---

*We continue to consider hypothesis 1 even though experiment 2 cannot be explained by it; scientists do not typically discard a hypothesis because of a single contradictory finding.

ANSWER SHEET

Experiment 1

Hypothesis 1   Frequency of presentation determines the response to the ambiguous figure

Hypothesis 2   _____

_____

Hypothesis 3   _____

_____

Hypothesis 4   _____

_____

Experiment 2

Hypothesis 1   _____

_____

Hypothesis 2   _____

_____

Hypothesis 3   _____

_____

Hypothesis 4   _____

_____

Experiment 3

Hypothesis 1   _____

_____

Hypothesis 2   _____

_____

Hypothesis 3   _____

_____

Hypothesis 4   _____

_____

Experiment 4

Which of the four hypotheses can account for these results? _____

_____

Which hypotheses can account for the results of all four experiments? _____

_____

Answers to Problem

EXPERIMENT 1

Hypothesis 2: It is possible that the interpretation of the ambiguous picture was entirely influenced by the perception of the immediately preceding picture of the old woman. If so, this would be called a "recency effect," because the most recently presented picture would have had the strongest influence on perception of the ambiguous picture.

Hypothesis 3: An alternative possibility has to do with what the participant might be expecting to be presented on the last trial. He or she has just seen eight consecutive pictures of the old woman and so might reasonably expect that the next picture will also be that of an old woman. Thus, if this were the case, the participant's cognitive expectations would be guiding his or her perceptions.

Hypothesis 4: A final possibility is that participants in general have a bias to respond with the name "old woman." One might suppose that such a bias exists (for some reason) even independently of what the participant actually sees. That is, participants are biased to call the ambiguous version an "old woman" regardless of what precedes it.

EXPERIMENT 2

This experiment rules out Hypothesis 1, the frequency hypothesis. Both unambiguous versions were presented equally frequently before the ambiguous version was presented. Thus, a participant's perception of the ambiguous version could not have been influenced by the more frequently presented unambiguous version. None of the alternative hypotheses is ruled out by these results: (a) The response to the ambiguous version was the same as that to the most recently presented unambiguous version. Thus, recency is a viable interpretation of these results. (b) Because the responses to the sixth through tenth stimuli were "old woman," the participants may have built up an expectation that the eleventh stimulus would be an old woman as well. So cognitive expectations may well have guided their response to the ambiguous item. (c) The fact that most participants identified the ambiguous picture as an old woman is consistent with the possibility that they have a bias to call it that regardless of their immediately prior perceptual experience.

EXPERIMENT 3

Once again this experiment disconfirms the frequency hypothesis. This time participants responded to the test picture with the name of the *least* frequently presented unambiguous picture. Also, the experiment rules out Hypothesis 4, which states that participants have a predisposing bias to call the ambiguous version an old woman. Both the recency and the cognitive expectation hypotheses can account for the results.

EXPERIMENT 4

The cognitive expectation hypothesis probably is ruled out. In responding to the unambiguous versions, participants were following a regular pattern of two "young woman" responses followed by one "old woman" response. The last unambiguous picture was that of the old woman; thus participants should have been expecting a young woman next. Instead, most responded "old woman," a result that can be explained only by noting that the most recently presented unambiguous picture was that of the old woman. Thus, the recency explanation is compatible with these results. Once again the frequency hypothesis is disconfirmed because the most frequently presented unambiguous picture was the young woman. The response bias explanation might be brought up to explain the results of this experiment except that it was ruled out by Experiment 3. Thus, the only explanation that can explain the results of all four experiments satisfactorily is Hypothesis 2, which claims that the picture a participant sees most recently will affect his or her current perception.

This exercise demonstrates how it is sometimes possible to start with several potential explanations of a phenomenon and successfully rule out the incorrect ones with further experimentation. Initially there were four plausible interpretations of the results of hypothetical Experiment 1. The results of hypothetical Experiments 2 through 4, however, rule out all but one of the alternatives.

Even though the experiments described above are only hypothetical, they illustrate this process of narrowing down alternative interpretations. You may want to try out any of these experiments to determine the actual results. On page 75 you will find sets of pictures of both the unambiguous versions and the ambiguous version of the figure. Cut them out and return to the previous pages of this section. Perform the experiments as described there and record the results. Do your results correspond to the hypothetical data? Do the same hypotheses apply?

Reference

Epstein, W., & Rock, I. (1960). Perceptual set as an artifact of recency. *American Journal of Psychology, 73,* 214–228.

Cut these out to perform the experiments. On the back of each figure are the letters Y (young woman), O (old woman), or A (ambiguous).

Y   Y   Y   Y   Y

Y   Y   Y   Y   Y

O   O   O   O   O

O   O   O   O   O

A   A

CHAPTER 7

Memory

Learning Objectives

1. Be sure you see the parallel between perception and memory in the active role that perceiver or memorizer plays.
2. Understand the central role that memory plays in cognitive life.

ACQUISITION, STORAGE, RETRIEVAL

3. What is meant by the terms acquisition, storage, and retrieval? How do these processes differ from one another?
4. Know that both recall and recognition are used to measure retrieval. How do these two methods differ from one another?
5. What are causes of failures to retrieve?

ENCODING

The stage theory of memory
6. What motivates a stage theory of memory, both historically and introspectively?
7. How is the relationship between desktop and bookshelves relevant to working and long-term memory?
8. What is the capacity of working memory? How is it measured?
9. There are two mechanisms that account for forgetting from working memory. What are they, and how do they work?
10. Rehearsal is a process important to working memory. Describe its function in relation to both working and long-term memory.
11. One of the most robust phenomena in the study of memory is the appearance of primacy and recency effects in free recall. Describe these, and indicate what causes them. Be sure you can cite evidence that supports the presumed causes.
12. What is a chunk, and how does this concept apply to the capacity of working memory? How do chunks get created?

A changed emphasis: active memory and organization
13. How do findings about rehearsal challenge the stage theory of memory?
14. What is maintenance rehearsal? Does the amount of maintenance rehearsal affect the probability of information's entering long-term memory? Cite the relevant evidence.
15. What is the concept of "working memory," and how does it differ from the concept of "short-term memory"?

16. Understand the concept of depth of processing and how it affects memory. Give examples of processing at different depths.
17. What role does meaning play in remembering?
18. Mnemonics are tools to increase the capacity of memory. Describe some mnemonics, and understand how they work to affect memory capacity. What are the practical limitations of mnemonics? How do mnemonics create retrieval paths?

RETRIEVAL

19. Understand the role of retrieval cues in increasing the accessibility of memory traces.

The relation between original encoding and retrieval
20. What is the concept of encoding specificity, and how does it influence successful retrieval? Understand the range of contexts in which this principle operates.
21. The importance of matching encoding and retrieval contexts has to do with mental, not physical contexts. Explain.

Elaborative rehearsal
22. Contrast maintenance and elaborative rehearsal. Give examples of elaborative rehearsal.

Implicit memory
23. Be aware of the difference between implicit and explicit memory retrieval. What is the essence of an implicit measure, and what are some examples?
24. Describe how repetition priming and fragment completion show implicit retrieval effects.
25. Describe evidence showing that implicit memory can influence whether you believe something is true.
26. Be aware of how variations in depth of processing and in peripheral aspects of the stimulus produce differential effects on explicit and implicit tests of memory.
27. What are some theoretical accounts of the difference between implicit and explicit memory?

WHEN MEMORY FAILS

Forgetting
28. What is the shape of the forgetting curve?
29. Recount the evidence both for and against a decay theory of forgetting.

30. What is an interference theory of forgetting, and how does it differ from a decay theory?
31. Give some accounts of the forgetting of childhood memories and why there may be individual differences in this forgetting.
32. What are some of the characteristics of having a word on the tip of your tongue?
33. Some memories seem to last quite a long time. Give examples. What factors affect this?
34. How are flashbulb memories claimed to be different from other memories? Are these memories really treated differently by the memory system? Discuss the evidence.

Conceptual frameworks and remembering

35. What effects did Bartlett document in his studies of recollection?
36. Describe some effects that schemas have on memory.
37. Memory is an important issue in the courtroom. What does research tell us about the fallibility of eyewitness testimony? Describe how eyewitness memory may be a reconstruction of earlier events.
38. What is source confusion and when does it occur?
39. Can the fallibility of eyewitness testimony be overcome?
40. Is hypnosis a reliable way of helping a witness remember an event? What is the evidence on whether hypnosis improves retrieval?
41. What is the verdict on the tape-recorder theory of memory?
42. Why is there reason to be cautious about the concept of "repressed memories"? What issues should one be concerned about in examining cases of this alleged phenomenon?

43. Discuss the limits to which our memories are distorted. How do top-down and bottom-up processes play a role in enhancing and limiting distortion?

Disordered memories

44. What are the symptoms of anterograde amnesia, and what are some of its causes?
45. How does retrograde amnesia differ from anterograde amnesia? What mechanism has been proposed to account for retrograde amnesia?

What amnesia teaches us

46. What sorts of learning are spared in anterograde amnesia? How is the distinction between declarative and procedural knowledge relevant to this issue?
47. The distinction between implicit and explicit memory has also played a prominent role in accounting for anterograde amnesia. Explain why. Why is it difficult to distinguish between the declarative/procedural versus explicit/implicit accounts of amnesia?
48. Be prepared to give examples of amnesias that selectively disrupt either episodic or genetic memory.
49. Distinguish between associate and strategic retrieval. Give evidence that these two types of retrieval are mediated by different brain circuits. Be sure you understand how evidence from patients who confabulate is relevant to this distinction.
50. How does evidence from brain imaging help us distinguish among different types of memories?t

Programmed Exercises

AQUISITION, STORAGE, AND RETRIEVAL

1. The first stage of memory is _____, in which information is acquired and brought into the system.　　encoding

2. The records of experience made on the nervous system are called memory _____.　　traces

ENCODING

3. The second stage of memory is _____, during which information is filed away. The final stage is _____, the point at which one tries to remember.　　storage / retrieval

4. A _____ test is a test of retrieval in which a participant is asked to produce an item from memory.　　recall

5. A _____ test is a test of retrieval in which several items are presented and the participant must decide which ones were presented earlier as part of a studied list.　　recognition

6. Learning that takes place without intention is called _____ learning.　　incidental

7. Translating raw input to memory into an intellectual record of the input is called _____ memory.　　encoding

8. The theory of memory that argues for separate memory systems working together is called the _____ theory.　　stage

9. _____ memory holds information for a brief interval. _____-_____ memory stores information for longer periods of time.　　Working, Long-term

10. The _____ capacity of working memory has been estimated as about 7 items.   storage

11. The _____ _____ is the number of items an individual can recall after just one presentation.   memory span

12. _____ is one way of either keeping an item in working memory or allowing it to pass into long-term memory.   Rehearsal

13. The method of _____ _____ allows a participant who is presented with a list of unrelated items to report them in any order desired.   free recall

14. Of a long list of presented items, a participant is most apt to remember the first few (known as the _____ effect) and the last few (known as the _____ effect).   primacy, recency

15. The process that allows the contents of working memory to expand is called _____. Using this process results in the creation of _____ of information.   organization chunks

16. _____ rehearsal consists of repeating items over and over to keep them in memory for a short time, as in repeating a telephone number.   Maintenance

17. _____ memory holds information for short intervals, while we are processing it.   Working

18. One theory of memory asserts that the extent to which information is subject to semantic analysis, as opposed to analysis of its surface features, will determine how firmly the information will be held in memory. This theory attributes permanence in memory to _____ of _____.   depth, processing

19. The various devices designed to improve memory are collectively called _____.   mnemonics

20. When it comes time to recall something memory, connections linking one memory to another become retrieval _____.   paths

21. The method of _____ requires learners to visualize each of the items they want to remember in a different spatial location.   loci

22. The most effective kind of image for remembering is one in which the elements of the image are _____.   interacting

RETRIEVAL

23. When you know a piece of information (i.e., you have stored it), but you cannot retrieve it at the moment, the trace is said to be _____.   inaccessible

24. A stimulus that provides a trigger to get an item out of memory is called a(n) _____ _____.   retrieval cue

25. The principle of _____ _____ states that retrieval success is most likely if the context at the time of retrieval approximates that during original encoding.   encoding specificity

26. _____ rehearsal consists of the organization of information in working memory so that it can be transferred to long-term memory.   Elaborative

27. Instances in which we tap our memory quite consciously to retrieve something are called _____ memory. By contrast, when our memory is used in an indirect way in the service of some other task, this is termed _____ memory.   explicit / implicit

28. Recall and recognition are both _____ measures of memory, whereas word fragment completion is an _____ measure.   explicit / implicit

29. _____ priming is a technique used to study implicit memory; words that appear on a study list are identified more readily than words that do not.   Repetition

WHEN MEMORY FAILS

30. The _____ curve was first plotted by Ebbinghaus who tested himself on the relearning of lists of nonsense syllables.   forgetting

31. If it was found that items faded from working memory even though no new information entered, this would support a _____ theory of forgetting.   decay

32. Animals forget when their internal temperatures are higher; this is evidence for a _____ theory of forgetting.   decay

33. One cause of forgetting is _____, in which some items in memory cause the forgetting of others.   interference

34. One possible reason we can't recall childhood memories is the drastic change in _____ cues between childhood and adulthood. This phenomenon is called childhood _____.   retrieval / amnesia

35. The _____-_____-_____ -_____ phenomenon is an example of unsuccessful retrieval in which the participant comes close to the searched-for item in his or her memory but cannot quite find the right memory location.   tip-of-the-tongue

36. When one learns a language in school, at least some of this material seems to enter a _____, lasting many years after the learning has ceased.   permastore

37. Certain salient and emotional events produce what are called _____ memories, which are quite vivid.   flashbulb

38. The conceptual framework that a person builds on the basis of his or her knowledge of the world is called a _____.   schema

39. Eyewitnesses to crimes seem to reconstruct the past from their partial knowledge of it in the process of trying to remember it. This leaves them open to memory _____.   errors

40. Getting a witness into the "mind-set" that he was in at the time of the incident is called context _____.   reinstatement

41. Eyewitness _____ of a culprit from a police lineup are subject to mistakenly identifying someone who is innocent.   identifications

42. Sometimes an observer can recall an event but not the origin of that event. This is called _____ confusion.   source

43. _____ seems to make people overly willing to cooperate with their questioner, not to substantially improve retrieval of information from memory.   Hypnosis

44. The _____-_____ theory of memory asserts that all we have heard or seen is stored in memory.   tape-recorder

45. _____ memories are alleged to occur when an emotionally traumatic event happens in early childhood and can't be easily retrieved.   Repressed

46. Lesions in the temporal cortex result in _____ amnesia, in which the patient has difficulty learning new material.   anterograde

47. _____ syndrome occurs after extended bouts of alcohol abuse.   Korsakoff's

48. A patient has suffered an accident involving trauma to the head. Following this, his ability to learn things is unimpaired, but he seems to have forgotten some things that happened prior to the accident. This is an example of _____ _____.   retrograde amnesia

49. One theory to account for the loss of prior memories after a trauma to the brain is based on the notion of _____ _____, according to which newly acquired memories undergo gradual change until they become more firmly established.   trace consolidation

50. An amnesic's memory is relatively unaffected when the memory task involves _____ knowledge, but her memory is drastically impaired when it involves _____ knowledge.   procedural / declarative

51. _____ tests of memory show great performance declines in amnesic patients, whereas _____ tests show little difference from the performance of people with normal memory capacity.   Explicit, implicit

52. There are amnesic patients who lose _____ memory while preserving episodic memory.   generic

53. Sometimes retrieval is effortless and automatic; at other times it is quite effortful. The former is called _____ retrieval and the latter is called _____ retrieval.   associative, strategic

54. The _____ plays a role in memory of emotional events.   amygdala

Self-Test

1. For us to remember something, we must first engage in the process of
   a. storage.
   b. rehearsal.
   c. encoding.
   d. recall.

2. An enduring physical record of a memory is called
   a. a memory trace.
   b. a chunk.
   c. short-term memory.
   d. none of the above.

3. Suppose you are given a choice between a multiple-choice test and a short-answer test for the final exam in this course. You want to maximize the chance of doing well. Based on what you know about recall and recognition, all other things being equal, which test should you choose?
   a. short answer
   b. multiple choice
   c. either, there is no difference
   d. It depends on the difficulty of the material.

4. Complete the following analogy: Multiple-choice questions are to fill-in-the-blank questions as
   a. recognition is to recall.
   b. recall is to retention.
   c. recognition is to retention.
   d. learning is to memory.

5. In principle, the stages of memory processes must be arranged in which of the following orders?
   a. memory trace—encoding—storage—retrieval
   b. encoding—memory trace—storage—retrieval
   c. encoding—storage—memory trace—retrieval
   d. encoding—memory trace—retrieval—storage

6. The following are all characteristics of working memory except
   a. limited capacity.
   b. contents lost without rehearsal.
   c. displacement causes forgetting.
   d. none of the above

7. It has been found that people can hold about seven items in working memory. When more items are presented, complete recall is generally not possible. This demonstrates the _____ of working memory.
   a. retention interval
   b. memory trace
   c. displacement
   d. memory span

8. What is true about forgetting from working memory?
   a. It can be caused by erosion of the memory trace with time.
   b. The memory trace can be knocked out of short-term memory by another trace.
   c. It can be inhibited by rehearsal of the material stored there.
   d. all of the above

9. Suppose you are given driving directions by a gas station attendant and you repeat them over and over to yourself, "First left, second right, left at the first light, third right." Now suppose that your repetition of the directions is interrupted by an emergency driving maneuver. This would likely cause you to forget the directions, thereby demonstrating the importance of _____ in preserving working memory.
   a. storage capacity
   b. retrieval
   c. accessibility
   d. rehearsal

10. Suppose cryogenics (freezing patients and awakening them at some future time) were possible. If you were to discover that after being awakened, the patients had retained very accurate memories of what they had experienced immediately before freezing, this would be evidence for which hypothesis of forgetting in working memory?
    a. interference
    b. decay
    c. neither displacement nor decay
    d. either displacement or decay

11. At a party you are taken around the room by the host and are introduced to the other guests. Some time after the introductions are finished, one of these people comes up to talk to you. All other things being equal, you have the best chance of remembering her name if she was one of the _____ people you met. This phenomenon is called _____.
    a. first, primacy
    b. middle, inhibition
    c. last, recency
    d. first or last, the opposition effect

12. Now imagine the same situation (as in No. 11) except that the person comes up to you immediately after you have been very quickly introduced to everyone. Again, other things being equal, you would have the worst chance of remembering her name if she was one of the _____ people you met and the best chance if she was one of the _____.
    a. first, last
    b. middle, last
    c. first, middle
    d. last, first

13. Suppose a participant is asked to memorize the following list of words: *apple, horse, desk, carpet, mug, milk, parrot, disk, street, tree*. Which of the following will occur?
    a. The word *street* will be rehearsed more than the word *horse*, causing *tree* to be stored in long-term memory.
    b. The word *parrot* will be rehearsed more than the word *mug*, causing *parrot* to be stored in working memory.
    c. The word *apple* will be rehearsed more than the word *carpet*, causing *apple* to be stored in long-term memory.
    d. The word *desk* will be rehearsed more than the word *parrot*, causing desk to be stored in working memory.

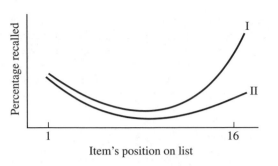

Item's position on list

14. The figure above depicts recall curves for a list of 16 items. Two conditions were employed, I and II. What was the difference between the conditions?
    a. The interval between items was longer for II than I.
    b. The interval between items was longer for I than II.
    c. The interval between the last item and the recall test was longer for I than II.
    d. The interval between the last item and the recall test was longer for II than I.

15. Increasing the capacity of working memory is a misnomer because
    a. all one does is to rehearse the material already there, keeping it fresh while new material is added.
    b. the number of items stored is the same, about 7; just the content of each item has changed.
    c. it is the number of chunks that has changed, not the capacity of working memory.
    d. it is not possible to increase the capacity of working memory.

16. Suppose you run an experiment in which you present one word, say *rabbit*, and the participant has to repeat it. Then you present another word, say *pear*, and the participant has to repeat *rabbit, pear*. Then you present a third word, and the participant has to repeat all three, and so on. At the end of your list, you test the participant's memory for all words on the list. Based on what you know about the effect of maintenance rehearsal on long-term memory, you predict that
    a. *rabbit* should be entered into long-term memory with higher probability than the last word on the list.
    b. *rabbit* should be entered into long-term memory with lower probability than the last word on the list.
    c. *rabbit* should be entered into long-term memory with the same probability as the last word on the list.
    d. none of the above

17. Working memory is to short-term memory as
    a. storage is to processing.
    b. processing is to storage.
    c. recall is to recognition.
    d. recognition is to recall.

18. The concept of depth of processing is intended to account for the fact that
    a. deeper structures in the brain are involved in memory in contrast to the more surface cortical structures that are involved in other aspects of cognition.
    b. deeper levels of analysis of material yield better memory for it.
    c. deeper organization of material into hierarchically organized chunks produces a better long-term memory for that material.
    d. none of the above

19. Which of the following processes will not result in the effective storage of memory traces in long-term memory?
    a. maintenance rehearsal
    b. clustering
    c. elaborative rehearsal
    d. organization by phrases

20. A follow-up to the experiment in which participants recalled the passage about washing clothes found that telling them the title of the paragraph after they had read it did not improve recall compared to not telling them the title at all. This result, taken together with the effect of telling participants the title of the paragraph before it is presented, suggests that
    a. chunking is not an effective strategy to memorize material.
    b. chunking is effective if it can be accomplished at the time of encoding.
    c. chunking is effective if it can be accomplished at the time of retrieval.
    d. chunking is effective if it can be accomplished during storage.

21. Mnemonic devices (memorizing aids) use the principle of
    a. consolidation of retrieval.
    b. recoding.
    c. retrieval of consolidation.
    d. all of the above

22. Which of the following images would produce the greatest increase in recall performance for the pair of items *horse-rock*?
    a. a horse standing next to a rock
    b. a horse dragging a rock
    c. a horse and rock pictured separately
    d. All of the above would be equivalent.

23. You have been trying to remember the name of a street that a friend lives on. Despite all of your efforts you are unable to recall it. While in the kitchen looking for a snack (to console yourself) you reach for a can of nuts, and suddenly the street name comes to you—Walnut. This is an example of the role of _____.
    a. anterograde amnesia
    b. retrograde amnesia
    c. mnemonics
    d. retrieval cues

24. Retrieval cues are most effective if they
    a. coincide with the way in which a trace was originally encoded.
    b. are presented at the time of recall, not at encoding.
    c. are quite concrete.
    d. elicit visual images.

25. The kind of rehearsal that establishes long-term memories is
_____. The type of rehearsal that holds material in
working memory temporarily is _____.
a. mnemonics, chunking
b. maintenance rehearsal, elaborative rehearsal
c. elaborative rehearsal, maintenance rehearsal
d. method of loci, mnemonics

26. The major role that elaborative rehearsal plays in improving
memory, as opposed to maintenance rehearsal, is
a. to increase the number of retrieval cues.
b. to increase the number of times an item is rehearsed.
c. to speed up the encoding time.
d. all of the above

27. Repeating word pairs aloud and forming images of words in
a pair are respectively examples of
a. maintenance rehearsal, and maintenance rehearsal.
b. maintenance rehearsal, and elaborative rehearsal.
c. elaborative rehearsal, and elaborative rehearsal.
d. elaborative rehearsal, and maintenance rehearsal.

28. The tip-of-the-tongue phenomenon provides us with
evidence concerning
a. the hierarchical organization of long-term memory.
b. accessibility in working memory.
c. the search process in long-term memory.
d. the use of retrieval cues in working memory.

29. Having something "on the tip of the tongue" indicates a
problem
a. in the way the item was chunked.
b. with reconstruction.
c. with proactive inhibition.
d. with retrieval.

30. What is the relationship between implicit and explicit
memory tests?
a. They must be correlated because they both measure
memory.
b. They can be uncorrelated as shown by demonstrations
of implicit memory without explicit memory.
c. They must be correlated because the tests measure
different aspects of memory.
d. Available evidence does not permit an answer.

31. Evidence that implicit and explicit memory tests may tap at
least some different aspects of the memory trace comes from
a. studies showing that implicit tests lead to better retrieval.
b. studies showing that forgetting as indicated by implicit
tests is slower than forgetting indexed by explicit tests.
c. studies showing that learning instructions affect tests of
explicit but not implicit memory.
d. all of the above

32. Each of the following is a test of explicit retrieval except
a. fragment completion.
b. repetition priming.
c. free recall.

d. memory span.
e. more than one of the above

33. According to one view, explicit retrieval is to implicit
retrieval as
a. conscious is to unconscious.
b. bottom-up processing is to top-down processing.
c. repetition priming is to recognition.
d. none of the above

34. If you read the Memory chapter in the text, which of the
following people should you now think of as more famous
than you would have if you had not read the text, assuming
that you didn't remember having encountered these names in
the text itself?
a. Esther Williams
b. Ted Williams
c. Johnny Carson
d. Sebastian Weisdorf

35. When Ebbinghaus tested himself on memory for nonsense
syllables, he found that
a. forgetting was fastest immediately after learning.
b. his episodic and generic memory were equivalent.
c. his implicit memory was better than his explicit memory.
d. none of the above

36. According to a decay theory of forgetting, if a participant
learning a list of words was then subjected to one of the
following procedures, he would forget the greatest number
of words if
a. he slept for four versus two hours.
b. he learned other lists for four versus two hours.
c. he performed arithmetic problems for four versus two
hours.
d. All of the above would be comparable.

37. One hypothesis about forgetting is that it is due to a change
in retrieval cues. Which of the following would be
counterevidence for this hypothesis?
a. demonstration of proactive inhibition
b. demonstration of retroactive inhibition
c. demonstration that decay caused forgetting
d. none of the above

38. One of the potential causes of childhood amnesia is that the
retrieval cues change massively between childhood and
adulthood. Another plausible cause might be
a. the poor quality of the initial encoding of memory traces.
b. retroactive inhibition.
c. decay.
d. all of the above

39. The concept of a permastore arises from the observation that
a. some memories are not subject to any forgetting.
b. some memories, while they decline initially after
learning, remain relatively intact thereafter.
c. some memories have a flashbulb character to them.
d. all of the above

40. The compelling nature of flashbulb memories has caused some to argue that they are caused by a special memory mechanism. Contrary to this hypothesis, though,
    a. the accuracy of these memories may not be all that impressive.
    b. some of the good memory may come from conversations about the event after it has occurred.
    c. both of the above
    d. none of the above

41. Distortions of memory seem to be accentuated as a function of time between original acquisition of the information and testing. Such distortions could be due to effects of
    a. encoding.
    b. storage.
    c. retrieval.
    d. b and c, but not a

42. Bartlett's experiments and evidence about the fallibility of eyewitness testimony highlight the importance of which of the following factors about recall?
    a. reconstruction
    b. proactive inhibition
    c. retrieval cues
    d. retroactive inhibition

43. Suppose two groups of participants watched a videotape of a minor theft, in which someone in a room full of people reached into a drawer and took a $20 bill. After the video-tape, Group 1 was asked, "Did you see the custodian reach into the drawer?" while Group 2 was asked, "Did you see a custodian reach into the drawer?" (Actually, there was no custodian in the room.) Which group is more likely to accuse the custodian of the theft?
    a. Group 1
    b. Group 2
    c. Group 1 and Group 2 will be equally likely to accuse the custodian
    d. can't tell from the available detail

44. Suppose an eyewitness to a crime was hypnotized and asked to recall as much as she could of the events of the crime. She would most likely
    a. recall more of what she had seen.
    b. recall less of what she had seen.
    c. recall about the same as if she had not been hypnotized, but report more.
    d. resist recalling more about the crime because of its emotional impact.

45. There are reasons to believe that some of the recent reports of repressed memories of childhood sexual abuse are not correct. Several factors may be exaggerating the number of such reports:
    a. Some of the therapists involved in eliciting them are using hypnosis, which is known to cause the patient to report more things that may be confabulations in the hopes of pleasing the therapist.
    b. Some of the therapists who work on this problem have a bias to find childhood causes of adult problems even when there may be no such causes.

    c. Highly charged memories such as those of childhood abuse are not likely to be repressed for such a long time without having come out before.
    d. all of the above

46. Retrograde amnesia may be caused by
    a. a disruption in the mechanism that causes new material to be placed into long-term memory, thus preventing any new learning.
    b. a disruption of trace consolidation at the time of the trauma.
    c. a difficulty in retrieving events that occurred just prior to the trauma.
    d. more than one of the above

47. One experiment has shown that while amnesic patients get better at reading mirror-reversed text, they cannot recognize the words they have read later on, whereas people with normal memories can. This indicates that
    a. amnesics lose the ability to learn new information.
    b. amnesics lose the ability to learn declarative information, but not procedural information.
    c. amnesics can learn procedural skills, but only if the very same stimuli are repeated over and over.
    d. anterograde amnesics are different from retrograde amnesics.

48. Three major symptoms characterize anterograde amnesia. They are
    a. accurate memory for pretrauma events, normal working memory, inaccurate memory for most posttrauma events.
    b. inaccurate memory for pretrauma events, normal working memory, inaccurate memory for most posttrauma events.
    c. accurate memory for pretrauma events, abnormal working memory, accurate memory for most posttrauma events.
    d. inaccurate memory for pretrauma events, normal working memory, accurate memory for most posttrauma events.

49. Milner's patient H. M. (an anterograde amnesic) was tested for his memory span for unrelated nouns. What is your best guess about his span?
    a. 0
    b. 4
    c. 7
    d. 10

50. A theory of memory that says that memory needs time to be fixed into a permanent form is called
    a. rehearsal.
    b. spreading activation.
    c. trace consolidation.
    d. memory priming.

51. You witness an automobile accident in which one of the drivers hits his head on the windshield. He appears unin-jured, but when a police officer asks him what happened just prior to the accident, the man seems confused and is unable to answer. The police officer is about to haul the man off to

jail (assuming that he must be drunk) when you step forward and (having studied your psychology text) say, "This man is suffering from _____ _____!"

   a. trace consolidation
   b. anterograde amnesia
   c. retrograde amnesia
   d. Korsakoff's syndrome

52. Patients with anterograde amnesia may experience
   a. impaired explicit memory but normal implicit memory.
   b. impaired declarative learning but normal procedural learning.
   c. impaired long-term memory processes but normal working memory processes.
   d. all of the above
   e. none of the above

53. Associate retrieval is to strategic retrieval as
   a. explicit memory is to implicit memory.
   b. anterograde amnesia is to retrograde amnesia.
   c. working memory is to long-term memory.
   d. top-down processing is to bottom-up processing.
   e. none of the above

54. Studies of patients with brain lesions and studies of normals using brain-imaging techniques has revealed a number of regions of the brain that seem to be critical for memory. These include
   a. the prefrontal cortex for working memory.
   b. the amygdala for emotional memory.
   c. the occipital lobes for visual memory.
   d. the temporal lobes for episodic memory.
   e. all of the above

Answer Key for Self-Test

1.	c	28.	c
2.	a	29.	d
3.	b	30.	b
4.	a	31.	c
5.	b	32.	e
6.	c	33.	a
7.	d	34.	d
8.	d	35.	a
9.	d	36.	d
10.	d	37.	d
11.	a	38.	d
12.	b	39.	b
13.	c	40.	c
14.	d	41.	d
15.	b	42.	a
16.	c	43.	a
17.	b	44.	c
18.	b	45.	d
19.	a	46.	d
20.	b	47.	b
21.	b	48.	a
22.	b	49.	c
23.	d	50.	c
24.	a	51.	c
25.	c	52.	d
26.	a	53.	e
27.	b	54.	e

Investigating Psychological Phenomena

THE EFFECT OF IMAGERY INSTRUCTIONS ON MEMORY

Equipment: None
Number of participants: One
Time per participant: Fifteen minutes
Time for experimenter: Twenty minutes

As the text discusses, there are several mnemonic techniques that will improve memory performance. One of these is the use of images. By now there is a good deal of research that demonstrates the memorial effectiveness of asking participants to create images of the objects or events that they are trying to commit to memory. In the present experiment you will have an opportunity to demonstrate the effectiveness of imagery instructions for yourself in an experiment that involves learning paired-associate lists.

The procedure is quite simple. Below you will find two lists of twenty noun pairs each that you can use as stimuli for the experiment. You will need just one person to participate in the experiment. The procedure is as follows.

First, read the following instructions to the participant:

This is a memory experiment in which you will be required to memorize and recall two lists of words, each of which is composed of twenty pairs of fairly common nouns. First I will read aloud the twenty noun pairs from List 1 at the rate of one pair every seven seconds or so. While I am reading the pairs, just sit quietly and listen to them, trying as well as you can to memorize the words in each pair. After I have presented all the pairs, I shall go through the list again, this time reading only the first noun in each pair. As I read each of these nouns, I would like you to recall the appropriate second noun that was paired with it when I originally presented the list. You will have seven seconds or so to recall the second noun for each pair and to write it in the space provided on your answer sheet. Do you have any questions?

After you have read these instructions to the participant, give him or her the report sheet for this chapter from Appendix 2. Then follow the testing procedure outlined in the instructions. After you have completed the procedure for List 1, read the following instructions to the participant:

Now I shall present you with another list of twenty noun pairs that I would like you to memorize. The procedure for this list will be identical to that for the first list except for one change: This time, when you are presented with each pair, try to form a mental image of the words in which there is some sort of interaction. For example, if you were presented with the pair "horse-rock," you might form an image of a horse that is harnessed to a large boulder, dragging the boulder along the ground. Such images should help you memorize the words. Do you have any questions?

Now give the participant another answer sheet for List 2 and present List 2 exactly as List 1 was presented.

To score the participant's performance, count up the number of items that were answered correctly on each list. If all went well, the participant should have scored better on List 2 (unless the participant was already forming mental images for the nouns in List 1).

At this point you may raise a question. Was the participant's performance on List 2 better because of the influence of the imagery instructions, or could it have been better for some other reason? For example, it may already have occurred to you that performance on List 2 may have been better than List 1 because List 2 was presented *after* List 1, and therefore the participant may simply have been better practiced at memorizing words. Before reading on, try to think of a way that you might have run this experiment that would have avoided this problem.

One way to have avoided a practice effect would have been to use two different participants. This first participant would have received only List 1 with its instructions; the second would have received only List 2 with its imagery instructions. If performance on List 2 was still better than on List 1, you might feel more confident in attributing this difference to the effect of the instructions (assuming that your two participants were fairly comparable in their overall memory ability). At least practice could not account for the difference.

But, you might object, there might *still* be an explanation for the difference between lists that has nothing to do with the effect of imagery instructions. Suppose, for instance, List 2 was composed of words that were more common or concrete than the words on List 1 (e.g., horse versus liberty). This alone might make List 2 more memorable. There are two ways that you might control for this possibility. The first is to choose words for the two lists that are equated for frequency of usage and concreteness (and, for that matter, whatever else you might think of that would affect the memorability of words). The second method is to balance experimentally which word lists are paired with which instructions. The following table shows one arrangement that should work in which you would have to run at least four participants:

	Neutral instructions	Imagery instructions
Word list 1	Participant 1	Participant 2
Word list 2	Participant 3	Participant 4

If you were to run this experiment, then you could tell whether the word lists differ from one another in memorability and/or whether there is an effect of instructions. If Word list 2 is more memorable than Word list 1, then Participants 3 and 4 should perform better than 1 and 2. If imagery instructions produce better performance than neutral instructions, then Participants 2 and 4 should perform better than 1 and 3. If List 2 is more memorable than List 1 *and* imagery instructions produce better performance than neutral instructions, then Participant 4 should perform best of all.

If you want to check on the possible influence of practice in the experiment that you ran, and if you want to be sure that the word lists are comparable (they have actually been balanced for meaningfulness and commonness of the words), then you should try this last experiment. Whether you try it or not, however, you should realize that one of the points of this exercise was to show that even a fairly simple experiment such as the one that you ran with the word lists is sometimes open to several interpretations. To find the right one requires careful experimentation.

Noun pairs for List 1	Noun pairs for List 2
1. building-letter	1. sail-bowl
2. grass-meat	2. coffee-lake
3. animal-village	3. girl-flood
4. house-lip	4. corn-river
5. sky-seat	5. stone-bottle
6. dress-apple	6. paper-shore
7. fur-mountain	7. dust-army
8. flag-coast	8. ocean-fire
9. sugar-ship	9. clothing-board
10. mother-city	10. door-king
11. market-church	11. butler-tree
12. plant-baby	12. gold-chair
13. sea-iron	13. flower-car
14. woods-engine	14. bird-skin
15. arm-boulder	15. hall-child
16. woman-forest	16. garden-book
17. table-wood	17. money-shoes
18. queen-college	18. cat-camp
19. bar-diamond	19. wife-storm
20. cotton-street	20. dollar-machine

CHAPTER 8

Thought and Knowledge

Learning Objectives

1. What is directed thinking, and how does it differ from other senses of the word "thinking"?

ANALOGICAL REPRESENTATIONS

2. Be able to define a mental representation and to distinguish it from an external representation.
3. Understand the difference between analogical and symbolic representations. Be able to give examples of each.

Mental images

4. Why is introspection not completely trustworthy as evidence about imagery?
5. What does evidence about mental rotation and mental scanning tell us about imagery?
6. What does neuroimaging evidence contribute to our understanding of the relationship between imagery and perception? How does this evidence blend with evidence from transcranial magnetic stimulation?

Spatial thinking

7. Be familiar with the evidence showing that some spatial knowledge is imagelike in quality; but also be familiar with the evidence showing that some spatial knowledge is more symbolic and conceptual.

SYMBOLIC REPRESENTATIONS

Symbolic elements

8. Be able to describe the definition of a concept and to give examples.
9. Be familiar with the term *proposition* and with its elements (the subject and the predicate).

Knowledge and memory

10. Describe the differences between episodic and generic memory. What is semantic memory, and how is it related to episodic and generic memory?
11. What is meant by the claim that semantic memory is organized hierarchically? Explain how judgments of typicality contradict this claim.

12. What is a parallel distributed processing model, and how does it compare with a spreading activation model? Understand the metaphor of the master spy and how it helps to explicate the principle underlying PDP models.

THE PROCESS OF THINKING: SOLVING PROBLEMS

Organization in problem solving

13. How is problem solving best conceived as a search? How is means-end analysis relevant to this search?
14. How is thinking goal directed?
15. How is thinking hierarchical? How are the concepts of subgoal and subroutine related to the hierarchical nature of thought?
16. What is the shape of the learning curve in the development of a skill, and what does this shape tell us about the course of learning?
17. Be able to describe how chunking ability differentiates novices from experts. What is the role of automaticity in skill development?
18. Describe the Stroop effect and discuss its relevance to automaticity.
19. What are the major differences between masters and beginners in problem solving? What skills do masters have that novices don't?

Obstacles to problem solving

20. Be aware of the effects of set on problem solving. How does set influence solution strategies?

Overcoming obstacles to solutions

21. How can the strategy of working backward help in problem solving? Why don't experts use it much?
22. What is the role of analogy in problem solving? What factors govern whether people will retrieve analogies from memory and use them?

Restructuring

23. What is restructuring? How is it related to creative thinking?
24. How is incubation related to the effects of set? Understand how it is related to creative thinking.

25. How is restructuring in problem solving similar to the process required to appreciate certain kinds of humor?

THE PROCESS OF THINKING: REASONING AND DECISION MAKING

26. Are the laws of logic the laws of thought?
27. Be able to explain the difference between deductive and inductive reasoning and give examples of each.

Deductive reasoning
28. What is a syllogism? What reasons cause many participants to do poorly in solving syllogisms?
29. What sorts of strategies do people use to solve syllogisms?
30. Describe the selection task and the errors people make on it.
31. When is performance on the selection task improved? What are two accounts of this?

Inductive reasoning
32. What is the availability heuristic and how do people use it to make judgments?
33. How is the representative heuristic used to make judgments about instances?
34. What is the confirmation bias? Why are disconfirmations more helpful in testing hypotheses than confirmations? Can you give an example of the confirmation bias?
35. How does formal training in statistics help people to reason inductively? What else can be done to improve reasoning?

Decision making
36. Give examples of errors in reasoning that are due to the way a problem is framed. How do people feel about gains and losses in their willingness to take on risk?

THE THINKING BRAIN

37. Be aware of the approach used by the field of cognitive science.

Localization of thought
38. Give some examples of regions of cortex used in different thinking tasks.
39. Be able to describe some of the deficits of patients with damage to prefrontal cortex.
40. What is the role of prefrontal cortex in working memory? What are some theories about the organization of prefrontal cortex?

Cognition and consciousness
41. Why is the study of consciousness so difficult?
42. Be able to distinguish between unconscious and nonconscious.
43. Be familiar with the phenomenon of blindsight and what its implications are for consciousness in perception.
44. What does it mean to use memory unconsciously? Give examples of the use of memory in comprehension that show its influence even when we're not conscious of it.
45. Describe how actions may be taken without conscious awareness.
46. Understand what it means to be aware of the products of processing without being aware of the processing itself.
47. How might consciousness be useful in situations requiring flexibility?
48. What are some views about the neural correlates of consciousness?

Programmed Exercises

1. The word _____ may be used as a synonym for remembering, attention, or belief. *thinking*

2. If one is talking about _____ thinking, one is referring to reasoning or reflecting on some problem, with some goal in mind. directed

ANALOGICAL REPRESENTATIONS

3. Mental _____ refer to internal codes that stand for external _____. representations representations

4. An _____ representation is one that captures some of the characteristics of what it represents; a _____ representation stands for what it represents, but does not resemble it in any simple way. analogical symbolic

5. Mental _____ seems to be analog in that the time it takes to effect a transformation is related to the number of degrees of transformation. rotation

6. You can show that people can _____ images by showing that the time it takes them to traverse from one part of an image to another is linearly related to the distance that must be traversed, as if they were looking over an actual map of the space. scan

7. _____ thinking is sometimes picturelike and sometimes requires conceptual representations. This is illustrated by examining several phenomena of mental maps. Spatial

8. _____ _____ stimulation is a technique used to disrupt normal brain activity at some site by applying magnetic pulses to the scalp. Transcranial magnetic

9. Mental images are just like _____, the representations of the world around us.   percepts

SYMBOLIC REPRESENTATIONS

10. A _____ is an internal representation of a class or category for which some instances can be enumerated.   concept

11. A _____ asserts a relationship between concepts such that it relates a _____ and a _____, the former of which is what the _____ is about and the latter of which is what is asserted.   proposition, subject predicate, proposition

12. It is generally believed that there are two kinds of memory representations: ones that tag an event with its time or place of occurrence (called _____ memory), and ones that constitute memory for items of knowledge (called _____ memory).   episodic generic

13. One type of generic memory is _____ memory, which concerns the meanings of concepts.   semantic

14. One popular type of model for semantic memory involves a representation called a _____, in which various _____ are linked together by lines and arrows in a complex system of relationships to show how they are interrelated.   network nodes

15. A network in which one concept was stored under others that subsumed it throughout would be called _____.   hierarchical

16. Semantic _____ occurs when a word activates mental representations of related words.   priming

17. Parallel _____ processing models have as one central assumption that the representation of a concept is spread out throughout a network, rather than being concentrated in a single node.   distributed

THE PROCESS OF THINKING: SOLVING PROBLEMS

18. One conceptualization of problem solving has solvers beginning in an _____ state and traversing a path to a _____ state.   initial goal

19. How to fall in love is an example of an _____-_____ problem; solving a crossword puzzle is an example of a _____-_____ problem.   ill-defined well-defined

20. The use of master plans to organize subsidiary actions suggests that thought is organized into _____.   hierarchies

21. _____ _____ analysis is a method of problem solving that involves minimizing the distance between a current state and a goal state.   means-ends

22. The ability to organize many details into larger _____ is one of the crucial features of directed activity, including thinking.   chunks

23. As Adrian de Groot demonstrated with chess, master problem solvers use _____ that contain more information than do those of beginners.   chunks

24. Much of the difference between a master and an apprentice is in the degree to which subcomponents of an activity have been chunked hierarchically; to the master, the substeps have become _____.   automatic

25. The _____ effect is an example of how reading letter strings has become an automatized activity for adults. Reading incompatible color names interferes with naming colors in which the color words are printed.   Stroop

26. When a person becomes _____ on one approach to a task, it is hard for him or her to approach it any other way.   fixated

27. A person who attempts to solve a problem by thinking along a line of thought created by previous thinking is operating under a _____ _____.   mental set

28. In general, the greater the motivation toward reaching a solution, the greater the _____ _____ with which the problem is approached.   mental set

29. _____ _____ is a problem-solving strategy that frequently helps because one can work from the solution.   Working backward

30. When two problems have a similar structure, using one as a(n) _____ to the other can be an effective problem-solving strategy.   analogy

31. Solutions of difficult problems often involve a perceptual _____ of the problem in order to break a false perceptual set.   restructuring

32. The phenomenon whereby one arrives at an insightful solution to a problem after intense preparation followed by rest is called _____.   incubation

33. It has been suggested that both _____ and _____ involve a dramatic shift from one cognitive organization to another.   humor, insight

THE PROCESS OF THINKING: REASONING AND DECISION MAKING

34. A _____ contains two premises and a conclusion.   syllogism

35. In _____ reasoning we apply a general rule to a particular case.   deductive

36. In _____ reasoning we consider different cases and try to find the rule that covers them all.   inductive

37. In the _____ task, subjects are given cards and they must turn over some to determine whether a rule they have been given is violated or not.   selection

38. _____ statements are of the "if-then"sort.   conditional

39. An _____ perspective on psychology attributes failure at the selection task to its failure to make contact with adaptively significant problems.   evolutionary

40. Reasoning _____ allow us to reason about problems that involve the concepts of obligation, permission, and cause-and-effect.   schemas

41. When people use the _____ heuristic to make frequency judgments, they rely on ease of retrieval from memory.   availability

42. The _____ heuristic may lead to error if you are making a judgment about an atypical case.   representativeness

43. The fact that people primarily seek evidence that will confirm their hypotheses suggests that there is a strong _____ _____.   confirmation bias

44. One _____ shows that a hypothesis is false, but countless _____ cannot prove that it is true.   disconfirmation, confirmations

45. The way a problem is _____ can influence the way people will solve it.   framed

46. People are more prone to take risks to limit _____ than to achieve _____.   losses, gains

47. There is a good deal of evidence that throws a poor light on human _____; we make all sorts of reasoning errors. But many important intellectual judgments are rational because they come about by _____ effort.   rationality   collective

THE THINKING BRAIN

48. Patients with frontal lobe damage have a difficult time in _____ situations that require some new plan, and they also show distinct patterns of _____, in which they continue the same action repeatedly.   novel   preservation

49. One important role of the frontal lobes has to do with _____ memory, the memory that is used in problem solving and planning situations.   working

50. The study of _____ has proven very difficult in psychology because mental events are private and not subject to external observation.   consciousness

51. Major advances in the study of consciousness have come about through the study of when it is _____.   absent

52. Freud's conception of the _____ included the notion that memories were actively kept out of our awareness.   unconscious

53. There are patients with damage to the occipital lobe of the brain who experience _____, the ability to make judgments about visual objects with no conscious experience of those objects.   blindsight

54. By and large, we seem to be unaware of mental _____; but, by contrast, we are sometimes aware of the _____ of mental operations.

processes
products

55. In relying on automatic routines, we give up _____.

flexibility

Self-Test

1. All of the following are examples of directed thinking *except*
   a. discovery of a geometric proof.
   b. deciding on the next move in a chess game.
   c. daydreaming about last night's meal.
   d. trying to figure out why a car will not start.

2. A hand drawing of a tractor is what kind of representation, as compared to an actual tractor?
   a. analogical
   b. symbolic
   c. both of the above
   d. neither of the above

3. The relationship between the quality of mental images and the ability to perform tasks that require imagery is
   a. positive.
   b. negative.
   c. sometimes positive, sometimes negative.
   d. unstudied.

4. You have probably seen standardized tests in which you are given a picture of a flat piece of paper in which folds are drawn in. You have to mentally fold the paper and compare it to several objects shown to determine which of the objects will be formed after the folding is completed. Studies of this skill show that the more folds that have to be executed, the longer it takes to perform the task. The task thus produces performance analogous to
   a. mental search of a hierarchical network.
   b. mental solution of a water jug problem.
   c. mental solution of a syllogism.
   d. mental rotation.

5. It appears that the relationship between scanning mental images and scanning actual pictures is
   a. symbolic.
   b. representational.
   c. haphazard.
   d. analog.

6. Studies of mental images for ambiguous figures show that
   a. participants can "see" either form of the figure.
   b. participants cannot reverse the figure in their mind's eye.
   c. participants can see both versions of the figure simultaneously, in contrast to what they see when they are viewing such a figure.
   d. none of the above

7. Brain lesions that disrupt vision often disrupt
   a. hearing.
   b. touch.
   c. smell.
   d. imagery.

8. Studies of the time it takes to estimate distance in a familiar environment result in data very much like studies of
   a. mental rotation.
   b. deductive reasoning.
   c. mental scanning.
   d. functional fixedness.

9. A concept
   a. may designate a quality.
   b. must have a finite number of instances.
   c. must not refer to a relationship.
   d. all of the above

10. Various theories argue that concepts should be represented by
    a. a representation that is abstract.
    b. features that characterize them.
    c. memories of the individuals within the category.
    d. all of the above

11. A proposition
    a. can be simply a mental image.
    b. can be simply a sentence.
    c. has a truth value.
    d. none of the above

12. A proposition must have
    a. a subject and a predicate.
    b. a product and a process.
    c. a node and a relation.
    d. none of the above

13. Remembering what you did on your last birthday is an example of
    a. semantic memory.
    b. generic memory.
    c. hierarchical memory.
    d. episodic memory.

14. A hierarchical network theory of semantic memory won't work because
    a. *apple* and *olive* are not coequal members of the category *fruit*.
    b. *red* is a more typical color than *mauve*.
    c. people rate *chairs* as being more representative of the category *furniture* than *ottomans*.
    d. all of the above

15. One difference between a parallel distributed processing (PDP) model of memory and a spreading activation model is that
    a. the knowledge of a concept in PDP is in single nodes.
    b. the knowledge of a concept in PDP is spread throughout the network.
    c. the knowledge of a concept in PDP is hierarchical.
    d. none of the above

16. Organization in problem solving is often
    a. lacking.
    b. ill-defined.
    c. determined working backward.
    d. goal-determined.

17. The Stroop effect clearly shows that
    a. certain mental activities become automatized.
    b. colors are named faster than words.
    c. words are named faster than colors.
    d. none of the above

18. Research has shown that master chess players are better than novices in
    a. solving algorithms.
    b. chunking chess moves.
    c. memorizing in general.
    d. memorizing random patterns of chess pieces.

19. A person is asked to solve a series of math problems. The first five problems can be solved only one way, each the same. The sixth problem can also be solved using this method, but there is also a much simpler solution. The participant solves this problem in the way he solved the first five. This person's problem-solving ability has been hampered by
    a. working backward.
    b. a lack of motivation.
    c. mental set.
    d. an improper heuristic.

20. The use of analogy in problem solving
    a. seems to be a habitual characteristic of the human problem solver.
    b. seems to work only when the analogy is somehow pointed out to the problem solver by someone else.
    c. requires that there be several potential analogs in memory for a single problem.
    d. depends on the problem solver's noticing a structural similarity between two problems.

21. All of the following often contribute to insights *except*
    a. a period of intense preparation.
    b. a period of retreat.
    c. a different environment.
    d. working backward.

22. One likely reason that incubation helps in reaching a problem solution is that
    a. it allows for perceptual restructuring.
    b. it helps break mental set.
    c. it gives time to set up subgoals.
    d. none of the above

23. The concept of an incubation period (in the explanation of insight) is unsatisfactory because
    a. it tells us nothing of the underlying processes.
    b. the term *unconscious thought* is too vague.
    c. it has been demonstrated to be false.
    d. a and b but not c

24. Insight and humor are similar in that
    a. both involve heuristics.
    b. both can be based on cognitive restructuring.
    c. neither will work if the participant is mentally set.
    d. none of the above

25. Restructuring seems to be an important component in humor and in problem solving. In both cases
    a. the person is caught off guard by the unexpected.
    b. some cognitive reorganization is required.
    c. there is usually some incongruity between the way things seem to be initially and the way they resolve themselves.
    d. all of the above

26. Ill-defined problems differ from well-defined problems in that
    a. ill-defined problems have more difficult and complex solutions.
    b. well-defined problems always have solutions; ill-defined problems are unsolvable.
    c. it is hard to define what changes are needed to reach the goal stated in ill-defined problems.
    d. all of the above

27. All A are B
    Some B are C
    Therefore, some A are C. This is a(n)
    a. invalid syllogism.
    b. valid syllogism.
    c. invalid algorithm.
    d. valid algorithm.

28. Results from the selection task tell us that
    a. people are poor in reasoning about abstract problems that are not set in a concrete context.
    b. people's reasoning may be governed by whether the problem masks contact with some evolutionarily important problem that their ancestors faced.
    c. people's reasoning is improved if a problem is couched in terms of some social schema that is relevant, such as a schema having to do with obligation.
    d. all of the above

29. Which of the following statements is true?
    a. People often attempt to see whether their hypotheses are false.
    b. People rarely attempt to see whether their hypotheses are false.
    c. People do not seek evidence that will confirm their hypotheses.
    d. none of the above

30. In making predictions about the outcome of situations, people seem to make too little use of
    a. salient information that is presented in the form of a memorable scenario.

b. base-rate information that tells them the past history of a situation.

c. deductive reasoning.

d. none of the above; people appropriately balance these sources of information

31. Consider the following experiment (which is similar to one actually performed). Participants were shown a series of slides on each of which there was a male or female name. The females were relatively famous people; the males were not. Unknown to participants, 20 males and 20 females were included in the list. At the end of the presentation, participants were asked to judge whether there had been more male names on the list or more female names. According to the availability heuristic, the results should have been

a. that female names were judged more frequent because they were more retrievable.

b. that the male names were judged more frequent because they were more retrievable.

c. that the female names were judged more frequent because they were more representative of famous people.

d. that the female and male names were judged equally frequent because they were equally retrievable.

e. none of the above

32. According to the representativeness heuristic, if you were told that Sam L. is hard working, conservative, meticulous, and exact in his behavior, you would be most likely to judge him to be

a. a poet.

b. an engineer.

c. a high school teacher.

d. a creative writer for an advertising firm.

e. any of the above

33. Participants are involved in an experiment in which they have to test whether the following rule is true: If a box contains red, black, or green balls, then it also contains yellow balls. To test out the rule, the participants are given a choice of a number of boxes from which to select. The fact that people are subject to the confirmation bias suggests that they will not select

a. a box that they are told contains red balls.

b. a box that they are told contains green balls.

c. a box that they are told contains yellow balls.

d. a box that they are told contains black balls.

34. One thing that improves reasoning ability is stating a problem in terms of

a. probability.

b. frequency.

c. heuristics.

d. representativeness.

35. Statistical training does seem to improve people's inductive reasoning. This is probably due to

a. its providing them with formal training on such issues as sample size effects.

b. its allowing them to apply their own intuitions more appropriately about such things as chance to situations.

c. its showing them links between their intuitions and formal statistical effects.

d. all of the above

36. When a decision is affected by events that come readily to mind, this is a manifestation of

a. inductive reasoning.

b. framing.

c. the representativeness heuristic.

d. the availability heuristic.

37. Problem framing has an effect on decision making because

a. people are very risk-averse when they face losses.

b. people are not very risk-averse when they face losses.

c. people are risk-seeking when they face gains.

d. none of the above

38. One common marketing technique by consumer electronics stores is to advertise frequent sales (some as frequent as every week!). With sales this frequent, one could think of pricing as not involving discounts on the weeks of the sale but as price markups on the weeks when no sale is advertised. But marketing would not be as successful this way because

a. people are more willing to accept losses than to forgo gains.

b. people are more willing to forgo gains than to accept losses.

c. people are generally irrational and will not see the symmetry in these two modes of marketing.

d. people will use the marked-up price as the reference point in the alternative scenario.

39. All of the following are shortcomings of human rationality except

a. people cannot perform the operations of addition, subtraction, multiplication, and division adequately.

b. people make errors in deductive reasoning.

c. people make errors in inductive reasoning.

d. people are not concerned with demonstrating that their hypotheses are wrong.

40. Studies of patients with frontal lobe damage have implicated these structures in

a. planning novel actions.

b. working memory.

c. being able to switch from one action to another rather than perseverating on just one action.

d. forming strategies.

e. all of the above

f. a, b, and d only

41. The study of consciousness has been aided by the study of

a. blindsight.

b. incubation.

c. functional fixedness.

d. mental set.

42. Which of the following phenomena has been instrumental in the study of consciousness?

a. perception without awareness

b. memory without awareness

c. action without awareness

d. all of the above

43. It has been suggested that consciousness is needed for

a. flexibility in processing.

b. automaticity in processing.

c. avoiding the deleterious effects of mental set.

d. promoting the use of analogy in reasoning.

Answer Key for Self-Test

1.	c	23.	d
2.	a	24.	b
3.	c	25.	d
4.	d	26.	c
5.	d	27.	a
6.	b	28.	d
7.	d	29.	b
8.	c	30.	b
9.	a	31.	a
10.	d	32.	b
11.	c	33.	c
12.	a	34.	b
13.	d	35.	d
14.	d	36.	d
15.	b	37.	b
16.	d	38.	b
17.	a	39.	a
18.	b	40.	e
19.	c	41.	a
20.	d	42.	d
21.	d	43.	a
22.	b		

Investigating Psychological Phenomena

THE STROOP EFFECT

Equipment: Included (see insert)
Number of participants: One
Time per participant: Thirty minutes
Time for experimenter: Forty minutes

It is frequently observed that as people are given more experience at the task of reading, the skill becomes more and more automatic in character. One symptom of this increasing automatization is that it is difficult to prevent a skilled reader from reading material that he is exposed to. This appears to be a general characteristic of skills that become automated. Given the proper conditions for the occurrence of such a skill, it is difficult to inhibit it.

Since automatization is a prominent characteristic of skilled activities ranging from reading to motor behavior to problem-solving routines, it is useful to investigate it to determine its characteristics. One task that has been studied extensively in this regard is the Stroop task (turn to p. 291 in the text for a full description of the task; Stroop, 1935). The following three experiments are designed to demonstrate the basic Stroop effect and to extend it somewhat so that you can develop some intuitions about why it occurs.

EXPERIMENT 1

First, before performing Stroop's actual demonstration you should conduct a simple version of it that will provide some baseline data on the effectiveness of our ability to ignore irrelevant information (see Chapter 6, "Perception," for a full discussion of this ability). In this experiment participants are required to name colors. In the control condition of the experiment the colors are simply displayed in patches. In the experimental condition the colors are presented by having randomly ordered

letter strings, each string of a different color. The question is whether having the letters present interferes with a participant's ability to name the colors. In principle, if the participant is capable of selectively attending to color, having the letters present should not interfere with his or her color-naming performance. Thus, naming the colors of the letter strings should be as easy as naming the colors of the color patches. On the other hand, the extent to which the participant cannot ignore the letter information is the extent to which his or her performance in color naming will decline.

Your measure of ease of color naming will be the amount of time it takes a participant to name a string of fifteen colors. To obtain reliable data you should have the participant name the colors in five lists of color patches and in five lists of letter strings, alternating between the two kinds of lists (see the number below each list).* The procedure is as follows: cut out the ten lists of stimuli for Experiment 1. On each trial have the appropriate list in front of the participant turned over so that he or she cannot see the stimuli (see book insert for these lists). Then read the following instructions:

When I say "go," turn over the list in front of you and name the colors in the list from top to bottom. There will be fifteen colors total. Name these colors as fast but as accurately as possible. After you have named the last color, say "Stop!" We will do this with ten different lists. Five have the colors printed in patches of ink; the other five have the colors printed in strings of randomly arranged letters. You should *ignore* how the colors are presented and simply name them. Any questions?

You should keep time from when you say "Go" until when the participant says "Stop." Make sure to present the ten lists in the order indicated by the number under the list. Record the time elapsed for each list and the number of errors for each list in the spaces provided on the report sheet.

Average the times for each type of list and total the errors. Does it appear that there is a difference between the average naming time or the total number of errors comparing the two types of lists? How would you interpret the data?

EXPERIMENT 2

In this experiment you are going to duplicate Stroop's demonstration. In the previous experiment you probably found either no effect or a very small effect of list type. The question we now ask is, Are there any conditions under which the participant cannot selectively attend well? In this experiment we have constructed such a condition by having the letters in the experimental condition spell color words themselves. Participants are still required to name the color of the word, not what it spells, but now the name of what it spells is itself going to be a color name. If selective attention is not very effective, these names should interfere with the participant's response and slow him or her down relative to a control condition that has neutral (noncolor) words printed in color.

---

* Notice that the two types of lists are matched for the length of the stimulus. That is, the color patches of Lists 1, 3, 5, 7, and 9 are matched in length to the Letter Strings of Length 2, 4, 6, 8, and 10. Why is this an important control? How have the lists of Experiments 2 and 3 been matched? Why?

Use the same procedure as before, but read the following set of instructions:

> In this experiment you are going to perform the same task as in the previous experiment. This time, however, the ink colors will be printed in the form of words. For half the lists, the words will be randomly chosen. For the other half, they will be color words. In both lists, however, you are to ignore the meaning of the words themselves and simply name the colors in which they are printed from the top to the bottom of each list. Remember that you should be as fast and as accurate as possible. Don't turn over each list until I say "Go," and when you have finished be sure to say "Stop!"

When you record the data, keep track of both the time to read the list and the number of errors made. Average the time and errors for each type of list. Is the difference in average time and total errors between list types greater than the difference found in Experiment 1? How would you interpret this?

EXPERIMENT 3

Now we will try a somewhat more subtle version of the Stroop experiment to get a better idea of the extent to which the participant can selectively attend. In the experimental condition, the words printed in color represent nouns whose referents themselves have a characteristic color (this color is never the same as the color in which the word is written). If the word suggests the characteristic color of its referent to the participant, this color might interfere with naming the color in which the word is printed (Majeres, 1974).

Use the same procedure as in Experiments 1 and 2, but read the following instructions to the participant:

> In this experiment you are going to perform the same task as in the previous experiment; that is, you will be naming colors. This time the ink colors will be printed in the form of words that themselves are not colors. For example, one of the lists might contain the word "stove" printed in green ink. Disregard the word that is present and simply name the ink color of each word in the list. Remember that you should not turn over the list until I say "Go," you should name the colors as quickly as possible, and you should say "Stop" when you have finished.

Conduct this experiment as you did the others. Is there a difference in performance between the lists? It it larger or smaller than in Experiment 2? What does this suggest about selective attention? What does it suggest about the automaticity of the reading process? *(If your instructor collects the data, fill out the report sheet in Appendix 2.)*

References

Stroop, J. R. (1935). Studies of interference in serial verbal reactions. *Journal of Experimental Psychology, 18,* 643–662.

Majeres, R. L. (1974). The combined effects of stimulus and response conditions on the delay in identifying the print color of words. *Journal of Experimental Psychology, 102,* 868–874.

REPORT SHEET

Experiment 1

Color patch list	Letter string list

Color patch list
List 1 _____ sec. _____ errors
List 3 _____ sec. _____ errors
List 5 _____ sec. _____ errors
List 7 _____ sec. _____ errors
List 9 _____ sec. _____ errors
Average = _____ sec.
Total errors = _____

Letter string list
List 2 _____ sec. _____ errors
List 4 _____ sec. _____ errors
List 6 _____ sec. _____ errors
List 8 _____ sec. _____ errors
List 10 _____ sec. _____ errors
Average = _____ sec.
Total errors = _____

Experiment 2

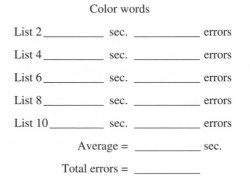

Neutral words
List 1 _____ sec. _____ errors
List 3 _____ sec. _____ errors
List 5 _____ sec. _____ errors
List 7 _____ sec. _____ errors
List 9 _____ sec. _____ errors
Average = _____ sec.
Total errors = _____

Color words
List 2 _____ sec. _____ errors
List 4 _____ sec. _____ errors
List 6 _____ sec. _____ errors
List 8 _____ sec. _____ errors
List 10 _____ sec. _____ errors
Average = _____ sec.
Total errors = _____

Experiment 3

Neutral words
List 1 _____ sec. _____ errors
List 3 _____ sec. _____ errors
List 5 _____ sec. _____ errors
List 7 _____ sec. _____ errors
List 9 _____ sec. _____ errors
Average = _____ sec.
Total errors = _____

Color referent words
List 2 _____ sec. _____ errors
List 4 _____ sec. _____ errors
List 6 _____ sec. _____ errors
List 8 _____ sec. _____ errors
List 10 _____ sec. _____ errors
Average = _____ sec.
Total errors = _____

CHAPTER 9

Language

Learning Objectives

THE BASIC UNITS OF LANGUAGE

The sound units

1. What are the major hierarchical levels of linguistic structure?
2. What is a phoneme? Give examples of phonemes.
3. Given what you know about phonemes, why is it difficult for humans to understand speech in a language that is not very familiar to them?
4. Are phonemes combined haphazardly? Give examples to support your answer.
5. How do phonemes vary among languages?

Morphemes and words

6. What is a morpheme? Give examples of morphemes.
7. How are morphemes combined?
8. What are content and function morphemes? How do the two kinds of morphemes differ from each other?

Phrases and sentences

9. How is the organization of words into phrases related to meaning?
10. How do the rules of syntax help convey meaning?
11. What is syntax, and how is it related to the acceptability of sentences?
12. What is phrase structure and how is it related to meaning?
13. How are phrases governed by rules?
14. What role do function morphemes play in organizing phrase structure?
15. Understand how the great complexity that is possible in sentence structure relies on the hierarchical structure of morphemes, words, and phrases.
16. Notice how the organization of some phrases leaves the meaning of a sentence ambiguous. Can you devise other ambiguities?

HOW LANGUAGE CONVEYS MEANING

The meanings of words

17. Describe the different kinds of word classes and how some aspects of the meaning of a word are conveyed by the class to which it belongs.
18. According to a definitional theory of meaning, how are words stored in memory? What is the role of semantic features?

What is the relationship between a definitional theory and a dictionary definition?

19. Name two observations about a definitional theory of meaning that suggest it is incomplete. How does the concept of a prototype deal with these observations?
20. How does a prototype theory differ from a definitional theory? What is the role of features? What is a family resemblance structure?
21. How does a prototype view of meaning work around the problem that many words do not seem to have necessary and sufficient features?
22. What evidence compels us to believe that we store both definitional representations of words as well as prototype representations? Describe the concept of a "grandmother" to illustrate this.
23. How is it that our understanding of word meanings confers constraints on our beliefs about the properties of objects?

The meanings of sentences

24. What is the significance of calling sentence meanings propositions? How can two propositions differ even if they contain the very same words?
25. How do sentence diagrams help convey the meaning of a sentence?
26. English uses word order heavily to signal meaning, but how do other languages signal meaning without being as reliant on word order?
27. Be able to give examples of how different verbs require different sentence structures to convey their meaning.
28. Explain the role of function morphemes in helping to encode meaning in complex sentences.

How we understand

29. Why is it that we are sometimes led down a garden path in interpreting the meaning of a sentence? What causes such effects, and how can they be reduced by changing grammatical construction?
30. Explain how often the conversational setting prescribes what sort of sentence should be constructed, giving just the information that is needed for comprehension.
31. Note that speakers do not speak in linear form, filling in all the details of an utterance that they are trading with a partner. They often leave large blanks that have to be inferred. What is the consequence of this? What savings does it produce?

How comprehension works

32. Describe the various cues to word meaning, and describe two views of how these cues are amassed in the service of sentence comprehension.

THE GROWTH OF LANGUAGE IN THE CHILD

33. Describe the course of word and syntax acquisition in children starting around age 2.

The social origins of language learning

34. Describe an example showing how children use social context as a guide to word learning.

Discovering the building blocks of language

35. Describe evidence about the brains of newborns suggesting that they already have a propensity to listen to human speech.
36. Beyond recognizing speech, within a short time, infants can discriminate the speech of one language from that of another. What is the evidence to support this claim?
37. Every baby eventually learns its native language, but at the outset, there is nothing to tell the baby which language this will be. How does the baby's innate capacity compensate for this in the first year of life?
38. Parsing out the words of a language is difficult because speech is continuous. How do babies solve this problem by paying attention to the relative frequencies of syllables and their combinations?

The growth of word meaning

39. What words do children learn first and what parts of speech are not learned at all early on?
40. What is the difficulty in explaining how young children come to understand what words mean? Do they not simply associate a word with an object?
41. Describe evidence that words are tied to the context in which they are spoken for children learning language. They seem to understand that words refer to things in the world.
42. What is a basic level of word understanding? Describe evidence that children focus on the basic level as they learn new words.
43. To what properties of an object will a child generalize a new word—color, shape, size?
44. Apparently, one of the powerful principles of word-learning is that children assume that each new word applies to a new thing. Describe evidence to support this claim.
45. Discuss evidence supporting the claim that children have primitive theories of the essence of objects, allowing them to discriminate man-made things from living things.
46. There is evidence that children also use grammatical class to differentiate what objects are; be able to describe this evidence.
47. Describe evidence showing that even children as young as 18 months have some sensitivity to the function morphemes even though they do not produce them.
48. Even children who utter only single words seem to have some evidence of the importance of word order; what evidence supports this?

The progression to adult language

49. What is the evidence that children do not learn to utter sentences by memorizing ones they have heard?
50. Describe the course of learning the past tense and why children at one point revert to incorrect forms (e.g., saying "runned" rather than "ran").

LANGUAGE LEARNING IN CHANGED ENVIRONMENTS

51. What is the value of studying language learning in very different environments from the ones children normally experience?

Wild children

52. How does early wild rearing affect language learning in the children who have been reared this way?

Isolated children

53. What does the study of isolated children tell us about language acquisition? How does the study of these children reveal the importance of early language learning?

Language without sound

54. Describe the characteristics of American Sign Language. Why is this an important example of language from a theoretical point of view?

Language without a model

55. Describe the language-learning studies with deaf children of hearing parents. What do the results imply?
56. What happens to children who are in a language-impoverished environment? Do they develop any language at all?

Children deprived of access to some of the meanings

57. Theoretically, blind children should learn sentence meanings more slowly than sighted children because blind children are cut off from opportunities to observe word referents. Nevertheless, evidence shows that the rate of language acquisition is not significantly different. Explain this finding.

LANGUAGE LEARNING WITH CHANGED ENDOWMENTS

58. What do cases of children with specific language impairment and Williams syndrome reveal about the relationship between language and other cognitive functions?

The critical period hypothesis

59. Summarize the evidence that points out the importance of critical periods in language learning.
60. Describe the initial difference between young learners of a second language and older learners. How does this difference change over time?
61. How does age relate to achieving native-level fluency in a language?

Language in nonhumans

62. Compare vocabulary learning in chimpanzees and humans. Which method works best to teach chimpanzees vocabulary?
63. What evidence has suggested early syntax acquisition in chimpanzees? Be able to evaluate the quality of this evidence.
64. If we say that trained chimpanzees use language, what does our definition of language exclude?

LANGUAGE AND THOUGHT

65. Give some examples of how languages differ from one another and how this might influence differences in thought among the linguistic groups.

How language connects to thought

66. Name some obvious ways in which language influences thought.

Do people who talk differently come to understand the world differently?

67. Realize that the connection between language and thought may be one that is mutually influenced by a common environment.

How can we study language and thought?

68. Is there universal agreement about the perception of colors regardless of the terms used to refer to individual colors? Give an example.

69. Is there universal agreement about the perception of space regardless of the terms used to refer to spatial relations? Give an example.

70. Understand the logic behind the tests of spatial priming to test for effects of mental representations of time.

Programmed Exercises

THE BASIC UNITS OF LANGUAGE

1. We can think of language as existing at a number of levels, from sounds to ideas. The structure of language is therefore _____.

   hierarchical

2. The spoken words bed and dead difffer only in the "b" and "d" sounds at the beginning. This is a difference in one _____.

   phoneme

3. English uses about _____ speech sounds.

   forty

4. Some of the facts about how phonemes combine in words are accidental choices. Others are _____ choices.

   systematic

5. Morphemes are the smallest language units that carry _____.

   meaning

6. "Strange," "er," and "s" are all _____.

   morphemes

7. An organized grouping of words is known as a _____, the unit from which sentences are composed.

   phrase

8. A tree structure of phrases and words is referred to as a _____ _____ _____ of a sentence.

   phrase structure description

9. In the sentence, "The boy saw the ice cream truck," the phrase "the boy" is called the _____ phrase.

   noun

10. A _____ _____ is a useful way of partitioning a sentence to show its hierarchical structure.

    tree diagram

11. Very often a single use of language can be interpreted in more than one way. That is, language is often _____.

    ambiguous

HOW LANGUAGE CONVEYS MEANING

12. The theory that argues that words are organized in our minds much as they are in a dictionary is the _____ theory of meaning.

    definitional

13. According to the theory described in question 12, the meaning of a word is a set of _____ that are essential for something to be a member of the class specified by a word.

    features

14. The _____ theory of meaning argues that words are defined by features, but the features are not necessary and sufficient.

    prototype

15. Many times members of a category share features that overlap but none of which is necessary or sufficient for membership in that category. Rather, the features share a _____ _____ structure.

    family resemblance

16. Sentences introduce a topic, the _____ of the sentence, and they offer a comment about that topic, the _____ of the sentence.

    subject
    predicate

17. In English and many other languages, word _____ is important to convey the semantic role of the words.

    order

18. Sometimes, case _____ provide important grammatical information, and they are usually function morphemes.

    markers

19. Sentences in which one is led to one interpretation but that switch to another interpretation are called _____ _____ sentences. — garden path

20. One technique for understanding the processes used by readers is to record with an _____-_____ the motion of their eyes as they read sentences. — eye-tracker

21. Language comprehension is influenced by syntax, semantics, _____ context, and _____ that speakers and listeners make about what each of them knows and intends to communicate. — extralinguistic, inferences

THE GROWTH OF LANGUAGE IN THE CHILD

22. Language appears to be _____ and interpersonal at its very outset; even the tone of voice of a speaker of a language that is not a child's will elicit a response in the child. — social

23. Recording _____ flow in two-day-old babies' brains reveals that the babies are sensitive to natural language input. — blood

24. One technique that has proven valuable in detecting what language sensitivity infants have is to record the rate of their _____ when they hear novel or familiar language sounds. — sucking

25. By the age of two months, infants are sensitive to distinctions among _____. — phonemes

26. The way infants are prepared to learn the sounds of any language when they are born is that during the first year of life, they can distinguish all the _____ of any language. — phonemes

27. One way that infants learn the words of a language is that they keep a record of the frequency with which _____ co-occur in speech that they hear. — syllables

28. Young children acquire _____-_____ words for whole objects before learning the superordinates or subordinates. — basic-level

29. Preschoolers apparently believe that no word can have a _____; that is, they act as if any one concept has only one word that refers to it. — synonym

30. Toddlers as young as 15 months seem to know how _____ words are used in English even though they do not use any themselves yet. — function

31. Children at about 18 months seem to have some grasp of the part of _____ that involves word order; they can tell the difference between a sentence in which X is doing something to Y versus Y's doing something to X. — syntax

32. Learning of past tense in English is subject to _____ errors in young children; they learn that –ed added to a word makes it refer to the past, but they then apply this rule to irregular forms of the past as well, such as "ranned." — overgeneralization

LANGUAGE LEARNING IN CHANGED ENVIRONMENTS

33. Cases of wild children raised by animals show that a proper environment is important for normal _____ development. — language

34. One thing is clear about language learning: Children do not produce sentences by simply _____ ones they have heard and then simply uttering them. — memorizing

35. Evidence that language can develop without sound comes from studies of _____ children. — deaf

36. A widely used manual communication system among deaf people is _____ _____ _____. — American Sign Language (ASL)

37. A biological _____ enables children to learn language, whether they invent the basics themselves (if there is no language model) or follow the model that they are exposed to. — predisposition

38. It is remarkable that _____ children come to use words such as "look" and "see" as early as _____ children. — blind sighted

LANGUAGE LEARNING WITH CHANGED ENDOWMENTS

39. When language capacities are lost or diminished because of damage to a cerebral hemisphere (usually the left), this state is termed _____. — aphasia

40. Patients who have a deficit in language only may have a _____ language impairment; by contrast, patients with _____ syndrome have other cognitive deficits, but their language is normal. — specific Williams

41. One hypothesis of language learning postulates an ideal time to learn languages, after which the learning process is significantly more difficult. This time is known as the _____ _____.　　critical period

42. In comparing adults with children, it is clear that _____ pick up a second language more effectively than _____ do.　　children / adults

43. There is evidence that the brain loci of _____-learned languages is different from _____-learned languages　　late, first

44. After four years of training, the chimpanzee Washoe had learned 130 _____ for objects, actions, and action modifiers.　　signs

45. Even if chimpanzees were shown to have some sense of sequence this would not be sufficient evidence to claim that they have knowledge of _____.　　syntax

LANGUAGE AND THOUGHT

46. Studies of the perception of _____, facial _____, or _____ position suggest that perception is universal, and all that differs among cultures is the words that are assigned to perceptions　　color, expression, spatial

47. There are cases, such as the phenomenon of framing discussed in Chapter 8, in which _____ guides thought. In this case, describing an outcome in positive or negative terms influences how people choose among alternatives.　　language

48. Experiments have shown that _____ can facilitate thinking, but that a small bit of training on them can change which ones a thinker uses.　　metaphors

Self-Test

1. When we say that language is hierarchical, we mean that
   a. different languages uses demonstrate social class differences.
   b. language structure exists at many levels.
   c. language has developed from other cognitive functions.
   d. modern languages are descended from other languages.

2. Which of the following represents the actual hierarchy of language structures from the smallest to the largest unit?
   a. phrase, word, phoneme, morpheme
   b. word, morpheme, phrase, phoneme
   c. phoneme, morpheme, word, phrase
   d. morpheme, phoneme, word, phrase

3. The perceptual units of speech are
   a. phonemes.
   b. morphemes.
   c. syllables.
   d. words.

4. One reason that foreign languages sound strange is that
   a. the same phonemes are pronounced differently.
   b. other languages are spoken more rapidly.
   c. there are fewer "gaps" in foreign languages than in English.
   d. some of the phonemes are different from those of English.

5. New words are being coined every day. Some sound combinations are not used, though. This is due to _____ rules.
   a. syntactic
   b. semantic
   c. pragmatic
   d. none of the above

6. A morpheme is a
   a. word.
   b. single sound.
   c. perceptual unit.
   d. unit of meaning.

7. A phrase is
   a. several sentences put together.
   b. unrelated to the meaning of a sentence that contains it.
   c. an organized group of words.
   d. always delineated by grammatical markings.

8. There are two kinds of morphemes that represent what kinds of information in a sentence?
   a. content and function
   b. sound and content
   c. semantic and sound
   d. pragmatic and semantic

9. At its most detailed level of specification, the phrase structure description of the sentence "A boy lost his ball" would contain which of the following elements?
   a. a noun phrase and a verb phrase
   b. a noun phrase, a verb, and a noun phrase
   c. a noun phrase and two verb phrases
   d. two noun phrases and two verb phrases

10. A two-branch tree diagram of a sentence structure would include these parts:
    a. principle rules and prescriptive rules
    b. verb phrase and noun phrase
    c. morphemes and phonemes
    d. pragmatic rules and verb phrases

11. Almost every child learns to speak grammatically, yet when a teacher tries to teach the grammatical structure of a language, this is difficult for a child to learn. The lesson from this is that
    a. grammar does not exist psychologically.
    b. grammar may be an implicit but not an explicit skill.
    c. grammar is not the same as syntax.
    d. grammar is unnatural for humans to understand and use.

12. The sentence "Flying planes can be dangerous" is ambiguous because
    a. there are three possible phrase structure descriptions.
    b. there are alternative possible phoneme descriptions.
    c. there are alternative ways of grouping the phrases.
    d. there are ambiguities of word meaning contained in the sentence.

13. The definitional theory of meaning attempts to define the _____ attributes that are included in a given concept.
    a. necessary
    b. sufficient
    c. both of the above
    d. none of the above

14. One problem with the definitional theory of meaning is that
    a. some words are used to describe more than one attribute.
    b. some concepts involve more than one attribute.
    c. some concepts have no attributes.
    d. some members of a category seem to be better examples of that category than other members.

15. The major characteristic of a prototype theory of meaning is that
    a. no feature is individually necessary.
    b. no feature is individually sufficient.
    c. a whole set of features describes word meaning.
    d. all of the above

16. A family resemblance structure is an analogy to support which theory?
    a. prototype
    b. definitional
    c. interpersonal
    d. language attribution

17. According to a definitional theory of meaning, the concept of a "semantic feature" is similar to the concept of an
    a. attribute of a concept.
    b. function morpheme.
    c. content morpheme.
    d. all of the above

18. Some words such as grandmother, bachelor, and six
    a. have only prototype representation.
    b. are function morphemes.
    c. have no pragmatic value.
    d. do have necessary and sufficient semantic features.

19. Sentences contain topics or comments about some subject which are called
    a. prototypes.
    b. predicates.
    c. paraphrases.
    d. phonemes.

20. If one utters the sentence "Mary bought John a ball" one is intending to convey that a ball was purchased for John by Mary. This meaning is called a
    a. prototype.
    b. predicate.
    c. proposition.
    d. phoneme.

21. Which sentence has a different proposition from the others?
    a. The girl kissed the boy.
    b. The boy was kissed by the girl.
    c. The boy kissed the girl.
    d. All of the above include the same proposition.

22. Case markers allow a language to have flexibility in
    a. morphemes.
    b. phonemes.
    c. word order.
    d. all of the above

23. Complex sentence meanings are often made easier to understand by adding
    a. function morphemes to guide understanding.
    b. content morphemes to guide understanding.
    c. pragmatics to guide understanding.
    d. none of the above

24. One of the factors that makes it easier for people to comprehend complex sentences is that they take into account which of the following things?
    a. the number of content morphemes in a sentence
    b. the frequency with which events happen
    c. the number of function morphemes in a sentence
    d. all of the above

25. Which of the following are contributors to sentence understanding?
    a. the context in which a sentence is uttered
    b. the likelihood that an event might happen
    c. the placement of function morphemes in a sentence
    d. all of the above

26. Garden path sentences are defined by
    a. ambiguous words in a sentence that can be interpreted in either of two ways.
    b. an initial semantic interpretation based on the first few words that is then changed by the remaining words.
    c. descriptions of flowers growing along a path.
    d. none of the above

27. Language comprehension is influenced by more than syntax and semantics. In addition, listeners make heavy use of
    a. the order of words in a sentence.
    b. the meanings of individual words in a sentence.
    c. the context in which a conversation occurs.
    d. a and b, but not c

28. Speakers and listeners appear to honor a set of unwritten rules when they converse. For example,
    a. a speaker would normally specify which of several possible objects in a room is the topic of an utterance.
    b. a listener would normally honor a rrequest that was given indirectly rather than answering "Yes" or "No" to a question such as, "Can you pass the butter?"
    c. a speaker would normally not utter a comment that is not relevant to an interchange that is currently occurring.
    d. all of the above

29. Language comprehension is guided by
    a. syntax.
    b. semantics.
    c. extralinguistic context.
    d. inferential activity by the listener.
    e. all of the above
    f. a and b, but not c or d
    g. a, b, and c but not d
    h. c and d, but not a and b

30. The number of words in an average adult vocabulary is
    a. 10,000.
    b. 40,000.
    c. 80,000.
    d. 150,000.

31. If French infants are playing and are scolded by an English speaker, they will
    a. not understand the scolding because of the language difference and therefore not change their behavior.
    b. begin laughing.
    c. stop their play because of the intonation of the speaker regardless of the fact that they cannot understand the words.
    d. speak back in English to the speaker because they imitate everything they hear.

32. One indication that language is not mere imitation, but that young children pay attention to the social context in which utterances occur is that
    a. when children hear a new word, they will try to figure out what object was being referred to.
    b. young children will talk with each other using a different language from the one they use to adults.
    c. children emit utterances that have nothing to do with the social situation in which they occur.
    d. none of the above

33. Which of the following statements is true about sound discrimination in early language learning?
    a. Initially, infants respond to all sounds in all languages.
    b. Initially, infants respond only to the sounds of their own language.
    c. Initially, infants cannot respond to sound distinctions at all.
    d. Initially, infants respond only to the most common sound distinctions in their own language and they ignore other sounds.

34. An indication of the interest level that an infant has is
    a. a decrease in the rate at which it sucks a nipple.
    b. an increase in the rate at which it sucks a nipple.
    c. the amount of habituation it shows toward a familiar stimulus.
    d. the amount of dishabituation is shows when given a novel stimulus.
    e. all of the above

35. A way to show that infants can discriminate phonemes is to show that
    a. their rate of sucking when they hear "ba" repeatedly goes down but then rebounds when they hear "pa."
    b. their rate of sucking when they hear "go" repeatedly goes down but then rebounds when they hear "mo."
    c. their rate of sucking when they hear "fi" repeatedly goes down but then rebounds when they hear "ti."
    d. their rate of sucking when they hear "du" repeatedly goes down but then rebounds when they hear "lu."
    e. all of the above
    f. none of the above

36. The reason children will often say "Carry you" when they mean "Carry me" is
    a. that they hear their parents say the former to them.
    b. that they want to carry their parents.
    c. that they do not understand the pronoun "me" but only understand the pronoun "you."
    d. none of the above

37. Which of the following is most likely to be among a child's first words?
    a. push
    b. and
    c. the
    d. pain

38. Children learn new words at about the rate of how many words per day?
    a. 1
    b. 10
    c. 100
    d. 1000

39. If a two-year-old child is asked where the kitty is when no cat is present, she will
    a. do nothing because she will respond only to objects that are present in the environment.
    b. stare blankly at the person asking the question.
    c. stare at an object that is most similar to a kitten in the environment.
    d. search for a kitty by shifting her eyes around.

40. Which of the following is a "basic level" word?
    a. beagle
    b. animal
    c. poodle
    d. dog

41. Suppose a child has a fish tank in her house in which there is a goldfish named "Max" that is often called by his name by the child's parents. The child will likely
    a. learn the word "fish" before the word "Max."
    b. learn the word "Max" and apply it to any animal.
    c. learn the word "Max" and apply it to any fish.
    d. learn the word "fish" and apply it to any animal whose name is "Max."

42. Suppose a child knows the word for "dog" and you point to a Dalmation dog and say "This is my rif." If you then ask the child to show you more "rifs," she will
    a. point to more dogs.
    b. point to other spotted things.
    c. point to nothing because the word "rif" is not a word in English.
    d. point aimlessly to lots of things in the environment.

43. Children seem to understand the "essentialism" of some objects. That is, they know that
    a. you could not turn a toaster into a frog.
    b. you could not turn a lawnmower into a scooter.
    c. you could not turn a dog into a cat.
    d. you could not turn a hat into a pillow.

44. Children eighteen months of age appear to be somewhat sensitive to the use of function morphemes in sentences as indicated by the fact that they
    a. find the sentence, "Bill is running" odd.
    b. find the sentence, "Bill can running" odd.
    c. find the sentence, "Bill can run" odd.
    d. find the sentence, "Bill ran" odd.

45. Children of eighteen months know that which of the following pairs of sentences mean different things?
    a. John pulled Mary. Mary pulled John.
    b. John hit Mary. Mary hit John.
    c. John touched Mary. Mary touched John.
    d. all of the above
    e. none of the above

46. The use of a word form such as "sitted" by a child is known as
    a. telegraphic.
    b. undergeneralization.
    c. overgeneralization.
    d. syntactics.

47. Evidence from wild children who have been found reveals that
    a. some can be rehabilitated to use language without problems.
    b. some can learn to speak a few words.
    c. all can learn to speak a few words.
    d. none of the above

48. Language development does not depend on hearing language, as evidenced by
    a. wild children learning language.
    b. children learning ASL.
    c. isolated children learning language.
    d. retarded children learning language.

49. Deaf children whose parents did not teach them sign language demonstrated language development similar to that of hearing children in that
    a. the children went through one-word production, two-word production, and so on.
    b. they invented a communication system of their own.
    c. they eventually put signs together in predictable serial order.
    d. all of the above

50. As compared to sighted children, blind children
    a. will not learn language as quickly.
    b. will not be able to learn words related to sight such as "look."
    c. will learn language later in life.
    d. all of the above
    e. none of the above

51. The loss of language function is known as
    a. aphasia.
    b. anorexia.
    c. asphyxia.
    d. aphaeresis.

52. The following individuals were deprived of exposure to language since birth. Which one has the best chance of learning to speak?
    a. an eight-year-old boy
    b. a fourteen-year-old boy
    c. a twenty-year-old man
    d. a thirty-year-old woman
    e. all are equivalent in their language learning ability

53. First-language learning, second-language learning, and recovery from aphasia may all depend on
    a. intelligence.
    b. the particular language involved.
    c. generalization.
    d. the critical period.

54. In bilinguals, there is evidence that
    a. when they learn their languages at the same time, the languages are represented in different areas of the brain.
    b. when they learn their languages one after another, the languages are represented in the same area of the brain.
    c. when they learn their languages one after another, the languages are represented in different areas of the brain.
    d. none of the above

55. People who learn American Sign Language late in life will
    a. have all the same facility with the language as those who learned it early in life.
    b. not have all the elaborations of the language as those who learned it early in life.
    c. have diffficulty learning much of the language.
    d. only be able to learn it if they have not learned another sign language beforehand.

56. Studies in which experimenters have attempted to teach chimpanzees language have led us to the conclusion that
    a. chimpanzees can learn words.
    b. chimpanzees can learn to express propositions.
    c. can learn to use syntax to express thoughts.
    d. all of the above
    e. a and b, but not c
    f. b and c, but not a
    g. a and c, but not b

57. Some have argued that the many words Eskimos have for snow has shaped their perception of snow. However, this argument is flawed because
    a. Eskimos don't perceive snow any differently than do residents of the southern United States.
    b. Eskimos don't have more than one word for snow.
    c. Eskimos don't have as many words for snow as English has.
    d. all of the above

58. Various experimental studies have been conducted that cast doubt on Whorf's claim about the relation of language to thought. For example, studies have shown
    a. that people of different cultures perceive colors the same regardless of the words they use to name colors.
    b. that people of different languages have similar perceptions of spatial position even if their languages are inconsistent in assigning names to particular spatial relationships.
    c. that people of different cultures perceive time differently but that this perception can be changed by minimal training and is not immutable.
    d. all of the above
    e. a and b, but not c
    f. a and c, but not b

Answer Key for Self-Test

1.	b	30.	c
2.	c	31.	c
3.	a	32.	a
4.	d	33.	a
5.	d	34.	e
6.	d	35.	e
7.	c	36.	a
8.	a	37.	a
9.	b	38.	b
10.	b	39.	d
11.	b	40.	d
12.	c	41.	c
13.	c	42.	b
14.	d	43.	c
15.	d	44.	b
16.	a.	45.	d
17.	a	46.	c
18.	d	47.	b
19.	b	48.	b
20.	c	49.	d
21.	c	50.	e
22.	c	51.	a
23.	a	52.	a
24.	b	53.	d
25.	d	54.	c
26.	b	55.	b
27.	c	56.	e
28.	d	57.	c
29.	e	58.	d

Investigating Psychological Phenomena

IMPLICIT LEARNING

Equipment: A stopwatch or a watch that indicates seconds, index cards
Number of participants: One
Time per participant: Thirty minutes
Time for experimenter: Forty minutes

One of the most impressive aspects of language is its acquisition: children learn an enormous amount about their language without ever being explicitly taught. Consider syntax, for instance. Not until children have already learned a substantial number of syntactic rules do parents correct syntactic constructions that their children use. Somehow the growing child manages to induce the syntactic rules of language from the variety of utterances that he or she happens to encounter. This ability to induce complex rules from examples is an ability that we use all the time, but its use without intention, or even awareness, and with complex linguistic construction is what makes it impressive as a characteristic of language acquisition. Having just learned about language acquisition, you can now begin to appreciate how complex the language-learning process must be, especially since it is largely mediated by implicit induction.

You can demonstrate this implicit induction process using the following experiment modeled after one by Arthur Reber (1967). There are two phases to the experiment. In the first phase, your participant will memorize a series of strings of letters after being told only that he or she is a participant in a memory experiment. In the second phase, the participant will be told that the letter strings from the first phase were constructed using a rule. Then the participant will be shown twenty-four new strings that she has never seen before and asked to judge which twelve of these were constructed from the same rule used in phase 1. If the participant correctly categorized more of these twenty-four strings than we would expect by chance alone (twelve by chance, since there are only two responses the participant can make), then we can conclude that the participant has learned something about the rule even though he or she wasn't trying to in Phase 1.

PHASE 1

Instruct your participant as follows:

> This experiment concerns memory for unmeaningful material. You will be presented with twenty strings of letters that you must memorize and recall. These strings of letters will be presented in groups of four that you can study for fifteen seconds. Then the groups will be taken away and you will be required to recall all four strings (in any order). Following this you will be presented with the same strings again for another fifteen-second study period. This will be followed by another recall attempt. In all, the five groups of strings will be presented five times each for study and recall.

The stimulus materials for this first phase are at the end of this section. Write each of the five lists of strings on index cards and present them to the participant individually. Provide the participant with twenty slips of paper on each of which he or she can recall one quadruplet of strings. Be sure to remove each recall attempt before showing the next repetition of a set of strings or before going on to a new set of strings.

PHASE 2

Instructions:

> The strings of letters were constructed according to a rule. The rule dictated the orders in which letters were allowed to follow one another. In the second phase you will be shown twenty-four new strings of letters, and you must decide for each one whether it was or was not constructed according to the same rule for the letter strings in Phase 1. When you

decide, you should place your answer in the appropriate place on the answer sheet.

Score the participant's answers after he or she has completed Phase 2, using the answer key provided. Did the participant do better than chance? Ask whether he or she has any guesses about what the rule is. You will probably be surprised to discover how little the participant appears to be aware of the rule even though he or she can use it (in some sense) to make judgments about individual instances.

A diagrammatic representation of the rule is shown below. It works as follows: If you begin at "start" and trace through the diagram along any path in the direction of the arrows, you can get to "end." By noting the order of the letters that you pass along the way, you can construct a string. Notice that because of loops, some strings may be quite long but still permissible according to the rule.

Think about some of the following issues: In what way does this experiment mimic language learning? In what way is language learning different? As a model of language learning, why was it important not to tell participants about the rule until the end of Phase 1? What do the results suggest about language learning?

Reference

Reber, A. S. (1967). Implicit learning of artificial grammars, *Journal of Verbal Learning and Verbal Behavior, 6,* 855–863.

PHASE 1: STIMULUS LISTS

(Write these on index cards or pieces of paper for presentation to the participant.)

List 1	List 2	List 3	List 4	List 5
VVTRXRR	VVRXRR	VTRRR	VVTRXR	XMVTRX
XMVTTRX	XXRR	XMVRXRR	VTRR	XMTRRRR
XMVRXR	VVRMVRX	VVTTRMT	VVRMTRR	XMVRX
VVTRX	XMVRMT	VVRMTR	XMVTRMT	XXRRR

PHASE 2: LIST OF ALTERNATIVES FOR RECOGNITION TEST

(Write these on index cards as well.)

1.	RXTTVMXR	13.	VVTTRX
2.	XMTR	14.	VVRX
3.	MXXR	15.	VVRRRTX
4.	XMVRXRRR	16.	MT
5.	VVRXR	17.	VVTRMVRX
6.	VTTX	18.	VM
7.	MVTTXVR	19.	XXR
8.	XX	20.	XMT
9.	VRT	21.	RXTMV
10.	VVTTTRX	22.	XXM
11.	TTV	23.	TTRXXM
12.	VT	24.	VTR

ANSWERS

1.	no	13.	yes
2.	yes	14.	yes
3.	no	15.	no
4.	yes	16.	no
5.	yes	17.	yes
6.	no	18.	no
7.	no	19.	yes
8.	yes	20.	yes
9.	no	21.	no
10.	yes	22.	no
11.	no	23.	no
12.	yes	24.	yes

RECOGNITION TEST REPORT SHEET

(You can find this report sheet in Appendix 2; cut it out and give it to the participant.)

RULE FOR LETTER-STRING CONSTRUCTION

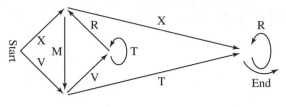

CHAPTER 10

Cognition and Social Behavior

Learning Objectives

THE SOCIAL SELF

1. Describe the self-concept and indicate how it is shaped by, and how it shapes, the social world.

Knowing ourselves
2. Contrast introspection and self-perception theory as accounts of how we come to know ourselves.

Behaviors shape attitudes
3. Explain the mutual relation between attitudes and behavior.
4. Describe the foot-in-the-door technique, and how it demonstrates the influence of behavior on attitudes.
5. Explain how aspects of cognitive dissonance, particularly bringing one's own behavior into line with one's attitudes, causes attitude change. Include forced compliance and justification of effort in the discussion.

Do attitudes predict behavior?
6. Define attitudes, and review the evidence for the value of attitudes as predictors of behavior.
7. Summarize the factors that determine the degree to which attitudes predict behavior.
8. Distinguish implicit and explicit attitudes.
9. Indicate how priming and the implicit attitudes test (IAT) are used to probe implicit attitudes.

SELF-CONCEPT AND SELF-DEFENSE

The above-average effect
10. What is the above-average effect, and what are some accounts for it?

The self-serving bias
11. What is the self-serving bias? How does it extend beyond the self

Impression management
12. Describe impression management, including self-handicapping, and indicate how it involves more than the "actor."

Embarrassment
13. What is embarrassment, and how might it relate to impression management?

PERSON PERCEPTION

Forming impressions
Person perception as discerning patterns
14. Describe Asch's experiments on impression formation.
15. What is a "central trait" and in what sense are people perceived as more than the sum of their attributes?
16. Why are first impressions so important?

Person perception and cognitive schemas
17. What are the parallels between cognitive constructions of the physical and social worlds?
18. Indicate the role of schemas and implicit theories of personality in social cognition and impression formation.
19. What are stereotypes, and what is the role of illusory correlation in maintaining inaccurate stereotypes?
20. Describe the outgroup homogeneity effect.
21. Explain how ingroup favoritism can account for why stereotypes are often derogatory

ATTRIBUTION

Attribution as a rational process
22. Indicate the parallels between scientific thinking and the attribution process.
23. What are situational and dispositional factors in causal attribution?

Errors in the attribution process
24. Evaluate the roles of situational and dispositional factors in judgments of other people. What is the fundamental attribution error?
25. What is the actor-observer difference?
26. Why are people more inclined to make situational attributions about their own behavior, as opposed to the behavior of others (the actor-observer difference)? Indicate the role of different information and different perspectives.

CONFORMITY AND THE SOCIAL CONSTRUCTION OF REALITY

27. What is social cognition?
28. Describe Asch's experiment on the social basis of physical "reality," and indicate its importance for understanding the social construction of the world.

Social referencing and social comparison
29. What is social comparison, and how does it function in ambiguous situations?

Persuasive communications
30. What accounts for the effectiveness of persuasive communications? Review the role of the message source.
31. Describe the central and peripheral routes to persuasion, and indicate the role of heuristics.

Conformity and beyond
32. Discuss the motivation to conform, including the avoidance of embarrassment.

Majorities and minorities
33. Discuss the importance of a unanimous opinion versus a judgment in which there is at least one dissenter in addition to the target participant.

Obedience
34. What characterizes the authoritarian personality?
35. Describe Milgram's basic study on obedience.
36. Discuss the importance of seeing oneself as another's agent. Relate this to the Nazi massacre of the Jews or other atrocities.
37. Discuss how dehumanization, psychological distance, and gradual escalation (slippery slope) influence blind obedience. Illustrate these influences with examples from the Milgram experiments.
38. Contrast personality factors with situational factors as causes of blind obedience.
39. Describe the Zimbardo prisoner study as another example of situational factors causing normal persons to behave in a cruel manner.

SOCIAL IMPACT: THE CONVERGENCE OF SOCIAL FORCES

40. What is social impact theory? What environmental factors increase and decrease social impact?
41. Describe social loafing and social facilitation. Indicate the sense in which they are opposites.

LEADERSHIP

Great person or social forces
42. Compare situational and dispositional approaches to the determination of leadership.

Leadership in the laboratory
43. Illustrate how leadership has been studied in the laboratory. What personality and situational factors promote leadership?

GROUP DECISION MAKING

44. Indicate how group decisions may systematically differ from individual decisions. Include discussion of group polarization, risky shift, and groupthink.
45. Discuss some of the reasons for the occurrence of group polarization and risky shift.

CROWD BEHAVIOR AND PANDEMONIUM

The emphasis on the irrational: deindividuation
46. What is deindividuation? How does it influence crowd behavior?

Cognitive factors and the panicky crowd
47. In what ways can one account for apparently irrational behavior by a crowd in terms of the rational behavior of the individuals in the crowd? What is the role of trust in this?
48. What is the prisoner's dilemma? Provide examples of payoff matrices as illustrations.
49. Show how the prisoner's dilemma analysis can account for panic in crowds.
50. Discuss the prisoner's dilemma analysis of social dilemmas, such as air pollution, and indicate strategies that might produce more cooperation.
51. Evaluate the statement that "people become 'primitive' or irrational in crowds."

CULTURE AND SOCIAL INFLUENCE

Collectivism versus individualism and views of the self
52. Describe the difference between individualist and collectivist cultures, and how cross-cultural studies might provide a different perspective on social cognition.

Cutural context of above average
53. Describe and explain the evidence for the reversal of the above-average effect in some collectivist cultures.

Attributions about causes of behavior
54. How do people from collectivist cultures differ from those from individualist cultures on the balance between dispositional and situational attributions? What might cause this difference?

In-groups and out-groups
55. Why are members of collectivist cultures usually more influenced by ingroups than members of individualist cultures? Discuss differences in the number and structure of in-groups in collectivist versus individualist cultures.

Programmed Exercises

THE SOCIAL SELF

1. The _____-_____ is composed of who we want to be, how we wish to be perceived, and how we perceive outselves.

   self-concept

2. A direct approach to knowing the self is to look within ourselves, or _____.

   introspect

3. A less direct approach is to learn about ourselves by inferring features of our selves from our behavior, as proposed by _____-_____ theory.

   self-perception

4. There is evidence that not only do attitudes affect behavior, but that _____ affects _____.

   behavior
   attitudes

5. The "_____-_____-_____-_____" technique is an example of how behavior can lead to attitude change.

   foot-in-the-door

6. If people behave inconsistently with their beliefs under _____ _____, they are unlikely to change their attitudes.

   forced compliance

7. According to _____ _____ theory, a goal will be valued all the higher, the harder it was to reach.

   cognitive dissonance

8. Attitudes toward a goal often become more positive after a person makes sacrifices to attain the goal. This is called _____ of effort.

   justification

9. An _____ is a stable set of mental views and assessments about some object, idea, or person.

   attitude

10. Attitudes are typically measured using a _____.

    questionnaire

11. An attitude is more likely to predict a behavior if the attitude is _____ and _____ pressures are minimal.

    strong, situational

12. Directly expressed attitudes are called _____ attitudes whereas those that are not recognized by a person are called _____ attitudes.

    explicit
    implicit

13. Two techniques that are used to explore implicit attitudes are _____ and the _____ _____ test.

    priming, implicit
    attitudes

SELF-CONCEPT AND SELF-DEFENSE

14. The tendency to overrate the self in terms of ability compared to others is called the _____-_____ effect.

    above-average

15. The tendency to attribute success to one's ability, and failure to the situation is called the _____- _____ bias.

    self-serving

16. When we show the self-serving bias for those close to us as well, we are demonstrating the _____ self.

    extended

17. One account of the self-serving bias is that it is a form of face-saving, or _____ _____.

    impression management

18. Goffman holds that much human behavior is "putting up a front," that is, behaving in accordance with the expectations for some role. This is called _____ _____.

    impression management

19. One strategy for impression management is _____- _____, in which, anticipating a poor performance, a person arranges an excuse in advance.

    self-handicapping

20. _____ is an unpleasant feeling that may be related to a loss of public or self-esteem.

    Embarrassment

21. Another interpretation of embarrassment is that it occurs when there is a _____ of a social interaction that no one knows how to repair.

    disruption

PERSON PERCEPTION

22. According to Asch, both form perception and person perception result from combinations of attributes into _____ wholes.

    organized

23. Asch's experiments on impressions of others showed that certain attributes had an organizing effect on the integration of other attributes. Such "organizing" attributes were called _____ _____.

    central
    traits

24. Because we gradually build up an impression of a person, using what we already know, there is special importance in _____ impressions.

first

25. Impressions of others can be seen as patterns, based on the relations among elements. One basis of this process is a set of organized expectations about the way in which different behaviors of people hang together, called a _____ or an _____ _____ of personality.

schema, implicit theory

26. Schemas are part of our _____ cognition, and provide us with _____ so that we can quickly form impressions of people.

social, shortcuts

27. Simplified schemas applied to whole groups are called _____.

stereotypes

28. People tend to see expected relations even if they do not exist. This is called _____ _____ It can lead to the maintenance of _____ stereotypes.

illusory correlation
inaccurate (derogatory)

29. As a result of _____-_____ favoritism, stereotypes of others are often derogatory.

in-group

30. The tendency to perceive groups other than one's own as more alike than members of one's own group is called the _____-_____ _____ _____.

out-group homogeneity effect

ATTRIBUTION

31. _____ is a process through which people infer the causes of other people's behavior.

attribution

32. Studies of attribution show that in judging others people tend to rely too much on internal causation, or _____ factors, as opposed to _____ factors, in explaining behavior. This is called the _____ _____ _____.

dispositional, situational
fundamental attribution error

33. People are more likely to attribute their own (as opposed to others') behavior to situational factors. This is called the _____-_____ _____.

actor-observer difference

34. A cognitive account of the actor-observer difference focuses on different _____ about the self and other; a perceptual account focuses on a different _____ toward the self and other.

information
perspective

CONFORMITY AND THE SOCIAL CONSTRUCTION OF REALITY

35. The way we try to interpet and understand social events, that is, _____ _____, is like the way we comprehend nonsocial events.

social cognition

36. In Asch's experiment on judging line length, participants become disturbed because the behavior of the confederates challenged their shared sense of _____ _____.

physical reality

37. When people have to make difficult judgments, they often seek the opinion of others, demonstrating the need for _____ _____.

social comparison

38. Messages that openly try to convince us of something, called _____ communications, are more effective if they come from a _____ and _____ source.

persuasive
credible, trustworthy

39. There may be two routes to persuasion. One, the _____ route, involves careful consideration of arguments. The other, the _____ route to persuasion, demands less attention and makes use of shortcuts, or _____.

central
peripheral
heuristics

40. Sometimes we pay attention to and agree with the opinions of others because we are _____ about our own opinion.Other times, we may agree with the majority because we want to avoid _____.

uncertain

embarrassment

41. A minority of as few as _____ can have a big effect on whether a person with a deviant view conforms to the majority.

one

42. People who emphasize the importance of power, dominance, and obedience have been described as having an _____ personality.

authoritarian

43. In Milgram's first experiment on obedience, approximately _____ percent of participants shocked the learner up to the maximum amount.

65 (50–75 percent would be acceptable)

44. Milgram's experiments suggest that it is not necessary to have an _____ personality to exhibit blind obedience.

authoritarian

45. An important factor that causes people to perform acts that they might otherwise consider abhorrent is the feeling that they are another person's _____.

agent

46. Blind obedience is more likely when _____ _____ between the "participant" and the "victim" is increased.

psychological distance

47. The obedient person who causes pain to another person may treat that person as an object. This is called _____.

dehumanization

48. The cognitive reorientation required in producing obedience is best accomplished by a _____ _____ in obedience requirements. This is called the _____ _____.

gradual increase
slippery slope

49. The Milgram studies emphasize that contrary to the _____ accounts of most people who try to predict the results of the study, the major determinant of the obedience results is _____.

dispositional
situational

SOCIAL IMPACT: THE CONVERGENCE OF SOCIAL FORCES

50. According to _____ _____ theory, social influences can be explained in terms of a combination of the effects of a variety of social forces.

social impact

51. In _____ _____, individuals working as a group on a common task, all doing the same thing, generate less effort than they would alone.

social loafing

52. Sometimes, people perform better when they are in a group than when alone. This is called _____ _____.

social facilitation

LEADERSHIP

53. Evidence suggests that part of leadership depends on dispositional characteristics, so that there is an effect for _____ _____ as well as situational factors.

great persons

54. Leadership is associated with dispositional characteristics, such as _____ and _____.

(2 of) dominance, intelligence, sociability (extra-version, "outgoingness")

55. Situational factors that encourage leadership include _____ and _____.

(2 of) clear-cut task, good interpersonal relations, possibility for expressing authority

GROUP DECISION MAKING

56. Group decisions are often more extreme than the decision that would be made individually by the members of the group. This is called _____ _____.

group polarization

57. Often, group decisions are not only more extreme but also _____. This is called the _____ shift.

riskier, risky

58. Threatened and cohesive groups may downplay dissent, and sometimes generate faulty decisions, by a process called _____.

groupthink

CROWD BEHAVIOR AND PANDEMONIUM

59. _____, a weakened sense of personal identity, disinhibits impulsive actions that are normally under restraint. It occurs more often in _____.

Deindividuation
crowds

60. The prisoner's dilemma presents an individual with a choice in a situation with mixed risks and benefits, described in a _____ _____.

payoff matrix

61. The prisoner's dilemma analysis is an attempt to explain the apparently _____ behavior of a crowd in terms of the _____ behavior of individuals.

irrational
rational

62. The prisoner's dilemma can be applied to problems of society, such as industrial pollution and other _____ dilemmas.

social

CULTURE AND SOCIAL INFLUENCE

63. In _____ cultures or ethnic groups, the emphasis is on interdependence, and there is a focus on the group.

collectivist

64. In _____ cultures or ethnic groups, the emphasis is on independence, and the self is seen as the central focus.

individualist

65. In general, it is the cultures of _____ or _____ that are most collective.

(2 of) Asia, Africa, Latin America

66. Whereas individuals in individualistic cultures seem to enhance their self-esteem, as shown in the
_____-_____ effect, this does not occur for individuals in collectivist cultures.   above-average

67. People from collectivist cultures are more likely to explain an individual's behavior with _____   situational
attributions than are people from individualist cultures.

68. People from individualist cultures tend to have (be members in) more _____-_____ but to   in-groups
be less committed to them than people in collectivist cultures.

69. Generally, collectivists seem to conform more than individualists to their _____-_____   in-groups
and are less influenced by _____-_____.   out-groups

Self-Test

1. The distinction between introspection (I) and self-perception
theory (SPT) as ways of coming to know the self is that
   a. I is inherently social and SPT is not.
   b. I involves direct examination of the mind whereas SPT
   involves inferring the mind from behavior.
   c. I assumes the mind and SPT holds that there is no mind.
   d. I assumes the self-concept is self-evident whereas SPT
   holds that only others can know us.
   e. a and c

2. According to cognitive dissonance theory, which of the
following would be the best way to cause people to change
attitudes?
   a. pay them a lot to make them believe they hold the new
   attitude
   b. force them to behave as if they support the new attitude
   for at least a few weeks
   c. tell them that they will be prejudiced if they continue
   with their current attitude
   d. show them that their current attitude is inconsistent with
   their actual behavior
   e. urge them to consult with an appropriate social
   comparison group

3. The accompanying graph illustrates the relation between

   a. attitudes and beliefs.
   b. cognitive dissonance and forced compliance.
   c. cognitive dissonance and cognitive consistency.
   d. social comparison and ambiguity.
   e. cognitive dissonance and beliefs.

4. After working as a volunteer for a political candidate for a
month, Jonathan finds that his support for the candidate has
increased even though he has never met her. This is an
instance of
   a. forced compliance.
   b. justification of effort.
   c. persuasive communications.
   d. a and b
   e. all of the above

5. Attitudes are
   a. usually measured by questionnaire.
   b. almost unrelated to behavior.
   c. an unstable set of mental views.
   d. usually almost identical to platitudes.
   e. a and b

6. An attitude is more likely to predict behavior if
   a. the attitude is strong.
   b. situational forces are not very strong.
   c. the attitude is implicit.
   d. a and b
   e. all of the above

7. Implicit attitudes are
   a. stronger than explicit attitudes.
   b. usually unconscious.
   c. the only type that show cognitive dissonance.
   d. a and c
   e. all of the above

8. A group of people report that they think the two sexes
(genders) are equally "good." In an implicit attitude (IAT)
test, they must categorize words as either good or bad, or
male or female. The male or female words are male or
female names. The people take longer to respond to the
female names when they are paired with the "good" key than
when paired with the "bad" key, and the opposite is true for
male names. These results suggest that
   a. most of these people have racial prejudices.
   b. most of these people do not have an implicit attitude to
   gender.
   c. implicit attitudes to gender conflict with explicit
   attitudes.
   d. cognitive dissonance is operating.
   e. the implicit attitude to gender is not strong.

9. The self-serving bias and above-average effect have in common
   a. reducing cognitive dissonance.
   b. self-enhancement.
   c. that both are forms of self-offense.
   d. that both depend on implicit attitudes.
   e. b and d

10. One can explain both self-serving bias and the above-average effect in terms of
    a. a general motive to enhance the self.
    b. interpretation of the meaning of abilities and characteristics in a way that is favorable to the self.
    c. a biased search of memory for examples on which to base a judgment.
    d. a and c
    e. all of the above

11. A senior lawyer tells a novice lawyer: "It is important to convey to your client on the first meeting that you are extremely experienced and well informed as to the law in the area of the client's problems." This advice illustrates
    a. implicit attitudes.
    b. embarrassment.
    c. impression management.
    d. the above-average effect.
    e. c and d

12. Having become bored with the guests at a dinner party, Kermit excuses himself by saying that he has to get up very early the next morning (which is not true) to take a trip out of town. According to Goffman's analysis, this performance can be explained as
    a. an example of Kermit's theatrical sense.
    b. an example of attitude formation.
    c. an attempt to leave without seeming rude and without insulting the guests.
    d. an attempt to alter the social perception of the audience by providing them with an ambiguous social stimulus.
    e. a stereotype.

13. In a high school classroom, a teacher selects a student at random and asks her a difficult question. She confidently gives the correct answer but feels embarrassed. This episode is *most* consistent with
    a. the loss of public esteem theory of embarrassment.
    b. the disrupted and irreparable social interaction view of embarrassment.
    c. the idea that embarrassment results when attention is called to the self.
    d. a and b
    e. b and c

14. The reason(s) that first impressions are particularly important is (are) that
    a. they may create "central traits" that influence later interpretations.
    b. subsequent information is interpreted in light of existing information.
    c. first impressions are less subject to impression management.
    d. a and b
    e. all of the above

15. Herman meets Sylvia and after a few minutes concludes that she is warm and selfish. He is troubled by his impression, and decides that perhaps Sylvia isn't really selfish, but rather very self-protective when it comes to certain issues that are important to her. Herman has
    a. invoked his implicit theory of personality.
    b. resolved cognitive dissonance.
    c. illustrated how we construct our concept of individual people.
    d. treated "warm" as a central trait.
    e. all of the above

16. Perception of objects and people have this in common:
    a. Both involve construction of an entity from individual features.
    b. Both are fixed in their nature by first impressions.
    c. Both rely almost exclusively on vision.
    d. Both involve resolution of cognitive dissonance.
    e. Both are subject to the above-average effect.

17. Stereotypes
    a. are always innaccurate.
    b. may be distorted because of illusory correlation.
    c. are always implicit.
    d. are a part of the normal construction of the person.
    e. b and d

18. Which of the following could explain the outgroup homogeneity effect?
    a. People have more information about their in-group.
    b. Out-groups actually are more homogeneous.
    c. People usually value consistency.
    d. a and c
    e. b and c

19. Jonathan, deep down, believes that unlike most people, most Germans have a great deal of respect for authority, although he claims that he doesn't think Germans are any different from anyone else in respect for authority. This illustrates what we might call
    a. an out-group homogeneity effect.
    b. an implicit stereotype.
    c. an effect of selective memory.
    d. another example of the above-average effect.
    e. all of the above

20. In-group favoritism could result from
    a. the outgroup homogeneity effect.
    b. selective memory for positive experiences with the ingroup.
    c. general self-enhancing tendencies.
    d. a and b
    e. b and c

21. The decision by a person that another person's behavior was internally caused (e.g., as a result of his or her aggressive nature) is an example of
    a. impression management.
    b. illusory correlation.
    c. stereotypes.
    d. attribution.
    e. situational factors.

22. People have a tendency to believe that actors in the theater are really like the roles that they play. This is an example of
    a. the resolution of cognitive dissonance.
    b. the dominance of dispositional over situational factors in attribution.
    c. the primacy effect in impressions.
    d. the distinction between the bodily self and the social self.
    e. the interaction of social and biological factors in the determination of behavior.

23. The actor-observer difference describes the fact that people are *less* likely to make _____ attributions about themselves than others.
    a. dispositional
    b. correct
    c. cognitively consistent
    d. situational
    e. c and d

24. In Asch's experiment on the effect of social pressure on judgments of noticeably different line lengths, he found that
    a. many participants yielded to social pressure, but their perception of line length did not necessarily change.
    b. the actual perceptions of line length were changed in the participant.
    c. the perceptions of line length were changed in the confederates.
    d. the shared sense of physical reality can affect perception.
    e. a and b

25. Indicate which of the following statements about social comparison is *false:*
    a. Social comparison is more likely to occur when someone is faced with a difficult decision.
    b. Social comparison is more likely to occur in a situation in which there is some ambiguity.
    c. Social comparison is more likely to occur when people feel they need more information.
    d. Social comparison is more likely to occur when the decision involves social issues.
    e. none of the above are false

26. Oddly, a major and respected religious figure comes out with a statement favoring Macintosh computers over PCs. One could categorize this as a case of a(n) _____ source.
    a. optimistic
    b. dissonant
    c. central
    d. trustworthy
    e. neither credible nor incredible source

27. Cynthia is making preparations for her marriage and a round the world honeymoon. Rose is trying to decide whether to get a Japanese- or American-made car. Both look at an article providing statistics and opinions about the relative quality of Japanese and American cars. The bottom line of this article is that American cars are now about as reliable as Japanese cars. In reading this article,
    a. Cynthia is more likely than Rose to be subject to the peripheral route of persuasion.
    b. Cynthia is more likely than Rose to be subject to the central route of persuasion.

c. Both are likely to be influenced primarily through the peripheral route.
    d. Both are likely to be influenced primarily through the central route.
    e. Neither is likely to be persuaded by the conclusion of the article.

28. Which of the following factors would increase the likelihood that someone would conform:
    a. a desire to avoid being embarrassed
    b. a feeling that others in the group are more expert than oneself
    c. all others in the group take the same position
    d. b and c
    e. all of the above

29. An explanation of blind obedience that emphasizes the authoritarian personality of the person in question relies on
    a. situational factors.
    b. dispositional factors.
    c. cognitive dissonance.
    d. cognitive consistency.
    e. attribution of emotional experience.

30. Both Milgram's obedience experiment and Asch's line judgment studies show the importance of _____ in determining behavior.
    a. attribution
    b. cognitive dissonance
    c. compliance
    d. dispositional factors
    e. none of the above

31. Which of the following would tend to *prevent* obedience in a situation of the type that Milgram studied?
    a. making a person feel like the agent of another
    b. dehumanizing the person being punished
    c. describing the experiment as a scientific enterprise
    d. decreasing the psychological distance between the participant and the person being punished
    e. none of the above

32. It is probably easier for a bombardier to drop bombs on an inhabited building than for the same person to kill someone standing in front of him. This presumed fact can be accounted for in terms of
    a. anonymity.
    b. psychological distance.
    c. dehumanization.
    d. all of the above
    e. none of the above

33. The fact that people underestimate the percentage of people who comply in the Milgram obedience study can be accounted for in terms of
    a. the fundamental attribution error.
    b. conformity.
    c. dehumanization.
    d. decreased psychological distance.
    e. b and c

34. Zimbardo's prison experiment
    a. proves that the Milgram study is correct.
    b. extends the range under which situational factors can cause cruelty.
    c. casts doubt on the situational interpretation of Milgram's studies.
    d. creates a situation in which college students behave in a cruel manner to other students.
    e. b and d

35. According to social impact theory, which of the following factors contribute to the total social influence in a situation?
    a. number of "influencers"
    b. number of people being influenced
    c. status of "influencers"
    d. a and c
    e. none of the above

36. Social loafing is somewhat contradictory to the principle of
    a. conformity.
    b. attribution.
    c. social impact.
    d. social facilitation.
    e. blind obedience.

37. The tendency to account for leadership almost entirely in terms of "great persons" can be explained by
    a. leadership theory.
    b. social impact theory.
    c. the fundamental attribution error.
    d. the above-average effect.
    e. statistics.

38. Which of the following makes it *less* likely that Cynthia will emerge as a leader?
    a. She is in a position of authority.
    b. The goal (situation) is ambiguous.
    c. She is sociable.
    d. She is dominant.
    e. There are good relationships among members of the group.

39. Groupthink differs from both group polarization and risky shift because only groupthink
    a. requires the presence of a leader.
    b. leads groups to more extreme decisions.
    c. is explained by social impact.
    d. usually leads to faulty decisions.
    e. leads to more conservative decisions.

40. Anonymity promotes
    a. social exchange.
    b. the fundamental attribution error.
    c. the actor-observer difference.
    d. social facilitation.
    e. deindividuation.

41. Brown suggests that panic is more likely in situations in which
    a. a serious danger is perceived.
    b. the escape routes appear to be inadequate.
    c. the people involved have well-defined roles.
    d. a and b
    e. all of the above

42. The prisoner's dilemma analysis explains
    a. the use of payoff matrices.
    b. how obedience is based on a past history of stern parental treatment.
    c. how maladaptive crowd behavior can result from rational behavior of individuals.
    d. the importance of roles in controlling the crowd panic reaction.
    e. b and c

43. From what we know about collectivist versus individualistic cultures, we might expect individuals from collectivist cultures to be lower in
    a. in-group aggression.
    b. out-group aggression.
    c. parenting.
    d. impression management.
    e. situational attributions.

44. Individualism is to collectivism as
    a. in-group is to out-group.
    b. society is to culture.
    c. independence is to interdependence.
    d. autonomy is to community.
    e. c and d

45. Americans, unlike Japanese, are reported to be more likely to enhance their self-picture. This tendency might be accounted for, at least in part, by
    a. the smaller number of in-groups among the Japanese.
    b. Japanese kinship patterns.
    c. a greater tendency to conform among the Japanese.
    d. a and c
    e. none of the above

46. Differences between individuals in individualist and collectivist cultures, in the area of social cognition, have been reported for all but which one of the following?
    a. the above-average effect
    b. primacy in impression formation
    c. the fundamental attribution error
    d. degree of conformity
    e. b and c

47. Suppose it was reported that 80 percent of Dutch people show the fundamental attribution error, and 55 percent of Hindu Indians do. This finding would
    a. be evidence that there is no cultural difference on this characteristic, since both groups score above 50 percent.
    b. suggest that increasing college education among Indians makes them more inclined to dispositional attributions.
    c. support the argument for cultural difference in an aspect of attributions.
    d. cast doubt about the existence of the fundamental attribution error.
    e. by itself, be no evidence for anything.

Answer Key for Self-Test

1.	b	25.	e
2.	d	26.	d
3.	b	27.	a
4.	b	28.	e
5.	a	29.	b
6.	d	30.	c
7.	b	31.	d
8.	c	32.	d
9.	b.	33.	a
10.	e	34.	e
11.	c	35.	d
12.	c	36.	d
13.	c	37.	c
14.	d	38.	b
15.	e	39.	d
16.	a	40.	e
17.	e	41.	d
18.	a	42.	c
19.	b	43.	a
20.	e	44.	c
21.	d	45.	c
22.	b	46.	b
23.	a	47.	c
24.	a		

Investigating Psychological Phenomena

PERSON PERCEPTION: THE EFFECT OF CONTEXT OR SET ON FIRST IMPRESSIONS

Equipment: Paper and pencil, a stopwatch or a watch that indicates seconds
Number of participants: At least eight
Time per participant: Five minutes
Time for experimenter: Forty minutes

Social perception bears many analogies to more traditional areas of perception. In both cases, information is taken in selectively and put together into some organized percept. This aspect of person perception was illustrated in the text with special reference to the classic studies of Solomon Asch. Asch's work argued for an organizational basis for impression formation. This approach is in keeping with the position of Gestalt psychology. In Asch's view, impressions were not formed by "summing" different items of information about a particular person. One particular aspect of the active process of impression formation is the effect of set. One is constantly forming impressions of people. New information on any person is integrated with an already existing impression: the new information will be interpreted to be as consistent as possible with the existing impression. Under the circumstances, one would expect that the first information one gets about a person would be especially important, since it might color what comes in later. Therefore, an organizational view

would predict that the *order* of items of information about a person would affect the resulting impression, whereas a simple *summation* hypothesis would not matter.

Asch tested his hypothesis in a very simple manner: he gave college students a list of six adjectives that ostensibly described someone and recorded the impressions that they subsequently formed of this imaginary person. By manipulating the types of adjectives used and the order of their presentation, Asch attempted to produce systematic changes in the elicited impression formations. We will repeat his experiment on word order in precisely the same way that it was performed by Asch.

Try to get at least eight (student) participants. It might be useful for you to team up with a few friends from the course and run up to twenty participants so that your results might be more meaningful. Participants must be divided into two groups. You can run as many participants as you want at the same time, so long as they are all from the same group. Since this experiment will compare the results of participants from one group with the results from another group, it is important that the two groups be similar in general characteristics. For example, keep the percentage of females the same in both groups, and try not to run a group of friends together, since they may share many similar characteristics. If you run one participant at a time, simply assign the first participant to Group A, the second to Group B, and so on. This should give you a random and "unbiased" sample.

The list for Group A	The list for Group B
intelligent	envious
industrious	stubborn
impulsive	critical
critical	impulsive
stubborn	industrious
envious	intelligent

Note that the adjectives in Group B are in the reverse order of Group A. This arrangement is designed to enhance any effect of order, by putting adjectives that would lead to quite different impressions on opposite ends of the adjective list.

Participants should be seated comfortably and should have in front of them a blank piece of paper and a pencil. Make sure to put the group letter (A or B) on the paper and on the checklist. The experimenter reads the following instructions:

I shall read you a number of characteristics that belong to a particular person. Please listen to them carefully and try to form an impression of the kind of person described. You will later be asked to give a brief characterization of the person in just a few sentences. I will read the list slowly and will repeat it once.

Read the list of six adjectives out loud in a steady voice, with an interval of five seconds between terms. Then say:

I will now read the list again.

(Repeat the reading of the list)

Now please write a brief characterization of this person.

(Participant writes)

Finally, tell the participants while handing them the checklist (see pages 121 and 123);

Here is a list of pairs of adjectives. For each pair, please circle the adjectives that better characterize the person we have been describing.

After the participant has completed this task, he or she is finished.

NOTES ON PROCEDURE

In setting up any experiment, many decisions must be made. Here, these include selecting the adjectives for the list, and for the checklist, deciding on the number of adjectives in the list, and so on. In most cases there are specific reasons for making these decisions. In this experiment, for example, ask yourself:

1. Why does the experimenter read the list instead of allowing the participant to read the list?
2. Why is the participant asked to write an impression before seeing the checklist rather than after filling out the checklist?

RESULTS

You should end up with eight or more written sketches and eight or more marked checklists. About half should be in each group. There is no simple way to score the written impressions. Read them over and try to summarize the impressions written by the two groups (the procedure used by Asch). You could also give the written impressions to another person and ask that person to sort them into piles, about equal in size. One pile would be for the more desirable impressions (persons) and the other for the less desirable ones. See if the impressions based on the adjective list with more desirable traits first are usually classified as more desirable. (It would be a good idea to fold back the part of the impressions paper with the group letter on it before reading and analyzing the character summaries.)

It is easier to analyze the data from the checklists. Simply record the percentage of participants who selected the more favorable adjective of each pair for each group. This is the procedure used by Asch. His results, based on twenty-four student participants in Group A and thirty-four in Group B, are presented in the accompanying table. Record your data in the columns next to his data. Compare your results with his. If we take a difference of 20 percentage points as worthy of note, he reported big differences, in favor of Group A, on happy, humorous, sociable, popular, good-looking, and restrained.

(You can increase the significance of your data by combining it with data from a few friends in the class, so that you would have 20 or more participants in each group.)

Based on your results, what is the conclusion about the validity of the organization (set, Gestalt) versus simple summation explanations of impression formation?

Try to explain why some particular adjectives show clear effects and others do not. Obviously, in real life people form impressions from interactions with other people or by hearing about them from other people. To what extent do you think that Asch's procedure gives an indication of how people actually form impressions? The hallmark of a good experiment is that it simplifies a situation but still preserves its essential features. Is that true of this experiment?

FURTHER STUDY

You can use Asch's technique to address other questions. You can change specific adjectives on the list. You can use brief statements about a person's *behavior* (e.g., John consistently drives over the speed limit; John is always on time) rather than general characteristics. You can see which types of adjectives cause a participant to guess that a person is male or female. There are many possibilities, should this problem interest you. Some of the possibilities that you will come up with may never have been investigated.

Reference

Asch, S. E. (1946). Forming impressions of personality. *Journal of Abnormal and Social Psychology, 41,* 258–290.

Percentage of participants checking favorable adjective at left

| | Asch's data | | Your data | |
| | Group A (24 students) | Group B (34 students) | Group A (__ students) | Group B (__ students) |
Adjective pair				
generous	24	10		
wise	18	17		
happy	32	5		
good-natured	18	0		
humorous	52	21		
sociable	56	27		
popular	35	14		
reliable	84	91		
good-looking	74	35		
serious	97	100		
restrained	64	9		
honest	80	79		

Circle the most relevant adjective:

generous–ungenerous

shrewd–wise

unhappy–happy

irritable–good-natured

humorous–humorless

sociable–unsociable

popular–unpopular

unreliable–reliable

good-looking–unattractive

frivolous–serious

restrained–talkative

dishonest–honest

Group _____

Circle the most relevant adjective:

generous–ungenerous

shrewd–wise

unhappy–happy

irritable–good-natured

humorous–humorless

sociable–unsociable

popular–unpopular

unreliable–reliable

good-looking–unattractive

frivolous–serious

restrained–talkative

dishonest–honest

Group _____

-- *Cut here* --

Circle the most relevant adjective:

generous–ungenerous

shrewd–wise

unhappy–happy

irritable–good-natured

humorous–humorless

sociable–unsociable

popular–unpopular

unreliable–reliable

good-looking–unattractive

frivolous–serious

restrained–talkative

dishonest–honest

Group _____

Circle the most relevant adjective:

generous–ungenerous

shrewd–wise

unhappy–happy

irritable–good-natured

humorous–humorless

sociable–unsociable

popular–unpopular

unreliable–reliable

good-looking–unattractive

frivolous–serious

restrained–talkative

dishonest–honest

Group _____

Circle the most relevant adjective:

generous–ungenerous

shrewd–wise

unhappy–happy

irritable–good-natured

humorous–humorless

sociable–unsociable

popular–unpopular

unreliable–reliable

good-looking–unattractive

frivolous–serious

restrained–talkative

dishonest–honest

Group _____

Circle the most relevant adjective:

generous–ungenerous

shrewd–wise

unhappy–happy

irritable–good-natured

humorous–humorless

sociable–unsociable

popular–unpopular

unreliable–reliable

good-looking–unattractive

frivolous–serious

restrained–talkative

dishonest–honest

Group _____

-- *Cut here* --

Circle the most relevant adjective:

generous–ungenerous

shrewd–wise

unhappy–happy

irritable–good-natured

humorous–humorless

sociable–unsociable

popular–unpopular

unreliable–reliable

good-looking–unattractive

frivolous–serious

restrained–talkative

dishonest–honest

Group _____

Circle the most relevant adjective:

generous–ungenerous

shrewd–wise

unhappy–happy

irritable–good-natured

humorous–humorless

sociable–unsociable

popular–unpopular

unreliable–reliable

good-looking–unattractive

frivolous–serious

restrained–talkative

dishonest–honest

Group _____

CHAPTER 11

Biology, Emotion, and Social Behavior

Learning Objectives

THE BIOLOGICAL ROOTS OF SOCIAL BEHAVIOR

1. Explain the Darwinian principle of natural selection, and indicate how it presumes there is variation.

Personal and genetic survival
2. Distinguish personal from genetic survival. Give examples in which they seem to be opposed to one another.

SOCIAL BEHAVIOR AND REPRODUCTION

Advertising for a mate
3. Indicate the essential importance of advertising for a mate in genetic survival.
4. Illustrate both physical and behavioral means of advertising, including courtship rituals.

Attraction
5. Review arguments for physical attractiveness as determined by our primate heritage or by culture.
6. Describe the dating-dance study that shows the importance of physical attractiveness in mate choice.
7. Discuss the effects of physical attractiveness on the perception of other traits (the halo effect).
8. Explain the matching hypothesis.

What is physically attractive?
9. Mention some physical features that seem to universally contribute to physical attractiveness in humans.
10. Discuss the possible adaptive value of some of these features, such as symmetry, and certain waist-hip ratios in women.

Proximity
11. Why is proximity a major determinant of attraction?

Similarity
12. Review the evidence for the importance of similarity (homogamy) in mate attraction? Why is the similar more attractive?

Who chooses whom?
13. Explain why the female is generally more selective in mate selection than the male.

Mating systems
14. Define polygamy, polygyny, polyandry, and monogamy. Explain why most bird species are monogamous while most mammals are polygynous.
15. What is the relation between polygyny and sexual dimorphism?
16. What is the evolutionary explanation of the predominance of polygyny in human cultures, and the widespread tendency of men to be more interested in multiple sexual partners than women? What is the culturally oriented rejoinder to the evolutionary explanation?

LOVE

Romantic love
17. Describe the phenomenon of romantic love.
18. Indicate how cognitive arousal theory explains romantic love.
19. What factors affect the intensity of romantic love? Include a discussion of the Romeo-and-Juliet effect.

Companionate love
20. Distinguish romantic from companionate love.

PARENTING

The infant's attachment to the mother
21. Discuss the function of the infant's attachment to the mother, how it is manifested, and the extent to which the attachment depends on the mother's fulfillment of the child's basic biological needs.

The mother's attachment to the infant
22. What is the function of maternal attachment?
23. What characteristics of the infant are important in establishing maternal attachment?

AGGRESSION

Aggression and predation
24. Is aggression related to predatory attack? Explain

Male aggression and hormones
25. Discuss the relation between testosterone and aggression, in animals and humans.

26. Describe the complex relation between serotonin and both aggression and position in a dominance hierarchy.

Territoriality

27. What is a territory and how does it function to control aggression?
28. What is the evidence for territory or personal space in humans? Discuss the contributions of our genes, and individual and cultural experience to the manifestations of territory.

Constraints on aggression

29. Explain mechanisms for limiting aggression, including sizing up the strength of the "enemy" and dominance hierarchies.

Patterns of human aggression

30. Illustrate the way humans express aggression, both physically and symbolically.
31. Describe how culture influences the expression of aggression, using the culture of honor in the southern United States as an example.

Aggression and the media

32. Discuss the evidence supporting and arguing against an effect of violence in the media on actual levels of violence.

ALTRUISM AND SELF-SACRIFICE

33. Why is altruism a problem for evolutionary theory?

Altruism in animals

34. Explain how altruism or self-sacrifice is consistent with evolutionary theory. Distinguish in this discussion between personal and genetic survival.
35. Distinguish between kin selection and reciprocal altruism as accounts for altruistic behavior.
36. What is the relation of mutual grooming to reciprocal altruism and social bonding?

Reciprocity and human altruism

37. What is social exchange?
38. Explain the reciprocity principle.
39. How is the reciprocity principle used in bargaining and persuasion? What are reciprocal concessions?
40. Discuss self-disclosure in the context of reciprocity, and possible gender differences in the United States in self-disclosure.

Fairness

41. Describe how reciprocity can be seen as a basis for fairness.
42. Explain the ultimatum game, the basic results of the game, and the relation of this to fairness.
43. Indicate how reciprocity and fairness change in communal relationships.

Helping

44. Compare communal and exchange relationships, and indicate how helping might be expected to occur in both.
45. What is the bystander effect?
46. Under what circumstances do people fail to help others in distress? Consider the role of ambiguity, pluralistic ignorance, and diffusion of responsibility.
47. Indicate the possible costs that someone who offers aid might incur.

EMOTION

Emotional experience: interpretations of internal states

48. Describe the James-Lange theory of emotion and the major objections to it.
49. Describe the attribution-of-arousal theory of emotion. Contrast this theory with the James-Lange theory. What is the role of physiological state in each theory?
50. Discuss the misattribution of arousal in light of the attribution-of-arousal theory. How do results from excitation transfer effects support this theory?
51. Describe the evidence, from both animals and humans, indicating a special role for the amygdala in the integration of appraisal and arousal, particularly with respect to fear.

Emotional expressions

52. What is Darwin's universality thesis? What is the cross-cultural evidence for it, and what are some problems with the evidence?
53. Describe cultural display rules, and indicate how they relate to the universality thesis.
54. Describe the view that facial expressions are communicative displays, in addition to or instead of expressions of an inner state. What is the evidence for this position, including audience effects, and what are some problems with this view?

Are there basic emotions?

55. Explain the idea of basic emotions, and the criteria that have been suggested for distinguishing them. Indicate the problems with the idea of basic emotions.

Complex emotions

56. Indicate the role of attributions of controllability and moral issues in the experience of anger, guilt, and pity.
57. What is regret, and how does the ease of reconstructing a scenario that would have avoided a negative event help to explain the circumstances that elicit regret?

Culture and emotion

58. Discuss cultural differences in emotion vocabulary, and the problem of determining whether people in different cultures experience different emotions.

Programmed Exercises

THE BIOLOGICAL ROOTS OF SOCIAL BEHAVIOR

1. According to Darwin, evolution proceeds because _____ of a species with superior characteristics are more likely to survive. This process is called _____ _____.

variants
natural selection

2. Essentially, natural selection is not about literal survival, or _____ survival, but about reproductive success, which amounts to _____ survival. The latter leads to selection of traits that produce an advantage in _____ competition.

personal
genetic
sexual

SOCIAL BEHAVIOR AND REPRODUCTION

3. In order to survive genetically, a sexually reproducing adult must _____ both its _____ and its _____.

    advertise
    availability, sex

4. A prominent form of behavioral advertisement indicating readiness to mate are _____ _____.

    courtship rituals

5. Perhaps the most important initial feature that attracts one potential human mate to another is _____ _____.

    physical attractiveness

6. People tend to believe that good traits go together, so that physically attractive people are thought to be, for example, more intelligent. This is called the _____ _____.

    halo effect

7. People tend to link up with and mate with others who are at about the same level of physical attractiveness. This is called the _____ _____.

    matching hypothesis

8. Some universal features contributing to physical attractiveness are _____ and _____.

    (2 of) symmetry, shiny hair, certain waist-hip ratios in females, clear skin

9. Some of the universal features may be adaptive because they are predictive of _____ or _____.

    health fertility

10. Two people who have spent a fair amount of time in physical _____ to one another are more likely as a result to be friends or mates.

    proximity

11. People also tend to prefer as mates others who are _____ to them.

    similar

12. The strong tendency for people to marry other people very similar to themselves is called _____.

    homogamy

13. In most species, the _____ (male or female) has the major role in deciding whether or not to mate.

    female

14. In mammals, birds and some other groups, the female is more selective in mating because she has a greater _____ in the offspring.

    investment

15. In general, in terms of mating systems, bird species are _____, whereas mammal species are _____.

    monogamous polygamous

16. There is usually more structural difference between the sexes, that is _____ _____, in species that are _____.

    sexual dimorphism polygynous

17. The evolutionary view predicts that because of the lower investment that male mammals have in any reproductive act, the mating system of _____ will be more common than its opposite, _____, and that males will seek more _____ in sexual partners than will females.

    poloygyny polyandry, variety

LOVE

18. According to a cognitive arousal theory, romantic love involves a state of physiological and/or sexual _____, and a set of culturally instilled beliefs and attitudes that causes a person to interpret this arousal as _____.

    arousal passion

19. Parental opposition tends to intensify romantic love. This is called the _____-_____-_____ effect.

    Romeo-and-Juliet

20. Two contrasting types of love are a passionate type, or _____ love, and another type that emphasizes mutual trust, care, and sharing, called _____ love.

    romantic companionate

PARENTING

21. The human infant's _____ or the chirp of a newly hatched bird are examples of distress calls.

    cry

22. Human parents have a special sing-song mode of speaking to their infants, called _____.

    motherese

23. The _____ is the human infant's built-in means of communicating with adults and maintaining their attention while indicating a generally positive state.

    smile

AGGRESSION

24. An attack by a lion on a zebra seems qualitatively different from a fight or threat sequence between two members of the same species. We call the fomer _____ and the latter _____.   predation, aggression

25. The generally higher level of aggression seen in males of most species has been attributed to higher levels of the male hormone _____.   testosterone

26. In some species, greater aggression is associated with low levels of the neurotransmitter _____, although high levels of this same neurotransmitter may be associated with higher positions in the _____ hierarchy.   serotonin   dominance

27. Animals often defend a particular area against other members of their species. This area probably serves to guarantee them essential _____ and is called a _____.   resources, territory

28. A person walks up to a stranger, approaching her until their bodies are just inches apart. This can be considered a violation of _____ _____.   personal space

29. In a _____ _____ a group of animals of the same species develops a stable social order based on the establishment of rank as a result of mutual aggressive encounters.   dominance hierarchy

30. In humans, aggression is not only physical, but also _____.   symbolic

31. Aggression seems to be more likely in persons with high _____-_____.   self-esteem

32. In the American South, aggression is sometimes prescribed by particular situations, as when someone is insulted, a violation of his or her _____ _____ _____.   culture of honor

33. Many, but not all investigators, believe that violence portrayed in the _____ encourages actual violence in individuals.   media

34. The problem is partly that a correlation between the two can result from violence on TV causing violence, or people who are already more _____ preferring to watch violent TV.   violent

ALTRUISM AND SELF-SACRIFICE

35. Self-sacrifice by a parent animal can be understood within an evolutionary framework, since it may ultimately serve to increase the number of the parent's _____ that are passed on.   genes

36. One form of altruistic behavior in animals involves _____ calls, which warn other members of the species of the presence of the predator, at some risk to the caller.   alarm

37. When an altruistic behavior can be shown to spare the lives of relatives, it may considered an example of _____ selection.   kin

38. "Unselfish" acts may also be adaptive because the recipients of these acts may later return the favor. This is called _____ _____.   reciprocal altruism

39. Mutual _____ behavior in animals can be interpreted as reciprocal altruism, and promotes social _____.   grooming   bonding

40. According to the principle of _____ _____, each partner in a relationship gives something to the other, and expects to receive something in return.   social exchange

41. The notion that favors and gifts must be repaid is embodied in the _____ principle.   reciprocity

42. After a person refuses a large request, he or she is more likely to assent to a smaller request from the same person. This is explained by _____ _____.   reciprocal concession

43. In the non-material domain, _____-_____ is an example of reciprocity. At least in the United States, it is more common in _____.   self-disclosure   females (women)

44. Reciprocity can become the basis for _____.   fairness

45. The importance of fairness is illustrated in the results of the _____ game.   ultimatum

46. Keeping track of reciprocal exchanges is less common in _____ _____, in which the parties involved are part of an extended _____.

communal relationships
self

47. Three factors that account for people's failure to help people in distress are _____ _____ _____, and _____ _____ _____.

ambiguity
pluralistic ignorance
diffusion of responsibility

48. The larger the size of a group a person is in, the less likely he or she is to come to a victim's assistance. This is called the _____ _____.

bystander effect

49. The costs of helping include loss of _____ and _____ _____.

time, physical danger

EMOTION

50. According to the _____-_____ theory, the subjective experience of emotion results from our awareness of bodily changes in the presence of certain stimuli.

James-Lange

51. According to Schachter and Singer's _____-_____-_____ theory of emotion, emotion depends on the interpretation of autonomic _____ by an individual, in light of the total situation.

attribution-of-arousal
arousal

52. According to attribution-of-arousal theory, when a person believes that arousal actually caused by one factor (e.g., exercise, an arousing drug) is caused by another (e.g., sexual excitation), this is an example of _____ _____.

excitation transfer

53. A part of the brain that is involved in important ways with the integration of appraisal and arousal is the_____. It seems to play a particularly important role in the emotion of _____.

amygdala, fear

54. According to Darwin's _____ _____, at least some aspects of emotional facial expressions are present in all humans.

universality thesis

55. Learned and deeply ingrained conventions that govern what facial expressions should be displayed or suppressed in different situations are called _____ _____ _____.

cultural display rules

56. According to the _____ _____ view of facial expressions, they are primarily social signals indicating actions that the displayer is about to take, or actions that the displayer is calling for in others.

communicative display

57. Evidence for the communicative display view comes from the fact that facial expressions are more common in social situations, called the _____ _____.

audience effect

58. According to some investigators, such as Ekman, there are certain fundamental emotions, called _____ _____. These can be identified because of universal _____ expressions, specific_____ circuitry devoted to them, or the fact that they cannot be decomposed into other _____.

basic emotions, facial
neural
emotions

59. Whether one experiences pity, guilt, or anger depends in part on whether one thinks the behavior in question was _____.

controllable

60. The experience of anger and guilt may be related to _____ factors.

moral

61. _____ is the emotion of the might-have-been.

Regret

62. The tendency to feel regret is _____ in near-miss situations, as a result of a tendency to replay such situations.

greater

63. Cultures differ in the _____ they use to describe emotions.

words (vocabulary)

64. The Japanese emotion of _____ represents a desire to be dependent and cared for.

amae

65. We cannot be certain whether differences in the words used to describe emotions mean that different emotions are _____.

experienced

Self-Test

1. In order for Darwinian evolution to occur, it is necessary to have
   a. variation on some relevant characteristic.
   b. a difference in survival value among the variants.
   c. a wide selection of natural products.
   d. a and b
   e. all of the above

2. Animal A lives 10 years and has 6 offspring. Animal B lives 8 years and has 10 offspring.
   a. A has greater personal survival.
   b. B has greater personal survival.
   c. B has greater genetic survival.
   d. a and c
   e. b and c

3. Courtship rituals are an example of
   a. an action to increase personal survival.
   b. an action to increase genetic survival.
   c. a form of sexual advertisement.
   d. b and c
   e. a and c

4. In a first impressions study, four groups of participants each hear a different list of adjectives describing a person. The lists are as follows:
   Group 1: trustworthy, sensitive, subtle, detached, stingy, envious
   Group 2: same as group 1, but in the opposite order
   Group 3: same as group 1, but with physically attractive added as the first adjective (making this a seven-adjective list)
   Group 4: same as group 2, but with physically attractive added at the end of the list
   Participants are then asked to rate how charming the person is. We would expect the participants in which group to give the highest charm rating?
   a. 1
   b. 2
   c. 3
   d. 4
   e. 3 and 4 equally

5. The prediction in Question 9 is based on
   a. similarity.
   b. the importance of firstr impressions.
   c. the importance of physical attractiveness.
   d. the matching hypothesis.
   e. b and c

6. In a particular culture, relatively thin males tend to marry relatively plump females. According to the matching hypothesis, this implies that
   a. relative thinness in males is as desired (attractive) as is relative plumpness in females.
   b. physical attractiveness is not important in this culture.
   c. body shape is not important in this culture.
   d. the plumpness and thinness of relatives is important in this culture.
   e. c and d

7. Features that contribute to physical attractiveness more or less universally in humans include
   a. clear skin.
   b. symmetrical face.
   c. small nose.
   d. long hair.
   e. a and b

8. Arguments for biological determinants in some features of physical attractiveness in humans is
   a. the matching hypothesis.
   b. the existence of variation in most features.
   c. the universality of attractiveness of some features.
   d. the fact that hair length attractiveness may vary with gender.
   e. a and b

9. Proximity is an important factor in attraction. There is evidence that this relation results from the fact that
   a. one must ordinarily meet someone in order to be attracted to him or her.
   b. familiarity promotes attraction, and familiarity is increased by proximity.
   c. proximity explains the matching hypothesis.
   d. a and b
   e. all of the above

10. Mildred and Herb have been dating for years. Both are physically unattractive, and one acquaintance wonders what they see in each other. Which of the following factors could contribute to their mutual attractiveness?
    a. proximity
    b. similarity
    c. matching
    d. a and c
    e. all of the above

11. Predictions about male-female differences in mammalian mating systems and variety seeking in sexual partners are based on the fact that female mammals have a greater investment in reproduction because they
    a. carry the offspring during pregnancy.
    b. take the greater responsibility for the early care of infants.
    c. account for a greater part of the genetic material of their offspring.
    d. all of the above
    e. a and b

12. There is a tendency for human males to seek more variety in mates ("male promiscuity") than females. Which of the following is *not* evidence that this difference has a biological basis?
    a. Males have higher economic and social status in almost all cultures.
    b. Male promiscuity appears cross-culturally.
    c. Male promiscuity occurs in most mammalian species.
    d. Male mammals have a lower investment than females in any particular offspring.
    e. Female mammals carry and nurse their young.

13. If you knew that in a particular species the males sought more variety in sexual partners than did the females, you would guess that this species had a _____ mating system.
    a. monogamous
    b. polyandrous
    c. polygynous
    d. dimorphic
    e. b or c

14. According to the evolutionary account, a human female is inclined to emphasize financial/social security in selecting a mate because
    a. this improves the prospects for a successful upbringing of her children.
    b. males with higher status are more likely to be fertile.
    c. she is likely to give birth to more children.
    d. males with higher status are less likely to prefer polygyny.
    e. b and c

15. Romantic love
    a. occurs only in certain cultures and at certain periods in history.
    b. is intensified by parental approval.
    c. can be completely explained in terms of sexual arousal.
    d. differs from companionate love in that romantic love depends heavily on similarity.
    e. c and d

16. Romantic love has been described as having three components: intimacy, passion, and commitment. In comparison, companionate love would differ most from romantic love in that it would have less of
    a. intimacy.
    b. passion.
    c. commitment.
    d. b and c
    e. a and c

17. Features of the human infant, such as the smile, cries, upturned nose, and chubby cheeks, are
    a. the stimuli through which we learn to recognize specific children.
    b. the vehicles for the establishment of basic trust.
    c. releasers of parental behavior.
    d. instances of distress displays.
    e. more common in monogamous cultures.

18. Aggression is increased in most mammals by
    a. higher levels of testosterone.
    b. higher levels of all sex hormones.
    c. lower levels of serotonin.
    d. a and b
    e. a and c

19. High levels of serotonin seem to be associated with a higher position of an animal in a dominance hierarchy. This is puzzling because
    a. this is supposed to be the effect of testosterone.
    b. the comparative method says this should not be true.
    c. high levels of serotonin are associated with less aggression.

    d. a and c
    e. a and b

20. Aggressive encounters between members of the same species are often concerned with the establishment of
    a. distributed testosterone levels.
    b. territories.
    c. predation.
    d. appropriate defense mechanisms.
    e. a and c

21. The adaptive value of territories is that they
    a. increase the aggressiveness of the territory holder.
    b. provide resources for the territory holder.
    c. prevent threat displays.
    d. decrease personal space and allow for greater reproduction.
    e. c and d

22. Human territories
    a. have a biological basis.
    b. are transformed and elaborated by cultures.
    c. must be distinguished from personal space.
    d. a and b
    e. b and c

23. Dominance hierarchies
    a. exist only in males.
    b. are the basis of personal space.
    c. confer reproductive advantages on those at the top.
    d. guarantee equal distribution of resources.
    e. increase aggressive encounters.

24. Human aggression
    a. is often verbal.
    b. is often symbolic.
    c. is culturally channeled, as in the culture of honor.
    d. may be physical.
    e. all of the above

25. Most studies on TV violence and actual violence report that they are positively correlated. From this we can conclude that
    a. TV violence causes actual violence.
    b. People who are actually violent prefer to watch violence on TV.
    c. Human aggression is almost entirely generated by culture.
    d. b and c
    e. none of the above

26. Consider a case in which an animal risks death from a predator by distracting it from the children of the animal's sister. Which of the possibilities listed below is the most likely account of this "altruistic" behavior?
    a. kin selection
    b. reciprocal altruism
    c. emancipation from hormonal control
    d. all of the above
    e. none of the above

27. Consider a different case, one in which an animal A risks death from a predator by distracting the predator from another adult, B, of its species. And suppose that B is not related to A, and furthermore, that B is not a member of A's group, and is only transiently in A's presence. This apparently altruistic act would be easily accounted for as
    a. kin selection.
    b. reciprocal altruism.
    c. emancipation from hormonal control.
    d. a and b
    e. none of the above

28. The idea of social exchange is
    a. tit-for-tat (exchange of favors).
    b. the money economy.
    c. the slavery system.
    d. forced compliance.
    e. altruism.

29. Both gift-giving and self-disclosure
    a. are altruistic.
    b. encourage reciprocity.
    c. encourage ambiguity.
    d. b and c
    e. a and c

30. Reciprocal exchange can become the basis of
    a. fairness.
    b. communal relationships.
    c. ultimatums.
    d. ambiguity.
    e. b and c

31. In communal relationships
    a. the ultimatum game operates efficiently.
    b. principles of reciprocal exchange may be suspended.
    c. altruism does not occur.
    d. the self is extended beyond an individual.
    e. b and d

32. The bystander effect is accounted for by
    a. reciprocity.
    b. diffusion of responsibility.
    c. altruistic tendencies.
    d. a and c
    e. all of the above

33. Diffusion of responsibility is
    a. an example of social exchange.
    b. an example of cost of intervention.
    c. less if there are fewer observers.
    d. b and c
    e. a and c

34. After running for a quarter mile, a person shows increased heart rate and various other signs of arousal but may not feel any strong emotion. This fact is particularly damaging to which of the following theories?
    a. the attribution-of-arousal theory
    b. the James-Lange theory

    c. Cannon's idea that subjective emotion leads to physiological responses
    d. a and b
    e. all of the above

35. An experiment has shown that participants alter their ratings of the attractiveness of nude photos in response to feedback about the increase or decrease of their heart rate. This result can be taken to support
    a. the attribution-of-arousal theory of emotion.
    b. the James-Lange theory.
    c. Cannon's theory (subjective emotion leads to the physiological responses, but the latter do not cause the former).
    d. a and b
    e. all of the above

36. The idea that there is a set of universal facial expressions
    a. was proposed by Darwin.
    b. is supported by some cross-cultural data.
    c. is supported by the existence of cultural display rules.
    d. a and b
    e. all of the above

37. The existence of cultural display rules presents serious problems for
    a. the idea of basic emotions.
    b. the communicative display view.
    c. the attribution-of-arousal theory.
    d. the idea of impression management.
    e. none of the above

38. Facial expressions can be considered as primarily communicative displays. Audience effects are used as evidence for this position. Consider the following statements, and then indicate which of the combination of alternatives represents both a criticism of the audience effect evidence, and a counter to that criticism.
    i. Facial expressions are made when people are unobserved.
    ii. An audience of only one observer is sufficient to induce more facial expressions.
    iii. Facial expressions increase when a person is alone but imagines the presence of another.
    iv. Facial expressions are distinctive only for basic emotions.

    a. ii, iv
    b. i, iii
    c. i, ii
    d. iii, ii
    e. none of the above

39. People in social and obviously emotional situations are often not expressive. This observation causes problems for the _____ view of emotions, but can be accounted for in terms of _____.
    a. communicative display, cultural display rules
    b. communicative display, basic emotions
    c. basic emotions, cultural display rules
    d. James-Lange theory, facial feedback
    e. basic emotions, communicative displays

40. Suppose an investigator claims that disgust is a "basic emotion." Which of the following would be evidence for this claim?
    a. Disgust has a characteristic, universal facial expression.
    b. Disgust is specifically interfered with by certain types of brain lesions.
    c. Disgust cannot be decomposed into a combination of other emotions.
    d. a and c
    e. all of the above

41. Anger and guilt share
    a. the same facial expression.
    b. a basis in transgression.
    c. consideration of controllability.
    d. a sense of near-miss.
    e. the fact that both evoke pity.

42. Regret is enhanced by
    a. near-miss situations.
    b. a tendency to replay experiences.
    c. feelings of pity.
    d. its own unique facial expression.
    e. a and b

43. Regret and guilt differ from anger and disgust in that regret and guilt
    a. are uniquely human.
    b. are always complex emotions.
    c. do not have a unique facial expression.
    d. a and b
    e. all of the above

44. Complex emotions
    a. have their own distinct facial expressions.
    b. involve appraisals and attributions.
    c. may be combinations of basic emotions.
    d. b and c
    e. a and b

45. Rather unique emotion words, such as *amae* in Japanese or *Schadenfreude* in German, show that
    a. there are actually different emotions in different cultures.
    b. cultures have different emotion vocabularies.
    c. only basic emotions are constant across cultures.
    d. there cannot be basic emotions.
    e. b and d

46. Understanding of human social life involves evaluating the oppositions between
    a. biology and culture.
    b. reasons and passion.
    c. self and other.
    d. a and c
    e. all of the above

Answer Key for Self-Test

1. d		24. e
2. a		25. e
3. d		26. a
4. c		27. e
5. e		28. a
6. a		29. b
7. e		30. a
8. c		31. e
9. d		32. b
10. e		33. c
11. e		34. b
12. a		35. d
13. c		36. d
14. a		37. e
15. a		38. b
16. b		39. a
17. c		40. e
18. e		41. c
19. c		42. e
20. b		43. e
21. b		44. d
22. d		45. b
23. c		46. e

Investigating Psychological Phenomena

PERSONAL SPACE: BEHAVIOR IN ELEVATORS

Equipment: A bank of at least two public elevators
Number of participants: None
Time per participant: None
Time for experimenter: Thirty minutes to one hour

Whatever one's view of the precise way in which the basic phenomena of territoriality in animals are experienced in humans, it is clear that humans prefer to avoid close contact with strangers. Strangers interact at respectable distances, and one typically feels uncomfortable when a stranger approaches to within much less than a meter. Observations of this sort lead to the notion of personal space, a "territory" around the body. The distance spacing of students seated at libraries or riders on public transportation speaks to the same issue.

In this study we will attempt to gather direct evidence for the idea of personal space. To do so, we must find a common situation in which strangers find themselves in close confinement. Elevators seem particularly suited for this study.

Our study will be based on observations of where people stand in elevators. Given that an elevator already requires that all riders stand in close proximity, a personal space approach would certainly predict that *strangers* would maximize the distance between them. In order to test this idea, we will have to make some decisions about where, when, and how to make observations. (Although it would seem easy to just go and observe people in elevators, to do so without some thought, planning, and preliminary casual observation, would almost surely result in unreliable and not very meaningful data.)

What are the predictions? We must realize that elevators are typically asymmetrical: There is a door on one wall, and there is usually a button panel on one or both sides of the door. When people enter, they normally go to the panel to see if their floor has been pressed. Since it is likely that each person who gets on will go to the panel, it would be natural to maximize the distance from the panel in anticipation of the arrival of the next person. A personal space approach would also predict that strangers would not look at each other, but rather would tend to look straight ahead (toward the door) or up or down. On the basis of personal space, we would make the following predictions with respect to the positions in the schematic elevator diagrammed below.

1. In elevators with only one rider, the rider would usually stand along the back wall. In anticipation of a second rider, the first rider would be expected to stand in one back corner, thus leaving the other back corner for the second rider (and keeping both away from the button panels, which an additional rider would approach on entering). In terms of the schematic elevator layouts on the next page, a single person should be located either in Square 7 or Square 9.

2. The second rider would be inclined to maximize distance from both the first rider and a potential third rider, who would be expected to approach the button panel(s) on entering the elevator. Therefore, in the schematic elevator layout below, two people should occupy Squares 7 and 9. (Note: Squares 7 and 6, 4 and 9, and 4 and 6 would also constitute reasonable distributions, but would not be as optimal as 7 and 9.)

1	2	3
4	5	6
7	8	9

Schematic elevator, divided into a 3 × 3 unit array.
The door is at 2.

Conditions of Observation: The observer cannot be on the elevator, as he or she would then be influencing the results. Therefore, observations must be made when an elevator arrives or departs and the door is open. Since people are likely to be leaving or entering, quick observations will be necessary at a stable moment: just as the doors open or just as they close. (If you are lucky enough to be near an office or other building with video security monitors for the elevators in the lobby, you can use the monitors to record the positions of people between floors.)

Personal space rules would not necessarily hold among friends, and certainly not between lovers. Therefore, a fair test of personal space should eliminate any data including people who know each other well. To do this as well as possible, we will adopt two policies:

1. We will eliminate any observation (i.e., the data collected from any particular elevator at a particular time) if any two people in the elevator are talking to one another or showing personal involvement in any way (e.g., holding hands).

2. We will try to make observations at places and at times when the number of people knowing each other well would be minimal. Ideal locations would be elevators in department stores or office buildings. Time would also be an important

factor. We should avoid taking observations around the noon hour. (Why? Because it is very common to go out to lunch with friends, so the level of friend pairs or groups in elevators might be particularly high. This holds as well for people returning from lunch.)

Finally, precise conditions of measurement must be determined. Record only stable patterns: No one should be moving. Your critical time for observation is the moment before the doors close (it is harder to use the moment they open, because it is likely that a passenger intending to exit has moved toward the door as the elevator comes to his or her floor). If, at the time of departure, the elevator contains one or two people who have settled into position and if they do not appear to be friends (by the criteria above) then record their location on the data sheet. Assign each person to whichever of the nine squares best locates him or her.

To minimize data collection time, try to find a bank of elevators (at least two), and try to go at a time of moderate use, so you won't have to deal with infrequent or empty elevators. But don't use the lunch period, as discussed above. Normally the first floor is the natural place to make observations, but if you have a great deal of trouble with participants moving in the elevator, you could go to another floor and push the call button, so that the elevator will stop on your floor. (The second floor would be best for these purposes. Why?)

Make sufficient observations so that you can get fifteen cases of elevators with one rider and fifteen of elevators with two riders. Indicate on the two data sheets the plan of the elevator, its location, and the time of day. Record one-person elevators on one data sheet and two-person elevators on the other.

When you have fifteen observations of each type, enter your data in the boxes in the table below. Do your data support the personal space theory? In order to help you make this evaluation, we have given you an indication of what would be statistically significant findings.

For the one-person elevator, there are nine possible positions. The theory predicts that one of two positions (7 or 9) will be occupied. If people positioned themselves randomly in the elevator, we would expect them to be at 7 or 9 2/9 of the time, or for fifteen cases, $2/9 \times 15 = 3.3$ times (see table). By statistical calculations, we have determined that if there was actually an equal chance of someone's standing in any square, the chances of finding nine or more participants out of fifteen in Squares 7 or 9 is less than one in 100. This seems highly unlikely, so we would reject the idea that people stand randomly in the elevator and claim that the results supported the personal space hypothesis. These calculations are worked out in the table.

For the case of two people in the elevator, we have made similar calculations. It turns out that there are thirty-six different pairs of spaces that could be occupied in our 9-square elevator. The 7-9 combination is just one of them, and hence, if people were standing in random positions, there would only be one case in thirty-six where the 7-9 position was occupied. Therefore, the expected number of 7-9 locations in fifteen trials would be $15 \times 1/36 = 0.4$. A value of three or more people in this pair of locations would come about by chance less than one time in 100.

We can use one other measure with the two-person elevators. Personal space theory predicts, in general, that these people will stand far apart. We can translate this into the prediction that two people will not stand in boxes that are touching (even on the diagonal). Pairs 7-9, 4-6, 1-9 and others would meet this criterion, although, of the thirty-six pairs of locations, twenty are touching (contiguous). Thus, we would expect that (since there are sixteen nontouching pairs), in $16/36 \times 15$ cases, we would expect people in nontouching pairs, assuming that people distributed themselves randomly. A score of twelve or more pairs in nontouching squares would come about less than one time in 100 by chance and would be evidence for the personal space hypothesis. (See calculations in table below.)

For comparison purposes, we have made measurements like those we asked you to make in this study. We took advantage of a special situation that allows unusually easy data collection. The data we present comes from elevators in an office building in New York City. In this building, there is a video security camera in the ceiling of each elevator. Therefore, we could watch the bank of video monitors, and record the location of people. Furthermore, we could make the measurements between floors, so that there was no movement to or from the door. *(If your instructor collects the data, fill out the report sheet in Appendix 2.)*

ANALYSIS OF RESULTS

Elevator type	Location prediction	# in predicted place/Total	Expected random #	# significant[*]
1 person	7 or 9	□/15	3.3	9
2 person	7 and 9	□/15	0.4	3
New York data				
1 person	7 or 9	28/57	12.7	20
2 person	7 and 9	15/32	0.9	5

		# in noncontiguous squares/Total	Expected random #	# significant[*]
2 person	16 noncontiguous pairs out of 36 total pairs	□/15	6.7	12
New York data				
2 person	16 noncontiguous pairs out of 36 total pairs	31/32	14.2	21

* # significant means that one would expect this or a larger number of cases by chance no more than one time in one hundred.

Indicate panel location and other unusual features on diagram below.

Name _____   Location _____

1 Person in Elevator   Time _____

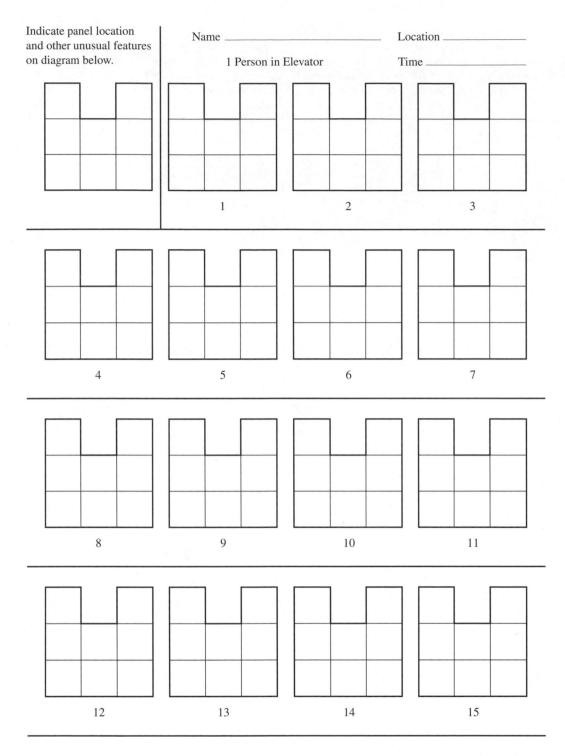

1   2   3

4   5   6   7

8   9   10   11

12   13   14   15

Indicate panel location and other unusual features on diagram below.

Name _____   Location _____

2 Persons in Elevator   Time _____

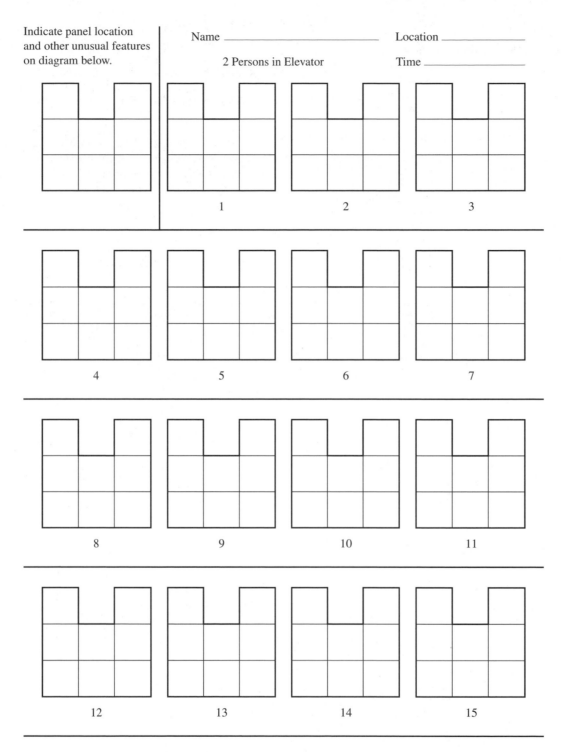

FURTHER STUDIES

1. You can extend these observations. In elevators with a button panel on one side of the door, you can make the further predictions that: 1. the first person will stand in the back corner opposite to the panel; 2. in three-person elevators, the third person should stand in the front corner that does not have the button panel.

2. You can extend this study to elevators with three persons. In elevators with two-button panels, it is hard to make precise predictions about where people will stand (see item 1 above, for predictions in single-panel elevators). However, personal space theory would predict that people would stand as far apart as possible, so that they should not stand in contiguous squares. There are eighty-four possible arrangements of three people, assigned to three of the nine squares. Only nine of these eighty-four arrangements involve no person in a square contiguous to another (e.g., 1, 3, 9; 6, 1, 7; 1, 3, 8).

Run another fifteen elevators, this time with three persons. How many have no one in a square contiguous with any other? We would predict, based on random location of people, $9/8 \times 15 = 1.6$ cases of people in noncontiguous squares. A significant result (less than one time in 100, by chance) would be six or more cases out of fifteen with no one in continguous squares.

3. You can make observations like the elevator observations in any place where strangers are in an enclosed area. Library tables or seats on vehicles of public transportation are natural places to see if distance between strangers are maximized.

4. What do you think would happen if the rules of personal space were purposely violated? How would the desire for privacy and isolation from strangers affect the behavior of the person violated? Also, do you think that the gender of the participants, in cases when there are two or more persons per elevator, would be influential in any way?

Investigating Psychological Phenomena

MATCHING FOR INTELLIGENCE AND ATTRACTION

Equipment: None
Number of participants: One, yourself
Time per participant: Twenty minutes
Time for experimenter: Twenty minutes

As described in the text, one of the major features of romantic couples is that they are similar along a wide variety of dimensions. Much of this similarity seems to be a reason for the formation of the relationship, rather than a consequence of it. Although certain characteristics may become more similar the longer a couple is together, this cannot be so for the many characteristics unlikely to change in adulthood, such as height. Furthermore, individuals are likely to seek a partner with a high rating on characteristics for which there can be a clear positive or negative evaluation (such as intelligence or attractiveness), with competitive selection and fear of rejection tending to sort people out with others at their own level of achievement, ability, beauty, and so forth. Thus, one would expect similar ratings on almost all traits.

This study will demonstrate the principles of homogamy and matching by examining the similarity of couples on two characteristics: physical attractiveness and intelligence. You will be the one participant in this study. First, select ten heterosexual couples that you know fairly well. The couples should be selected according to the following criteria:

1. All should be romantically involved: married or together for at least one year.

2. The couples should be about the same age in two senses: The members of the couple should be no more than ten years apart in age and the oldest person should be no more than twenty years older than the youngest person of the same gender on the list. (If you cannot generate the ten couples that this study calls for, you can ask a friend to generate the data for you.)

DO NOT INCLUDE YOURSELF IN ANY OF THESE COUPLES.

List the couples (by first name of each partner) in the accompanying tables. Now rank the ten women and the ten men separately for both physical attractiveness and intelligence. Thus, for physical attractiveness, rank the most attractive man number one, the next most attractive number two, and so on until all ten numbers have been assigned. Rank the women in the same fashion.

Now calculate a rank-order correlation, a statistic that represents the correlation between the ranking for men and women in each couple. (See the Statistical Appendix in the text, but use the formula on page 140 to calculate the correlation.) If the members of a couple match perfectly on a characteristic (i.e., if the man ranked number one for attractiveness is involved with the woman ranked number one in this same trait, etc.), the correlation coefficient would equal 1.00—the highest possible value for correlation. If the members of a couple are inversely matched (i.e., if the man ranked number one for attractiveness is involved with the woman ranked number ten on that trait), then the correlation coefficient would equal –1.00 (the lowest possible value). If there is no relation between the ranking of the man and woman in a couple on the trait in question, then the correlation coefficient would be 0. (For a sample calculation and table, see page 141.)

Attractiveness

Couple (man's/woman's name)	Man's Rank	Woman's Rank	Difference	Difference^2
1 _____	_____	_____	_____	_____
2 _____	_____	_____	_____	_____
3 _____	_____	_____	_____	_____
4 _____	_____	_____	_____	_____
5 _____	_____	_____	_____	_____
6 _____	_____	_____	_____	_____
7 _____	_____	_____	_____	_____
8 _____	_____	_____	_____	_____
9 _____	_____	_____	_____	_____
10 _____	_____	_____	_____	_____

Correlation for attractiveness = _____

Intelligence

Couple (man's/woman's name)	Man's Rank	Woman's Rank	Difference	Difference^2
1 _____	_____	_____	_____	_____
2 _____	_____	_____	_____	_____
3 _____	_____	_____	_____	_____
4 _____	_____	_____	_____	_____
5 _____	_____	_____	_____	_____
6 _____	_____	_____	_____	_____
7 _____	_____	_____	_____	_____
8 _____	_____	_____	_____	_____
9 _____	_____	_____	_____	_____
10 _____	_____	_____	_____	_____

Correlation for intelligence = _____

Use the formula below to calculate the correlation, r.

$$r = 1 - \frac{6(\text{sum of the difference in ranking between couple members}^2)}{\text{number of couples (number of couples}^2 - 1)}$$

Sample data on intelligence:

| | | Intelligence | | |
Couple (man's/woman's name)	Man's Rank	Woman's Rank	Difference	Difference^2
1 A/B	1	2	−1	1
2 C/D	5	3	2	1
3 E/F	3	1	2	4
4 G/H	9	6	3	9
5 I/J	2	7	−5	25
6 K/L	7	5	2	4
7 M/N	4	4	0	0
8 O/P	8	9	−1	1
9 Q/R	10	8	2	4
10 S/T	6	10	−4	16

Sum of difference^2 = 65

Correlation for intelligence = .61

For the sample table, the equation would read:

$$r = 1 - \frac{6(65)}{10(100 - 1)} = -.61$$

Compare your results to those in the list below generated by other students in introductory psychology. These correlation coefficients were calculated by eleven students for intelligence and thirteen students for attractiveness and have been arranged in order of increasing correlation. How do your values compare to theirs?

Correlations

Attractiveness	Intelligence
−.16	−.01
−.01	.18
.02	.26
.07	.35
.36	.39
.45	.42
.46	.56
.50	.63
.55	.68
.60	.75
.60	.76
.76	
.76	

Finally, try to think of the characteristic that would be most likely to show similarity in mates, as well as the characteristic that might, perhaps because of its lack of importance, not show matching in mates. Calculate the correlation coefficient for each of these characteristics, using the same ten couples you have already used. You might also consider doing a similarity/matching score for ten same-gender couples or nonromantic friends. Would you expect them to show similarity/matching effects as well? Would you expect this on the same characteristics as with heterosexual romantic partners?

CHAPTER 12

Physical and Cognitive Development

Learning Objectives

WHAT IS DEVELOPMENT?

Development as growth

1. Review the major events in physical growth of humans from conception to adulthood.
2. How does humans' physical growth (especially of the nervous system) compare with that of other animals? What is the effect of the difference?
3. Review the basic sensory and response capacities of the human infant.

THE PHYSICAL BASIS OF DEVELOPMENT

The mechanism of genetic transmission

4. Define chromosomes. Indicate how gender is determined by chromosomes.
5. Define genes. Distinguish between dominant and recessive genes, giving an example. How many genes do humans have?
6. Distinguish between genotype and phenotype.
7. Describe polygenic inheritance.

Environments at different points in development

8. Review gene-environment interactions in the embryo, including the role of both the cellular and hormonal environments in development.
9. Define and describe critical periods and sensitive periods.
10. Describe how development depends on a complex interaction of genes and environment.
11. How do studies of adopted children underscore the importance of genes in cognitive development?

COGNITIVE DEVELOPMENT

12. What are the major philosophical positions on development? How does Piaget's theory relate to these? What are the four developmental stages, according to Piaget?

Sensorimotor intelligence

13. Describe the hallmarks of this stage. How do children see themselves and objects around them? What distinctions develop during this period?
14. Why is object permanence seen as an end to this stage of development?
15. What do the terms *assimilation* and *accommodation* mean according to Piaget? What is a schema?

16. What does Piaget mean by the term *representation*? What are some examples of representations?

The preoperational period

17. How is the name of this period derived?
18. Be familiar with various tests of conservation. How does the child's conservation ability develop during this period? Why do children fail to conserve at the beginning of this period? What operations are crucial for conservation?
19. Describe egocentrism.

Concrete and formal operations

20. What is the difference between these stages? How does Piaget describe formal operations?

WHAT IS THE COGNITIVE STARTING POINT?

21. What are the two principal challenges to Piaget's views?

Space and objects in infancy

22. What is occlusion? How does it affect adult object perception?
23. What is the habituation procedure, and how has it been used to study infant perception?
24. What evidence suggests that infants have some notions of the principles that govern objects in space?
25. How do studies of the effects of removing supports from objects reveal a developmental progression in object learning?
26. Cite the evidence that indicates that infants do have a notion of object permanence, but that they have incomplete control over their motor responses.

Number in infancy

27. What is Piaget's position on the conception of number? What do studies of "threeness" in infancy say about this position?
28. Describe an experiment showing that primitive ideas of addition and subtraction are also present in infancy.

Social cognition in infancy: the existence of other minds

29. Describe the evidence that very young infants are capable of discriminating a face from other stimuli, a skill that is fundamental to early social interaction.
30. What is the evidence about facial imitation in young infants? What is the significance of this evidence?
31. A next important step in social interaction is sharing attention with another person. Be familiar with the data showing that this skill develops early as well.

32. What is the evidence that infants can separate an object from a physical movement toward that object?

COGNITIVE DEVELOPMENT IN PRESCHOOLERS

The meaning of mental stage
33. What are the characteristics of a developmental "stage" as Piaget uses the term? How is this contradicted by modern evidence?

Numerical skills in preschoolers
34. Even though preschoolers may use idiosyncratic counting terms, how does evidence show that they may nonetheless have a rudimentary understanding of counting principles?
35. How do modern studies of number cast doubt on the Piagetian concept of a stage? Why do these studies differ in their results from Piaget's work?

Social cognition in preschoolers: developing a theory of mind
36. What are some basic assumptions of a theory of mind?
37. How has it been shown that young children have the rudiments of an understanding of some of these assumptions?
38. What is the course of development of a theory of beliefs about what others know?
39. In what sense can one claim that young children have a theory of mind?
40. Describe some evidence about the idea that humans have a brain module concerned with reasoning in social situations.

Sequence or stages?
41. Understand the argument that Piaget's fundamental conception of stages as transitions still has plausibility even in spite of modern evidence about his tasks.

THE CAUSES OF COGNITIVE GROWTH

The role of biological inheritance
42. What are three sources of evidence on the importance of biological factors in understanding cognitive development?

The cultural context of development
43. Realize that the culture in which a child develops can have substantial influence on the course of development.

Differences in competence
44. What is the evidence about the development of formal operations in different cultures? Do tests of formal operations tell us all about the sophisticated reasoning skills of people?

The cultural context of testing
45. How can the kinds of questions that are asked in cognitive testing influence what one infers about development of cognitive skills?

Social and cultural influences on development
46. How do the surrounding cultural influences help determine what a child will learn?

The child's role in shaping the impact of culture
47. How do changes in parental questioning about past events help shape the child's memory of those events?
48. Understand how questioning by adults can shape a child's memory so much that it can distort it if the adults are not careful.
49. What are examples of cultural influences of adult questioning on children's memory?

The information-processing approach
50. What are the memory skills of young children? Can they sometimes remember as much as adults?
51. Describe some strategies for remembering that adults and children use. How do young children approach a memory task, and how does their approach change as they mature?
52. What is meant by the term *metacognition*? How is metacognition manifested in memory, perception, language, thinking, and problem solving?

COGNITIVE DEVELOPMENT IN OLD AGE

Aging and intelligence
53. What is the study of life-span development?
54. Distinguish between fluid and crystallized intelligence.
55. What are some possible causes of decline in fluid intelligence?
56. How does bodily health influence mental status and its change with age?

Aging and memory
57. What are some possible causes of memory decline with age?

Programmed Exercises

WHAT IS DEVELOPMENT?

1. Physical growth continues until approximately the end of the _____ decade of life.

    second

2. The part of the human body that grows at a disproportionately high rate before birth is the _____.

    head (brain)

3. Because of extensive growth of the brain after birth, humans have a longer period of _____ than most other species.

    dependency

4. Human growth does not occur smoothly, but in _____.

    spurts

5. The _____ reflex is elicited in an infant by a touch to the cheek, which makes the infant turn his head toward the stimulating object.

    rooting

6. The _____ reflex is elicited by a touch of the palm.

    grasp

7. In general, the infant's sensory capacities are _____ advanced at birth than are his or her _____ capacities.

    more
    response (motor)

THE PHYSICAL BASIS OF DEVELOPMENT

8. The genetic material of humans is arranged in pairs of structures called _____.

   chromosomes

9. In contrast to a female, who has two X chromosomes, a male has a(n) _____ and a(n) _____ chromosome in each body cell.

   X
   Y

10. The unit of hereditary transmission is the _____.

    gene

11. A gene that exerts its effect regardless of the identity of the other member of its pair is called _____. A gene that will express itself only if the other member of its pair is comparable is called _____.

    dominant
    recessive

12. The observed characteristics of an organism are called its _____, while the underlying genetic blueprint is called its _____.

    phenotype
    genotype

13. When an attribute is determined by multiple genes, this is called _____ inheritance.

    polygenic

14. In mammalian embryos, the genitals will develop as _____ unless the body is exposed to a _____ sex hormone, called _____.

    female
    male, androgen

15. Consider a person with a male (XY) genetic makeup, but whose tissues are not sensitive to male hormone. Such a person will develop female genitals. Unlike a typical male, such a person shows a disparity between _____ and _____.

    phenotype, genotype
    (either order)

16. During _____ periods in development, certain important events will have an impact that they would not have (or would have to a much lesser extent) at earlier or later times.

    critical (sensitive)

17. Adopted children are more similar to their _____ parent than to their _____ parent.

    biological, adoptive

COGNITIVE DEVELOPMENT

18. Piaget regards cognitive development as a dynamic process in which the child progresses through several _____.

    stages

19. A child has begun to learn that he lives in a stable world that can be distinguished from his sensory impressions. This child is most likely in the _____ stage.

    sensorimotor

20. Children develop the notion of _____ _____ near the end of the sensorimotor stage as they become aware that objects exist independently of their sensory experience and motor manipulations.

    object permanence

21. Perhaps the most significant accomplishment of children in the last phase of the sensorimotor stage is their ability to _____ objects or events in their absence, rather than merely reacting to their presence.

    represent

22. Recurrent action patterns (such as sucking, swallowing, and head and eye movement) are the first mental elements, or _____. It is in terms of these that the infant organizes the world.

    schemas

23. According to Piaget, development proceeds by infants' _____ new objects to existing schemas and by changing those schemas appropriately, a process called _____.

    assimilating
    accommodation

24. Representations may be internalized actions, images, or words; in all cases they function as _____, which stand for whatever they may signify.

    symbols

25. According to Piaget, a conceptual system of thought can be constructed only by means of higher-order schemas. These _____ allow the internal manipulation of ideas according to a stable set of rules and emerge at age seven or so; the period from two to seven is therefore termed _____.

    operations
    preoperational

26. A characteristic of children in the preoperational stage is their inability to _____ quantity, as shown by their lack of knowledge about relative quantities of liquids in two glasses.

    conserve

27. One of the crucial concepts that children must grasp if they are to conserve is that manipulations upon objects are _____.

    reversible

28. A preoperational child believes his or her point of view is the only one. Such a belief is known as _____.

    egocentrism

29. A child can determine whether a given number is odd or even and can also add one to any number. The child finds that 3 + 1 is even, and 5 + 1 is even, but doesn't understand that any odd number added to one results in an even number. This child would be categorized as being in the _____ _____ stage.

    concrete operations

30. The ability to entertain hypothetical possibilities and deal with potential relationships is characteristic only of the stage of _____ _____. formal operations

WHAT IS THE COGNITIVE STARTING POINT?

31. The fact that an infant can perceive an object that is partially blocked by another object gives evidence that infants are capable of reacting appropriately to the perceptual effect of _____. occlusion

32. The procedure in which a perceptual display is kept in view until an infant becomes bored is called _____. habituation

33. It appears that young infants have some knowledge of the fact that two objects cannot occupy the same _____ at the same time. space (place)

34. Young infants believe that any contact with an object will provide _____ for it, keeping it from falling. support

35. Modern investigators believe that although infants may believe that objects exist, they do not actively search for them. Much of the proof for this theory comes from studies on the _____ effect. A-not-B

36. Studies show that infants have a primitive notion of _____: they can distinguish two items from three items. number

37. Studies of the knowledge of number in infants have relied on the _____ method, which depends on showing a stimulus repeatedly and then testing with it and a novel stimulus. habituation

38. Studies of numerical reasoning show that infants as young as five months had a primitive understanding of _____ operations: they could distinguish when a stimulus had been added to an array. arithmetical

39. Investigations of infants minutes after birth have demonstrated that they have a preference for looking at normal rather than scrambled _____. faces

40. Infants will turn their _____ in the direction in which the mother is looking. attention

COGNITIVE DEVELOPMENT IN PRESCHOOLERS

41. According to Piaget, cognitive development is characterized by a series of _____, each qualitatively different from the others. stages

42. Even though children may use idiosyncratic symbols to denote given numbers of objects, they may still have the basic principle of _____. counting

43. Piaget had demonstrated failure of young children to _____ number, in that if a number of items was stretched out, the children thought there were more items present. conserve

44. Recent studies of cognitive development suggest that stages are not _____ or _____ in nature. The demarcations between stages are not sharp. all, none

45. The fact that young children will turn a photograph in the proper orientation when showing it to another person suggests that they have a rudimentary theory of _____. mind

46. At about two-and-a-half years of age, children can predict what another child will want. They understand something about the mental state of _____. motive (desire)

47. There are two crucial components to the notion of a _____. One is that they can be true or false; the other is that different people can have different ones. belief

48. The _____ _____ test asks a child to predict what another being will know in a certain situation. This test compares the child's own knowledge with what the child knows about another's knowledge. false belief

49. Some have argued that natural selection would favor people with the ability to predict the actions of others. So, evolution may have promoted the development of a _____ _____ module. social cognition

50. Most developmental psychologists would say that Piaget's cognitive milestones are not a succession of mental stages, similar to those found in embryological development, but rather a _____ of mental steps. sequence

THE CAUSES OF COGNITIVE GROWTH

51. Piaget was probably wrong in thinking that all development stemmed from a few reflexes. The role of biological _____ appears to be much more extensive than that.

    inheritance

52. People from different _____ appear to differ on tests of formal operations even though ones who fail these tests still show sophisticated reasoning skills.

    cultures

53. _____ differ in the activities to which children are exposed, as it is hardly surprising that children who live near the water will be good swimmers.

    Cultures

54. The zone of _____ _____ refers to the tasks that are just out of reach of children but that they are capable of attaining with guidance.

    proximal development

55. A more current approach to cognitive development asserts that it results from a change in _____ _____.

    information processing

56. According to this approach, mental growth is partly based on the acquisition of various _____ for thinking and remembering.

    strategies

57. Working memory capacity is often measured with the _____ _____ task.

    memory span

58. The fact that adults can reflect on the cognitive operations whereby they gain knowledge shows that they are capable of _____.

    metacognition

COGNITION DEVELOPMENT IN OLD AGE

59. The study of development at all ages, not just in children, is called _____-_____ development.

    life-span

60. _____ intelligence refers to the ability to reason quickly and efficiently about novel problems.

    Fluid

61. _____ intelligence refers to a person's accumulated knowledge.

    Crystallized

62. Both _____ and _____ memory show little change with age.

    implicit, semantic

63. Both _____ and _____ memory show declines with age.

    working, episodic

Self-Test

1. All but one of the following are distinctive features of human development, in comparison with most other mammals. Which is not a distinctly human feature?
   a. long period of dependency on the parent
   b. being born at a very immature stage
   c. presence of reflex at birth
   d. continuation of growth until about twenty years of age
   e. b and c

2. Major features of motor, language, and other types of development often occur in a fixed order in children who develop at different rates. A major reason for this is that
   a. development must occur in stages.
   b. some capacities depend on the existence of other capacities.
   c. sense organs mature before response capacities.
   d. language depends on locomotion ability.
   e. the infant begins with reflexes like grasping before it can learn.

3. The ability to taste a certain chemical called PTC is genetically determined, and controlled by a single pair of genes. All children of nontasters are nontasters, but some of the children with two taster parents are also nontasters. This suggests that the gene that codes for tasting is
   a. polygenic.
   b. on at least two chromosomes.
   c. dominant.
   d. recessive.
   e. rare.

4. Phenotype and genotype are not always in close correspondence because
   a. some genes are recessive.
   b. some inheritance is polygenic.
   c. only females have two X chromosomes.
   d. a and c
   e. all of the above

5. A genetic female who is exposed to androgen as a fetus and develops male genitals illustrates
   a. that behavior is inherited.
   b. that recessive traits can occur in both gender and intelligence.
   c. that inborn, genetically determined traits can be changed by environmental factors.
   d. that environmental factors, under some circumstances, have no influence on behavior.
   e. that behavior is related to gender chromosomes.

6. Phenotype is to genotype as
   a. building is to building plan.
   b. maturation is to motor development.
   c. fetus is to embryo.
   d. recessive is to dominant.

7. The fact that at different ages organisms perceive their environment differently and the existence of critical periods together argue for the view that
   a. it is not possible to describe the meaningful environment for an animal by just listing all the physical and social events that are occurring.
   b. initially behavior is controlled by genes, and later by environment.
   c. it is not possible to evaluate the role of environment in determining behavior.
   d. b and c
   e. all of the above

8. Adopted children are an important source of information about the interplay of heredity and environment in the development of cognition. Study of these children shows that
   a. they are more similar to their adoptive than their biological parents.
   b. their similarity to their adoptive parents increases the longer they live with those parents.
   c. their similarity to their biological parents decreases as they grow older.
   d. none of the above

9. A child has learned that whether a toy box is open or closed, there are toys inside. It could be said that the child has attained the concept of
   a. object permanence.
   b. representations.
   c. directed action.
   d. solipsism.

10. When a child just becomes aware that objects exist independent of her own sensory experience, she would most likely have completed which Piagetian stage?
    a. sensorimotor
    b. preoperational
    c. concrete operations
    d. formal operations

11. Recurring action patterns, such as sucking and swallowing, are
    a. simple reflexes that have little developmental interest.
    b. the first mental elements with which the infant organizes the world.
    c. examples of intentional acts.
    d. none of the above

12. The two processes that Piaget sees as being responsible for cognitive development are
    a. deferred imitation and assimilation.
    b. schemas and representations.
    c. assimilation and accommodation.
    d. none of the above

13. A toy is hidden under a box in the presence of a child. The child is prevented from reaching the box for a few seconds. When he is released he immediately lifts the box off the toy. The earliest stage that this child could be in is _____.
    a. sensorimotor
    b. preoperational
    c. concrete operations
    d. formal operations

14. When a child searches for an object in a location where it was previously present, but from which she saw it moved, she demonstrates
    a. the A-not-B effect.
    b. deferred imitation.
    c. object permanence.
    d. all of the above

15. Demonstrations of the child's understanding that symbols (i.e., internalized actions, images, or words) may stand for objects but are not equivalent to them include all of the following *except*
    a. object permanence.
    b. deferred imitation.
    c. make-believe play.
    d. metacognitions.

16. The concept unknown to a child who doesn't conserve quantity is
    a. reversibility.
    b. accuracy.
    c. size.
    d. weight.

17. Children who don't conserve are
    a. unable to attend to all of the relevant dimensions of a stimulus.
    b. usually in the concrete operations stage.
    c. usually in the formal operations stage.
    d. none of the above

18. One of the features of the world for which children fail to show conservation is number. They apparently believe
    a. that, say, the number 4 is the same as the number 5.
    b. that the number of items is equivalent to its length when laid out.
    c. that number and quantity are the same thing.
    d. that the number of items that are present is the same as the number that were present a few minutes ago.
    e. all of the above

19. The social counterpart of an inability to attend to more than one dimension in a conservation task is
    a. aggressive behavior.
    b. having only one friend during a particular time interval.
    c. egocentrism.
    d. none of the above

20. The major difference between a child in the concrete operations stage and one in the formal operations stage is
    a. the former is incapable of following the rules.
    b. the former cannot deal with numbers.
    c. the former cannot deal with abstract concepts.
    d. all of the above

21. The idea behind using habituation to study knowledge of occlusion is
    a. to have an infant habituate to an occluded stimulus and then see whether it sees the whole unoccluded stimulus as novel.
    b. to have an infant habituate to an unoccluded stimulus and then see whether it sees the whole occluded stimulus as novel.
    c. to have an infant see a stimulus and then see whether it habituates to that stimulus faster when it is occluded.
    d. none of the above

22. The experiment showing that infants have knowledge about objects and the fact that two objects cannot occupy the same place at the same time made use of a procedure in which a screen moved over an object and either stopped when it reached the object or seemed to pass through it. This procedure indicated that the infants had a sense of objects because
    a. they habituated to the moving screen.
    b. they spent more time looking at the screen when it stopped at the object behind it.
    c. they moved their hands and arms more while the screen was moving, indicating that they anticipated its stopping when it hit the object.
    d. they spent less time looking at the screen when it stopped at the object behind it.

23. One problem in interpreting results from the A-not-B effect is that
    a. it gives an infant too many places to search for a hidden object.
    b. it does not allow habituation sufficient time to develop.
    c. the results may simply depend on an infant's preference to avoid a place where it has just searched for an object.
    d. none of the above

24. A major claim of Piaget's theory that has been challenged is
    a. development proceeds by transitions.
    b. the boundaries between developmental stages are sharp.
    c. infants have a wealth of built-in capacities.
    d. all of the above

25. Some developmental psychologists have challenged Piaget's view on what is given to the infant at the start of life. With which of the following would these critics agree?
    a. Four-month-old infants can perceive partially hidden objects similar to the way adults do.
    b. Young infants have a primitive notion of number, at least for small numbers.
    c. Young infants have a primitive notion of arithmetic operations.
    d. all of the above

26. What do three-month-old infants understand about what supports objects so they will not fall?
    a. nothing
    b. that any physical contact with an object provides support
    c. that contact with an object from below it provides support
    d. that contact with an object has to come from two sources to provide support

27. Studies of number and addition knowledge in young children
    a. confirm Piaget's view of the young child's cognitive competence.
    b. raise the possibility that young children are endowed with more cognitive sense than Piaget supposed.
    c. indicate that concrete operations can precede the preoperational period.
    d. none of the above

28. Piaget's demonstration of the failure of young children to conserve number
    a. has been called into question by more recent work on children's ability to focus attention on where the mother is focusing attention.
    b. has stood the test of time in that more recent investigations have also found the preoperational child to be unable to conserve number or any other quantity.
    c. is inconsistent with his demonstrations of other skills in conservation tasks at the same age.
    d. needs to be modified based on more recent evidence of number conservation of small numbers of items.

29. There is evidence that infants have primitive social abilities that will later develop more fully. This evidence includes
    a. the fact that infants are more responsive to faces than to other stimuli with the same features scrambled.
    b. the fact that infants are capable of taking another person's perspective in Piaget's problem where he asks children to predict what another person's perspective will be.
    c. the fact that infants are sensitive to where another person is concentrating attention.
    d. all of the above
    e. a and b, but not c
    f. a and c, but not b

30. What are two characteristics of a developmental stage as Piaget uses the term?
    a. consistent, continuous
    b. continuous, discrete
    c. consistent, concrete
    d. consistent, discrete

31. The fact that children younger than five count with unusually ordered numbers (e.g., one, two, eight, five) but assign a unique label to each item counted
    a. casts doubt on Piaget's discrete-stage view of development in which these children should be in a preoperational stage.
    b. suggests that the preoperational and concrete operational stages are one and the same.
    c. forces one to abandon the notion of sequentially ordered stages altogether.
    d. is inconsistent with the ability of even younger children to have a primitive notion of number and addition.

32. Evidence that young children have a primitive theory of mind is that they have an early sense of
    a. another person's beliefs.
    b. another person's perceptual capacities.
    c. another person's motives.
    d. all of the above

33. A rudimentary theory of mind has been demonstrated in young children by the result that
    a. they will appropriately orient a picture they are showing to an adult so that it faces the adult.
    b. they will be egocentric in trying to take the perspective of another person in how that person views a scene.
    c. they can recognize faces only minutes after birth.
    d. none of the above

34. Some have argued that a "social cognition module" may have evolved in human brains because
    a. brain damage sometimes causes impairments to a patient's theory of mind.
    b. different cultures make very similar assumptions about the mind and people's motives.
    c. adaptively it would make sense to be able to predict the actions of others.
    d. a and b but not c
    e. a and c but not b
    f. all of the above

35. The Piagetian theory of stages faces difficulty because
    a. children often display cognitive competence earlier than they should according to the theory.
    b. development is sometimes continuous rather than stage-like.
    c. both of the above
    d. neither of the above

36. Evidence that biological factors have a heavy influence on development includes
    a. that adopted children are more similar to their biological than their adoptive parents.
    b. certain cognitive capacities are tightly tied to particular neural structures.
    c. some cognitive skills are evident so early in life that it is implausible for the environment to have had much influence.
    d. all of the above

37. Cultures in which there is no formal schooling raise children
    a. with no object permanence.
    b. who fail tests of formal operations.
    c. who cannot count.
    d. all of the above

38. One way of reconciling modern evidence with Piaget's view of stages of development is to say that
    a. young children begin with very few cognitive capacities and need to learn them all.
    b. young children have some cognitive skills but cannot apply them to very many situations.
    c. Piaget was essentially correct in all of his assertions about stages, but he was wrong in when the stages begin.
    d. none of the above

39. An approach to cognitive development asserts that mental growth is based partly on the acquisition of better strategies for handling information. This approach explains cognitive development as a change in
    a. accommodation.
    b. information processing.
    c. phenotype.
    d. assimilation.

40. Which of the following is *not* an example of metacognition?
    a. being realistic about how many numbers you can recall at one time
    b. recognizing the difference between reality and illusion

    c. using strategies for reaching solutions
    d. reading and following directions for a recipe

41. Which of the following is true?
    a. Unschooled people are incapable of abstract thought.
    b. Schooled and unschooled people think alike.
    c. Schooled people cannot apply their knowledge to a variety of contexts or situations.
    d. none of the above

42. When parents are trying to elicit recalled memories in children, they often tailor their questioning to the age of the child by
    a. asking more specific questions the older the child.
    b. never asking young children to recall from memory because they know that young children do not have the appropriate strategies to answer.
    c. giving very explicit clues to young children about what to recall and more general cues to older children.
    d. changing their speech to older children to make clear that the child should only recall what she is confident about.

43. Fluid intelligence is to crystallized intelligence as
    a. genotype is to phenotype.
    b. assimilation is to accommodation.
    c. problem-solving is to word retrieval.
    d. heredity is to environment.

44. What might be a cause of the individual differences in people in fluid intelligence and the decline in fluid intelligence with age?
    a. differences in neuroanatomy with age and among individuals
    b. increased blood flow with age
    c. increases in working memory capacity with age
    d. all of the above

45. Many insults to bodily organs can have an important spillover effect on brain function because
    a. if overall health declines, then there will likely be a decline in brain function.
    b. the brain is an unusually large consumer of metabolic energy and so any compromise to the body's ability to metabolize oxygen and glucose will have a large effect on brain function.
    c. both of the above
    d. neither of the above

46. What sorts of memory performance will show declines with age?
    a. priming and other implicit measures of memory
    b. retrieval of facts about the world that are the province of semantic memory
    c. retrieval of autobiographical facts that are the provice of episodic memory
    d. retrieval of information from working memory
    e. all of the above
    f. a and b only
    g. c and d only

Answer Key for Self-Test

1.	c	24.	b
2.	b	25.	d
3.	c	26.	b
4.	a	27.	b
5.	c	28.	d
6.	a	29.	f
7.	a	30.	d
8.	d	31.	a
9.	a	32.	d
10.	a	33.	a
11.	b	34.	e
12.	c	35.	c
13.	b	36.	d
14.	a	37.	b
15.	d	38.	b
16.	a	39.	b
17.	a	40.	d
18.	b	41.	d
19.	c	42.	c
20.	c	43.	c
21.	a	44.	a
22.	d	45.	c
23.	d	46.	g

Investigating Psychological Phenomena

CONSERVATION OF NUMBER

Equipment: Thirty-three red poker chips and thirty-four blue ones
Number of participants: One, age four or five (preoperational
  stage, according to Piaget)
Time per participant: Fifteen minutes
Time for experimenter: Thirty minutes

In Chapter 12, the authors discuss the development of conservation ability as children move into what Piaget calls the stage of concrete operations. The characteristic of this ability is that children come to use a set of mental rules, or operations, to govern their thought about objects in the world. For example, they learn that a certain volume of water is unchanged by the characteristics of the container that happens to contain it. Thus, pouring a certain amount of water from a low and wide container into one that is tall and thin does not change its volume even though the water achieves a greater height in the tall container.

There is also research suggesting that Piaget may have underestimated the ability of children to conserve. Apparently, when faced with somewhat less demanding tasks, which nevertheless are formal tests of conservation ability, young children who should be in a preoperational stage show some signs of conservation. This has been shown most impressively with the conservation of number. The problem that preoperational children face in conserving number is that they confuse numerosity with the physical length of the series that contains the items whose number must be judged. For example, they frequently judge that a row of items contains more items if it is simply longer than another row of items.

The present exercise allows you to take an empirical look at this issue. One of the variables that may influence whether children show evidence of conservation is the number of items that are included in a test. Common sense suggests that the more objects in a set whose number must be judged, the more difficult will be the judgment. We shall test this hypothesis in the context of a number conservation test in which the number of objects whose number must be judged will vary. In both conditions of the experiment, your participants will be asked to judge which of two rows contains more objects. In one condition, the number of objects in each row will be less than in the other condition.

In order to conduct this experiment most efficiently, and with the greatest chance of keeping the attention of your participant, prearrange the stimulus arrays before you begin. The accompanying figure shows you the five stimulus arrangements for each of the two numerosity conditions. Each letter in the figure represents a chip of the appropriate color (B = blue, R = red). On the left are the arrangements for the lower numerosity condition. The first arrangement is the control condition in which each row contains the same number of chips, and in which the two rows are of equal length. In the second figure, the two rows contain the same number, but the lengths of the rows differ. In the third figure, the lengths are equal, but one row contains more chips than the other. The fourth arrangement pits the two variables against one another: The row that is longest also contains fewer chips than the shorter row. On the right are comparable arrangements for the condition in which more chips are used. The four arrangements are in the same order as the ones on the left of the figure.

Make each of the eight arrangements on a separate piece of cardboard, and place them out of sight. Then seat your participant comfortably and explain to him or her that you are going to play a game in which the child has to say which row of chips has more chips. Take out Arrangement 1 first and ask the child, "Which row has more, the one with red or the one with blue, or are they the same?" If the child answers that they are not the same, then lengthen or shorten one of the rows so that the child agrees that they are equal. Be sure that the red and blue chips are equal. Be sure that the red and blue chips line up above one another, so there is a one-to-one correspondence.

Now move on to Arrangement 2. Continue with the same line of questioning, asking which row contains more, the red one or the blue one. After getting an answer, which you should record on the answer form that is given on p. 152, ask your participant to explain his or her response. That is, ask why the participant judged one of the rows as having more (or less, or equal, depending upon the answer) chips, and record the substance of this answer on the answer form. Continue with Arrangements 3 and 4, after which you should move on to Arrangements 5 through 8. In each case, record the data in the spaces provided on the answer sheet. For each arrangement decide whether your participant was paying attention to the number or the length of the series in making his or her judgment. Which condition shows better number conservation overall?

The critical comparison that is of interest in this experiment is whether your participant shows evidence of competence in number conservation with fewer chips, but falters with a greater number of chips. If this is so, how does it fit in with the discussion in the text about the development of conservation? What does it imply about a stage theory of development?

Some other questions that might be raised by this exercise are the following: Would your results have been any different if the two conditions had been run in the opposite order, from the more to the less difficult? Is there something inherent in the questioning of the participant that may bias him or her to attend to length rather than number? Why might number conservation be better with fewer chips in the stimuli? What kinds of operations did your participant seem to be using as the basis for his or her judgment? What kinds of tests could be constructed to discover whether other conservation skills might also develop earlier than previously thought?

STIMULI FOR NUMBER CONSERVATION EXPERIMENT

Small Numbers

1. B B B
    R R R

2.   B   B   B
     R   R   R

3. B   B
    R R R

4. B   B
      R R R

Large Numbers

5. B B B B B
    R R R R R

6.   B B B B B
    R R R R R R

7. B B B B B
    R R R R R R

8. B B B B   B
    R R R R R

ANSWER SHEET FOR A NUMBER CONSERVATION EXPERIMENT

1. More blue _____
    More red   _____
    Both equal _____

    Explanation:

2. More blue _____
    More red   _____
    Both equal _____

    Explanation:

3. More blue _____
    More red   _____
    Both equal _____

    Explanation:

4. More blue _____
    More red   _____
    Both equal _____

    Explanation:

5. More blue _____
    More red   _____
    Both equal _____

    Explanation:

6. More blue _____
    More red   _____
    Both equal _____

    Explanation:

7. More blue _____
    More red   _____
    Both equal _____

    Explanation:

8. More blue _____
    More red   _____
    Both equal _____

    Explanation:

CHAPTER 13

Social Development

Learning Objectives

ATTACHMENT

The roots of attachment
1. Describe the view (the "cupboard" theory) that attributes the infant's love for the mother to the fact that she fulfills basic biological needs.

Bowlby's theory of attachment
2. Explain Bowlby's theory of attachment. Contrast Bowlby's theory with Freud's "cupboard" theory.
3. Discuss the importance of fear of the unfamiliar and contact comfort.
4. How do Harlow's experiments on monkeys cast doubt on the "cupboard" view and support Bowlby's view?

Imprinting and attachment
5. Describe the process of imprinting in animals. Is there imprinting in humans?
6. Review the evidence for sexual imprinting in animals and humans, including discussion of the role of odor and the major histocompatibility complex (MHC).

PATTERNS OF ATTACHMENT

7. What is separation anxiety and when does it first occur?

Assessing attachment
8. Describe Ainsworth's procedure for measuring attachment. What characterizes the securely attached child?
9. To what extent are attachment styles stable across childhood? What kinds of events are likely to cause changes in attachment styles?
10. What is the evidence that the early parent-child relationship, as assessed in the Strange Situation, is a major determinant of later social and emotional adjustment? What are some counterarguments?
11. Discuss the problems of inferring causation from correlation in developmental studies.

Attachment to the father
12. What is the evidence of attachment to the father? What is the difference between paternal and maternal attachment, and what are possible causes of this difference?
13. How have changes in modern Western societies affected father and mother relations with their children?

Early maternal separation and day care
14. What are the effects of maternal separation and the effects of career mothers and day care on later social adjustment?

Disrupted attachment: domestic conflict and divorce
15. Summarize the effect of divorce on child adjustment, and indicate the possible role of domestic conflict as a causal agent.

When there is no attachment at all
16. Summarize the effects of maternal deprivation on young monkeys and humans. To what extent are the effects similar in monkeys and humans?

Are the effects of early social deprivation reversible?
17. Describe the circumstances under which it is possible to reverse effects of early maternal deprivation in monkeys and humans.
18. Evaluate the Freudian claims that early experience is a critical factor in social development, and that its effects are irreversible. Describe the general process of social development.

CHILDHOOD SOCIALIZATION

Cultural values and child rearing
19. What are some values that are socialized in all cultures? How do the characteristics of a culture or social class influence the values that are socialized?

Mechanisms of socialization
20. What is the reinforcement approach to socialization?
21. Describe social learning theory and observational learning. Indicate the way in which this process differs from instrumental learning.
22. Outline the cognitive (developmental) approach. Indicate how it views imitation.
23. Summarize the basic differences among the Freudian-reinforcement, social learning, and cognitive (developmental) approaches to socialization.

The first agents of socialization: the parents
24. Describe the autocratic, permissive, and authoritative-reciprocal patterns of child rearing. What are the characteristic behaviors of children raised under each of these approaches? Might there be culture differences?

The child's effect on the parents

25. Explain the interaction between the child's temperament and the parent's pattern of child rearing, and indicate how this interaction complicates the task of relating patterns of child rearing to the child's personality.

THE DEVELOPMENT OF MORALITY

Not doing wrong

26. What does it mean to internalize moral values? What is the role of punishment in internalization, and what is the principle of minimal sufficiency?

Doing good

27. What is empathy, and how does it function in supporting altruistic behavior? Is it sufficient?

Moral reasoning

28. Describe Kohlberg's stages of moral reasoning.
29. According to Gilligan, what is the fundamental sex difference in moral attitudes or reasoning? What is the evidence on this potential sex difference?
30. Discuss cultural differences in moral reasoning and moral behavior.
31. What is the relation between moral reasoning and moral behavior? To what extent do Kohlberg's stages represent the ability to describe principles, rather than guidance of behavior by these principles?

THE DEVELOPMENT OF SEX AND GENDER

32. Distinguish among gender roles, sexual orientation, and gender identity.

Gender roles

33. What is gender typing and what are gender role stereotypes?

Sex differences in gender roles

34. Review physical and physiological differences in male and female development, and in adults.
35. Consider common misinterpretations of the meaning of sex differences.
36. Evaluate the role of nature (biological-genetic) factors and experience in establishing gender differences in aggression. In what ways is aggression expressed differently in males and females?
37. Review the types of evidence suggesting a biological basis for gender differences in patterns of intellectual abilities, especially spatial abilities. What are suggested roles for testosterone and cultural factors?

Gender identity

38. Review the development of gender identity in the first six years of life.
39. Describe pseudohermaphrodites, and indicate what they tell us about gender identity. Describe the nature and justification for sex reassignment.
40. What are the effect of early exposure to sex hormones, or their absence, on gender identity and gender role?
41. Is there a critical period for gender identity determination? Include a discussion of the guevedoces syndrome.

Sexual orientation

42. Discuss the incidence of homosexuality at different historical times and in different cultures.
43. Describe the varieties of bisexuality.
44. What is the psychoanalytic account of homosexuality? What is the evidence on age of onset of homosexuality and the effects of early experience?
45. Discuss some possible biological causes of homosexuality, or, more generally, sexual orientation. Include consideration of genetic effects, brain differences, and effects of prenatal and adult hormone levels.
46. Discuss evidence about the possibility of changing sexual orientation.
47. Review arguments against considering homosexuality a psychological disorder.

DEVELOPMENT AFTER CHILDHOOD

48. Describe Erik Erikson's conception of human growth. What are his "eight ages of man"?

Adolescence

49. Discuss the particular problems of adolescence as a transition to adulthood in the United States and in other cultures. Is adolescence always turbulent?
50. In what sense is there an adolescent identity crisis?

Adulthood

51. Describe the mid-life transition.
52. Indicate how changes in American society have markedly altered the experience of old age.
53. Evaluate the extent to which Erikson's stages may be considered to be universal.

Programmed Exercises

ATTACHMENT

1. According to Freud, love for the mother derives from the fact that she is associated with the _____ of hunger, thirst, and pain. This is sometimes called the _____ theory.

    alleviation (reduction, decrease), cupboard

2. According to Bowlby's theory of attachment, fear of the _____ forms one basis of attachment. Another basis is a tendency to engage in _____ _____.

    unknown (unfamiliar) social interaction

3. According to Bowlby, proximity to an attachment figure provides _____ and _____, and separation from it leads to _____.

    comfort, security distress

4. Harlow's experiments with terry-cloth mothers suggest that in monkeys, the nutrient provided by the mother is less important for attachment than the _____ _____ that she provides.

    contact comfort

5. The formation of strong attachments by the young of a species to objects (typically the parent) encountered early in life is called _____.

imprinting

6. This type of attachment (imprinting) tends to occur during a special time, early in life, called the _____ _____.

sensitive (critical) period

7. There is evidence for sexual imprinting in animals and humans based on the _____ _____ _____ and detected by the sense of _____.

major histocompatibility complex (MHC), smell

PATTERNS OF ATTACHMENT

8. Specific recognition of the mother and distress at her departure, called _____ _____, occur at about the same time across cultures. This time is from _____ to_____ months of age.

separation anxiety, six, eight

9. In Ainsworth's "Strange Situations" measurements, a child who explores freely when the mother is present, shows some distress at her leaving, and greets her return with enthusiasm is called _____ _____.

securely attached

10. In Ainsworth's "Strange Situation" measurements, a child who doesn't explore even in the mother's presence, becomes intensely upset when she leaves, and shows ambivalence during reunion is called _____.

anxious (resistant)

11. In Ainsworth's "Strange Situation" measurements, a child who is distant and aloof toward his or her mother, shows little distress when she leaves, and ignores her when she returns is called _____.

avoidant

12. While attachment style is moderately consistent across childhood, it can be changed by events such as _____ or _____.

(2 of) divorce, marital problems, birth of a sibling, serious illness, unemployment

13. In examining the long-term effects of attachment, it is difficult to infer _____ from correlations.

causation

14. In the "Strange Situation," disappearance of the father also produces some _____.

distress

15. While mothers are preferred sources of care and comfort for most children, fathers are often the preferred _____.

playmate

16. The consequences of early separation from the mother, such as placement in _____ _____, have not been clearly established.

day care

17. Attachment may be disrupted by_____. This may have a causal effect, or the effect may be explained by _____ conflict.

divorce
domestic

18. Evidence indicates that the effects of maternal separation in humans are _____, and that maternal _____, with consequent day care, may not compromise social adjustment.

reversible
employment (careers)

19. Motherless monkeys and humans reared in some _____ show marked deficits in social performance.

institutions

20. Maternal deprivation has severe long-term effects in both monkeys and humans, but not if it occurs for no more than a few _____.

months

21. Studies using younger monkey therapists with motherless monkeys and studies on children put in nurturant environments after being in institutions indicate that many of the effects of maternal deprivation are _____ to some degree.

reversible

22. In general, early deprivation of parental contact, or poor parental contact, produces poorly adjusted children. But later interventions can partially _____ these effects, and high-_____ substitutes for parental contact, as in some day care, can reduce or eliminate the effects.

reverse, quality

CHILDHOOD SOCIALIZATION

23. _____ is the process by which the child acquires the patterns of thought and behavior that are characteristic of the society in which he or she is born.

Socialization

24. Both Freudian and reinforcement theories explain socialization in terms of the opposite influences of _____ and _____.

pain (punishment), pleasure (reward)

25. Researchers who believe that the basic Pavlovian and instrumental learning process must be supplemented to explain socialization are called _____ _____ theorists.

social learning

26. Such theorists (see previous question) add to the basic learning processes the mechanism of _____ learning.

observational

27. In order to perform an observed act, there must be something to _____ that is called the model.

imitate

28. The _____ approach to socialization emphasizes the role of understanding or competence in the socialization process.

cognitive

29. The cognitive approach recognizes the importance of _____, but emphasizes its cognitive complexity.

imitation

30. Important early Freudian features of development—such as _____ or_____ feeding, or harsh or relaxed _____ training—seem to have little effect on later development.

breast, bottle
toilet

31. The child-rearing style in which the parent controls the child strictly, and does not explain the justification for the governing rules to the child, is called the _____ pattern. The opposite extreme is called the _____ pattern. An intermediate approach, in which the parents exercise power, but also recognize the child's point of view, is called the _____-_____ pattern.

autocratic
permissive
authoritative-reciprocal

32. Of these patterns (see above), the one that leads to the best-adjusted children is the _____-_____ pattern.

authoritative-reciprocal

33. Some differences in the pattern of child rearing may result from differences in _____ in children, some of which are present at birth.

temperament

THE DEVELOPMENT OF MORALITY

34. We say a moral value is _____ when an individual avoids transgressions because he or she feels that they are wrong, and not because the individual is afraid of being punished.

internalized

35. According to the principle of _____ _____, internalization occurs best under mild social pressure.

minimal sufficiency

36. The _____-_____ child-rearing style is most compatible with the minimal sufficiency principle and successful internalization.

authoritative-reciprocal

37. A direct emotional response to another person's emotions is called _____.

empathy

38. Kohlberg has interviewed both adults and children in an attempt to describe the development of _____ _____.

moral reasoning

39. Kohlberg describes this development in a series of successive _____.

stages

40. According to Kohlberg, moral reasoning develops along a course in which right and wrong are defined by, first: _____ or _____; second: _____; and third: _____ _____ _____.

1. fear of punishment, desire for gain; 2. convention 3. internalized (or abstract) moral principles

41. According to Gilligan, in making moral decisions, men tend to emphasize _____, while women tend to be more influenced by _____.

justice, compassion (caring)

42. A criticism of Kohlberg's cognitive approach to moral behavior is that although it may be able to _____ moral rules, these rules may not actually guide _____. Furthermore, the Kohlberg results may measure one's _____ to describe moral rules rather than one's tendency to believe them.

describe, behavior
ability

THE DEVELOPMENT OF SEX AND GENDER

43. A definition of maleness or femaleness would have to consider three different "domains" or aspects. One is our inner sense of being male or female, called _____ _____.

gender identity

44. A second aspect (see above) is a group of behavior patterns that our culture deems appropriate for each sex, called _____ _____.

gender roles

45. A third aspect (see previous) is our choice of sexual partner, called _____ _____. — sexual orientation

46. The expectation that someone "labeled" as male will be more aggressive and more interested in things than people is an example of _____ _____. — gender typing

47. The idea that girl babies should be dressed in pink and boy babies should be dressed in blue is an example of a gender role _____. — stereotype

48. Characteristics of the female gender role stereotype in American society include (list 3) _____, _____, and _____. — submissiveness, interest in people, emotionality, gentleness

49. There are many physical and physiological differences between males and females, including the fact that their brains are sexually _____. — dimorphic

50. There seems to be a biological basis for some sex differences; for example, in the area of motivation, males tend to be more _____ than females. — aggressive

51. Although males exceed females in _____ aggression, females are at least the equals of males in _____ aggression. — physical / relational

52. There may also be a biological predisposition for male superiority in _____ ability. — spatial (spatial-mathematical)

53. There is evidence that higher _____ levels lead to better spatial abilities. — testosterone

54. By age five or six, children have a basic understanding of fundamental sex differences and their permanence, or _____ _____. — gender constancy

55. A child who has reproductive organs that are difficult to classify as male or female is called a _____. — pseudohermaphrodite

56. People who are genetically male but raised as female from infancy usually show normal female gender _____, but a tendency to a masculine gender _____. — identity, role

57. A female who sees herself as female and is sexually attracted to males but is aggressive and athletic could be said to have some characteristics of the male _____ _____. — gender role

58. Most sex reassignment studies indicate that if the reassignment is made within the first _____ years of life, the child will grow up with a normal gender _____, appropriate to his or her sex rearing. However, studies on the _____ syndrome suggest that successful sex reassignment can occur at _____. — two (three, four) / identity / guevedoces / puberty

59. The majority of men and women are _____ in that they seek sexual partners of the opposite sex. The minority who seek partners of the same sex are called _____. — heterosexual / homosexuals

60. The 1948 Kinsey study found the incidence of exclusive male homosexuality in the United States to be about _____ percent of all adult males. — 4

61. _____ experience erotic or romantic feelings toward both sexes. — Bisexuals

62. According to Freud, homosexuality follows from the _____ of the young child with the opposite-sex parent. — identification

63. Research indicates no major differences between homosexuals and heterosexuals in _____ experience. Overall, it seems homosexuals experience an attraction to the same sex _____ (before/after) having sexual experiences. — early / before

64. _____ studies suggest a genetic influence on homosexuality. — Twin

65. There is evidence for a difference in _____ structure between male heterosexuals and homosexuals. — brain (hypothalamus)

66. There is little evidence for differences in _____ hormone levels between homo- and heterosexuals, but it is possible that there is a difference in _____ hormone levels. — adult / prenatal

DEVELOPMENT AFTER CHILDHOOD

67. Erikson's "Eight Ages of Man" span the entire life cycle, each stage accompanied by a critical _____. — conflict (or crisis)

68. The stage of transition from childhood to adulthood is called _____.   adolescence

69. In some cultures, the transition to adulthood is marked clearly, with a ceremony or more extended set of
    activities called _____ _____.   initiation rites

70. In adolescence, the major conflict is described as a(n) _____ _____.   identity crisis

71. In the _____ _____, people of middle age reappraise what they have done with their   midlife transition
    lives, and may reevaluate their marriage and career.

72. In Erikson's scheme, although there are some important biological markers in growth past childhood,
    such as _____, the quality and duration of each stage is substantially influenced by   puberty (or menopause)
    _____.   culture

Self-Test

1. Bowlby's theory of attachment
   a. focuses on contact comfort.
   b. assumes that infants fear unfamiliar objects.
   c. assumes that infants enjoy social interaction.
   d. all of the above
   e. none of the above

2. Harlow's results, showing a preference by infant monkeys for a "terry-cloth mother" over a wire mother that provides food, argue
   a. in favor of Freud's view of attachment.
   b. in favor of Bowlby's view of attachment.
   c. that nutrition has no effect in producing attachment between infant and mother.
   d. a and b
   e. all of the above

3. Which of the following statements about imprinting is false?
   a. Imprinting depends on the fact that the parents will be the most salient objects around the offspring in the first part of life.
   b. Imprinting is based on experience.
   c. Animals may lose the capacity to imprint after a certain age.
   d. One would not expect to find imprinting in a "parasitic" species that is typically raised by adults of another species.
   e. none of the above

4. Proximity is to comfort as separation is to
   a. imprinting.
   b. critical periods.
   c. providing nutrients.
   d. distress.
   e. satisfaction.

5. A major difference between sexual imprinting (mediated by the major histocompatibility complex) and imprinting on parents, is that the former
   a. depends more on odor.
   b. has no sensitive period.
   c. involves learning what *not* to be attached/attracted to.
   d. a and b
   e. a and c

6. Attachment theorists suggest that a good parent-child relationship at an early age, as assessed in the Strange Situation, is a major determinant of later social emotional adjustment. However,
   a. later adjustment may result from the current relation between parent and child.
   b. the father also plays a major role in adjustment.
   c. adjustment involves the parent-child relation, not just the child.
   d. imprinting may be the cause of later adjustment.
   e. b and c

7. In Ainsworth's Strange Situation, infants show less distress at their father's than their mother's departure. Which of the following would be most likely to increase the infants' distress response to the father's disappearance?
   a. dress the father as a woman
   b. dress the father as a strange man
   c. find a father who had much more contact with his child
   d. find a child who had been severely punished by his or her mother
   e. feed the child bananas

8. The effects of maternal deprivation for more than a few months on subsequent behavior of monkeys and humans are
   a. severe, and similar.
   b. severe for humans, mild for monkeys.
   c. severe for monkeys, mild for humans.
   d. minimal.
   e. irreversible.

9. A conclusion that can be drawn from monkey and human maternal deprivation studies is that
   a. adequate nutrition is not sufficient to produce normal social behavior.
   b. behavior to peers is unaffected by maternal deprivation.
   c. imprinting does not have anything to do with later sexual or maternal behavior.
   d. the effects of maternal deprivation are very different in humans and monkeys.
   e. maternal deprivation effects are especially severe if the deprivation occurs in the first few months of life.

10. Monkeys deprived of mothers in about the first six months of life
    a. show a temporary depression in social behavior.
    b. are abnormal in social behavior, but will usually be successful parents.
    c. are permanently deficient in all domains of social behavior.
    d. show severe deficits in social behavior that are completely irreversible.
    e. show severe deficits in social behavior that can be at least partly cured by carefully designed "therapy."

11. Institutionalized human children and motherless monkeys show social abnormalities characterized by
    a. a "critical period" beginning at the time of birth and ending at about three months.
    b. social withdrawal.
    c. long-term effects that are irreversible.
    d. a and b
    e. all of the above

12. Freud claimed that early experience had (1) a critical and (2) an irreversible effect on social development. Results from research up to this time suggest that
    a. these two principles are basically correct.
    b. early experiences have important effects, but many are reversible.
    c. these two principles are totally incorrect.
    d. early experiences have some significant effects, and these effects are irreversible.
    e. none of the above

13. Both the Freudian approach and social learning or reinforcement theory agree that _____ is a major factor in socialization.
    a. imitation
    b. toilet training
    c. the child's understanding of the importance of older people
    d. gender identity
    e. none of the above

14. According to social learning theory, a critical aspect of socialization is
    a. observational learning.
    b. making models.
    c. Pavlovian conditioning.
    d. imprinting.
    e. none of the above

15. Wendy sees her big sister smoking a cigarette. A few hours later she sneaks over to a pack of cigarettes, takes one out, holds it with two fingers, and puts it into her mouth, looking as debonair as possible. Then she lights it up, and inhales her first breath, coughing and gagging. But she continues to smoke the whole cigarette. This performance presents problems for a simple reinforcement view of socialization because
    a. there is observational learning without immediate performance.
    b. there seems to be negative reinforcement (gagging) for smoking.

    c. there seems to be no basic biological reinforcement for her smoking.
    d. it is not clear why she would want to imitate her sister.
    e. all of the above

16. The cognitive approach emphasizes the difficulty of imitation. Complexities in the process of imitation include
    a. what the child sees is a reflection (180-degree rotation) of what he or she has to do.
    b. the child must determine what of many actions performed by the model is relevant.
    c. one has to explain why the child wants to imitate in the first place.
    d. a and b
    e. b and c

17. Ironically, children raised in the opposite autocratic and permissive styles share some common behavioral characteristics. Both types of children tend to
    a. be socially responsible.
    b. be more attached to their father.
    c. lack independence.
    d. be high in originality.
    e. a and c

18. Imagine that a study reports that most cranky five-year-olds had parents who closed the door to their infants' bedrooms at night so the baby wouldn't wake them. What might be possible explanations of this result?
    a. Isolating infants causes them to be cranky later in life.
    b. Cranky infants are more likely to be isolated by their parents.
    c. Parents who isolate their children in this way also do other things in child rearing that cause crankiness.
    d. Crankiness is inherited; cranky parents are more likely to be irritated by a crying child, and so are more likely to isolate it.
    e. all of the above

19. Authoritative-reciprocal rearing style is to optimal adjustment as mild social pressure is to _____.
    a. doing good
    b. not doing wrong
    c. maximum internalization
    d. permissive rearing style
    e. autocratic rearing style

20. Forced compliance is an ineffective way of producing attitude change. This finding is in accord with
    a. the permissive rearing style.
    b. the principle of minimal sufficiency.
    c. the principle of imitation.
    d. attachment theory.
    e. none of the above

21. The occurrence of unselfish helping behavior by A suggests that A
    a. experiences empathic distress.
    b. is at a high stage of moral reasoning.
    c. knows how to be helpful in the particular situation.
    d. a and b
    e. a and c

22. Consider the following three objections to making three reservations on different airlines at the same time for one person: A. It is against the unwritten rules of the airlines. B. It interferes with the access of others with no tangible gain to the party in question. C. It can be detected, and penalties can be assessed. According to Kohlberg, how would these three reasons be arranged in terms of the development of moral reasoning; indicate the earliest stage first.
    a. A, B, C
    b. B, C, A
    c. C, B, A
    d. B, A, C
    e. C, A, B

23. A person says that one shouldn't double park because it is against the law. This explanation is an example of
    a. fear of punishment.
    b. conventional morality.
    c. abstract principle.
    d. empathy.
    e. none of the above

24. According to Gilligan, moral reasoning in men is relatively more influenced by justice, while in women it is relatively more influenced by compassion. But men and women don't differ on scores on Kohlberg's tests of moral reasoning. Why?
    a. Kohlberg's tests value compassion as much as abstract principles.
    b. Compassion is more abstract than justice.
    c. The male-female difference has more to do with emphases than abilities.
    d. a and b
    e. a and c

25. Seymour speaks eloquently on the issue of equal rights for all races and religions but is actually quite racially prejudiced when he hires workers at his business. This illustrates
    a. the effects of reinforcement.
    b. the influence of the Freudian unconscious.
    c. the distinction between moral reasoning and moral conduct.
    d. the conflict between the social learning view and more traditional reinforcement explanations of moral behavior.
    e. egocentrism.

26. Which of the following is illustrative of gender role?
    a. thinking of oneself as a female
    b. attraction to the opposite sex
    c. submissiveness and emotionality in a female
    d. homosexual tendencies
    e. none of the above

27. From the clear demonstration of a biological (genetic) component to a gender difference, we can conclude
    a. that all of one gender is superior on this characteristic to all of the other gender.
    b. that the gender difference cannot be eliminated.
    c. that the gender difference is irreversible.
    d. b and c
    e. none of the above

28. In American culture, females have been shown to express emotion more readily than do males. This finding should be interpreted to mean
    a. that females are biologically more inclined to express emotions.
    b. that our society teaches females to be more expressive.
    c. that the average female is more emotionally expressive than the average male, but that there is a great deal of overlap.
    d. that gender typing is not a sufficient explanation of sex difference, and one must also consider gender identity.
    e. a and d

29. The idea that there is a biological factor contributing to sex differences in aggression is (or would be) supported by all but which of the following?
    a. In early humans, the stronger male was responsible for almost all hunting and fighting.
    b. These differences are seen in many cultures.
    c. Some of these differences are also seen in animals.
    d. Male hormone increases aggression.
    e. all of the above

30. Studies of early sex reassignment indicate that
    a. gender identity and role are completely shifted to the new sex.
    b. sexual orientation is usually not changed.
    c. gender identity fails to shift, but there are some effects of the original gender role.
    d. all three aspects of sex (role, gender, and orientation) show significant resistance to change.
    e. none of the above

31. The presence of hormones of the opposite "sex" in young children is most likely to influence their
    a. gender identity.
    b. gender role.
    c. sexual orientation.
    d. all of the above
    e. none of the above

32. Male homosexuality
    a. is not stigmatized in all cultures.
    b. was quite acceptable in ancient Greece.
    c. seems to be more common than female homosexuality.
    d. is almost always associated with male gender identity.
    e. all of the above

33. The psychoanalytic view suggests that male homosexuality may result when the child resolves fears aroused during the Oedipal conflict by identifying with the mother instead of the father. This theory would have difficulty explaining
    a. the absence of evidence for differences in the early experience of homosexuals and heterosexuals.
    b. the occurrence of a normal homosexual phase in adolescents in some cultures.
    c. the fact that, typically, male homosexuals have traditional male gender identity and roles.
    d. all of the above
    e. a and b

34. The data from sex reassignment and the fact that in most cases homosexuals report homosexual tendencies early in life both argue for
    a. the psychoanalytic approach.
    b. attachment to the mother at the time of the Oedipal crisis.
    c. a genetic basis for important aspects of sexual orientation and gender identity.
    d. all of the above
    e. none of the above

35. Evidence for a biological predisposition to homosexuality comes from all but one of the following. Which of the following is *not* evidence?
    a. twin studies
    b. male hormone level differences between male homosexual and heterosexual adults
    c. male hormone level differences between male homosexuals and heterosexuals prenatally
    d. differences in brain structure between male homosexuals and heterosexuals
    e. a and b

36. The transition from childhood to adolescence
    a. occurs at the same age in all cultures.
    b. is always a turbulent period.
    c. usually occurs at the onset of sexual maturity.
    d. all of the above
    e. none of the above

37. Initiation rites, retirement parties, and marriages have in common that they
    a. explicitly mark important life transitions.
    b. occur in virtually all cultures.
    c. are explicitly predicted by Erikson's scheme.
    d. match Freud's views of major life events.
    e. make for gradual transitions from one stage to another.

38. In some societies, children gradually assume adult responsibilities, and in some societies, old family members live in the home, taking care of grandchildren (or great-grandchildren) and giving advice. These traditions
    a. emphasize transitions from one stage of life to another.
    b. ease transition from one stage of life to another.
    c. emphasize the importance of biological factors in life history.
    d. prove the correctness of Erikson's stages.
    e. none of the above

Answer Key for Self-Test

1.	d	20.	b
2.	b	21.	e
3.	e	22.	e
4.	d	23.	b
5.	e	24.	c
6.	a	25.	c
7.	c	26.	c
8.	a	27.	e
9.	a	28.	c
10.	e	29.	e
11.	b	30.	e
12.	b	31.	b
13.	e	32.	e
14.	a	33.	d
15.	e	34.	e
16.	d	35.	b
17.	c	36.	c
18.	e	37.	a
19.	c	38.	b

Investigating Psychological Phenomena

SEX DIFFERENCES

Equipment: None
Number of participants: Twelve
Time per participant: Five minutes
Time for experimenter: Sixty minutes

Sex differences can be analyzed into three different categories:
1. Gender identity—thinking of oneself as male or female.
2. Sexual orientation—sex of desired sexual partners, leading to the heterosexual-homosexual distinction.
3. Gender role—behavior patterns or attitudes associated with one or the other sex.

The relative role of experience (nurture) and genes (nature) has been debated for each of these aspects of sex. But before such studies can be done definitively, we must be clear on the nature of the differences to be explained. This is more or less clear for gender identity and sexual orientation. But the major behavioral and attitudinal differences between the sexes are not obvious and surely differ across cultures.

This study is an attempt to define some reliable sex differences among American college students. We have developed seventeen questions that promise to reveal sex differences (we will use as a criterion a question that discriminates between the sexes with a response pattern in which there is at least a 25 percentage point difference between males and females).

First: Answer the questionnaire. *Do not read on until you finish it.*

Questionnaire on Sex Differences

> Sex: Male   Female
> (Circle one)

1. Would you be willing to kill a cockroach by slapping it with your hands?
   a) yes   b) no
2. What is Queen Anne's lace?
   a) flower   d) doily
   b) embroidery   e) spice
   c) perfume
3. How many times in the last twenty-four hours have you used the word "shit"?
   a) fewer than 5 times   b) 5 or more times
4. Can you sew well enough to make clothes?
   a) yes   b) no
5. Do you believe in sexual intercourse only after a spiritual love exists between you and your partner?
   a) yes   b) no
6. Do you walk around freely in the nude in a locker room?
   a) yes   b) no
7. How often do you cry?
   a) very often   d) very infrequently
   b) often   e) never
   c) only with good reason
8. At times I feel like smashing things.
   a) true   b) false
9. Do you know your chest measurement?
   a) yes   b) no
10. Can you change a tire easily?
    a) yes   b) no
11. I spend no more than one hour during an average school day playing the radio or listening to records.
    a) true   b) false
12. Would you prefer to be the dominant one in a relationship?
    a) yes   b) no
13. Do you think that you are overweight?
    a) yes   b) no
14. When you get depressed, does washing your hair make you feel better?
    a) yes   b) no
15. Do you sleep in the nude?
    a) yes   b) no
16. Which parent are you closest to?
    a) mother   b) father
17. I try to keep my room as neat as possible.
    a) true   b) false

These questions have been made up by faculty and students in introductory psychology courses. Each question has been "tested" with at least 100 undergraduate students in psychology courses. Therefore, we know how well these questions discriminate between college-age males and females (at least in 1971–1973, when the questions were tested). Of the seventeen questions, we know from past testing that five do not discriminate males from females. Try to guess, in advance, which questions would not discriminate. Then, check your guesses against the data presented on the final page of this study. *Guess before you read on.*

List questions that would not discriminate.

Note the type of successful questions in this questionnaire. Some relate to traditional male-female differences. Thus, males are more aggressive (Item 12 on dominance, but note no difference on Item 8—smashing things). Similarly males are less squeamish (Item 1, cockroach) and more restrained emotionally (Item 7, crying).

Other questions refer to knowledge or abilities that tend to go with gender in our society. This would include information about flowers (Item 2, Queen Anne's lace), sewing ability (Item 4), ability to change a tire (Item 10), and knowledge of body measurements (Item 9).

There are in addition some "miscellaneous" questions that tap into reliable differences (Item 5, attitudes to intercourse; Item 6, attitude to walking around nude in a locker room; Item 13, perception of fatness in self; Item 14, washing of hair as a response to depression; and Item 17, neatness).

Second, collaborate with at least one or two other students in the class so that you can collect enough data. Give the twelve copies of this questionnaire, located on pp. 167–177, to twelve undergraduates, six males and six females. (Try to get them to fill out the questionnaire when you give it to them; otherwise, you will find that you don't get a very high return rate.) Aim for a minimum of five completed questionnaires for each sex. Combine your results with the results of as many classmates as you can: it would be desirable to end up with at least fifteen students of each sex.

Third, tabulate your results (see p. 164) in the following way. For the "yes" or "no" questions (e.g., Item 1), add up the number of participants who answered "yes." Then calculate what percentage answered "yes." For the "true" or "false" questions (e.g., Item 8), record those who answer "true." For other items (e.g., Item 2), add up the number of participants whose answers are the same as those indicated in parentheses under "Item" (e.g., Item 1—flower).

Fourth, we have devised a "femaleness" score, by indicating the more common female response to each of the questions that discriminates sex. Compute such a score for each of your participants by counting one point for each of the following answers:

1.	no	9.	yes
2.	flower	10.	no
4.	yes	12.	no
5.	yes	13.	yes
6.	no	14.	yes
7.	very often, often, or with good reason	17.	yes

Indicate here the total number of participants of each sex from whom you have collected data:

Male _____   Female _____

	Your data (combined with classmates' data)				U. of Pa. Students[**]	
	Male		Female		Male	Female
Item	#	%	#	%	%	%
1. Killing cockroach	_____	_____	_____	_____	37	[*] 7
2. Queen Anne's lace (correct answer: flower)	_____	_____	_____	_____	50	[*]82
3. Using word "shit" (less than 5 times)	_____	_____	_____	_____	49	50
4. Sew clothes	_____	_____	_____	_____	4	[*]59
5. Intercourse only after spiritual love	_____	_____	_____	_____	30	[*]75
6. Nude in locker room	_____	_____	_____	_____	72	[*]31
7. Crying frequently (very often, often, or only with good reason)	_____	_____	_____	_____	22	[*]78
8. Feel like smashing things	_____	_____	_____	_____	75	70
9. Chest measurement	_____	_____	_____	_____	28	[*]78
10. Change tire	_____	_____	_____	_____	76	[*]13
11. Playing radio	_____	_____	_____	_____	41	42
12. Prefer dominance in relationship	_____	_____	_____	_____	72	[*]10
13. Overweight	_____	_____	_____	_____	17	[*]60
14. Washing hair when depressed	_____	_____	_____	_____	19	[*]53
15. Sleep in nude	_____	_____	_____	_____	39	44
16. Closest parent (mother)	_____	_____	_____	_____	61	72
17. Keep room neat	_____	_____	_____	_____	51	[*]77

[*] A male-female difference of a least 25 percentage points.

[**] Responses to items in the sex difference questionnaire by undergraduate introductory psychology students at the University of Pennsylvania (1971–1973). Percentages are based on responses from 70 to 270 males and from 88 to 292 females, depending on the item.

SCORES OF MALES AND FEMALES ON "FEMALENESS" SCORE

Plot the number of males and females with each score. Use solid lines for the males and broken lines for the females. The graph at the left contains data gathered from fifteen undergraduate males and seventeen undergraduate females in 1980. Plot your data on the blank graph on the right. How well does this score separate biological females from biological males? What percentage of females scores less than the highest male? How would you go about making a better behavioral discriminator of the sexes? (Note: We have avoided asking questions that might trivially distinguish males from females, such as Do you wash the hair on your chest? or Do you ever wear dresses?)

You may note some major differences between your data and the data we reported in 1971–1973. In fact, we tried the questionnaire on fifteen male and seventeen female undergraduate students in 1980 (the participants used in the femaleness ratings), and found some differences from our 1971–1973 study. The biggest effects were that male-female differences disappeared for Queen Anne's lace (Question 2), overweight (Question 13: Over half of the men as well as women thought they were overweight), and washing hair when depressed (Question 14: Practically no one in our recent sample answered "Yes" to that).

There are basically three ways to explain discrepancies (our recent data or your data) from the original large sample of 1971–1973.

1. A general change in society over the last decades. It would seem fair to say that female gender roles have become more like male gender roles in this period. Do your data show this trend for any items? (Note that this would mean that female scores could move closer to male scores, and *not* that male scores would move closer to female scores. Of course, it is also possible to argue that the roles are becoming less distinct, but not necessarily moving toward the traditional male role.)

2. A difference in the populations sampled. Students from different parts of the country or from institutions with different styles or emphases might differ markedly in gender roles. Do you think your student sample would be likely to be very different from University of Pennsylvania students? In what ways? Is this reflected in differences on any scores? (Note that the differences might not just appear as male-female differences, but as generally higher or lower levels of response. For example, one might expect a generally higher positive response on sewing or changing a tire in people from rural backgrounds.)

3. Sampling error. Some observed differences may simply result from the fact that all samples from the same population don't have precisely the same scores (see the statistical appendix to the textbook). With a small sample such as you have collected (as opposed to the large sample that we originally used), a wider variation from sample to sample would be expected. We would ordinarily use statistical methods to indicate how confident we would be that a difference between samples was not due to chance.

FURTHER ACTIVITIES

You might wish to try out some other questions that would relate gender identity to gender role. You could get a suggestion as to whether your questions were good discriminators with samples as low as twenty.

You can also try to use behavior rather than verbal responses to questionnaires. Can you think of obvious differences in such activities as manner of walking or eating, facial expressions, behavior in front of mirrors, motorcycle riding, and so on? Test your hypothesis by direct observation.

(If your instructor collects the data, fill out the report sheet in Appendix 2.)

Questionnaire on Sex Differences

Sex: Male   Female
(Circle one)

1. Would you be willing to kill a cockroach by slapping it with your hands?
   a) yes   b) no
2. What is Queen Anne's lace?
   a) flower   d) doily
   b) embroidery   e) spice
   c) perfume
3. How many times in the last twenty-four hours have you used the word "shit"?
   a) fewer than 5 times   b) 5 or more times
4. Can you sew well enough to make clothes?
   a) yes   b) no
5. Do you believe in sexual intercourse only after a spiritual love exists between you and your partner?
   a) yes   b) no
6. Do you walk around freely in the nude in a locker room?
   a) yes   b) no
7. How often do you cry?
   a) very often   d) very infrequently
   b) often   e) never
   c) only with good reason
8. At times I feel like smashing things.
   a) true   b) false
9. Do you know your chest measurement?
   a) yes   b) no
10. Can you change a tire easily?
    a) yes   b) no
11. I spend no more than one hour during an average school day playing the radio or listening to records.
    a) true   b) false
12. Would you prefer to be the dominant one in a relationship?
    a) yes   b) no
13. Do you think that you are overweight?
    a) yes   b) no
14. When you get depressed, does washing your hair make you feel better?
    a) yes   b) no
15. Do you sleep in the nude?
    a) yes   b) no
16. Which parent are you closest to?
    a) mother   b) father
17. I try to keep my room as neat as possible.
    a) true   b) false

Questionnaire on Sex Differences

Sex: Male   Female
(Circle one)

1. Would you be willing to kill a cockroach by slapping it with your hands?
   a) yes   b) no
2. What is Queen Anne's lace?
   a) flower   d) doily
   b) embroidery   e) spice
   c) perfume
3. How many times in the last twenty-four hours have you used the word "shit"?
   a) fewer than 5 times   b) 5 or more times
4. Can you sew well enough to make clothes?
   a) yes   b) no
5. Do you believe in sexual intercourse only after a spiritual love exists between you and your partner?
   a) yes   b) no
6. Do you walk around freely in the nude in a locker room?
   a) yes   b) no
7. How often do you cry?
   a) very often   d) very infrequently
   b) often   e) never
   c) only with good reason
8. At times I feel like smashing things.
   a) true   b) false
9. Do you know your chest measurement?
   a) yes   b) no
10. Can you change a tire easily?
    a) yes   b) no
11. I spend no more than one hour during an average school day playing the radio or listening to records.
    a) true   b) false
12. Would you prefer to be the dominant one in a relationship?
    a) yes   b) no
13. Do you think that you are overweight?
    a) yes   b) no
14. When you get depressed, does washing your hair make you feel better?
    a) yes   b) no
15. Do you sleep in the nude?
    a) yes   b) no
16. Which parent are you closest to?
    a) mother   b) father
17. I try to keep my room as neat as possible.
    a) true   b) false

Questionnaire on Sex Differences

> Sex: Male   Female
> (Circle one)

1. Would you be willing to kill a cockroach by slapping it with your hands?
   a) yes   b) no
2. What is Queen Anne's lace?
   a) flower   d) doily
   b) embroidery   e) spice
   c) perfume
3. How many times in the last twenty-four hours have you used the word "shit"?
   a) fewer than 5 times   b) 5 or more times
4. Can you sew well enough to make clothes?
   a) yes   b) no
5. Do you believe in sexual intercourse only after a spiritual love exists between you and your partner?
   a) yes   b) no
6. Do you walk around freely in the nude in a locker room?
   a) yes   b) no
7. How often do you cry?
   a) very often   d) very infrequently
   b) often   e) never
   c) only with good reason
8. At times I feel like smashing things.
   a) true   b) false
9. Do you know your chest measurement?
   a) yes   b) no
10. Can you change a tire easily?
    a) yes   b) no
11. I spend no more than one hour during an average school day playing the radio or listening to records.
    a) true   b) false
12. Would you prefer to be the dominant one in a relationship?
    a) yes   b) no
13. Do you think that you are overweight?
    a) yes   b) no
14. When you get depressed, does washing your hair make you feel better?
    a) yes   b) no
15. Do you sleep in the nude?
    a) yes   b) no
16. Which parent are you closest to?
    a) mother   b) father
17. I try to keep my room as neat as possible.
    a) true   b) false

Questionnaire on Sex Differences

> Sex: Male   Female
> (Circle one)

1. Would you be willing to kill a cockroach by slapping it with your hands?
   a) yes   b) no
2. What is Queen Anne's lace?
   a) flower   d) doily
   b) embroidery   e) spice
   c) perfume
3. How many times in the last twenty-four hours have you used the word "shit"?
   a) fewer than 5 times   b) 5 or more times
4. Can you sew well enough to make clothes?
   a) yes   b) no
5. Do you believe in sexual intercourse only after a spiritual love exists between you and your partner?
   a) yes   b) no
6. Do you walk around freely in the nude in a locker room?
   a) yes   b) no
7. How often do you cry?
   a) very often   d) very infrequently
   b) often   e) never
   c) only with good reason
8. At times I feel like smashing things.
   a) true   b) false
9. Do you know your chest measurement?
   a) yes   b) no
10. Can you change a tire easily?
    a) yes   b) no
11. I spend no more than one hour during an average school day playing the radio or listening to records.
    a) true   b) false
12. Would you prefer to be the dominant one in a relationship?
    a) yes   b) no
13. Do you think that you are overweight?
    a) yes   b) no
14. When you get depressed, does washing your hair make you feel better?
    a) yes   b) no
15. Do you sleep in the nude?
    a) yes   b) no
16. Which parent are you closest to?
    a) mother   b) father
17. I try to keep my room as neat as possible.
    a) true   b) false

Questionnaire on Sex Differences

Sex: Male   Female
(Circle one)

1. Would you be willing to kill a cockroach by slapping it with your hands?
    a) yes   b) no
2. What is Queen Anne's lace?
    a) flower   d) doily
    b) embroidery   e) spice
    c) perfume
3. How many times in the last twenty-four hours have you used the word "shit"?
    a) fewer than 5 times   b) 5 or more times
4. Can you sew well enough to make clothes?
    a) yes   b) no
5. Do you believe in sexual intercourse only after a spiritual love exists between you and your partner?
    a) yes   b) no
6. Do you walk around freely in the nude in a locker room?
    a) yes   b) no
7. How often do you cry?
    a) very often   d) very infrequently
    b) often   e) never
    c) only with good reason
8. At times I feel like smashing things.
    a) true   b) false
9. Do you know your chest measurement?
    a) yes   b) no
10. Can you change a tire easily?
    a) yes   b) no
11. I spend no more than one hour during an average school day playing the radio or listening to records.
    a) true   b) false
12. Would you prefer to be the dominant one in a relationship?
    a) yes   b) no
13. Do you think that you are overweight?
    a) yes   b) no
14. When you get depressed, does washing your hair make you feel better?
    a) yes   b) no
15. Do you sleep in the nude?
    a) yes   b) no
16. Which parent are you closest to?
    a) mother   b) father
17. I try to keep my room as neat as possible.
    a) true   b) false

Questionnaire on Sex Differences

Sex: Male   Female
(Circle one)

1. Would you be willing to kill a cockroach by slapping it with your hands?
    a) yes   b) no
2. What is Queen Anne's lace?
    a) flower   d) doily
    b) embroidery   e) spice
    c) perfume
3. How many times in the last twenty-four hours have you used the word "shit"?
    a) fewer than 5 times   b) 5 or more times
4. Can you sew well enough to make clothes?
    a) yes   b) no
5. Do you believe in sexual intercourse only after a spiritual love exists between you and your partner?
    a) yes   b) no
6. Do you walk around freely in the nude in a locker room?
    a) yes   b) no
7. How often do you cry?
    a) very often   d) very infrequently
    b) often   e) never
    c) only with good reason
8. At times I feel like smashing things.
    a) true   b) false
9. Do you know your chest measurement?
    a) yes   b) no
10. Can you change a tire easily?
    a) yes   b) no
11. I spend no more than one hour during an average school day playing the radio or listening to records.
    a) true   b) false
12. Would you prefer to be the dominant one in a relationship?
    a) yes   b) no
13. Do you think that you are overweight?
    a) yes   b) no
14. When you get depressed, does washing your hair make you feel better?
    a) yes   b) no
15. Do you sleep in the nude?
    a) yes   b) no
16. Which parent are you closest to?
    a) mother   b) father
17. I try to keep my room as neat as possible.
    a) true   b) false

Questionnaire on Sex Differences

Sex: Male   Female
(Circle one)

1. Would you be willing to kill a cockroach by slapping it with your hands?
   a) yes   b) no
2. What is Queen Anne's lace?
   a) flower   d) doily
   b) embroidery   e) spice
   c) perfume
3. How many times in the last twenty-four hours have you used the word "shit"?
   a) fewer than 5 times   b) 5 or more times
4. Can you sew well enough to make clothes?
   a) yes   b) no
5. Do you believe in sexual intercourse only after a spiritual love exists between you and your partner?
   a) yes   b) no
6. Do you walk around freely in the nude in a locker room?
   a) yes   b) no
7. How often do you cry?
   a) very often   d) very infrequently
   b) often   e) never
   c) only with good reason
8. At times I feel like smashing things.
   a) true   b) false
9. Do you know your chest measurement?
   a) yes   b) no
10. Can you change a tire easily?
    a) yes   b) no
11. I spend no more than one hour during an average school day playing the radio or listening to records.
    a) true   b) false
12. Would you prefer to be the dominant one in a relationship?
    a) yes   b) no
13. Do you think that you are overweight?
    a) yes   b) no
14. When you get depressed, does washing your hair make you feel better?
    a) yes   b) no
15. Do you sleep in the nude?
    a) yes   b) no
16. Which parent are you closest to?
    a) mother   b) father
17. I try to keep my room as neat as possible.
    a) true   b) false

Questionnaire on Sex Differences

Sex: Male   Female
(Circle one)

1. Would you be willing to kill a cockroach by slapping it with your hands?
   a) yes   b) no
2. What is Queen Anne's lace?
   a) flower   d) doily
   b) embroidery   e) spice
   c) perfume
3. How many times in the last twenty-four hours have you used the word "shit"?
   a) fewer than 5 times   b) 5 or more times
4. Can you sew well enough to make clothes?
   a) yes   b) no
5. Do you believe in sexual intercourse only after a spiritual love exists between you and your partner?
   a) yes   b) no
6. Do you walk around freely in the nude in a locker room?
   a) yes   b) no
7. How often do you cry?
   a) very often   d) very infrequently
   b) often   e) never
   c) only with good reason
8. At times I feel like smashing things.
   a) true   b) false
9. Do you know your chest measurement?
   a) yes   b) no
10. Can you change a tire easily?
    a) yes   b) no
11. I spend no more than one hour during an average school day playing the radio or listening to records.
    a) true   b) false
12. Would you prefer to be the dominant one in a relationship?
    a) yes   b) no
13. Do you think that you are overweight?
    a) yes   b) no
14. When you get depressed, does washing your hair make you feel better?
    a) yes   b) no
15. Do you sleep in the nude?
    a) yes   b) no
16. Which parent are you closest to?
    a) mother   b) father
17. I try to keep my room as neat as possible.
    a) true   b) false

Questionnaire on Sex Differences

> Sex: Male   Female
> (Circle one)

1. Would you be willing to kill a cockroach by slapping it with your hands?
   a) yes   b) no
2. What is Queen Anne's lace?
   a) flower   d) doily
   b) embroidery   e) spice
   c) perfume
3. How many times in the last twenty-four hours have you used the word "shit"?
   a) fewer than 5 times   b) 5 or more times
4. Can you sew well enough to make clothes?
   a) yes   b) no
5. Do you believe in sexual intercourse only after a spiritual love exists between you and your partner?
   a) yes   b) no
6. Do you walk around freely in the nude in a locker room?
   a) yes   b) no
7. How often do you cry?
   a) very often   d) very infrequently
   b) often   e) never
   c) only with good reason
8. At times I feel like smashing things.
   a) true   b) false
9. Do you know your chest measurement?
   a) yes   b) no
10. Can you change a tire easily?
    a) yes   b) no
11. I spend no more than one hour during an average school day playing the radio or listening to records.
    a) true   b) false
12. Would you prefer to be the dominant one in a relationship?
    a) yes   b) no
13. Do you think that you are overweight?
    a) yes   b) no
14. When you get depressed, does washing your hair make you feel better?
    a) yes   b) no
15. Do you sleep in the nude?
    a) yes   b) no
16. Which parent are you closest to?
    a) mother   b) father
17. I try to keep my room as neat as possible.
    a) true   b) false

Questionnaire on Sex Differences

> Sex: Male   Female
> (Circle one)

1. Would you be willing to kill a cockroach by slapping it with your hands?
   a) yes   b) no
2. What is Queen Anne's lace?
   a) flower   d) doily
   b) embroidery   e) spice
   c) perfume
3. How many times in the last twenty-four hours have you used the word "shit"?
   a) fewer than 5 times   b) 5 or more times
4. Can you sew well enough to make clothes?
   a) yes   b) no
5. Do you believe in sexual intercourse only after a spiritual love exists between you and your partner?
   a) yes   b) no
6. Do you walk around freely in the nude in a locker room?
   a) yes   b) no
7. How often do you cry?
   a) very often   d) very infrequently
   b) often   e) never
   c) only with good reason
8. At times I feel like smashing things.
   a) true   b) false
9. Do you know your chest measurement?
   a) yes   b) no
10. Can you change a tire easily?
    a) yes   b) no
11. I spend no more than one hour during an average school day playing the radio or listening to records.
    a) true   b) false
12. Would you prefer to be the dominant one in a relationship?
    a) yes   b) no
13. Do you think that you are overweight?
    a) yes   b) no
14. When you get depressed, does washing your hair make you feel better?
    a) yes   b) no
15. Do you sleep in the nude?
    a) yes   b) no
16. Which parent are you closest to?
    a) mother   b) father
17. I try to keep my room as neat as possible.
    a) true   b) false

Questionnaire on Sex Differences

> Sex: Male   Female
> (Circle one)

1. Would you be willing to kill a cockroach by slapping it with your hands?
   a) yes   b) no
2. What is Queen Anne's lace?
   a) flower   d) doily
   b) embroidery   e) spice
   c) perfume
3. How many times in the last twenty-four hours have you used the word "shit"?
   a) fewer than 5 times   b) 5 or more times
4. Can you sew well enough to make clothes?
   a) yes   b) no
5. Do you believe in sexual intercourse only after a spiritual love exists between you and your partner?
   a) yes   b) no
6. Do you walk around freely in the nude in a locker room?
   a) yes   b) no
7. How often do you cry?
   a) very often   d) very infrequently
   b) often   e) never
   c) only with good reason
8. At times I feel like smashing things.
   a) true   b) false
9. Do you know your chest measurement?
   a) yes   b) no
10. Can you change a tire easily?
    a) yes   b) no
11. I spend no more than one hour during an average school day playing the radio or listening to records.
    a) true   b) false
12. Would you prefer to be the dominant one in a relationship?
    a) yes   b) no
13. Do you think that you are overweight?
    a) yes   b) no
14. When you get depressed, does washing your hair make you feel better?
    a) yes   b) no
15. Do you sleep in the nude?
    a) yes   b) no
16. Which parent are you closest to?
    a) mother   b) father
17. I try to keep my room as neat as possible.
    a) true   b) false

Questionnaire on Sex Differences

> Sex: Male   Female
> (Circle one)

1. Would you be willing to kill a cockroach by slapping it with your hands?
   a) yes   b) no
2. What is Queen Anne's lace?
   a) flower   d) doily
   b) embroidery   e) spice
   c) perfume
3. How many times in the last twenty-four hours have you used the word "shit"?
   a) fewer than 5 times   b) 5 or more times
4. Can you sew well enough to make clothes?
   a) yes   b) no
5. Do you believe in sexual intercourse only after a spiritual love exists between you and your partner?
   a) yes   b) no
6. Do you walk around freely in the nude in a locker room?
   a) yes   b) no
7. How often do you cry?
   a) very often   d) very infrequently
   b) often   e) never
   c) only with good reason
8. At times I feel like smashing things.
   a) true   b) false
9. Do you know your chest measurement?
   a) yes   b) no
10. Can you change a tire easily?
    a) yes   b) no
11. I spend no more than one hour during an average school day playing the radio or listening to records.
    a) true   b) false
12. Would you prefer to be the dominant one in a relationship?
    a) yes   b) no
13. Do you think that you are overweight?
    a) yes   b) no
14. When you get depressed, does washing your hair make you feel better?
    a) yes   b) no
15. Do you sleep in the nude?
    a) yes   b) no
16. Which parent are you closest to?
    a) mother   b) father
17. I try to keep my room as neat as possible.
    a) true   b) false

CHAPTER 14

Intelligence: Its Nature and Measurement

Learning Objectives

1. Explain the relationship between the rise of mental testing and the structure of society.

MENTAL TESTS

2. Distinguish between achievement and aptitude tests.
3. Describe the purpose of intelligence, neuropsychological, and personality tests.

The study of variation
4. Define frequency distribution, mean, median, variability, and normal curve.
5. Explain the importance of variability in evolution.
6. Explain the meaning of correlation, and describe the correlation coefficient.

Evaluating mental tests
7. Explain the concept of reliability and different measures of reliability.
8. Explain predictive and construct validity and the procedure of standardization.

INTELLIGENCE TESTING

9. Indicate the difficulties in defining intelligence.

Measuring intelligence
10. Describe the origin of intelligence testing.
11. Discuss the strategy behind constructing intelligence tests.
12. Describe a few types of intelligence tests.
13. Review the reliability and validity of intelligence tests.
14. Discuss problems in inferring causation from the correlation of intelligence tests with school grades or job performance.

WHAT IS INTELLIGENCE? THE PSYCHOMETRIC APPROACH

15. What is the psychometric approach?

The structure of mental abilities
16. What is a correlation matrix and what is factor analysis?
17. Describe the evidence for "g."
18. Distinguish fluid and crystallized intelligence.
19. Speculate on the neural and psychological ability basis of "g."

20. Discuss the distinction between g as a statistical as opposed to a theoretical entity.

THE INFORMATION-PROCESSING APPROACH

Simple cognitive correlates
21. Indicate the logic and evidence behind the suggestion that simple cognitive processes, such as performance on simple or choice reaction time tasks or on a lexical decision task, may be components of intelligence.

Complex cognitive components
22. What are the limitations on explanations of intelligence in terms of simple cognitive processes, and how does involvement of complex cognitive processes solve some of these problems?
23. Explain how analogical reasoning has been analyzed into components, and the possible relation of analogical reasoning to intelligence.

The role of working memory and attention
24. Indicate how working memory and attention may be components of intelligence, and describe active span tasks.

Strategies and intellectual functioning
25. Discuss the role of strategies and strategies for using strategies in intelligence. Compare retarded people, normal children, and normal adults on this dimension.

WHAT IS INTELLIGENCE? BEYOND IQ

Practical intelligence
26. What are the limitations of intelligence tests, in terms of the range of mental abilities measured?
27. Distinguish among practical, analytic, and creative intelligence.
28. What is tacit knowledge, and how does it contribute to practical intelligence?

The notion of multiple intelligences
29. What are Gardner's multiple intelligences, and what is the evidence for them?
30. What are some problems with the multiple intelligence idea? Refer to interpretations of the savant syndrome.

The cultural context of intelligence
31. How might cultural differences produce different performances on questions on intelligence tests?

32. Explain and evaluate the statement: "We may be able to measure intelligence, but we don't really know what it is."

NATURE, NURTURE, AND INTELLIGENCE

Some political issues

33. Review the history of positions on genetic factors in intelligence differences related to racial groups or social class.

Genetic factors

34. Explain why it is not possible for any trait to be determined completely by the genotype.
35. Review basic terms in genetics (phenotype, genotype) and the relation between genotype and phenotype.
36. Describe the cause and genetic basis of phenylketonuria, and know how it illustrates the fact that inborn characteristics may be changeable.
37. Explain why studies of the similarity in intelligence of members of the same family cannot be used to distinguish between genetic and environmental factors.
38. Explain how twin and adoption studies can be used to make this same distinction. Summarize the results of these studies.

Environmental factors

39. Describe the effects of deprived or enriched environments on IQ scores.
40. What is the Flynn affect, and why is it evidence for environmental factors?

41. Summarize the evidence for and against genetic and environmental explanations of differences in intelligence (IQ) in American whites, from twin and adoption studies, from situations where major environmental differences were studied, and from trends over time in IQ scores.

Heritability

42. Explain the idea of heritability, why it only makes sense to use it to explain differences across individuals, and how it can change markedly over time.

Group differences in IQ

43. Describe the mean differences and overlap in IQ between African Americans and European Americans.
44. Explain how heritability within groups can differ markedly from heritability of the same trait between groups.
45. What is stereotype threat, and how is it demonstrated in the laboratory?
46. Evaluate each of the following explanations of the reported difference between average IQ scores of African Americans and European Americans:

   1. the difference doesn't exist
   2. unfairness of the tests and test situations for African Americans
   3. differences in environments between the groups
   4. genetic differences between the groups
   5. stereotype threat

Programmed Exercises

MENTAL TESTS

1. Tests of _____ measure what an individual can do now—his or her present knowledge and competence in a particular area.   achievement

2. Tests of _____ predict what an individual will be able to do later.   aptitude

3. _____ tests measure general aptitude.   Intelligence

4. _____ tests assess effects of brain injury.   Neuropsychological

5. _____ tests assess behavioral dispositions.   Personality

6. The frequency with which individual cases are distributed over different intervals of some measure is called a(n)_____ _____.   frequency distribution

7. The sum of all cases (observations) divided by the number of cases is called the _____.   mean

8. The case located in the "middle" of the frequency distribution, such that 50 percent of cases are smaller and 50 percent are larger, is called the _____.   median

9. The more that individual cases differ from one another, the higher the_____.   variability

10. Many physical and mental attributes show symmetrical bell-shaped frequency distributions, which are described as _____ _____.   normal curves

11. In evolution, _____ provides the basis on which natural selection works.   variability

12. Each point in the figure here represents the weight and IQ of one person. This display is called a
_____ _____.   scatter diagram

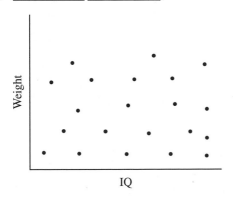

13. The _____ _____ is a statistic that describes the relations between two sets of measures.   correlation coefficient

14. The correlation between X and Y is –.70, that is, _____ = –.70. This means that the bigger X gets, the _____ Y gets, on the average. r

smaller

15. The consistency with which a test measures is called its _____.   reliability

16. This can be measured by calculating the _____ between scores on the same test at two different times, or _____-_____ reliability.   correlation

test-retest

17. Reliability can also be measured as the _____ between split halves of the same test.   correlation

18. The extent to which a test measures what it is supposed to measure is called its _____.   validity

19. The higher the positive correlation between the score on a driving test and the number of years driving without an accident, the greater the _____ _____ of this test.   predictive validity

20. In order to obtain _____ against which to evaluate a test score, the test is administered to a large number of people, called the _____ _____.   norms

standardization sample

INTELLIGENCE TESTING

21. The Wechsler Adult Intelligence Scale was in part a response to the emphasis on language in the Binet-Simon IQ tests. The Wechsler test has two parts, labeled _____ and _____.   performance, verbal

WHAT IS INTELLIGENCE? THE PSYCHOMETRIC APPROACH

22. In the _____ approach, the results of intelligence tests are studied and analyzed in an attempt to discover the structure of intelligence.   psychometric

23. The fact that scores from a variety of different intelligence tests, specific and general, are positively _____, led Spearman to introduce the factor of _____ _____.   correlated, general intelligence (g)

24. The technique used to try to extract the structure of intelligence from correlation matrices is called _____ _____.   factor analysis

25. It seems to be the case that as one ages, ability to deal with new problems or to respond rapidly, called _____ intelligence, tends to deteriorate, while the repertoire of basic cognitive skills, knowledge, and strategy, called _____ intelligence, remains intact.   fluid

crystallized

26. Since both _____ and _____ intelligence correlate with "g," it isn't clear whether "g" is a _____ theoretical concept, or just a _____ fact.   fluid, crystallized

unitary, statistical

THE INFORMATION-PROCESSING APPROACH

27. One possible cognitive correlate of intelligence is the speed with which a person responds to a stimulus, or _____ _____ _____.   simple reaction time

28. A better cognitive correlate is the speed of response when there are several responses and stimuli, or _____ _____ _____.   choice reaction time

29. Some have argued that basic abilities, such as the time it takes to access a word in long-term memory, or the _____ _____ task, are correlates of intelligence.   lexical decision

30. A problem such as "car is to garage as person is to _____ (house)" is an example of _____ _____. Some believe that such tasks can be analyzed into _____ _____.

    analogical reasoning
    cognitive components

31. Working memory and attention ability are measured in _____ _____ tasks.

    active span

32. Humans improve their performance by using flexible _____ to solve problems, learn, or remember.

    strategies

33. The idea that strategies are fundamental to intelligence is supported by the fact that retarded people do poorly in memory tasks that require _____.

    organization

WHAT IS INTELLIGENCE? BEYOND IQ

34. IQ tests measure principally _____ intelligence. But two other "types" of intelligence are _____ and_____.

    analytic
    practical, creative

35. _____ _____, derived from experience in specific domains, is an important part of practical intelligence.

    Tacit knowledge

36. Gardner's theory of _____ _____ holds that there are six different, _____ mental capacities.

    multiple intelligences,
    independent

37. Evidence for these independent capacities is the presence of retarded people who show outstanding performance on a task related to one of these activities. Such people have what is called the _____ syndrome.

    savant

38. People from different _____ may know different things, respond to tests differently, and make different interpretations of the meaning of the same question.

    cultures

NATURE, NURTURE, AND INTELLIGENCE

39. The observed characteristics of an organism are called its _____. But the underlying genetic blueprint is called the _____.

    phenotype
    genotype

40. At some level, any trait is a result of _____ between genotype and environment.

    interaction

41. A form of mental retardation that is caused by a single gene is _____.

    phenylketonuria (PKU)

42. The fact that PKU can be prevented by dietary interventions argues that heredity does not always imply _____.

    immutability
    (unadulterability,
    impossibility of change)

43. The fact that members of the same family have positively correlated intelligence and often share special abilities can be used as evidence for both _____ and _____ factors.

    hereditary (genetic),
    environmental

44. Two basic methods for estimating the role of inherited factors in intelligence or other traits are _____ and _____ studies.

    twin, adoption

45. The pattern of a higher correlation of IQ scores in _____ twin pairs than in _____ twin pairs, argue for a role for heredity in intelligence.

    identical, fraternal

46. The fact that the IQ of early-adopted children correlates more highly with the IQ of the biological as opposed to adoptive mother is evidence for _____ determinants of intelligence.

    genetic (biological,
    hereditary)

47. As adopted children grow older, the corelation of the IQ with their *biological* parents' IQ _____. This supports the importance of _____ factors in IQ.

    increases, genetic
    (hereditary)

48. The negative effects of poor environments on IQ are illustrated by data showing that the longer a child is in a deprived environment, the lower his or her IQ. This appears as a _____ correlation between IQ and age.

    negative

49. A number of studies have shown that _____ environments increase IQ.

    enriched

50. Evidence for environmental influence on IQ is the _____ effect, the gradual (few points/10 years) increase in worldwide mean IQ.

    Flynn

51. _____ is a concept that describes the percentage of the variation in a population that can be attributed to genetic factors. It does not apply to individuals.

Heritability

52. The difference between the mean IQs of European Americans and African Americans is _____ to_____ points.

10
15

53. Evidence from twin and adoption studies and other sources suggests that hereditability of IQ in American whites is about _____ .

.50

54. Some have argued that at least part of the European-American and African-American difference in average IQ scores can be attributed to the fact that the test was designed for the white middle class, that is to say, that the tests are not _____ fair. The evidence suggests that this _____ (is, is not) the case.

culture, is not

55. One cannot infer that if a trait has high heritability within two populations, then population differences will also be explainable as largely due to _____ .

heredity

56. A number of studies indicate that when differences in the environment of African Americans and European Americans during childhood are markedly reduced or equated, the African-American and European-American IQ difference is markedly _____ .

reduced (diminished)

57. As a result of _____ _____ , a group tends to perform in accordance with societal and its own expectations about ability in the relevant domain.

stereotype threat

58. Thus, in experiments, if African Americans are reminded of their race, their performance on IQ tests becomes _____ (lower, unchanged, higher).

lower

59. In a deomocratic society, individuals should be judged on their own _____ , and not on the basis of group _____ , or information about the _____ of a trait.

merits (abiltiy, performance), stereotypes, heritability

Self-Test

1. Mental testing is primarily an American product, dating from the beginning of this century. America was a natural place for mental testing because
   a. Americans embraced Freudian theory.
   b. the American idea that all people are created equal required mental tests to show up their subtle differences.
   c. of the high social and occupational mobility in America.
   d. reinforcement was a popular concept in America.
   e. Binet and Simon were Americans.

2. One group of five people gets the following scores on a mathematics test: 85, 85, 90, 95, 95. Another group gets these five scores: 80, 80, 90, 100, 100. Which of the following statements about these groups is true?
   a. Both have the same means and different variability.
   b. Both have the same means and the same variability.
   c. Both have different means and the same variability.
   d. Both have different means and variability.
   e. It is impossible to say which group has a bigger mean.

3. The accompanying diagram represents the hypothetical scores of individual participants on an IQ test and on a history achievement test. The correlation displayed would be closest to:
   a. +1.00
   b. + .50
   c. +0.00
   d. −.50
   e. −1.00

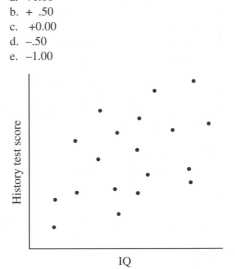

IQ

4. For which of the following pairs of variables would one expect to see a negative correlation?
   a. age and vocabulary
   b. height and visual acuity
   c. brain size and intelligence
   d. long-distance running ability and weight (among adults)
   e. social security number and intelligence (among adults)

5. If X is correlated with Y, then
   a. if we know X, we can guess better than chance at the value of Y.
   b. if we know Y, we can guess better than chance at the value of X.
   c. there is no variability in X and Y.
   d. X causes Y.
   e. a and b

6. A hypothetical air force needs a test to help select people for training as pilots. There is no adequate theory of the acquisition of flying skills, but air force investigators discover that the speed with which one can tap with the third finger correlates +.80 with good performance in flying school. On the basis of this observation, one could say that the test had
   a. high reliability.
   b. high predictive validity.
   c. a frequency distribution.
   d. good standardization.
   e. no mean validity.

7. An appropriate standardization sample for a test of artistic talent in elementary school children would be
   a. elementary school children.
   b. elementary school children fifty years ago.
   c. older children who have selected art as a career.
   d. elementary school children with artistic talent.
   e. representative adults from the same country.

8. Intelligence testers face special problems because
   a. intelligence changes with age.
   b. intelligence tests are not reliable.
   c. all questions require prior knowledge, so that past experience determines the test score.
   d. there is no agreement about what intelligence is.
   e. it is difficult to calculate a score.

9. A student takes the same test of reaction time at 10:00 A.M. on two consecutive days. She gets very different scores on these two days. If this was true of many other test takers, it would suggest that this test is not
   a. valid.
   b. standardized.
   c. reliable.
   d. none of the above
   e. all of the above

10. A test measuring participants' abilities to do jigsaw puzzles would be a _____ test.
    a. performance
    b. verbal
    c. fluid
    d. unreliable
    e. c and d

11. A psychometrician examines a verbal and a spatial intelligence test and finds that the scores on these two tests correlate +.38. From this he might conclude that
    a. performance on both tests is partly determined by "g" but mostly by specific factors.
    b. these tests measure very different things, and there is no "g" component here.
    c. both of these tests are excellent measures of "g."
    d. these results constitute proof that "g" is only a statistical fact.
    e. none of the above

12. Gordon is really pretty ignorant, but he has a way of seeing relationships among ideas and figures and quickly comes up with new ways of doing things. He could be described as
    a. high in "g."
    b. high in fluid, low in crystallized intelligence.
    c. evidence for one-factor theories of intelligence.
    d. someone who would do well on vocabulary tests.
    e. someone who would do poorly on Raven's progressive matrices.

13. Studies indicate that certain types of "intelligence" decline with age in adulthood and others do not. A type that improves or at least holds its own through most of adulthood is
    a. "g."
    b. fluid intelligence.
    c. crystallized intelligence.
    d. both b and c
    e. none of the above

14. Some believe that one can understand intelligence and predict IQs by analyzing intelligence into simple cognitive components, such as
    a. strategies of problem solving.
    b. reaction times.
    c. retrieval time of items from memory.
    d. all of the above
    e. b and c

15. Complex intelligence-related tasks, like analogical reasoning, can be broken down into components, such as identifying the common attribute of the first members of each pair in an analogy. This general route to the understanding of intelligence is called
    a. the simple cognitive component approach.
    b. the information-processing approach.
    c. the psychometric approach.
    d. the analogical approach.
    e. none of the above

16. In memory tasks, in contrast to retarded children, normal children or adults
    a. organize more.
    b. use strategies more.
    c. rehearse more.
    d. b and c
    e. all of the above

17. Cindy has to memorize the names of all of the American vice-presidents and the dates that they held office. She considers doing it in alphabetical order, but then decides it would be better to try to remember them in chronological order. She is demonstrating
    a. analogical reasoning.
    b. enhanced working attention.
    c. a psychometric effect.
    d. simple cognitive components.
    e. strategy for using strategies.

18. The hypothetical finding that artists and composers are generally poor at solving everyday problems, like organizing a group of people on a task, would argue in favor of
    a. the distinction between practical and analytic intelligence.
    b. the importance of strategies in intelligence.
    c. the importance of working memory in only some kinds of intelligence.
    d. the separation of practical and creative intelligence.
    e. b and d

19. One occasionally finds people who are highly intelligent but terrible at spatial relations. This fact supports
    a. Gardner's theory of multiple intelligence.
    b. practical intelligence.
    c. the concept of "g."
    d. the importance of working memory.
    e. a and b

20. One might expect that individuals in non-Western cultures might be superior to Westerners at some types of intelligence and inferior in others. One major variable might be the degree of literacy. Which of the following features of "intelligence," broadly conceived, might be relatively unaffected or even improved by an inability to read?
    a. spatial relations
    b. ability to memorize and repeat long narratives
    c. ability to solve analogy problems
    d. a and b
    e. b and c

21. The observation that people on the political left tend to think of intelligence as more under environmental control, while those on the right tend to think of it as more under genetic control suggests that
    a. one must distinguish between within- and between-group differences.
    b. the study of genetic and environmental influences on intelligence is inherently political.
    c. sociopolitical factors influence judgments about the role of heredity in intelligence.
    d. there is no way to study scientifically the issue of the role of heredity and environment in intelligence.
    e. c and d

22. In the period between the two World Wars, IQ scores of Eastern European immigrant groups improved the longer the immigrants were in the United States. This finding
    a. justified a policy of excluding Eastern Europeans from immigrating to the United States.
    b. raises questions about U.S. immigration policy in the period between the wars.
    c. demonstrates that intelligence is primarily under genetic control.

    d. demonstrates that intelligence is primarily under environmental control.
    e. none of the above

23. Jane and Phyllis have brown eyes. All of Jane's relatives have brown eyes. Phyllis's father has brown eyes, but her mother has blue eyes (brown eye color is dominant). From this information, we can guess that Jane and Phyllis have
    a. the same genotype and phenotype.
    b. the same genotype and different phenotypes.
    c. different genotypes and the same phenotype.
    d. different genotypes and phenotypes.
    e. c or d

24. A genetic female who is exposed to androgens as a fetus and develops male genitals, and a person with phenylketonuria who is treated at birth and develops no symptoms, both illustrate that
    a. inborn, genetically determined traits can be changed by environmental factors.
    b. sex-linked traits can occur in both sex and intelligence
    c. behavior is inherited.
    d. environmental factors, under some circumstances, have no influence on behavior.
    e. behavior is related to sex chromosomes.

25. The clustering of specific talents (e.g., music in the Bach family) or high intelligence in particular families, *across generations,* argues for
    a. a significant role for genetics in these abilities.
    b. a significant role for environment in these abilities.
    c. polygenic inheritance.
    d. a and b
    e. a and/or b

26. If, counter to the results actually found, it was reported that fraternal and identical twins had the same high correlation in intelligence and that this was *higher* than the correlation between other siblings (e.g., brothers and sisters of different ages), one would be most justified in concluding that
    a. the higher correlation in twins was due to environmental factors.
    b. the higher correlation in twins was due to genetic factors.
    c. fraternal twins are more closely related, genetically, than are other siblings.
    d. a and c
    e. b and c

27. Environmentalists explain the significant correlation between the IQ of adopted children and their biological parents in terms of *selective placement* of these children in adopted homes. (Children with higher-IQ biological parents are placed with higher-IQ adoptive parents.) This argument, however, is strongly weakened by
    a. the studies on identical twins.
    b. the fact that the IQ of adopted children correlates more highly with biological than adoptive parents.
    c. the fact that there is a positive correlation between the IQ of adopted children and their adoptive parents.
    d. b and c
    e. none of the above

28. All but one of these findings supports or is consistent with the idea of a hereditary component in intelligence differences. Which finding does *not* support such a view?
    a. higher IQ correlation in identical than fraternal twins
    b. higher IQ correlation between adoptive children and their biological parents than between these same children and their adoptive parents
    c. higher IQ correlation between siblings than between half-siblings (sharing only one parent)
    d. higher correlations in IQ between fraternal twins than between other siblings
    e. the stability of IQ over decades

29. On the whole, the IQs of biological parents giving children up for adoption are below those of adopting parents (since the latter are screened by agencies). The observation that whatever the correlation between IQ of adopted child and biological parent, the actual IQ of such adopted children tends to be considerably higher than that of the biological parents, is evidence for
    a. hereditary effects.
    b. environmental effects.
    c. a and b
    d. a heritability value.
    e. polygenic inheritance.

30. If intelligence (IQ scores) in a particular group showed a heritability of 1.0, this would mean that
    a. existing environments have no effects on intelligence.
    b. while existing environments have no effects on intelligence, presently nonexistent environments might have significant effects.
    c. genetic factors account for most of the variation in IQ in this particular group.
    d. genetic factors account for all of the variation in IQ in this particular group.
    e. none of the above

31. Which of the following traits would you expect to show the *lowest* heritability?
    a. eye color
    b. height
    c. length of hair
    d. visual acuity
    e. running speed

32. Many have argued that IQ tests and the circumstances under which they are given favor European Americans over African Americans. All but one of the following reported findings argue against this view—that is, all but one indicate that the tests are reasonably culture fair. Select the one reported finding that does *not* argue in favor of the culture fairness of tests or test situations.
    a. The African-American and European-American IQ difference remains about the same when the African-American version of the test is translated into African-American English.
    b. The African-American and European-American difference is about the same for verbal tests and for the abstract Raven's progressive matrices.

    c. The African-American and European-American difference remains about the same whether the tester is African American or European American.
    d. The African-American and European-American difference remains about the same for tests of verbal and tests of spatial intelligence.
    e. The African-American and European-American difference decreases in the children in families that have children of both races through adoption.

33. Assume two breeds of cattle: in both, size differences within the breed are completely determined by genes (heritability: 1.0). Assume further that one breed is found in New Zealand and the other in central Africa and that the New Zealand breed averages about 10 percent bigger than the African breed. What inferences can be made about the origin of this difference between breeds?
    a. It is certainly due to heredity.
    b. It is certainly due to environment.
    c. The heritability of the population difference would be at least .50.
    d. The heritability of the population difference would be at least .10.
    e. No certain inference can be drawn about the original breed differences from this information.

34. Following is a fair summary of studies on environmental matching or change, as applied to the African-American and European-American IQ difference:
    a. There is generally a decreased African-American and European-American IQ difference when attempts are made to equalize environments in the comparison groups, and an improvement in African-American IQs when the environment is improved.
    b. Appropriate manipulation of environments, to provide African Americans with the full advantages of the European-American environment, leads to elimination of the African-American and European-American IQ difference.
    c. There is very little effect of environmental change or equalization on African-American IQ or African-American and European-American differences.
    d. a and b
    e. none of the above

35. Which of the following statements about IQ differences is true?
    a. Within American whites, environment accounts for most IQ differences.
    b. There is no logical relation between with- and between-group heritability.
    c. Twin studies show no effect of environment on IQ.
    d. African-American versus white IQ differences disappear completely when attempts are made to equalize environment.
    e. none of the above

36. What would be educationally and scientifically *appropriate* sociopolitical responses to a *hypothetical* proof that a fair proportion of the difference in IQ scores between African

Americans and European Americans could be assigned to hereditary factors?
a. curtailment of early enrichment programs
b. establishment of racial quotas
c. inclusion of race as an important factor in determining the ability of applicants for jobs involving intelligence
d. cessation of affirmative action programs
e. none of the above

Answer Key for Self-Test

1.	c	19.	a
2.	a	20.	d
3.	b	21.	c
4.	d	22.	b
5.	e	23.	c
6.	b	24.	a
7.	a	25.	e
8.	d	26.	a
9.	c	27.	b
10.	a	28.	d
11.	a	29.	b
12.	b	30.	d
13.	c	31.	c
14.	e	32.	e
15.	b	33.	e
16.	e	34.	a
17.	e	35.	b
18.	d	36.	e

Investigating Psychological Phenomena

"INTELLIGENCE TESTS"

Equipment: None
Number of participants: One (yourself)
Time per participant: Thirty minutes
Time for experimenter: Thirty minutes

This is an experiment that will help you to understand the construction of intelligence tests. The procedure that you will go through will be like the procedure that might be used in the development of an intelligence test. The main concern is that you understand how a distribution of test scores is generated, and how an individual score is interpreted with respect to that distribution.

For this purpose, rather than making up a so-called intelligence test, we have chosen to try out a measure of a characteristic that is rarely tested: one's knowledge of foods and cooking. In this case, one begins with some idea of the ability or knowledge base that one is trying to assess. Questions or tasks are constructed that seem to measure these. Then, pilot tests, like those we will give you, are distributed to a representative sample of the population for which the tests are intended. In your case, your class might serve as a sample of college undergraduates. Of course, students differ in schools and in different regions, so this would not be anything like the random sample we would actually need were this a real test.

The results of the test are examined. Typically, most of the questions which all participants get right or all get wrong are discarded, because such questions do not help to measure *differences* among people in the abilities under study. Then, some sort of retest study is done to make sure the test is reliable, and a validity study is done to assure that the test measures what it is supposed to measure.

We will deal only with one phase of test construction here. We have made up a test that has never been used by psychologists before. (It is certainly not clear why a food knowledge test would be of interest to anyone in the real world.) We ask each of you to take the test. It is brief. The food knowledge test is in the format of a written test, with unlimited time. It is, of course, "closed book." Fill it out in a quiet place. Then score your answers, using the list of correct answers at the end of this section.

FOOD KNOWLEDGE TEST

Sex _____

Listed below are five countries
    Italy (southern Italy)
    China
    India
    Mexico
    Germany

Each of the following food items (1–14) is particularly characteristic of the cuisines of one of the five countries listed above. Write the name of the appropriate cuisine (country) beside the food item.

1. potatoes _____
2. corn _____
3. sesame oil _____
4. olive oil _____
5. soy sauce _____
6. cumin (two possible answers) _____
7. oregano _____

8. curry _____
9. chili pepper (two possible answers) _____
10. liverwurst _____
11. turmeric _____
12. yogurt _____
13. bean curd _____
14. ghee _____

Write in the name of the country associated with each of the following items:

15. sushi _____
16. lasagna _____
17. taco _____
18. paella _____
19. moussaka _____
20. goulash _____
21. sukiyaki _____

22. mousse _____
23. sate (pron: sa′ • tāy) _____
24. biryani _____
25. mole (pron: mo′ • lăy) _____
26. trifle _____
27. kim chee _____
28. champagne _____

29. What is the primary ingredient used in raising (leavening) bread? _____
30. What is yogurt made from? _____
31. What are raisins made from? _____
32. What is meringue made of? _____
33. What animal does bacon come from? _____
34. What are prunes made from? _____
35. What type of fish is lox made from? _____
36. What vegetable are pickles usually made from? _____
37. What fruit is wine usually made from? _____
38. What is sauerkraut made from? _____
39. What are chitterlings made from? _____
40. What does caviar come from? _____
41. What is marzipan made from? _____
42. What is the primary ingredient in guacamole? _____

Indicated below are five common cooking methods:

    baking
    sautéing or pan frying
    braising
    boiling
    broiling

For each dish or food below, indicate by writing in the correct term from those listed above the primary cooking method used.

43. chicken soup _____
44. bread _____
45. scrambled eggs _____
46. pot roast _____
47. shish-kebab _____

48. spaghetti _____
49. soufflé _____
50. hash-brown potatoes _____
51. collard greens _____

TEST RESULTS AND "IQ" CALCULATIONS

The food knowledge test was taken by 153 University of Pennsylvania undergraduates in the introductory psychology course and twenty-one students in a University of Michigan class in learning and memory. The results were

    Mean score: 35.9 for 174 participants
    Standard deviation: 5.03
    Range of scores: 22 (lowest) to 47 (highest)

Females do slightly better than males on this test (mean female score: 36.8; mean male score: 35.1).

CALCULATION OF A "CULINARY IQ"

As we will discuss below, much more work would have to be done with this test before it could actually be used in a meaningful way. For the sake of illustrating the scaling of psychological tests, we will use the data generated by undergraduates taking this test to develop a "deviation" scale like that used in IQ tests. You can then calculate your "culinary IQ."

The basic principle behind scaling of tests is the deviation score. Like a percentile score, it expresses where a particular score stands with respect to all of the other scores. The distribution of scores for tests usually falls into what is called a normal distribution. An ideal normal distribution is drawn in the next column. Normal distributions are typically described by their mean value and their standard deviation, a measure of the spread or variability of the curve (see the statistical appendix to the text). In a normal distribution, 68 percent of all observations fall within one standard deviation of the mean, and 96 percent of all observations fall within two standard deviations of the mean (see the accompanying figure). Test scores are measured in units of deviation from the mean. For all IQ type tests, 100 is set as the mean

value and 15 point as the standard deviation. Thus, an IQ of 115 corresponds to the score one standard deviation above the mean (85 to one standard deviation below); 130 corresponds to a score of two standard deviations above the mean (70 to two below), and so on. (An IQ of 105 would then be one-third of a standard deviation above the mean.) In percentile terms, an IQ of 130 would be at the 98th percentile, and an IQ of 85 would be at the 16th percentile (see figure).

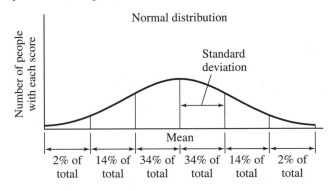

Applying these ideas to our test, the mean score (35.9) on the food test would be assigned a scaled score of 100. Subtracting one standard deviation (5.03) from this score, we get approximately 31, a score that would be assigned a scaled score of 85 (one standard deviation below the mean corresponds to 15 scaled points). We have performed the appropriate arithmetic for the food test, and provided the raw score (your actual score) and scaled score (converted to deviation units) equivalents in the table on the next page. Because the standard deviation for the food knowledge scores is almost exactly 5, each additional point on the test is worth one-fifth of a standard deviation, or 3 "IQ" points.

FOOD TEST

Raw score (your actual score)	Scaled score ("IQ")
18	46
19	49
20	52
21	55
22	58
23	61
24	64
25	67
26	70
27	73
28	76
29	79
30	82
31	85
32	88
33	91
34	94
35	97
36	100
37	103
38	106
39	109
40	112
41	115
42	118
43	121
44	124
45	127
46	130
47	133
48	136
49	139
50	142
51	145

The next step in developing a test would be to improve the first version. For example, in the food knowledge test, there are a number of useless items: these are items that do not contribute to the measurement of differences in people. For three items (number 16—lasagna, 37—wine, and 44—bread), all 174 participants got the right answer. Because of this, these items would normally be discarded. Three additional items were missed by less than 2% of the participants and might also be discarded. There were no questions that were missed by all participants. The "hardest" question was about the country of origin of sate (Number 23—Indonesia), and 8.6% of participants were correct on this item.

We would also eliminate any questions that turned out to be ambiguous. In this test, for example, some of the "What is X made from?" questions need clarification. Thus, for Number 39—chitterlings (chitlings), some people answered "pig," and others said "intestine." We scored both as correct, but should have been more specific in the question. Similarly, for Number 30—what is yogurt made from?—we intended that milk be the correct answer. But bacteria cultures are also components of yogurt. We should have asked, "What is the primary ingredient in yogurt?" (See if you can find some other ambiguous questions.) Finally, we would examine the correlation of correctness on each question with the total score on the test. Are there any items that don't seem to be measuring the same sort of thing as the rest of the test? (See the experiment on personality testing in the next chapter.) Such items might or might not be included but would at least be reexamined. Along these same lines, one might look at any questions that the top performers on the test all missed. Often such items are badly worded, or perhaps even in error. For the food test, there was no single item missed by all of the six top scorers.

Having streamlined the test, we would then use some type of test-retest procedure to determine reliability. (Will the same person score about the same on two different occasions?) The reliability measures would be complicated, since one would expect improvement on the second time through.

We would then perform some sort of validity test. Is the test measuring what it is supposed to measure? If the food knowledge test is supposed to predict likely candidates for success in a cooking school, does it actually do so?

Finally, having satisfied ourselves that we had a reliable and valid test, we would then administer the test to a large sample of people (hundreds to thousands of people) randomly selected from the population of people for whom the test was designed (e.g., high school seniors, all adults).

Ask yourself whether you believe the food test is meaningful. How would you validate it? What might it be used for? What would it correlate with?

FURTHER ACTIVITIES

Sketch out what you think would be an appropriate test for use in predicting success in a particular profession: for example, fighter pilot, baseball player, or architect. Then ask yourself how you would validate the test.

Answer Sheet

Score one point for each correct answer
(Listed next to each answer are the percentages correct out of 174 students.)

1. potatoes–Germany (83.9%)
2. corn–Mexico (78.7%)
3. sesame oil–China (28.2%)
4. olive oil–Italy (93.7%)
5. soy sauce–China (97.7%)
6. cumin–India or Mexico (78.2%)
7. oregano–Italy (90.2%)
8. curry–India (73.0%)
9. chili–India or Mexico (90.2%)
10. liverwurst–Germany (97.7%)
11. turmeric–India (48.3%)
12. yogurt–India (44.8%)
13. bean curd–China (44.8%)
14. ghee–India (60.3%)
15. sushi–Japan (55.7%)
16. lasagna–Italy (100%)
17. taco–Mexico (98.8%)
18. paella–Spain (40.2%)
19. moussaka–Greece (43.7%)
20. goulash–Hungary (73.6%)
21. sukiyaki–Japan (76.4%)
22. mousse–France (74.7%)
23. sate–Indonesia (8.6%)
24. biryani–India (37.4%)
25. mole–Mexico (14.9%)
26. trifle–England (47.7%)

27. kim chee–Korea (13.2%)
28. champagne–France (80.4%)
29. bread–yeast (97.1%)
30. yogurt–milk (88.5%)
31. raisins–grapes (96.0%)
32. meringue–egg white (74.1%)
33. bacon–pig (99.9%)
34. prunes–plums (77.0%)
35. lox–salmon (66.7%)
36. pickle–cucumber (97.7%)
37. wine–grapes (100%)
38. sauerkraut–cabbage (89.1%)
39. chitterlings–pig or intestine (29.3%)
40. caviar–fish eggs (91.4%)
41. marzipan–almond or sugar (31.0%)
42. guacamole–avocado (48.3%)
43. chicken soup–boiling (96%)
44. bread–baking (100%)
45. scrambled eggs–pan frying (98.3%)
46. pot roast–braising (46.6%)
47. shish kebab–broiling (57.5%)
48. spaghetti–boiling (97.7%)
49. soufflé–baking (83.3%)
50. hash-brown potatoes–pan fry or sautéing (96.6%)
51. collard greens–boiling (55.7%)

CHAPTER 15

Personality

Learning Objectives

METHODS OF ASSESSMENT

Structured personality tests
1. Understand the construction and the use of the Minnesota Multiphasic Personality Inventory (MMPI). What is the importance of score profiles and validity scales?
2. Why isn't the MMPI a commonly used test for normal people? What is one of the tests that is used instead?
3. Be familiar with predictive test validity.

Projective personality tests
4. What is the rationale for projective techniques? Describe some of the projective procedures.
5. What scoring categories are used in the interpretation of Rorschach inkblots, and what general rules are employed?
6. Be familiar with the difference in interpretation between the Rorschach and the Thematic Apperception Test (TAT) in regard to perceived content.
7. How is TAT interpretation impressionistic and global?
8. Summarize the issues and arguments in assessing the validity of the TAT and the Rorschach.
9. Of what value are projective tests in a clinical setting?

THE TRAIT APPROACH

10. What is the trait approach to personality?

The search for the right taxonomy of traits
11. What was Cattell's approach to developing a taxonomy of personality traits? What modifications of Cattell's analysis have been suggested and why? What are the "Big Five?"
12. Discuss Eysenck's taxonomy of neuroticism and extroversion-introversion. What personality differences are encompassed by this scheme? Do the two dimensions of Eysenck's classification apply to other cultures?
13. What are the arguments about the validity of a factor-analytic approach to personality?

Traits versus situation: the consistency controversy
14. What is the importance of cross-situational consistency, or inconsistency, in the argument against trait theory? How does this affect the validity of personality tests?
15. What is situationism, and how is it related to personality?
16. Review the evidence on the consistency of behavior across time and situations. Describe how superficially different expressions of a personality trait contribute to apparent behavioral inconsistency. What are the implications for trait theory?
17. Realize that consistency may be a personality trait. How does Snyder's self-monitoring scale measure behavioral consistency in different situations?

Traits and biology
18. What is the definition of the word *temperament*, and what effect does it have on a person's personality?
19. Be prepared to discuss how evidence from the study of twins contributes to our understanding of personality traits.
20. Discuss the evidence that personality traits may have a genetic component. What traits are most heritable?
21. What studies have been done to show that between-family differences in environment are not important in determining personality traits? In what situations do between-family environmental differences matter?
22. How can differences within a family environment affect its children?
23. Describe how Eysenck compares introverts and extroverts in terms of their arousal systems. What research on sensation seeking has Zuckerman done that correlates with Eysenck's findings?
24. What is known about the involvement of neurotransmitter systems in sensation seeking?

THE SOCIAL-COGNITIVE APPROACH

Behavioral roots of social-cognitive theories
25. What is the central assumption of the social-cognitive approach to personality?
26. What is Bandura's view of personality? How is it based on expectations of outcomes?

Cognitive roots of social-cognitive theories

27. How does the concept of "construals" govern Kelly's view of personality?

28. Be prepared to describe the five cognitive qualities that Mischel has proposed as dimensions on which people differ.

Control

29. What is the evidence that control over a situation is a cognitive dimension that people seek? What is the role of self-efficacy?

Explanatory style

30. How does explanatory style have an effect on such conditions as depression?

Self-control

31. Describe how self-control is seen as an important personality characteristic. Discuss evidence that children can be influenced in their self-control depending on physical and cognitive factors.

32. How is the early ability to delay gratification related to late coping ability?

Traits and social-cognitive theory

33. How are social cognitive theorists different from trait theorists?

THE PSYCHODYNAMIC APPROACH: FREUD AND PSYCHOANALYSIS

The origins of psychoanalytic thought

34. How did Freud view the process of taming the savage, selfish human nature?

35. Compare Freud's and Hobbes's views of human nature and its taming.

36. Describe the symptoms of hysteria. Why is this illness termed a psychogenic disorder?

37. What is free association?

38. What are repression and resistance?

39. What is psychoanalysis, and how does it relate to the understanding of psychopathology and the normal personality?

Unconscious conflict

40. Understand the nature of unconscious conflict and its effect on behavior.

41. What are the three divisions of personality according to Freud? How do these develop, and how do they interact to give rise to conflict and resolution?

42. Be cognizant of the major role of anxiety as a motivating force in keeping unacceptable urges repressed.

43. How does repression affect the realm of thought in addition to that of behavior?

44. What are defense mechanisms?

45. Describe the specific defense mechanisms (repression, displacement, reaction formation, rationalization, and projection).

Unconscious conflict and the formation of personality

46. What are Freud's stages of psychosexual development, and what is the relation of these stages to sexuality and pleasure?

47. What are oral and anal characters, and how, according to Freud, do they relate to psychosexual development?

48. In Freud's view, the Oedipus complex is the most important aspect of psychosexual development. Discuss this theory with respect to both sexes.

49. What are Freud's views of the psychosexual development of girls?

Windows into the unconscious

50. What is the psychopathology of everyday life, and how does it reflect underlying motives and conflicts?

51. Explain Freud's theory of dreams. Understand the motive of wish fulfillment and its symbolic expression, and the difference between the latent and the manifest dream context.

52. How have Freud's theories been used to interpret myths?

A critical look at Freudian theory

53. Recount some of the methodological and conceptual difficulties with Freud's theories.

54. Explain how interpretations of clinical evidence cast doubt on the testability of Freud's theory.

55. Review the evidence on the validity of the existence of anal and oral characters, and their link to childhood toilet training and feeding experiences.

56. How universal is the Oedipus complex? Summarize evidence from the Trobriand Islanders.

57. What evidence militates against Freud's emphasis on wish fulfillment in the interpretation of dreams?

58. Summarize the issues and arguments against and in favor of Freud's reliance on repression in dealing with unconscious conflicts. What is the evidence for repression, as opposed to a less "motivation-oriented" view of retrieval blocking?

59. What are Freud's major contributions to our understanding of human nature and to the field of psychology? What are the shortcomings of his approach and theory?

THE PSYCHODYNAMIC APPROACH: PERSONALITY DIFFERENCES

60. What are dominant patterns of defense, and what, according to the neo-Freudians, is their role in accounts of personality differences?

Patterns of conflict

61. Describe Karen Horney's views about patterns of neurotic conflict, including basic anxiety and vicious circles.

Coping patterns and mental health

62. What are coping mechanisms and how do they relate to Freudian defense mechanisms?

63. What do longitudinal studies tell us about the importance and consistency of coping patterns? What child-rearing patterns are associated with the best adjustment?

64. What is the relationship between coping mechanisms and Freud's view of the unconscious?

THE HUMANISTIC APPROACH

The major features of the humanistic movement

65. Describe the basic differences between the humanistic approach and all of the other approaches to personality that have been discussed.

66. Explain the hierarchy of needs, including self-actualization.

67. What is the self-concept according to Rogers?

Evaluating the humanistic approach

68. What are the empirical and conceptual problems of the humanistic approach?

Positive psychology

69. Describe the contributions and weaknesses of positive psychology.

THE SOCIOCULTURAL PERSPECTIVE

70. What are the basic sociocultural criticisms of the four personality theories already discussed?

Personality and human diversity

71. Indicate important cultural variations in basic personality features and gender roles.

Human sameness

72. Describe the cross-cultural method. What does it indicate about common themes in personality across cultures?

73. How do child-rearing practices differ by type of culture and socioeconomic class?

Collectivism and individualism

74. Describe collectivism and individualism. What are the different features of each? Indicate countries or areas of the world in which one or the other is dominant.

75. Review evidence indicating a different concept of self in some Asian cultures.

76. What are the consequences for current personality theory if the sociocultural critique is basically correct?

Programmed Exercises

1. The way that people differ in their desires, feelings, and in the expression of these feelings reflects _____ differences.

   personality

2. In the comic dramas that they performed, the Greeks and Romans thought of the different characters and their respective personalities as _____. The same characterizations were used in literature.

   types

METHODS OF ASSESSMENT

3. The first personality test was administered to army recruits and was meant to identify _____ disturbed soldiers.

   emotionally

4. The MMPI is termed multiphasic because it assesses a number of personality _____ simultaneously.

   traits

5. The MMPI is scored by comparing the scores on each of the ten major scales to those of the relevant _____ group.

   criterion

6. In interpreting scores on the MMPI, it is necessary to examine score _____, which present the scores on all the scales in graphic form.

   profiles

7. In order to detect whether or not participants are lying on test items or are trying to fake mental illness, the MMPI uses two _____ scales made up of items no one can honestly deny and of items so bizarre that few would endorse them.

   validity

8. It is difficult to interpret MMPI scores for _____ participants since the criterion groups used to define the scales were composed of _____ patients.

   normal
   psychiatric

9. One test that was developed using normal participants as the criterion group is the _____ _____ Inventory.

   California
   Psychological

10. The degree to which a test can predict real-world events is called its _____ validity.

    predictive

11. The use of _____ techniques was, in part, a protest against the highly structured nature of paper-and-pencil techniques.

    projective

12. One of the concerns of the originators of projective techniques was that a participant could _____ to _____ when taking a test like the MMPI.

    lie, himself (or herself)

13. The idea behind projective techniques is that in structuring unstructured materials, a participant will reveal deeper facets of his or her _____.

    personality

14. These categories used to score the Rorschach are the portion of the blot used, the _____ of the blot (such as color), and the _____ of the response.

    attribute
    content

15. In interpretations of Rorschach inkblots, use of the entire blot is said to reflect _____ thinking, while attention to details suggests _____.

    integrative (or conceptual)
    compulsiveness (or rigidity)

16. Rorschach responses using the white space as the foreground are interpreted as indicating _____, and those dominated by color suggest _____.

    rebelliousness
    (negativism), emotionality
    (or impulsivity)

17. The _____ _____ Test in which people tell stories about pictures, places a major emphasis on content.

Thematic Apperception (TAT)

18. _____ scoring of a Rorschach test appears to yield the best reliability.

Numerical

THE TRAIT APPROACH

19. The major task in determining the proper traits with which to classify personality is the development of a(n) _____ of personality difference.

taxonomy

20. Cattell's taxonomy of personality is based on _____, using factor analysis to discover how _____ words are interrelated.

language
trait

21. The "big five" dimensions of personality are _____, _____, _____, _____, and _____ to experience.

extroversion, neuroticism, agreeableness, conscientiousness, openness

22. Eysenck's classification scheme included _____ versus _____ stability and _____ versus _____.

neurotism, emotional
extroversion, introversion

23. Some psychologists have argued that the reason many tests are not good predictors of future behavior is that most people exhibit a lack of _____-_____ consistency.

cross-situational

24. _____ maintains that human behavior is largely determined by the situation a person is in rather than by the actual, internal traits of the person.

Situationism

25. When a person's reactions cannot be predicted adequately solely by situation or by individual differences, the critical factor may be the _____ of these two.

interaction

26. Since cross-situational consistency varies from person to person, it may be regarded as a _____ that only some individuals possess.

trait

27. One can assess how much a person adjusts his or her behavior to fit a situation by having that person complete the _____-_____ scale developed by Mark Snyder.

self-monitoring

28. It is believed that a person's _____ ultimately originates from his or her biological makeup.

temperament

29. Identical twins show more similarity of personality than do fraternal twins, indicating some _____ of personality traits.

heritability

30. It appears that _____-_____ differences in environment are unimportant in determining personality traits such as emotionality and extroversion. However, _____-_____ differences in environment (e.g., birth order and spacing, friends) faced by children in the same family will cause variations in personality between those siblings.

between-family
within-family

31. According to Eysenck, introversion corresponds to a high level of _____; thus, persons of this type are actually more awake than others.

arousal

32. Zuckerman's research on _____ _____ indicates that those people with a higher arousal system (introverts) have higher levels of the neurotransmitter _____ in their brains. Those with lower levels of this neurotransmitter are underaroused, and as a result are likely to seek thrills and take risks.

sensation seeking
norepinephrine

THE SOCIAL-COGNITIVE APPROACH

33. The social-cognitive approach, in contrast to _____ theory, emphasizes the importance of external forces in the determination of behavior.

trait

34. This view is a direct descendent of _____, an important movement early in this century that emphasized the role of learning, and de-emphasized the role of cognition.

behaviorism

35. Kelly called people's interpretation of a situation their _____ of it.

construal

36. Patients who are allowed the opportunity to _____ their environments are more active and feel better than patients who are not.

control

37. A person's _____ style indicates the extent to which he or she designates the causes of events as internal versus external.

explanatory

38. The _____-_____ questionnaire asks people about situations and what might have caused them. — attributional-style

39. Measures of _____ of gratification in young children show that this characteristic predicts behavior in adolescence. — delay

40. Social learning theorists can still be regarded as behaviorists in that they continue to stress the importance of the _____ in determining behavior, and they insist on the importance of _____ in acquiring various personality characteristics. — situation / learning

THE PSYCHODYNAMIC APPROACH: FREUD AND PSYCHOANALYSIS

41. According to the psychodynamic approach, understanding of human personality requires understanding of _____ psychological forces. — hidden (deep, unconscious)

42. The psychodynamic approach derives from _____, founded by Freud. — psychoanalysis

43. Freud has been compared to Hobbes, since both men believed that humans are basically _____. But Freud differs from Hobbes in that Freud believed that the taming force of society is _____ in each of us. — savage (selfish) / internalized

44. A patient exhibiting partial blindness, glove anesthesia, or memory gaps would likely be diagnosed as suffering from _____. — hysteria

45. If organic damage is ruled out in the above case (Question 44), then the origin of the symptoms must be _____. — psychogenic

46. Freud and Breuer believed that crucial memories that were repressed could be recovered through _____ _____. — free association

47. Although Freud began by using hypnosis, he later abandoned this approach, since not all of his patients were hypnotizable and since the same crucial memories could be obtained in the waking state through the method of _____ _____. — free association

48. A patient is told to say anything that enters his mind, yet struggles at times to change the subject or forgets what he was going to say. This subject is demonstrating _____ to the recovery of _____ memories. — resistance / repressed

49. According to Freud's view, forbidden impulses are never completely controlled, despite repressive measures by the individual. This division of the individual (one part fighting another) gives rise to _____ conflicts. — unconscious

50. Freud investigated unconscious conflicts: their origin, effects, and removal. He termed his exploration and interpretation of these phenomena _____. — psychoanalysis

51. The three distinct systems of the human personality, according to Freud, are the _____, the _____, and the _____. — id / ego, superego

52. The most primitive portion of personality is the _____. It operates according to the _____ principle, with the single goal being immediate satisfaction. — id / pleasure

53. As id-dominated infants encounter the frustration of the real world, they develop a(n) _____, which attempts to satisfy the urges of the id according to a _____ principle. — ego / reality

54. The young child refrains from doing wrong only through fear of being caught. Because the rules and admonitions of the parents are _____, however, the _____ develops and suppresses forbidden behavior even in the absence of negative consequences. — internalized, superego

55. _____ is the crucial factor in the mechanism underlying repression. Internal thoughts and feelings that evoke this state must be escaped and are thus suppressed. — Anxiety

56. Repression can be regarded as the primary, initial mechanism of _____. — defense

57. When fear of retaliation blocks the expression of anger, a person may vent his or her feelings on another recipient, resulting in _____ aggression. — displaced

58. When a repressed thought or wish manifests itself as a diametrically opposite wish or thought, it is a result of _____ _____. — reaction formation

59. _____ is another defense mechanism in which a repressed thought is reinterpreted in more acceptable terms. — Rationalization

60. Cognitive reorganization also plays a role in _____, in which forbidden urges are attributed to others rather than to the self.

projection

61. Freud's theory of _____ development postulates biologically determined stages of emotional and sexual development.

psychosexual

62. Seeking pleasure through the mouth is characteristic of the _____ stage, which yields to the _____ stage as toilet training begins. The _____ stage focuses on the stimulation of the genitals, while interest in the satisfaction of others as well as one's own satisfaction characterizes the _____ stage.

oral
anal, phallic

genital

63. A lingering attachment to pleasure-seeking of the type characteristic of a particular psychosexual stage is called a _____. This can sometimes be manifested in terms of opposite characteristics, mediated by the mechanism of _____ _____.

fixation
reaction formation

64. The _____ character recapitulates the pleasure and passive dependency of nursing at his or her mother's breast.

oral

65. The _____ character is typically excessively clean, obstinate, and stingy.

anal

66. The family drama from which grows the boy's internalized morality and identification with the same-sex parent is called the _____ _____.

Oedipus complex

67. According to the theory of the Oedipus complex, the _____ urges of the boy at ages three and four are directed toward the _____ as the source of previous gratification during the oral stage.

phallic (sexual)
mother

68. The young boy's _____ of the father leads to hostility and a fear of retaliation by the father.

jealousy

69. The renunciation of genital pleasures endures from about five to twelve years of age and is termed the _____ _____.

latency period

70. The weakest aspect of Freud's theory of psychosexual development concerns the young girl's progression of sexual interests. This is called the _____ complex. Specifically, why does the little girl desire the father instead of the mother? Freud attributed this transference of attachment to _____ _____.

Electra

penis envy

71. Through his study of dreams, Freud came to the conclusion that dreams are an attempt at _____ _____. Desires suppressed by considerations of reality and by the superego emerge and are gratified in dreams.

wish fulfillment

72. The _____ dream content is the disguised expression of the _____ dream content, which represents hidden and forbidden wishes.

manifest, latent

73. Some psychoanalytic practitioners acknowledge the importance of social factors in development. These psychologists are termed _____-_____.

neo-Freudians

74. Studies of Trobriand Islanders have suggested that the hostility of the young boy toward the father in our culture may be a product, not of sexual _____, but rather of the father's role as an _____.

jealousy, authoritatian

75. The same urge may sometimes be disguised and sometimes be expressed openly in a dream. Freud's assertion that the manifest dream represents a _____ disguise cannot handle this facet.

defensive

76. Despite the criticisms of Freud's theoretical proposals, his conception of _____ conflict and the sheer scope of his ideas rank him as one of the giants of psychology.

internal (or unconscious)

THE PSYCHODYNAMIC APPROACH: PERSONALITY DIFFERENCES

77. The neo-Freudians describe personality differences in terms of dominant _____ of defenses.

patterns

78. According to Horney, neurotic conflicts are caused by basic _____, an all-pervading feeling of being alone and helpless in a hostile world. These conflicts may harden into personality characteristics, because the conflicts create a self-perpetuating vicious circle.

anxiety

79. _____ _____ by Vaillant indicate consistency in coping patterns, with more _____ coping patterns in older and better-adjusted people.

Longitudinal studies
mature

80. The results of Block's longitudinal studies suggest that poorly adjusted adults had parents who were either _____ or _____.

overinvolved, rejecting
(dictatorial, indifferent)

THE HUMANISTIC APPROACH

81. In contrast to the behavioristic and psychoanalytic approaches to personality, _____   humanistic
    psychologists describe themselves as having a positive view of human motivation.

82. Maslow places the needs referred to above at the bottom of the _____ _____   hierarchy of
    _____. At the top is the desire to realize oneself to the fullest, called _____-   needs, self-
    _____.   actualization

83. According to humanistic psychologists, a basic part of one's subjective experience is one's sense of
    oneself as both agent and object, called one's _____-_____.   self-concept

84. According to Rogers, a solid sense of self-worth depends on a child's feeling of _____   unconditional
    _____ _____.   positive regard

85. According to Maslow, satisfaction of lower-level needs and a reasonable sense of self-worth allow for
    the expression of the desire for _____-_____.   self-actualization

86. One problem with the humanistic approach is that there is little _____ to support the assertions   evidence
    made about human nature.

87. Another problem is that, in an important sense, people like Adolf Hitler fit the description of being
    _____-_____.   self-actualized

88. The emerging field of _____ psychology is concerned with defining well-being and how it is   positive
    attained.

89. The phenomenon of _____ refers to the fact that humans grow accustomed to a static   adaptation
    stimulus.

THE SOCIOCULTURAL PERSPECTIVE

90. Evidence from _____ _____ suggests wide differences across cultures in   cultural anthropology
    _____ and gender _____.   personality, roles

91. The _____-_____ method compares different cultures, with the aim of extracting   cross-cultural
    common themes.

92. Cultures in which there is more emphasis on relations with and obligations to the family and
    community are called _____, as opposed to _____.   collectivist, individualist

93. Cultures differ in their concept of _____, referring to the origins of personal actions.   agency

Self-Test

1. Personality differences include
   a. intelligence, ability, and insight.
   b. desires, feelings, and modes of expressing these needs
      and feelings.
   c. none of the above
   d. both a and b

2. The first personality and intelligence tests were similar in
   that both were _____.
   a. invalid
   b. unstructured
   c. projective
   d. structured

3. An appropriate criterion group for a diagnostic test of
   paranoid schizophrenics would be
   a. normal individuals.
   b. paranoid schizophrenics.
   c. a mixture of a and b.
   d. No criterion group is needed when the test is used as a
      diagnostic tool.

4. The California Psychological Inventory (CPI) uses
   _____ criterion groups.
   a. no
   b. pathological
   c. normal
   d. random

5. When a test measuring a trait can foretell some real-world
   behavior, it is said to have
   a. face validity.
   b. incremental validity.
   c. predictive validity.
   d. unproven validity.

6. Projective techniques differ from tests such as the MMPI and
   CPI in that the former are more
   a. valid.
   b. quantitative.
   c. unstructured.
   d. all of the above
   e. none of the above

7. In structuring unstructured materials, it is expected that a participant
   a. will reveal his or her capacity for conceptual organization.
   b. will be relieved of objective test anxiety and will thus perform most effectively and honestly.
   c. will project his or her deepest feelings and conflicts upon the ambiguous stimulus.
   d. will be distracted from the psychologist's analysis of the participant's voice tone, body language, and gestures in responding.

8. Two examples of projective tests are
   a. the MMPI and the Thematic Apperception Test (TAT).
   b. the Rorschach and the TAT.
   c. the Rorschach and the CPI.
   d. all of the above

9. Three categories used in interpreting the Rorschach are
   a. location, negativism, color.
   b. content, attributes, and portion of the blotches.
   c. content, impulsiveness, use of white space.
   d. impulsiveness, happiness, truth value.

10. Which of the following is *not* an established piece of evidence against the validity of the Rorschach inkblot test?
    a. the failure of highly intelligent people to use the entire inkblot more than others do
    b. the lack of relation between Rorschach indices and psychiatric diagnosis
    c. the failure of artists to demonstrate a preponderance of human movement in their perceptions
    d. the fact that individual Rorschach indices show little relation to external validity criteria

11. While the TAT has not fared well as a diagnostic tool, it has shown some promise as an indicator of
    a. intelligence.
    b. hidden fears.
    c. imagination.
    d. none of the above

12. A taxonomy is a
    a. classification system.
    b. rating scale used in psychiatric diagnosis.
    c. type of mental disorder.
    d. class of stable personality traits.

13. Eysenck has formed a hypothesis that all personalities can be classified on the basis of a rating on two independent scales. They are _____ and _____.
    a. paranoid, schizophrenic
    b. shy-outgoing, anxiety
    c. neuroticism, extroversion-introversion
    d. psychopathic deviance, extroversion-introversion

14. Which of the following constitute problems for Eysenck's theory of personality based on neuroticism and introversion-extroversion?
    a. the dependence of factor analysis on the existing data set
    b. the possible nonindependence of these two dimensions
    c. the observation that introverted people tend to be more easily aroused than are extroverts
    d. a and b

15. Walter Mischel found that children are _____ in their behavior in different circumstances. He saw this as

evidence _____ the validity of personality traits.
    a. consistent, for
    b. inconsistent, for
    c. consistent, against
    d. inconsistent, against

16. The concept of situationism is most opposite to the assumptions underlying
    a. the MMPI and CPI.
    b. the Rorschach and TAT.
    c. all of the above
    d. none of the above

17. Situationists
    a. deny the existence of individual differences.
    b. believe that social roles play a large role in the situations people get into.
    c. claim that situations themselves are the best predictors of people's reactions.
    d. believe that past situational experiences determine personality traits.

18. In defense of trait theory, one could cite evidence that behavior is
    a. consistent over time.
    b. consistent across situations.
    c. both of the above
    d. none of the above

19. Tom is a gregarious and talkative person. He enjoys organizing activities with friends. Which of the following choices would not illustrate a reciprocal relation between Tom and the situation?
    a. Tom gives a party for his birthday.
    b. Tom's job is social director for a large singles' group in his city.
    c. On many evenings Tom likes to sit in his room and videotape sports events.
    d. Tom shares a house with five other guys from his college graduating class.

20. High self-monitors are
    a. not adaptable.
    b. inconsistent.
    c. consistent.
    d. rigid.

21. Which of the following traits is heritable?
    a. neuroticism
    b. agreeableness
    c. extroversion
    d. all of the above
    e. a and c

22. Studies have found that behaviors such as television watching or tendencies toward divorce are partially heritable. These findings need to be interpreted cautiously, however, because
    a. television watching is so recent that it couldn't have influenced genetic makeup.
    b. divorce, although hundreds of years old, is still too recent to have influenced genetic makeup.
    c. other, more fundamental traits such as extroversion may be the ones that are heritable, and they reveal themselves in such behaviors as television watching.
    d. all of the above
    e. a and b, but not c

23. One line of evidence suggesting a strong heritable component to personality traits is that
    a. identical twins have higher correlations (one to the other twin) in measures of personality traits than do fraternal twins.
    b. identical twins have lower correlations (one to the other twin) in personality traits than do fraternal twins.
    c. identical twins and fraternal twins have equal correlations (one to the other twin) in personality traits.
    d. fraternal twins have higher correlations (one to the other twin) than to siblings who are not twins.

24. Which of the following statements is true?
    a. Identical twins have less chance of being alike on various personality tests than do fraternal twins.
    b. Fraternal twins raised apart show a lower correlation of personality traits than do those raised together.
    c. Siblings raised in the same family are likely to have different personalities partly because the reciprocal interaction between each child's genetic makeup and his or her environment will be different.
    d. Identical twins raised together show a higher correlation of personality traits than do those raised apart.

25. Which of the following is true of sensation seekers?
    a. They have underactive norepinephrine systems in their brain.
    b. They are overaroused in certain systems of their brain.
    c. They have a low pain tolerance.
    d. They react more to external stimuli than those who are not sensation seekers.

26. The social-cognitive approach to personality does not attribute differences in personality to
    a. enduring traits in personality that may be a function of hereditary influences.
    b. differences in how a person will behave in different situations.
    c. learning that occurs during the life of an individual that may cause certain behaviors to appear in certain situations.
    d. classical and operant conditioning.

27. Mischel has proposed that people can differ on which of the following characteristics that determine their personality?
    a. their construal of external experiences
    b. their beliefs about the world
    c. their emotional response to situations
    d. their goals
    e. all of the above

28. The Attributional Style Questionnaire is an important instrument for measuring control because
    a. it assesses the extent to which an individual thinks the causes of events are internal to her or due to external forces.
    b. it has value in predicting clinical depression.
    c. it is related to the idea of learned helplessness in animals that may be related to depression.
    d. all of the above

29. The extent to which a child is willing to delay gratification is related to
    a. later academic performance.
    b. later social competence.
    c. later coping skills in adolescence.
    d. all of the above

30. Social-cognitive approach is to psychodynamic approach as
    a. psychiatry is to psychology.
    b. normality is to pathology.
    c. surface is to deep.
    d. airplane is to surface transportation.
    e. pleasure is to pain.

31. Which of the following adjectives would *not* be used by Freud to describe basic human nature?
    a. sexually motivated
    b. selfish
    c. pleasure-seeking
    d. conflict-free
    e. b and d

32. Freud and Hobbes agree
    a. about the basic savageness of human nature.
    b. that there is a taming of basic human nature.
    c. about the way that human nature is tamed.
    d. about the importance of unconscious conflict.
    e. a and b

33. Freud made a major contribution to the understanding of human nature when he suggested that the apparent irrationality of much human behavior was a symptom of _____ _____.
    a. basic insanity
    b. severe hysteria
    c. unconscious conflicts
    d. wish fulfillment
    e. internalized standards

34. Which of the following are symptoms of hysteria?
    i. partial or total blindness
    ii. paralysis
    iii. feelings of helplessness
    iv. anesthesia of a body part
    v. uncontrollable urges
    a. i, iii, v
    b. i, ii, iv, v
    c. ii, iii, iv
    d. i, ii, iv
    e. All are symptoms of hysteria.

35. Charcot and Freud believed that hysteria is _____.
    a. inherited
    b. psychogenic
    c. the result of physical trauma (injury to the brain)
    d. incurable
    e. unimportant

36. A patient is asked merely to say whatever comes to his mind during a therapy session. The term applied to this psychoanalytic technique is
    a. transference.
    b. free association.
    c. resistance formation.
    d. wish fulfillment.
    e. hypnosis.

37. All of the following statements (made by a patient during free association) are examples of resistance *except*
    a. "I really can't think of anything right now."
    b. "I just forgot what I was about to say."
    c. "I'm thinking of something that has nothing to do with my problem."
    d. "I just remembered a terrible experience from my childhood."
    e. "What I'm thinking about now is too unimportant to tell you."

38. According to Freud, repressed thoughts
    a. are connected to a wish or thought that a person is unable to face without intense anxiety.
    b. are linked to basic biological urges.
    c. often date back to early life.
    d. all of the above
    e. none of the above

39. Which of Freud's subsystems would be responsible for a desire to eat or drink?
    a. ego
    b. superego
    c. id
    d. a combination of ego and superego
    e. all of the above

40. If a child wants a drink, we often find that he or she asks for something rather than just taking it. This is evidence for the operation of
    a. the ego.
    b. repression.
    c. the id.
    d. a and c
    e. b and c

41. When children begin to think of themselves as if they were the parent, the _____ has begun to develop.
    a. ego
    b. superego
    c. id
    d. a and b
    e. impossible to tell from this description

42. Conflicts develop because the _____ and _____ often issue conflicting commands to the _____.
    a. id, ego, superego
    b. id, superego, ego
    c. ego, superego, id
    d. superego, ego, id
    e. All three systems issue commands to every other system.

43. On what is the mechanism underlying repression based?
    a. irrationality
    b. biological urge reduction
    c. anxiety reduction
    d. fear reduction
    e. ego expansion

44. A child is punished for something she did. She then hits her brother. This is an example of
    a. repression.
    b. transference.
    c. hysteria.
    d. displaced aggression.
    e. anxiety.

45. A child has deeply hidden feelings of hostility toward a younger sibling. However, the child treats his sibling with apparent love. This is an example of the defense mechanism known as
    a. projection.
    b. reaction formation.
    c. rationalization.
    d. displacement.
    e. repression.

46. A child who displays a behavior diametrically opposed to her frustrated true desires is demonstrating
    a. reaction formation.
    b. displacement.
    c. projection.
    d. isolation.
    e. none of the above

47. After failing to be offered a good job, an applicant decides that he wouldn't have liked the job anyway. This person is displaying a defense mechanism called
    a. rationalization.
    b. projection.
    c. reaction formation.
    d. isolation.
    e. repression.

48. When a person attributes his or her own thoughts and feelings to someone else, we call this
    a. rationalization.
    b. projection.
    c. reaction formation.
    d. repression.
    e. isolation.

49. Which of the following presents the correct stages of psychosexual development in the right order?
    a. oral, anal, erogenous, phallic, genital
    b. oral, anal, phallic, genital
    c. anal, oral, erogenous, phallic
    d. oral, anal, phallic, erogenous
    e. None are in the correct order.

50. An adult who dislikes eating, and avoids kissing and smoking, would, according to Freud, be described as
    a. fixated at the anal stage.
    b. showing a reaction formation from the oral stage.
    c. an oral character.
    d. an anal character.
    e. a remnant.

51. If a child experienced severe toilet training, and grew up to be messy, generous, and open minded, a Freudian would account for this by using the mechanisms of
    a. fixation and reaction formation.
    b. repression and fixation.
    c. projection and displacement.
    d. isolation and rationalization.
    e. a Freudian could not account for this.

52. The critical component(s) of Freud's theory of personality is (are)
    a. psychosexual stages.
    b. unconscious conflict.
    c. fixation and reaction formation.
    d. all of the above
    e. b and c only

53. The anal and oral characters have this in common
    a. reaction formation at a stage of development.
    b. fixation at a stage of development.
    c. a concern for orderliness.
    d. a lack of normal sexual interests.
    e. none of the above

54. The drama of the Oedipus complex unfolds according to the following progression of events
    a. identification, love, fear, hate, renunciation.
    b. love, fear, hate, renunciation, identification.
    c. hate, fear, renunciation, identification.
    d. love, hate, fear, renunciation, identification.
    e. none of the above

55. The stage following resolution of the Oedipus complex comprises
    a. the latency period.
    b. increased masturbation.
    c. puberty.
    d. genital stage.
    e. all of the above

56. Freud believed that the basis of every dream was
    a. projection.
    b. schizophrenia.
    c. wish fulfillment.
    d. day residues.
    e. castration anxiety.

57. Freud distinguished between two parts of the dream, which he termed
    a. conscious and unconscious.
    b. latent and manifest.
    c. normal and deviant.
    d. wish fulfillment and disguise.
    e. normal and abnormal.

58. Problems with the psychoanalytic view include
    a. lack of objectivity of clinical practitioners in reporting patients' statements.
    b. so much flexibility that an outcome or its opposite can be predicted.
    c. suggestion or influence of patients to report certain kinds of events or feelings.
    d. all of the above
    e. a and c only

59. For which claims of psychoanalytic theory is there specific positive evidence?
    a. universality of the Oedipus complex
    b. link between hostility to the father and his sexual link to the mother
    c. existence of a cluster of traits predicted by the anal character
    d. a link between toilet training and the anal character
    e. no evidence for any of the above

60. In a recent study, a test was made of Freud's view of the dream as an attempt at gratification. Most very thirsty participants reported
    a. dreams in which they drank.
    b. dreams in which they did not drink.
    c. no dreams whatsoever.
    d. dreams in which the act of drinking was represented symbolically.
    e. dreams about eating.

61. There is little evidence for all of the following assertions of psychoanalytic theory *except*
    a. the existence of unconscious conflict.
    b. the general theory of psychosexual development.
    c. the central importance of biology in determining stages of emotional development.
    d. personality is essentially fixed by the age of five or six.
    e. the Oedipus complex.

62. According to Horney, the vicious circle
    a. results from facing incompatible demands.
    b. is more likely if there is more basic anxiety.
    c. occurs in normal people.
    d. all of the above
    e. none of the above

63. Block finds that parents who are warm, self-assuring, and active, but provide firm guidelines, have the best-adjusted children. Which of the following might account for this relation?
    a. The parents' upbringing style leads to good adjustment in their children.
    b. Parents who practice a positive upbringing style are better adjusted, and pass this characteristic to their children via genes.
    c. Children who are disposed to be adjusted prompt good upbringing styles from their parents.
    d. Parents with good upbringing styles are also better educated, and it is the education of the parents that produces the adjustment in the child.
    e. all of the above

64. Coping is
    a. like a conscious mechanism parallel to unconscious defense mechanisms.
    b. somewhat consistent in style across decades in a given individual.
    c. an unsuccessful way of dealing with problems.
    d. all of the above
    e. a and b only

65. The humanistic approach differs from both the social-cognitive and psychoanalytic approaches in all but one of the following ways. Which of the choices below is *not* a difference between these approaches?
    a. emphasis on the positive side of human nature
    b. assumption of a hierarchy of needs
    c. acknowledgment of the existence of deficiency needs
    d. emphasis on self-actualization
    e. emphasis on free choice

66. In contrast to the social-cognitive approach, the trait, psychoanalytic, and humanistic approaches all
    a. emphasize internal causes of behavior.
    b. focus on the conflict between biological and social needs.
    c. posit a hierarchy of needs.
    d. take a basically statistical approach to personality.
    e. emphasize the role of the environment in shaping personality.

67. Self-actualization is
    a. at the top of the need hierarchy.
    b. associated with a higher frequency of peak experiences.
    c. dependent on satisfaction of lower-level needs.
    d. all of the above
    e. a and b

68. Unconditional positive regard in the humanistic scheme, and failure to fixate at the oral or anal phases in the psychodynamic scheme are both
    a. features of personality.
    b. contributing factors to adult psychopathology.
    c. dependent on repression.
    d. influenced by genetic predisposition.
    e. conditions for a well-adjusted adult personality.

69. Positive psychology is concerned with
    a. defining the good life.
    b. causes of making people happy.
    c. causes of making people healthy.
    d. all of the above
    e. none of the above

70. The sociocultural perspective differs from all other approaches considered in that only the sociocultural perspective
    a. does not assume the individual is necessarily the basic unit.
    b. considers the meaning of experience.
    c. acknowledges a major role for environmental factors.
    d. rejects a major role for biological factors.
    e. b and c

71. Humans across cultures show indications of diversity and common elements. Which of the following show marked commonalities across cultures?
    a. dimensions of personality
    b. degree of aggressiveness
    c. degree of cooperation
    d. frequency of common personality types
    e. a and c

72. The sociocultural approach compares parallel conditions in different cultures in order to
    a. discover dimensions of human diversity.
    b. extract common features of human nature across cultures.

c. test hypotheses (e.g., about the effect of early experience on later personality).
    d. all of the above
    e. a and c only

73. Collectivist cultures are more committed to
    a. charities.
    b. the extended family.
    c. community.
    d. self-expression.
    e. b and c

74. Dimensions along which the self might vary in different cultures include
    a. degree of belief in situational determinants of behavior.
    b. degree of belief in personality traits.
    c. permanence of personal names.
    d. degree of interdependence with others.
    e. all of the above

75. Overall, the five approaches to personality each
    a. represent valid alternative perspectives.
    b. present views that cannot, ultimately, coexist with all of the others.
    c. overemphasize the importance of culture.
    d. emphasize reason over feelings.
    e. assign a different role to the function of drama.

Answer Key for Self-Test

1.	b	33.	c
2.	d	34.	d
3.	b	35.	b
4.	c	36.	b
5.	c	37.	d
6.	c	38.	d
7.	c	39.	c
8.	b	40.	a
9.	b	41.	b
10.	a	42.	b
11.	d	43.	c
12.	a	44.	d
13.	c	45.	b
14.	a	46.	a
15.	d	47.	a
16.	c	48.	b
17.	c	49.	b
18.	c	50.	b
19.	c	51.	a
20.	b	52.	d
21.	d	53.	b
22.	d	54.	d
23.	a	55.	a
24.	c	56.	c
25.	a	57.	b
26.	a	58.	d
27.	e	59.	c
28.	d	60.	b
28.	d	61.	a
30.	c	62.	d
31.	d	63.	e
32.	e	64.	e

65. c
66. a
67. d
68. e
69. d
70. a

71. a
72. e
73. e
74. e
75. a

Investigating Psychological Phenomena

CONSTRUCTING A PERSONALITY INVENTORY

Equipment: None
Number of participants: One (yourself)
Time per participant: Forty-five minutes
Time for experimenter: Forty-five minutes

Constructing a test to assess a personality trait is an involved process. It requires the creation of test items and the validation of these items through administration of the test to large groups of participants. While it would be impossible to illustrate all the steps in this process through a short exercise such as this, it is possible to provide an idea about some of the issues that are involved. That is the purpose of this demonstration.

A first draft of a test for a particular personality trait has been created.* Before reading on, you should take this test. Listed below are twenty-one questions for you to answer. Try to put yourself in each of the following situations and on the answer sheet mark the choice that would best describe your reactions. Limit your replies to the choices given and answer every question.

* We thank Lisa Lange, John Prevost, Barb Merriam, Laurie Tunstall, and Julie Nuse for their permission to use the shyness inventory that was prepared as part of a course project supervised by Dr. Charles Morris. We also thank Dr. Morris for kindly supplying the correlational data.

Draft Personality Inventory

	strongly disagree	slightly disagree	slightly agree	strongly agree
1. I am in a crowded bar sitting with some friends. A good-looking individual comes up to me and asks me to dance. I like to dance but I notice that the dance floor is empty and answer no.	1	2	3	4
2. I get an important exam back and I disagree with the grading on one of the problems. But I accept my grade, avoiding a confrontation with the professor.	1	2	3	4
3. I enjoy attending seminars and discussion groups as opposed to large lectures.	1	2	3	4
4. I'm in a restaurant and receive some bad food. Instead of saying something, I stay quiet but leave a small tip.	1	2	3	4
5. My family is moving to another state and I will be attending a new school. I look forward to meeting new people and making new friends.	1	2	3	4
6. I find it easy to liven up a dull occasion.	1	2	3	4
7. I am required to form groups in a class and interact on a subject. The groups are formed but I tend to listen more than offer information.	1	2	3	4
8. If I were in the waiting room of a doctor's office and a stranger sat down next to me, introduced himself or herself, and started asking me questions, I would feel nervous and uncomfortable.	1	2	3	4
9. I can usually enjoy myself at a party even if I know almost no one there.	1	2	3	4
10. A teacher asks questions to which I know the answers, but I never raise my hand for fear that the answers might not be what the teacher is looking for.	1	2	3	4
11. I become uncomfortable and at a loss for words, usually blushing, when I am given a compliment.	1	2	3	4
12. I often find myself taking charge in group situations.	1	2	3	4
13. I prefer being with people and going to parties rather than spending my spare time alone pursuing personal interests or hobbies.	1	2	3	4
14. If someone was smoking a cigarette in a nonsmoking section and the smoke was bothering me, I wouldn't hesitate to ask the person to put out the cigarette.	1	2	3	4
15. I often look back at a situation and think of things I should have done or said.	1	2	3	4
16. I feel proud to be called on to give a toast at a social gathering.	1	2	3	4
17. I would go out of my way to make a stranger feel comfortable in a group in which the people are unfamiliar to him.	1	2	3	4
18. When I've been waiting in line for service for a long time and someone cuts in front of me, I feel angry but don't say anything about it.	1	2	3	4
19. I prefer not to answer the door when I know it's a salesperson because I have a hard time getting salespeople to leave once they're inside the door.	1	2	3	4
20. When I've struck up a conversation with the person sitting next to me, a long plane flight seems more enjoyable.	1	2	3	4
21. I consider myself to be a shy person.	1	2	3	4

Now that you have answered the questionnaire, you are probably aware that it is intended to assess shyness. The questions themselves were constructed as candidates that might have something to do with predicting how shy people are. How can one tell if the questionnaire accomplishes its purpose or which questions are the best predictors of shyness?

One possibility is to examine the face validity of each of the questions. Since you have just completed the questions yourself and since you are now aware that its purpose is to test for shyness, you can do this yourself. Examine each question and decide for yourself whether you think that it would be a good predictor of shyness. That is, does the question ask participants about a reaction that should depend on how shy the participants are? Try to pick out the four questions that you think would best predict shyness and the four that would be least relevant. Note, by the way, that the questions are constructed so that for some (Items 1, 2, 4, 7, 8, 10, 11, 15, 18, 19, and 21) a high score (e.g., 4) would indicate more shyness, while for the rest, a low score (e.g., 1) would indicate more shyness. This is only done to provide variety; your assessment of each question should be independent of this point.

Questions that would best predict shyness	Questions that would least predict shyness
1. _____	1. _____
2. _____	2. _____
3. _____	3. _____
4. _____	4. _____

Your judgment of the quality of a question is a measure of face validity (i.e., the extent to which a question, on the face of it, is a good predictor of shyness), but this is not the only possible measure of validity. Another criterion is to have some independent measure of a participant's shyness and correlate responses to each question with the measure (predictive validity). Presumably, if a question were a good predictor of shyness, it would correlate highly with this measure.

One such measure is a participant's response to Question 21. This question directly asks participants for their own assessment of whether they consider themselves to be shy. In order to determine how well each test question correlates with this self-assessment of shyness, sixty-nine participants were given this questionnaire and correlations of each question with Question 21 were calculated. They are presented in Table 1 below.

TABLE 1

Correlations of each question in the questionnaire with Question 21. A low correlation (a positive or negative value close to 0) indicates that there is little relationship between the answer to that question and the answer to Question 21; a high correlation (a value closer to −1 or +1) indicates a relationship between responses to that question and responses to Question 21. For example, Item 10 has a correlation of .42 with Item 21. This means that participants who tend to agree with the statement in Question 10 tend to agree also with the statement in Question 21.

Likewise, participants who tend to disagree with the statement in Question 10, also tend to disagree with the statement in Question 21. A negative correlation, such as in Question 6, indicates that participants who tend to agree with the statement in 6 tend to disagree with the statement in 21. Likewise, those who tend to disagree with the statement in 6 tend to agree with the one in 21 (note that even though a correlation is negative, it still means that there is a relationship between the two items in question, but a reverse relationship).

Question:	1	2	3	4	5	6	7	8	9	10
Correlation:	.23	.08	−.15	−.08	−.20	−.28	.38	−.24	−.24	.42
Question:	11	12	13	14	15	16	17	18	19	20
Correlation:	.29	−.22	−.20	−.27	.32	−.37	−.16	.17	.09	−.07

Compare your judgments of question quality against these correlations to see whether the ones you judged as good have either high positive or high negative values; also, check whether the questions you judged as poor have correlations near 0.

Another validity criterion that may be reasonable is the total score on the test. The logic of using this criterion is that individual questions may vary in how well they indicate shyness, but the test *as a whole* may be a much better indicator. If this were so, then it would be sensible to correlate scores on individual questions with those on the whole test to see which questions best predict the total test score. This was done for the same sixty-nine participants as above; the correlations are presented in Table 2.

TABLE 2

Correlations of each question with the total test score. As in Table 1, a low value means little relationship of that question with the total test score, while a higher value (either positive or negative) means that there is some relationship. For example, the correlation of .55 for Question 10 indicates that participants who tend to agree with the statement in Item 10 tend to have a high total score on the questionnaire, while participants who tend to disagree with the statement in 10 tend to score low on the whole questionnaire. Another illustration is the correlation of −.49 for Question 5. This means that participants who tend to disagree with the statement in 5 tend to get a high total score, while participants who tend to agree with the statement in 5 tend to have a low score.

Question:	1	2	3	4	5	6	7	8	9	10
Correlation:	.45	.41	−.54	.13	−.49	−.44	.46	.42	−.53	.55
Question:	11	12	13	14	15	16	17	18	19	20
Correlation:	.37	−.42	−.35	−.44	.40	−.46	−.27	.35	.25	−.01

Again, see how well your judgments of question quality are related to these correlations. Note also an interesting pattern in the two sets of correlations presented in Tables 1 and 2. Item 10 has both the highest absolute correlation with Question 21 and the highest correlation with the total test score. Also, Item 7 has very high correlations with both criterion measures. This consistency suggests that these two items may well be good, valid indices of shyness. How did you rate these items? Examine the items themselves to see if you can explain why they might be better than others.

Note also that two items, 4 and 20, have very low correlations with both criterion measures. How did you judge these items? Why to you think they have such low correlations?

If we were to continue to develop a "shyness inventory," we might well try to use other validity criteria as well as the three described above. For example, we might try to use the inventory to predict some behavior that is characteristic of shy people. This would allow us to assess the predictive validity of the test. Whatever the criteria, though, the objective of test construction is to find questions that best predict what you are trying to assess. This exercise should have given you some insight into the process by which this objective is reached.

CHAPTER 16

Psychopathology

Learning Objectives

1. Contrast statistical versus "qualitative (true illness)" conceptions of psychopathology.

DIFFERENT CONCEPTIONS OF MENTAL DISORDER

Psychopathology as demonic possession
2. Give examples from historical sources of the treatment of madness as demonic possession.

The decline of demonology
3. Describe the early history of the treatment of psychopathology as a disease.
4. Describe the somatogenic view of mental illness, referring to the example of general paresis.
5. Define psychogenic disorders, and explain the historical role of hysteria in clarifying the nature of these disorders.
6. Explain the somatic-psychogenic distinction.
7. Indicate problems with applying the somatic-psychogenic distinction.

THE MODERN CONCEPTION OF MENTAL DISORDER

8. Indicate the major features that define mental disorders, as developed in *DSM-IV*. What is the role of deviance, per se, in the definition?

Classifying mental disorders
9. Distinguish among symptoms, signs, and syndromes.
10. Describe the basic course of the diagnosis of mental disorders, including integration of the clinical interview information about symptoms, signs, course, and onset.
11. Describe how psychiatrists used to distinguish among organic brain syndromes, neuroses, and psychoses. Indicate how mental illnesses are now classified, referring to the changes in the latest taxonomy, *DSM-IV*.

Causal models of mental disorders
12. Explain the single pathology model of mental illness.
13. Briefly describe the biomedical, psychodynamic, and learning models as approaches to psychopathology.
14. Explain the multicausal model of mental disorders, using AIDS as an example.

15. Indicate how the multicausal model addresses some of the shortcomings of the single pathology model.

SCHIZOPHRENIA

16. What is the incidence of schizophrenia?

Signs and symptoms
17. Describe the major symptoms of schizophrenia in the areas of thought, social relationships, motivation, and behavior.
18. Define restitutional symptoms, delusions, hallucinations, and ideas of reference.
19. What are the most salient symptoms of paranoid, catatonic, and disorganized schizophrenia?

What goes wrong in schizophrenia?
20. Evaluate the idea that the major psychological disorder in schizophrenia is an inability to maintain a focus of attention.
21. Describe the dopamine hypothesis and indicate the types of evidence in favor of it. Suggest what types of experiments might strongly support it.
22. What is the evidence suggesting a modification of the dopamine hypothesis—the dopamine-serotonin interaction hypothesis?
23. What is the structural defect theory of schizophrenia, and what is the evidence for it?
24. Describe the multiple-syndrome hypothesis and indicate how it distinguishes positive and negative symptoms.
25. What is the evidence for three schizophrenic syndromes?
26. What are some problems with each of the accounts of schizophrenia?

Probable risk factors for schizophrenia
27. Review the evidence for genetic factors in schizophrenia? What is the evidence for genetic mutations?
28. Evaluate the importance of prenatal effects in schizophrenia. Include evidence linking it to prenatal trauma and exposure to viruses.
29. Describe the role of environmental effects in schizophrenia, including low social status and family pathology.
30. Evaluate the alternative possibilities that the environmental correlates of schizophrenia are caused by or are causes of schizophrenia.

Is schizophrenia a lifelong disorder?
31. Review the evidence indicating that schizophrenia is a lifelong disorder.

MOOD DISORDERS

32. Distinguish mood disorders from schizophrenia.

Bipolar and unipolar syndromes
33. Distinguish bipolar disorder from major depression.
34. Describe mixed states.
35. Discuss mania, including hypomania.
36. Describe the symptoms and degrees of depression, including depressive stupor and vegetative signs.
37. Consider childhood depression, and some difference in symptoms from adult depression.
38. What is the relation between suicide and depression?
39. What is seasonal affective disorder?

Organic risk factors
40. What are the biochemical hypotheses to explain depression, and what is the evidence for them?
41. Review the evidence for a genetic involvement in the causation of bipolar and unipolar disorders.

Psychological risk factors
42. Review the evidence for psychogenic factors in depression.
43. Describe Beck's cognitive theory of depression.
44. Describe the learned helplessness theory of depression, and summarize the evidence in favor of it that comes from both animal and human research.
45. Explain how the idea of despondent explanatory style as a cause of depression grew out of the concept of learned helplessness, and review the evidence for this position.
46. Discuss whether mood or cognitive disorders come first in the causation of depression.
47. Indicate features of depression that Beck's and Seligman's theories have difficulty explaining.

Sex differences in the prevalence of major depression
48. Indicate the explanations for the higher incidence of depression in American females, as opposed to males.

Mood disorders and multicausality
49. Describe the multiple causes of depression and their interaction.

ANXIETY DISORDERS

50. What defines the anxiety disorders?

Phobias
51. Describe phobias, including social phobias, and explain how they can be accounted for in terms of conditioning.
52. Describe the problems with conditioning accounts of phobia, the preparedness theory of phobias, and how it accounts for at least one problem with a conditioning approach.

Obsessive-compulsive disorder
53. Describe the symptoms of obsessive-compulsive disorders.
54. What are possible neurological and neurochemical causes?

55. Review recent evidence on infectious causes and linkages to other disorders.

Generalized anxiety disorder
56. Describe generalized anxiety disorder, and both conditioning and psychoanalytic explanations for it.

Panic disorder
57. What is panic disorder, and how does it differ from generalized anxiety disorder? How does it relate to agoraphobia? What are the cognitive autonomic explanations of this disorder?

REACTIONS TO EXTREME STRESS: ACUTE AND POST-TRAUMATIC STRESS DISORDERS

58. What is acute stress disorder and how does it relate to post-traumatic stress disorder?
59. What is post-traumatic stress disorder? How does dissociation fit into the development of this syndrome? How may low cortisol levels have a causative role?

DISSOCIATIVE DISORDERS

60. Describe dissociative amnesia, dissociative fugue, and dissociative identity disorder. What do they have in common?

Psychological factors underlying dissociative disorders
61. What is believed to be the psychological function of dissociative disorders?

Risk factors for dissociative disorders
62. Indicate a suspected predisposition for dissociative disorders and their controversial link to early traumas.

SOMATOFORM DISORDERS

Somatoform disorders
63. What are somatoform disorders, and what, in particular, is conversion disorder?
64. How can the decline in conversion disorders in recent decades be explained?

MENTAL DISORDER AND SOCIAL DEVIANCE

The psychopath
65. Discuss the distinctions between criminals and psychopaths.
66. Review the causes of psychopathy (antisocial personality disorder).

Psychopathy and the disorder concept
67. Discuss the advantages and disadvantages of making no legal distinction between psychopaths and criminals.

THE SCOPE OF PSYCHOPATHOLOGY

68. Discuss the problem of defining psychopathology and uncovering common principles underlying it. What, if anything, do all disorders described in this chapter have in common? What are the dangers of overextending the concept of psychopathology?

Programmed Exercises

DIFFERENT CONCEPTIONS OF MENTAL DISORDER

1. According to the _____ conception of psychopathology, it simply refers to deviance, or a relatively high frequency of intensity of certain behaviors.

    statistical

2. A dominant early social response to insanity, which resulted in practices such as trephining the skull, was based on the conception of insanity as _____ _____.

    demonic possession

3. Prior to the nineteenth century, people with severe mental illness were treated more or less as we currently deal with _____.

    criminals (or prisoners)

4. The disappearance of the psychological symptoms of _____ _____ following administration of penicillin provides strong evidence for a view of mental illness as a disease.

    general paresis (or syphilis)

5. A disorder that is characterized by symptoms that appear to be somatic but have no organic basis was once called _____.

    hysteria

6. Mental symptoms that can be directly explained by malfunction at the organic level are called _____. Those, like hysteria, that are best explained at the psychological level are called _____.

    somatogenic psychogenic

THE MODERN CONCEPTION OF MENTAL DISORDER

7. The commonly accepted definition for mental disorders is presented in _____. It does not require _____ as a condition for the diagnosis of a disorder.

    DSM-IV abnormality (deviance)

8. Rather, the *DSM-IV* defines mental disorder in terms of _____, _____, or increased risk of _____.

    disability, distress harm

9. In psychopathology, as in physical medicine, the diagnostic process begins with a _____ _____. This elicits a set of complaints, or _____.

    clinical interview, symptoms

10. The diagnostician also looks for _____, that is, indications that are not complaints but that are consistent with the symptoms.

    signs

11. A _____ is a pattern of signs and symptoms that go together.

    syndrome

12. In the course of the _____ _____, the diagnostician integrates information about _____, _____, _____, and _____ to arrive at a diagnosis.

    clinical interview symptoms, signs, course, onset

13. As a result of the diagnosis, one can often predict the _____ and _____ (cause) of the disorder.

    outlook (prognosis), etiology

14. In the older classification of mental illnesses, _____ were considered to be anxiety-related disorders in which there is good contact with reality, in contrast to the more severe disorders called _____. A third category was _____ _____ _____.

    neuroses psychoses, organic brain syndromes

15. In the most recent classification or taxonomy of mental illness, called _____, more emphasis is placed on the description of disorders than on _____ about their cause.

    DSM-IV theories

16. According to the _____-_____ _____, a particular disease is considered the underlying cause of specific mental symptoms.

    single-pathology model

17. According to the _____ model, mental illness has an organic basis, to be treated with somatic therapies. According to the _____ model, mental disorders are, in large part, the result of maladaptive learning. According to the _____ model, mental illness results from psychogenic factors.

    biomedical learning psychodynamic

18. According to the _____ model of mental disorders, they result from an accumulation of factors.

    multicausal

SCHIZOPHRENIA

19. The worldwide incidence of schizophrenia is about one person out of every _____.

    hundred

20. Schizophrenic symptoms include disorders in _____, _____, and _____.

    thinking, motivation, behavior

21. Schizophrenic persons often lose contact with other people as a result of social _____.

withdrawal

22. Schizophrenic symptoms include elaboration of the private world, or _____ symptoms, such as _____ of persecution and hearing voices or other _____.

restitutional
delusions, hallucinations

23. Schizophrenics typically show low _____.

reactivity (affect)

24. Some schizophrenics begin to believe that external events are specially related to them, personally. These beliefs are called _____ _____ _____, and may be elaborated into a _____ _____.

ideas of reference
delusional system

25. Delusions are typical symptoms in a common form of schizophrenia, _____ schizophrenia.

paranoid

26. A schizophrenic with unusual motor reactions, such as remaining motionless for long periods, is classified as _____. If the predominant symptoms are extreme incoherence in thought and inappropriateness in behavior, a person is classified as a _____ schizophrenic.

catatonic
disorganized

27. A cognitive theory of schizophrenia holds that many symptoms result from an inability to keep things in proper focus. This results in an inability to hold on to one _____ of thought or action.

line (train)

28. One argument for an organic basis for schizophrenia is the effectiveness of a group of drugs called _____ _____ in treatment.

classical antipsychotics
(major tranquilizers)

29. The _____ hypothesis of schizophrenia holds that it results from too much brain activity caused by the catecholamine neurotransmitter _____, which may cause the overstimulation characteristic of schizophrenia.

dopamine
dopamine

30. In accord with the theory that holds that neurons in the schizophrenic's brain are oversensitive to dopamine, the _____, which enhance dopamine activity, make schizophrenics worse and can induce a schizophreniclike _____ in nonschizophrenic individuals.

amphetamines
psychosis (syndrome)

31. The superior schizophrenia treatment effects of the _____ antipsychotics, such as Chlorazil, suggests the _____-_____ _____ hypothesis.

atypical, dopamine-
serotonin interaction

32. There are often _____ abnormalities in the brain associated with schizophrenia, and sometimes evidence of less total brain tissue, as indicated by enlarged_____.

structural
ventricles

33. A more modern classification of schizophrenia contrasts abnormal behavior, or _____ symptoms, with the absence of normal behaviors, or _____ symptoms.

positive
negative

34. According to the _____-_____ hypothesis, both anatomical deficits and neuro-transmitter excess are causes of schizophrenia. The anatomical deficits are thought to be associated with the _____ symptoms and the neurotransmitter excess with the _____ symptoms.

multiple-syndrome

negative, positive

35. There is evidence that there are three syndromes of schizophrenia, with the positive symptoms divided into those that represent _____ and those that represent _____ symptoms, like delusions and hallucinations.

disorganization,
psychotic

36. Twin studies indicate that there is a significant _____ factor in the causation of schizophrenia.

genetic (hereditary)

37. Identical twins show a _____ of 55 percent for schizophrenia.

concordance

38. The fact that schizophrenia is more common in children with older fathers suggests a role for _____ _____ in schizophrenia.

genetic mutation

39. Prenatal factors including _____ and exposure to _____ are linked to the occurrence of schizophrenia.

stress (trauma), viruses

40. According to the view of schizophrenia as a _____ disorder, pathological genes cause brain abnormalities in the fetus, which eventually lead to schizophrenia.

neurodevelopmental

41. Studies indicate that schizophrenia is much more common in _____ classes and that class status may be both a cause and an effect of schizophrenia.

lower

42. According to the _____ _____ view, there is a higher incidence of schizophrenia in lower classes because schizophrenia causes lower-class status, rather than lower-class status causing schizophrenia.

downward drift

43. There is evidence that _____ pathology may cause schizophrenia, but there is also evidence that it may be caused by schizophrenia.

family

44. There is no strong evidence for family attitudes and problems as _____ of schizophrenia, but they can affect how well schizophrenics _____.

causes
cope

MOOD DISORDERS

45. While schizophrenia can be regarded as essentially a disorder of thought, in the _____ disorders, the dominant disturbance is one of affect or mood.

mood

46. The two major types of mood disorders are _____ disorder and _____ _____.

bipolar, major depression

47. In _____ _____, a person shows symptoms of mania and depression at the same time.

mixed states

48. _____ is the opposite of depression and is characterized, among other things, by endless talking and overabundance of energy. In a milder form it is called _____.

Mania
hypomania

49. Depression is commonly associated with physical manifestations such as weakness, loss of appetite and interest in sex, and sleep disorders. There are called _____ symptoms.

vegetative

50. In severe depression, a person may become entirely unresponsive and may be in a _____ _____.

depressive stupor

51. Common symptoms more specific to childhood depression include _____ and _____.

school phobia, substance abuse, or belligerence

52. Depression is associated with a high rate of _____.

suicide

53. Depression associated with decreasing amounts of light as winter approaches is called _____ _____ _____. This may relate to changes in sleep cycles and the level of the pineal hormone, _____.

seasonal affective disorder
melatonin

54. There is evidence that low levels of three neurotransmitters, _____, _____, and _____, may account for depression.

serotonin, dopamine norepinephrine

55. Much of this evidence comes from the fact that antidepressant medication _____ levels of these three neurotransmitters.

increase

56. Twin studies indicate a higher role for genetic factors in _____ than in _____ disorders.

bipolar, unipolar

57. According to a number of psychogenic approaches to depression, the primary disorder is _____, which leads to changes in _____.

cognitive
mood

58. Beck asserts that depression results from a set of negative beliefs, called _____ _____ _____, and can be treated successfully with _____ therapy.

negative cognitive schema, cognitive

59. According to the _____ _____ theory of depression, depression is caused by an expectation that one's actions will have no significant effects.

learned helplessness

60. As a result of the difficulty in explaining symptoms such as self-blame in depression, emphasis on psychological causative factors has changed from learned helplessness to pessimistic _____ _____.

explanatory
style

61. In Western cultures, there is a much higher incidence of _____ _____ and _____ _____ in females.

major depression
bipolar disorder

ANXIETY DISORDERS

62. An irrational and intense fear of an object or situation is called a _____.

phobia

63. According to a _____ view, phobias are produced by a form of Pavlovian or classical _____.

conditioning
conditioning

64. A fear of embarrassment or humiliation in front of others is called a _____ phobia.

social

65. The _____ theory of phobias accounts for why snakes and spiders are more common phobic objects than flowers or pajamas.

preparedness

66. In _____-_____ disorders, anxiety is produced by persistent internal events (thoughts or wishes).

obsessive-compulsive

67. _____ are persistent thoughts. _____ are acts usually performed in an attempt to deal with these thoughts.

Obsessions, Compulsions

68. OCD is associated with damage to the _____ _____ and _____ _____, and with low levels of _____.

frontal lobes, basal ganglia, serotonin

69. Recent evidence links OCD to the _____ virus.

streptococcus (strep throat)

70. OCD is linked by inheritance and underlying cause to other diseases, called OCD _____ _____.

spectrum disorders

71. In phobias, anxiety is focused on a particular object or situation. In _____ _____ disorders, it is all-pervasive.

generalized anxiety

72. _____ disorder is more acute than generalized anxiety disorder, but like generalized anxiety disorder it doesn't focus on a particular object or situation.

Panic

73. Fear of having panic attacks causes some people not to venture away from their home, a condition called _____.

agoraphobia

74. Some have explained panic disorder as an overreaction to the bodily symptoms of _____.

fear

REACTIONS TO EXTREME STRESS: ACUTE AND POST-TRAUMATIC STRESS DISORDERS

75. Recurrent nightmares and flashbacks about a traumatic event characterize both _____ and _____-_____ _____ disorder. The latter has a much longer _____.

acute, post-traumatic stress, duration

76. Immediately after the trauma, people who will develop post-traumatic stress disorder often feel oddly unaffected by the event, or _____.

dissociated

77. Some have suggested that early adverse experiences may be a cause of PTSD, and that this may be mediated by low _____ levels.

cortisol

DISSOCIATIVE DISORDERS

78. In dissociative disorders, a whole set of mental events is removed from ordinary _____. These disorders include _____ and _____ (cite two types).

consciousness, dissociative fugue, dissociative amnesia, or dissociative identity disorder

79. Many believe that dissociative disorders are a psychological _____ against something the individual is unable to face.

defense

80. According to one formulation, the tendency to be able to be _____ forms part of the predisposition for dissociative disorders, and _____ _____ often triggers the disorder.

hypnotized
severe trauma (severe abuse, child abuse)

SOMATOFORM DISORDERS

81. In somatoform disorders, the principal symptom is a _____ disorder, such as paralysis.

somatic (bodily)

82. The four different types of somatoform disorders include (list two) _____ and _____.

hypochondriasis, somatization disorder, somatoform pain disorder, conversion disorder

83. Conversion disorders are declining in incidence. This probably results from more _____ child rearing and more general _____ sophistication.

permissive, medical

84. Psychophysiological disorders have primarily _____ symptoms and primarily _____ underlying pathology.

organic, mental

85. Schizophrenia has primarily _____ symptoms and primarily _____ underlying pathology.

mental, organic

MENTAL DISORDER AND SOCIAL DEVIANCE

86. Someone who behaves antisocially without signs of remorse is called an antisocial personality, or _____.

psychopath

87. Some explanations of psychopathy suggest that it may result from cortical _____, or cortical _____.

immaturity underarousal

88. Another account of psychopathy holds that psychopaths have little _____ for the consequences of their actions.

fear (concern)

89. The distinction between psychopathy and _____ is often hard to maintain.

criminality

Self-Test

1. Treatment of "mental disorders" in the past by such procedures as trephination or flogging is indicative of a conception of these disorders as caused by
   a. microorganisms.
   b. criminal impulses.
   c. degeneration.
   d. demonic possession.
   e. medical malpractice.

2. The discovery of a cure for general paresis gave support to the view of mental illness as
   a. demonic possession.
   b. akin to criminality.
   c. a disease of society.
   d. somatogenic.
   e. resulting from medical malpractice.

3. If a specific enzyme lack was pinned down as the cause of a previously poorly understood severe mental illness, it would change its classification from _____ to _____.
   a. psychosis, neurosis
   b. disease, pathology
   c. psychoanalytic, medical
   d. psychogenic, somatogenic
   e. minor, serious

4. According to the modern view, as expressed in *DSM-IV*, abnormality (deviance) is
   a. part of the definition of mental disorders.
   b. a frequent but not necessary feature of mental disorders.
   c. unrelated to mental disorders.
   d. directly linked to distress.
   e. serious only when it is somatogenic.

5. Which of the following goes along with symptoms, course, and onset in forming a mental disorder diagnosis?
   a. signs
   b. labeling
   c. deviance determination
   d. neurosis evaluation
   e. psychogenic evaluation

6. The diagnosis often leads to information about the
   a. signs.
   b. deviance.
   c. outlook.
   d. etiology.
   e. c and d

7. The fundamental difference between what was known as a psychosis and a neurosis was
   a. the psychosis involves more detachment from reality.
   b. the neurosis is easier to cure.
   c. all psychoses have a known biological cause.
   d. b and c
   e. a and c

8. Both the biomedical model and the psychodynamic model
   a. emphasize somatogenic disorders.
   b. fail to explain conversion disorders.
   c. are limited versions of the pathology model.
   d. emphasize psychogenic disorders.
   e. emphasize the role of learning.

9. It is probably true that most Swiss today are at least bilingual. Then a monolingual Swiss would be deviant or abnormal. Classification of such a person as suffering from a mental disorder would depend, according to the single pathology model, on
   a. the establishment of the deviance.
   b. demonstration that monolingualism seriously impairs functioning in Switzerland.
   c. description of a single underlying pathology that caused monolingualism.
   d. all of the above
   e. none of the above

10. Dr. A says disease W is caused by a toxin in the brain. Dr. A's account is an example of
    a. the biomedical model.
    b. the learning model.
    c. the single-pathology model.
    d. the multicausal model.
    e. a and c

11. Dr. B says disease W is caused by a comporomised brain system that cannot handle a particular set of unusual stresses that a person experiences. Dr. B's account is an example of
    a. the single-pathology model.
    b. the multicausal model.
    c. the psychodynamic model.
    d. a and b
    e. b and c

12. The general idea that schizophrenics have difficulty distinguishing between personal (internal) and external events can be used to explain some of the symptoms of schizophrenia. Which of the following schizophrenic symptoms can be explained in this manner?
    a. delusions
    b. hallucinations
    c. catatonic immobility
    d. a and b
    e. all of the above

13. Delusions differ from hallucinations in that
    a. delusions are associated with ideas of persecution.
    b. delusions are based on interpretations of real events.
    c. delusions are primarily visual while hallucinations are auditory.
    d. delusions are associated with apathy (indifference).
    e. delusions cause social withdrawal.

14. The idea that the fundamental disorder in schizophrenia is a cognitive deficit having to do with failure to keep things in proper focus, or to maintain selective attention, can explain all but one of the following. Which feature of schizophrenia *cannot* be easily explained?
    a. disconnected thought
    b. rhyming associations
    c. social withdrawal (as a consequence of overstimulation)
    d. apathy (indifference)
    e. c and d

15. Thorazine is a drug in the classical antipsychotic (major tranquilizer) family and is effective as therapy for schizophrenia. Antipsychotics are known to block the action of dopamine at the synapse. Dopamine is a neurotransmitter. Low levels of dopamine in animals lead to the neglect of stimulation. Taken together, these findings suggest
    a. that schizophrenia results from an excess of dopamine, leading to overstimulation or overload.
    b. that there is a strong, enzyme-based hereditary deficit in dopamine in schizophrenics.
    c. that schizophrenics have too little dopamine, leading to cognitive and affective symptoms.
    d. that there is probably no direct relation between dopamine levels and schizophrenia.
    e. that drugs should be given simpler names.

16. Penicillin is to general paresis as _____ is (are) to schizophrenia.
    a. dopamine
    b. amphetamines
    c. antipsychotics (major tranquilizers)
    d. norepinephrine
    e. genetics

17. According to the dopamine hypothesis of schizophrenia, a drug that opposes the effect of amphetamines would
    a. be likely to reduce positive symptoms of schizophrenia.
    b. be likely to reduce negative symptoms of schizophrenia.
    c. cause schizophrenic symptoms in normal people.
    d. oppose the effect of antipsychotics.
    e. a and b

18. Delusions in paranoid schizophrenics or bizarre behaviors in catatonic schizophrenics are examples of
    a. syndromes.
    b. signs.
    c. ideas of reference.
    d. negative symptoms.
    e. positive symptoms.

19. The multiple-syndrome hypothesis asserts that
    a. the positive and negative symptoms of schizophrenia have different causes.
    b. anatomical and neurotransmitter disorders produce different types of schizophrenia.
    c. there are two anatomical deficits underlying schizophrenia
    d. amphetamines and dopamine are the two causes of schizophrenia.
    e. a and b

20. The concordance rate among identical twins for schizophrenia is 55 percent, while the comparable figure for fraternal twins is 9 percent. These results suggest that
    a. genetic factors predominate as causes of schizophrenia.
    b. there is a very weak genetic component in the causation of schizophrenia.
    c. schizophrenia is essentially caused by environmental factors.
    d. the primary cause of schizophrenia is probably lack of a neurotransmitter rather than a genetic effect.
    e. both genetic and environmental factors play important roles in the causation of schizophrenia.

21. Evidence that schizophrenia may be caused or promoted by a virus is that
    a. it is more common in twins connected by a single placenta.
    b. in the temperate parts of the world, it is more common in children born during the winter.
    c. in the tropics, there is no relation between season of birth and incidence of schizophrenia.
    d. a and b
    e. all of the above

22. The incidence of schizophrenia is higher in the lower classes. This suggests that
    a. social class is a causal factor in schizophrenia.
    b. schizophrenics are lower in social class because they are schizophrenic.
    c. schizophrenia does not have a strong organic component.
    d. a and/or b
    e. all of the above

23. There are some reports of poorer mental health in the *adoptive* parents of schizophrenics. This, along with studies of differences in the behaviors of mothers to their schizophrenic and normal children, suggests that
    a. pathological home environments cause schizophrenia.
    b. schizophrenic children can induce pathological behavior in parents.
    c. there is an organic basis for schizophrenia.
    d. there is a psychogenic basis for schizophrenia.
    e. a and d

24. The biomedical, single-pathology model of schizophrenia presented in the text includes all but one of the following assumptions. Which assumption is *not* included?
    a. Family pathology leads to deficits in the function of brain neurotransmitters.
    b. Some genetic factors contribute to pathology in the function of certain brain neurotransmitters.
    c. Neurotransmitter deficits can lead to inability to focus in time or space.
    d. Inability to focus in time or space can lead to social withdrawal.
    e. Inability to focus in space and time can lead to inappropriate emotions.

25. Manic disorders share with some forms of schizophrenia which of the following symptoms?
    a. hallucinations
    b. social withdrawal
    c. shifting from one subject to another in conversation
    d. blunted affect in response to stimuli that would normally elicit affective responses
    e. enormous amounts of energy

26. A person shows little interest in the world around him. He shows little emotional response and has disconnected thoughts. On this basis, the most likely guess for a diagnosis would be
    a. mania.
    b. major depression.
    c. bipolar disorder.
    d. schizophrenia.
    e. a or c

27. Which of the following is *not* associated with some type of depression?
   a. shortening light cycles in winter
   b. hypomania
   c. disturbed sleep cycles
   d. suicide
   e. changes in levels of melatonin

28. According to the biochemical hypotheses, low levels of dopamine, norepinephrine, or serotonin are causative factors in
   a. mania.
   b. depression.
   c. schizophrenia.
   d. a and b
   e. a and c

29. All but one of the following provide evidence in favor of the theory that low levels of norepinephrine in the brain lead to depression. Which of these findings does *not* support this theory?
   a. Drugs that deplete norepinephrine cause depression in nonschizophrenic individuals.
   b. Helplessness training in animals depletes norepinephrine.
   c. Drugs which increase the availability of norepinephrine are effective in therapy for depression.
   d. Norepinephrine is involved with the systems in the brain that produce arousal and activation.
   e. Dopamine, a neurotransmitter related to norepinephrine, is implicated in the causation of schizophrenia.

30. In terms of the hypothesis that holds that high levels of norepinephrine (or serotonin) cause mania, which of the following should be an effective therapy for mania?
   a. a drug that mimics norepinephrine
   b. amphetamine
   c. a drug that increases reuptake of norepinephrine by the presynaptic neuron
   d. a drug that decreases the rate of breakdown of norepinephrine in the synaptic gap
   e. a drug that increases the rate of synthesis of norepinephrine in the synaptic terminals

31. There is evidence for a gene on the X chromosome that is associated with the occurrence of
   a. seasonal affective disorder.
   b. major depression.
   c. bipolar disorder.
   d. schizophrenia.
   e. none of the above

32. Parents with bipolar disorder tend to have children with bipolar disorder, and parents with unipolar disorder tend to have children with unipolar disorder. This suggests that
   a. parents are a stress.
   b. bipolar and unipolar disorders have a different basis.
   c. bipolar and unipolar disorders share a common cause.
   d. environmental events are the primary cause of mood disorders.
   e. bipolar disorder is more likely to be inherited than unipolar disorder.

33. According to Seligman's helplessness views, the low affect of depression results from
   a. low levels of norepinephrine.
   b. negative cognitions that produce affective changes.
   c. a tendency toward suicidal thoughts.
   d. bipolar mood change.
   e. self-hatred.

34. Which of the following symptoms of depression is particularly difficult to explain for both the biochemical and psychogenic (learned helplessness) theories?
   a. negative affect
   b. inactivity
   c. responsiveness to antidepressant drugs
   d. self-hatred
   e. none of the above

35. According to the learned helplessness theory of depression, which of the following would be the most relevant cause for depression?
   a. depletion of norepinephrine or serotonin
   b. past experiences in which a person could not control his or her environment
   c. genetic factors
   d. parents who gave the person too much responsibility as a child
   e. c or d

36. The advantage of the explanatory style explanation of depression over learned helplessness is that the former can explain
   a. inactivity.
   b. suicidal thoughts.
   c. self-blame.
   d. global depression.
   e. low levels of norepinephrine.

37. Which of the following hypothetical findings would oppose the organic explanations of a higher incidence of depression in adult females?
   a. equal incidence of schizophrenia in both sexes
   b. equal incidence of depression in both sexes in traditional cultures
   c. lower levels of brain norepinephrine in females
   d. lower levels of activity in adult females
   e. a and b

38. Which of the following lists of disorders is arranged in order of *increasing* importance of psychogenic causative factors?
   a. schizophrenia, depression, bipolar disorder
   b. schizophrenia, general paresis, phobias
   c. phobias, depression, bipolar disorder
   d. general paresis, depression, phobias
   e. schizophrenia, phobias, general paresis

39. One effective treatment for specific phobias is to expose the phobic person to weak instances of the phobic object while the person relaxes. The strength of the stimulus is gradually increased. Under these conditions, many phobias disappear, and no undesirable symptoms seem to replace them. This therapeutic success is an argument in favor of
    a. the conditioning view of phobias.
    b. preparedness.
    c. genetic factors in phobia.
    d. a biological basis for social phobias.
    e. none of the above

40. A disorder in which anxiety is handled by repetitive and ritualistic acts is called
    a. phobia.
    b. psychogenic fugue.
    c. obsessive-compulsive disorder.
    d. conversion disorder.
    e. generalized anxiety disorder.

41. OCD has been linked to
    a. low levels of brain ganglia.
    b. damage to basal ganglia.
    c. infection.
    d. a and c
    e. all of the above

42. If phobias are often about objects, and obsessions are about thoughts, then panic disorder can be said to be about
    a. physiological symptoms.
    b. lack of ability to escape.
    c. sexual objects.
    d. denial of fear.
    e. sympathy

43. Post-traumatic stress disorder and specific phobias share
    a. a conditioning explanation.
    b. causation by a traumatic event.
    c. dissociation.
    d. low anxiety.
    e. ritualistic behaviors.

44. Amnesia, fugue, and/or multiple identities may be symptoms of
    a. obsessive-compulsive disorders.
    b. psychoses.
    c. conversion disorders.
    d. dissociative disorders.
    e. none of the above

45. There has been a decline in the incidence of diagnosed conversion disorders in the United States. This might result from
    a. greater sophistication in making neurological diagnoses.
    b. increased medical sophistication of people.
    c. greater permissiveness in the upbringing of children.
    d. a and b
    e. all of the above

46. The fundamental distinction between anxiety disorders and somatoform or dissociative disorders is that
    a. anxiety disorders are more generalized.
    b. anxiety is an explanation only for anxiety disorders.
    c. organic factors are much more heavily involved in anxiety disorders.
    d. only in anxiety disorders is anxiety expressed overtly.
    e. a and b

47. A person is apprehended after committing a series of crimes. The question is whether she should be treated as a criminal or a psychopath. All but one of the following characteristics suggest that she is a sociopath. Indicate the characteristic that suggests a criminal, rather than psychopath, diagnosis
    a. She is a loner.
    b. She feels no guilt for the committed crimes.
    c. She is anxious.
    d. She is charming.
    e. She is intelligent.

48. There is actually evidence that low levels of brain serotonin are associated with high levels of violence. This might lead someone to hypothesize that levels of serotonin were a cause of sociopathy. Which of the following hypothetical findings would be evidence for this hypothesis?
    a. Drugs that block the action of serotonin reduce antisocial acts in sociopaths.
    b. There is a negative correlation between degree of psychopathy and levels of serotonin by-products in the blood.
    c. Many psychopaths are not more violent than normal people.
    d. There is a positive correlation between degree of psychopathy and levels of serotonin in the brain.
    e. None of the above are evidence.

49. Psychopathy differs from almost all other disorders considered as psychopathology in that
    a. there is no evidence that it runs in families.
    b. there is serious question as to whether it is a mental disorder.
    c. there is no accepted treatment for it.
    d. a and b
    e. all of the above

Answer Key for Self-Test

1.	d	26.	d
2.	d	27.	b
3.	d	31.	c
4.	b	32.	b
5.	a	28.	b
6.	e	29.	e
7.	a	30.	c
8.	c	33.	b
9.	d	34.	d
10.	e	35.	b
11.	b	36.	c
12.	d	37.	b
13.	b	38.	d
14.	d	39.	a
15.	a	40.	c
16.	c	41.	e
17.	a	42.	a
18.	e	43.	b
19.	e	44.	d
20.	e	45.	e
21.	e	46.	d
22.	d	47.	c
23.	b	48.	b
24.	a	49.	d
25.	c		

Investigating Psychological Phenomena

DEPRESSION AND NEGATIVE EXPERIENCES

Equipment: Pencil, paper, and stopwatch or watch with second indicator

Number of participants: One (yourself; you will need the cooperation of a friend to serve as a timer for about five minutes)

Time per participant: Twenty minutes

Time for experimenter: Twenty minutes

Depression is a very common disturbance. It can vary from almost universal "blue" moods to a serious, chronic, and incapacitating disorder. Because at least some of the characteristics of deep (psychotic) depression occur occasionally in most people, it is possible to study depression in a general population. In any population, there seems to be a more or less continuous distribution of people along a dimension running from depression to elation.

Severe depression is characterized by depressed mood; loss of interest in others and normally desirable things (such as food); feelings of hopelessness, helplessness, and worthlessness; and slowed-down thought and motor activity. Many of these symptoms appear in mild forms in the general population. It is reasonable to expect that mildly depressed people will show some of the same bases or causes of their symptoms as severely depressed people.

A number of theories of depression are outlined in the text. These include biochemical explanations (e.g., depletion of norepinephrine), and psychological theories emphasizing hopelessness or learned helplessness. In this study we will explore a particularly simple additional theory: people are depressed because bad things happen to them. Clearly, some people get depressed in the face of success and others remain nondepressed following a series of adverse events. Nonetheless, it seems very reasonable that negative experiences would contribute to the causation of depression. We will test the hypothesis that people who are more depressed have had relatively more adverse experiences in the recent past.

A major purpose of this exercise is to illustrate some of the difficulties that arise in the scientific study of psychopathology. More than in previous studies in this study guide, we want to make you aware of the problem of making definitive measurements that clearly support a particular hypothesis. We want you to appreciate the difficulty of research and at the same time realize that progress can be made.

The first problem that we face is this: How do we measure depression? A basic issue that arises is the matter of "subjective" or "objective" measurement. In the case of a mood disorder, one might be inclined to subjective measurement, and indeed, much of the diagnosis of depression is concerned with what people say about how they feel. More objective measurements would involve observation of people (facial expression, level of activity) or having them report on their own activities (e.g., how many hours they sleep each night). In this study we look at a totally subjective measure, the participant's rating of his or her own mood. Remember that we are dealing with the range of depression and elation seen in the general population, and not with people actually diagnosed as depressed. In the case of diagnosis, interview and observation by an experienced clinician is involved, sometimes along with administration of a question inventory. We will use only self-ratings of mood and will collect two such ratings: one for the participant's momentary mood (how depressed he or she feels now) and the other for how depressed he or she has felt, in general, over the past year.

The second problem is this: How do we develop a measure of the incidence of negative and positive events in the recent life of each participant? We will use as our measure the participant's recall of negative and positive events over the past year. There are many problems and alternative interpretations of the results of this procedure. We will discuss them after you have served as a participant in this study.

Fill out the two rating scales that follow and enter your self-ratings on the answer sheet at the end of this section. Then continue to the recall task.

Rate what you judge to be your mood, right now. Circle the most appropriate number.

Extremely depressed 9	Very depressed 8	Moderately depressed 7	Slightly depressed 6	Neither depressed nor happy 5
Slightly happy 4	Moderately happy 3	Very happy 2	Extremely happy 1	

Rate what you judge to have been your mood, on the average, over the last twelve months.

Extremely depressed 9	Very depressed 8	Moderately depressed 7	Slightly depressed 6	Neither depressed nor happy 5
Slightly happy 4	Moderately happy 3	Very happy 2	Extremely happy 1	

RECALL OF NEGATIVE AND POSITIVE EVENTS

For this measure you will need the assistance of a friend who will time two separate two-minute intervals for you. No one but you will see what you write down.

You will go through two recall tasks, in order. Get a pen or pencil and sit at a table. When you are comfortable, ask a friend to say "Go" when the second hand of a watch crosses 12. When your friend says "Go," turn to the next page, read the sentence at the top, and follow the instructions. Ask your friend to say "Stop" when two minutes have elapsed. You should then stop the task.

The next time the second hand passes 12 (i.e., a minute after you complete the first part of the task), have your friend time another two minutes. When he or she says "Go," turn to the page after the one you had just written on, read the instructions, and follow them for two minutes.

Do not read on until you have completed the above task.

You are asked to perform the following task for exactly two minutes.

Someone will time the two minutes. When he or she says "Go," read the sentence below and follow the instructions. Continue until you hear "Stop" at two minutes.

List below all of the negative things that have happened to you in the last twelve months.

_____

_____

_____

_____

_____

_____

_____

_____

_____

_____

_____

_____

_____

_____

_____

_____

_____

_____

_____

_____

_____

_____

_____

_____

_____

You are asked to perform the following task for exactly two minutes, following the performance of the "bad events" task.

Someone will time the two minutes. When he or she says "Go," read the sentence below and follow the instructions. Continue until you hear "Stop" at two minutes.

List below all of the positive things that have happened to you in the last twelve months.

Add up the number of negative and the number of positive events that you remembered. Put these numbers on the answer sheet at the end of this section. Also enter the difference between the number of negative events and the number of positive events (# negative events minus # positive events), and the total # of events recalled (# negative events plus # positive events).

ANALYSIS OF DATA

We obtained these same data (depression ratings and event scores) from sixty-four undergraduate students at the University of Michigan. We will present these data here. You will add your own results to theirs, and we will then discuss the results.

MEASURES OF DEPRESSION

We used two measures of depression: rated mood now and rated mood over the last twelve months. You might expect that momentary and long-term mood would be related but that the two could sometimes be different. That, in fact, is just what our data show. Below is a scatter plot that presents the data from all sixty-four participants (see the statistical appendix to the text to learn more about scatter plots). Each point on the plot represents the two mood scores for one participant. Enter your own data point.

There is a positive relation between the two measures of depression. All relations described in these results will be expressed as correlation coefficients (see the statistical appendix). A value of +1.00 indicates a perfect positive correlation; a value of −1.00 a perfect negative correlation, and a value of 0.00 indicates no relation at all.

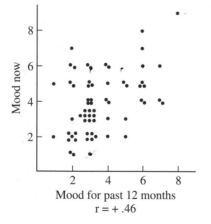

Mood for past 12 months
r = + .46

Our measure of "mood now" correlates +.46 with the measure of "mood over one year."

Looking at the scatter plot, you can see that there is some relation between the two mood measures. The general pattern of dots goes from lower left (happy on both scores) to upper right (depressed on both scores). But there are some exceptions. The correlation is positive, but far from perfect. Mark your point on the graph. Does your point fit in with the general pattern, or is it something of an exception? If an exception, can you explain this (e.g., it has been a very good year for you, but something unpleasant just happened to you)?

EVENT SCORES AND DEPRESSION

Before we test the major hypothesis (relatively more negative events in more depressed people), we can examine another prediction that can be made from the symptoms of seriously depressed people. Such people are characterized by a slowing down of action and thought. If this symptom also appears in milder form, in the low levels of depression in the student population, we would expect slowdown in memory search, along with other mental events. Therefore, we would expect that more depressed students would recall fewer events, positive or negative. (This type of finding would surely be true in a comparison of seriously depressed hospitalized patients versus "normal" participants.) We can test for this possibility by computing the correlation between self-rated depression (mood now) and the total number of events recalled (positive plus negative events). Note that because high scores on the depression rating mean more depression and high scores also represent large numbers of events recalled, we would expect a negative correlation: high depression scores go with low event recall scores.

For our sixty-four participants, the correlation between "mood now" and the total events is −.05: There is no evidence of any relation. Enter your score on these two measures in the scatter plot on the next page. You can see by examining the scatter plot that the two measures do not seem to be related. The relations between "mood over one year" and total events is also small. The correlation is +.14 (this is very small, but also in the direction opposite to the direction we predicted). There are two possible interpretations of our result. One is that our sample is not representative of the population, and that there actually is a negative depression–total event relation. Given the data we have, there is no reason to believe this. Another interpretation is that there is no relation, but that there might well be such a relation if we looked at severely depressed people as well—that is, the slowdown of mental function may only be marked in severe depression.

We now ask whether increased depression goes with a higher relative incidence of negative events. If this were true, we would expect a positive correlation between either depression score and the difference between number of negative and number of positive events recalled. We present below the scatter plot for both depression scores. Enter your own points on each of these plots. Just by inspecting these scatter plots you should be able to see that there is a positive relation: higher depression scores *tend* to go with higher negative minus positive event scores. In fact, the correlations are

Mood now versus negative−positive events r = +.46
Mood over one year versus negative−positive events r = +.32

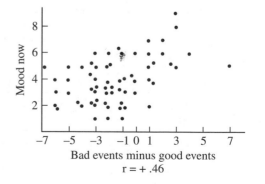

Bad events minus good events
r = + .46

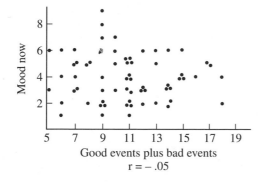

Mood now

Good events plus bad events
r = − .05

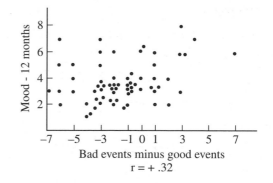

Mood − 12 months

Bad events minus good events
r = + .32

The relations are not overwhelming, but there is a clear relation. For example, the .46 correlation is significant at more than the .001 level: this means that a correlation this high could come about less than one chance in 1,000 if there were no relation between mood now and negative–positive events in the population (see the statistical appendix).

DISCUSSION AND COMMENTS

Our hypothesis—that in college populations, depression as measured by self-rating is positively related to relative recall of recent negative events—has been confirmed. We will now discuss a few problems in interpreting these results in order to make you more aware of the type of thinking that must go into research in general, and especially in this area.

First, our measure of events can be interpreted in a number of ways. We did not actually measure the number of positive and negative events that our participants experienced. We measured their *recall* for these events. A predominance of negative events could mean either that the participant experienced more of them or that the participant selectively remembers them . . . presumably because she is depressed. Remember that correlations show relations, but not causes (see the statistical appendix). Our hypothesis was that negative events cause depression. But the results of our study could be taken to indicate that in a relatively depressed mood, a person is more likely to remember negative events. The fact that the correlation was bigger between negative minus positive events and mood now, as opposed to mood over the last year, suggests that current mood may well influence what one thinks about. Of course, it is also possible that both effects exist: negative events lead to depression and depression leads to selective memory for negative events. There is some evidence in the literature for both of these effects. Under further activities, we will discuss ways of finding out whether both of these effects actually occur.

Second, even if more negative events do occur in more depressed people, the events may not be a cause of depression. Because a person is depressed, more negative events may occur to that person. For example, a depressed student will be less active, will be less inclined to study, and will probably not perform as well as he could in school.

Third, the same event that is evaluated as negative by someone who is depressed may not be considered negative by that same person when he is in a good mood (or by another person in a better mood). Many events may be both positive and negative (e.g., receiving a B in a course when one hoped for an A but did very little work and actually worried about getting a C, or the breakup of a relationship that had been unsatisfactory for some years). Read through your own events and decide how many could be seen as positive or negative.

We have just begun to scratch the surface, but we hope that you can appreciate the fact that a study like this would be just a beginning and that many more studies would have to be done to clarify the relation between negative events and depression. It should also be clear that whatever that relation is, there are many factors that influence depression. After all, the correlations we do have between depression and events are significant, but they are not that high. We might improve the correlations by getting better measures of depression and negative and positive events. But we also know from other studies, including those dealing with levels of catecholamines in the brain and specific types of past experiences (e.g., helplessness) that other factors are involved.

FURTHER ACTIVITIES

Try to think of some ways in which you could pull apart the effects of actual negative experiences and selective recall of them. After you decide on a few methods, read our suggestions below.

One approach is to get a more objective measure of the actual negative and positive events that a person has experienced. It is not practical to follow someone around for a year. But you could get a fair measure by giving the person a checklist of rather objective events, that are clearly negative or positive. Thus you could ask someone whether over the past year

A close relative or friend died
A course was failed
A job was lost
A favorite team had a disappointing season
A close relationship was broken

and so on, and, of course, a set of positive events.

You could then compare the negative minus positive recall score to the results of the checklist. What would you administer first to the participants: the free recall or the checklist? Why? You could try to make up an appropriate checklist for college students. It isn't easy.

A second approach is to test whether depressed people selectively remember negative events. For example, you could write a story that included a number of negative and positive events. It could be read to participants and you could measure their recall for the story, say one hour later. You could look at whether people who are more depressed remember relatively more of the negative events.

ANSWER SHEET

(If your instructor collects the data, fill out the report sheet in Appendix 2.)

Self-rating of mood now (enter number) _____

Self-rating of mood over last twelve months (enter number) _____

Number of negative events recalled _____

Number of positive events recalled _____

Negative minus positive events _____

Negative plus positive events _____

CHAPTER 17

Treatment of Psychopathology

Learning Objectives

BIOLOGICAL THERAPIES

1. Describe some early precursors to therapy for psychological disorders.

Pharmacotherapies

2. Discuss the effects of the classical antipsychotic medications, such as Thorazine, on schizophrenia. What symptoms do they affect and what symptoms do they leave largely untouched? What are the side effects?
3. Discuss the pharmacological effects of the atypical antipsychotics, such as Clozaril. How are they similar to more established antipsychotics, and how are they different?
4. What are the social side effects of treating schizophrenia with drugs, and why do they occur?
5. Discuss the effects of the monoamine oxidase inhibitors and the tricyclic antidepressants on the treatment of depression. How do the selective serotonin reuptake inhibitors differ from these? Why are they widely prescribed?
6. What are the atypical anti-depressants, and how do they work?
7. What is the effect of lithium salts and other antimanics?
8. What is the action of the anxiolytics and for what maladies are they prescribed?

Evaluating a medication

9. What are the drawbacks to using a before-and-after method to evaluate the effect of a therapy?
10. Describe placebo effects and discuss how they can have an impact in the evaluation of a drug therapy. What might cause placebo effects? How prevalent are they?
11. Discuss the double-blind technique and its usefulness in overcoming expectation effects. What are the limitations of this technique? How are these overcome when the goal of a study is to compare a new treatment with an existing one?
12. How is improvement assessed in the current medical climate?
13. Be aware of the limitations of pharmacotherapy and its impact on mental hospitals.

Psychosurgery

14. What has been the history of psychosurgery? When is it used today?

Electroconvulsive therapy

15. What is electroconvulsive therapy used for, and how effective is it? What are its side effects?

PSYCHOTHERAPY

16. What are the five major types of psychotherapy, and what are the theoretical underpinnings of each?

Classical psychoanalysis

17. What is the theory underlying classical psychoanalysis? What investigative techniques are used in classical psychoanalysis? Of what relevance is transference?

Psychodynamic therapy

18. What are the modern variations on traditional psychoanalysis that have been made by neo-Freudians? How do they differ from Freud's techniques? How are women now viewed?

Behavior therapy

19. What basic assumptions are made by behavior therapists? How are these assumptions translated into treatment techniques?
20. How does systematic desensitization use response incompatibility to eradicate phobias? How does an anxiety hierarchy figure into this therapy?
21. Describe aversion therapy and give examples of its use.
22. What is the major approach used in the application of operant techniques?

Cognitive therapy

23. How do cognitive therapies differ from traditional psychoanalysis? What are the assumptions of cognitive therapy?
24. How does confrontation figure into cognitive therapy?

Imterpersonal therapy

25. What is the underlying rationale for ITP?
26. Describe the areas of interpersonal relationships that IPT addresses.

Some common themes

27. What common themes underlie the various therapeutic schools?

Extensions of psychotherapy

28. How has psychotherapy been extended in recent years?

29. Understand the reasons for the development of group therapy.
30. What are shared-problem groups? Give examples.
31. What are the advantages of therapy groups for the patients who join them?
32. Describe the goals and techniques of couples and family therapy. How are they related to the relationship rather than to the individual?
33. How has psychotherapy reached beyond the original goals envisioned by Freud?
34. Describe how knowledge of and sensitivity to the cultural background of a patient can enhance the course of therapy.

EVALUATING THERAPEUTIC OUTCOME

35. What extraneous factors might influence the perception of whether a therapy is effective?

Does psychotherapy work?

36. What is the evidence concerning the effectiveness of psychotherapy? Describe meta-analysis, and its role in answering this question.
37. Why should there be a deterioration effect?

Comparing different therapies

38. Are there differences in the effectiveness of the various therapies? Describe the "Dodo bird verdict." How do placebo effects bear on this question?
39. What factors do the various psychotherapies have in common? Are there specific effects of individual therapies that go beyond their common effects?
40. How has the implementation of psychotherapy been influenced by practical considerations of accountability?
41. What is the issue surrounding discussions of "mental health parity?"

Programmed Exercises

BIOLOGICAL THERAPIES

1. Until the Middle Ages, _____ (the removal of pieces of skull bone) was a popular treatment for mental disorders. — trephining

2. _____ medications have their effects predominantly on mental conditions. — Psychotropic

3. _____ are drugs that have an effect on mental illness, and the effectiveness of these was among the first lines of evidence of the biochemical basis of schizophrenia. — Antipsychotics

4. Effective drug treatments for schizophrenia include _____ and _____. — Thorazine, Haldol

5. The advent of antipsychotic drugs led to the big movement in the 1960s to _____ mental patients. — deinstitutionalize

6. Atypical antipsychotic drugs, such as _____, have effects on both the positive and negative symptoms of schizophrenia. — Clozaril (or Risperdal)

7. The effects of the atypical types of antipsychotics seem to be lodged in their impact on the neurotransmitter _____, as well as its impact on the _____ system, which is affected by antipsychotics. — serotonin, dopamine

8. An individual feels extremely depressed most of the time. We would expect one of two types of drugs to have an effect on her: the _____ _____ _____ and the _____ _____. — monoamine oxidase inhibitors, tricyclic antidepressants

9. Recently, drugs such as Prozac have been developed for the specific treatment of depression. These drugs are called _____ _____ _____ _____. — selective serotonin reuptake inhibitors

10. Salts of _____ have an effect on bipolar disorder, both in causing manic episodes to subside, and also in preventing depressive episodes. These are called _____. — lithium antimanics

11. Valium and other _____ have become commonplace in treating anxiety in that they increase the transmission of the inhibitory neurotransmitter GABA. — anxiolytics

12. The major weakness of using before-and-after assessment techniques to evaluate the effect of a drug treatment is that the patient may _____ spontaneously. — improve

13. Sometimes merely giving patients what they think is a drug will cause an improvement in their condition; this is called a _____ effect. — placebo

14. It is hypothesized that a new drug will alleviate symptoms of air sickness. One hundred volunteers received an injection of this colorless liquid, while another 100 volunteers received an injection of saline solution (a colorless and totally inert liquid). All 200 participants took part in a simulated flight. Both subjective and objective indices of discomfort were recorded. Neither patient nor experimenter knew who received the drug. This study used a(n) _____-_____ technique to guard against any effects of expectations.   double-blind

15. The biggest cost associated with drug therapy is the likelihood of unpleasant _____ effects.   side

16. In evaluating the effectiveness of a drug, one must consider multiple _____ measures.   outcome

17. In a prefrontal lobotomy, the connections between the _____ and the _____ lobes are severed.   thalamus, frontal

18. Electroconvulsive shock treatment (ECT) is most effective in the treatment of _____; however, repeated shocks may cause _____ damage and _____.   depression, brain, amnesia

PSYCHOTHERAPY

19. According to the _____ school, neurotic ills stem from unconscious defenses against unacceptable urges.   psychoanalytic

20. A patient is asked to say whatever comes into his mind. This technique is known as _____ _____.   free association

21. During a therapy session involving free association a patient repeatedly changed the subject or forgot what she was about to say. This patient was displaying _____, an indication that she was about to remember something that she had previously tried to forget.   resistance

22. While Freud wanted patients to gain insight into their motives, he didn't want these insights to be merely _____; _____ involvement is necessary for genuine self-discovery.   intellectual, emotional

23. Freud considered _____ as the means for producing emotional involvement.   transference

24. The _____-_____ view emphasizes interpersonal and cultural factors rather than psychosexual development.   neo-Freudian

25. Behavior therapists hold that the condition Freud called neurosis is caused by maladaptive _____, which can be corrected through reeducation.   learning

26. The major goal of behavior therapists in treating phobias is to break the link between the _____ stimulus and the _____ response.   conditioned, fear

27. Sequential tensing and relaxing of the major muscles produces muscular relaxation, which is considered incompatible with fear response. Pairing the former with fear-evoking stimuli in order to eradicate phobias is part of the systematic _____ paradigm.   desensitization

28. Since fear-evoking stimuli can seldom be brought into the treatment room, systematic desensitization must depend on the patient's imagination of fear-evoking situations according to a(n) _____ _____.   anxiety hierarchy

29. In order to break compulsive fingernail biters of their habit, we coat their nails with a harmless but extremely bitter liquid so that they experience an unpleasant taste each time they bite their nails. This is an example of _____ therapy.   aversion

30. A _____ _____ uses operant reinforcement techniques to change patients' responses. This technique is usually most effective with in-patients.   token economy

31. One operant technique is _____ management, in which the patient learns of the consequences of his or her actions.   contingency

32. In contrast to behavior therapists, some therapists dispense with all conditioning techniques and, instead, help the patient acquire more appropriate ways of thinking. This is known as _____ therapy.   cognitive

33. _____ therapy is a technique for treating depression based on the idea that the disease stems from social isolation.   Interpersonal

34. One common feature of various therapies is the creation of a _____ alliance in which the patient feels as if he or she has a friend working with him or her.

    therapeutic

35. One common element of all therapists is _____ _____, as the patient is encouraged to rid himself or herself of intense and unrealistic fears.

    emotional defusing

36. An important part of therapy helps show patients how they react to others and is called _____ _____.

    interpersonal learning

37. One of the important components of psychotherapy is _____-_____, which may mean different things for different schools: for psychoanalysis, for example, it means insight into the patient's past.

    self-knowledge

38. All the psychotherapeutic techniques recognize the _____ nature of the therapeutic process. No progress is instantaneous.

    incremental

39. A new trend in psychotherapy is _____ _____, doing whatever works.

    technical eclecticism

40. In recent years, there has been a large shift in the delivery of therapeutic services from the one therapist-one patient model to _____ therapy.

    group

41. One example of _____ therapy is the _____-_____ group, in which a common affliction is present for all the patients.

    group, shared-problem

42. A form of group therapy that concentrates on the relationship of the attendees rather than on them as individuals is _____ therapy.

    couples

43. An important issue in therapy is the recognition that the _____ background of the patient may have an important effect on what techniques are likely to affect him or her.

    cultural

EVALUATING THERAPEUTIC OUTCOME

44. A valuable recent technique for investigating treatment effectiveness is _____, in which a comparison is made of studies that investigate those receiving treatment and those who have not been treated.

    meta-analysis

45. In general, a treatment group's scores on a test of emotional well-being will be more _____ following treatment than will a control group's, indicating a _____ effect in addition to improvement.

    variable deterioration

46. The _____ _____ verdict is that all therapies are equivalent in their effects.

    Dodo bird

47. By and large, while _____ have an effect on outcome, genuine psychotherapy seems to have more of an effect.

    placebos

48. _____ refers to the trend to recommend particular therapies for particular maladies.

    Prescriptionism

Self-Test

1. Classical antipsychotic drugs typically have effects on all but which of the following symptoms?
   a. delusions
   b. hallucinations
   c. apathy
   d. none of the above

2. Evidence that Thorazine is an antipsychotic drug and not merely a tranquilizer is
   a. that it improves the behavior of patients with hallucinations.
   b. that it improves the behavior of patients who are apathetic.
   c. that true tranquilizers have little effect on the symptoms of schizophrenia.
   d. all of the above

3. One of the important drawbacks to the antipsychotic drugs is that they
   a. have serious side effects such as the production of apathy.
   b. must be administered in a hospital setting only.
   c. produce side effects that keep patients from taking them.
   d. all of the above

4. The new generation of atypical antipsychotic drugs, such as Clozaril, is an advance on standard ones because
   a. they work on more than one neurotransmitter system.
   b. they work on both positive and negative symptoms.
   c. they are effective with a larger percentage of patients.
   d. all of the above

5. All of the following are effective treatments for depression, either alone or in combination with manic episodes, except for
   a. monoamine oxidase inhibitors.
   b. tricyclic antidepressants.
   c. lithium carbonate.
   d. selective serotonin reuptake inhibitors.
   e. all of the above

6. The action of Thorazine that makes it an effective drug for the treatment of schizophrenia is that it blocks dopamine receptors. This must mean that schizophrenia could be caused by
   a. too much dopamine being taken up by receptors at synapses.
   b. too little dopamine being taken up by receptors at synapses.
   c. too little dopamine being produced at synapses.
   d. too much dopamine being produced at synapses.

7. Antipsychotic drugs (e.g., Thorazine) reduce many symptoms of schizophrenia. Below are characterizations of five patients suffering from some form of mental illness. Which patients would be expected to improve with Thorazine treatment?
   i. this patient suffers from bizarre thoughts and beliefs
   ii. this patient is withdrawn and noncommunicative
   iii this patient has frequent hallucinations
   iv. this patient is easily agitated
   v. this patient is deeply depressed
   a. all of the above
   b. i, ii, v
   c. i, ii, iii, iv
   d. ii, iv, v

8. It has been suggested that lithium carbonate may
   a. be a general cure for forms of mental illness.
   b. be useless, acting only as a placebo.
   c. have a general activation and arousal effect rather than a specific treatment effect.
   d. effectively treat bipolar disorder.

9. Some drugs used to treat mental conditions have their action by increasing the amount of GABA that is released at synapses. This neurotransmitter is largely inhibitory in the nervous system, so one might assume that it reduces the amount of activity to the neurons with which it synapses. In view of this, which of the following drugs do you think have this action?
   a. Valium
   b. Xanax
   c. anxiolytics
   d. all of the above

10. Which of the following would be convincing evidence that antidepressants do more than just produce euphoria to counteract the depression that they are meant to treat?
    a. if they did not produce euphoria in normal individuals
    b. if they acted on normal people to increase euphoria
    c. if they had specific action on neurotransmitters
    d. if they had an influence on other illnesses such as panic disorder

11. The main problem in using a before-after design to evaluate the effectiveness of a drug treatment is
    a. the placebo effect.
    b. the effect of expectation.
    c. the effect of spontaneous improvements.
    d. the Dodo bird effect.

12. A researcher finds that after drinking nothing but milk for three months, three patients (out of nine) report that they no longer suffer from migraine headaches. The researcher proclaims the curative powers of milk. What critical questions cannot be answered due to the absence of a control group?
    a. What is the spontaneous recovery rate without treatment?
    b. How did the milk cure the headaches?
    c. Why were only one-third of the patients cured?
    d. Can this finding be repeated?

13. A motorist takes his car to the garage for a tune-up. Unbeknownst to him, the mechanic is dishonest and tells the motorist that he tuned the car when, in fact, he hadn't. The motorist feels that the car runs better. This is an example of
    a. the placebo effect.
    b. schizophrenia.
    c. a double blind.
    d. desensitization.

14. A new drug is believed to alleviate the symptoms of bipolar disorder. The drug is tested in the following manner: one group of patients receives the drug in pill form, and another similar group receives a sugar pill. No patient knows which group he or she is in. A panel of psychiatrists evaluates each patient before and after the treatment period. The panel is not told whether a patient is getting the drug or the sugar pill. This is an example of
    a. a placebo effect.
    b. simultaneous control.
    c. the double-blind technique.
    d. transference.

15. While drug therapy has produced a drastic decline in institutionalized patients, this has occurred at some cost. Patients on Thorazine, for example,
    a. experience varying side effects from their drugs.
    b. make only marginal adjustments to the outside world.
    c. must continue to take their drugs after release.
    d. all of the above

16. The original idea behind psychosurgery was to "liberate the patient's thoughts from the pathological influence of his or her emotions." This required
    a. localizing the area of the brain concerned with thought.
    b. localizing the area of the brain concerned with emotion.
    c. disconnecting the area of the brain concerned with thought from that concerned with emotion.
    d. all of the above

17. A treatment that was designed to liberate the patient's thoughts from his or her pathological emotions, but which produced ambiguous results and may impair foresight and attention, is
    a. electroconvulsive shock treatment (ECT).
    b. prefrontal lobotomy.
    c. lithium treatment.
    d. catharsis.

18. ECT was originally used to treat schizophrenia but was later found to be more effective in treating
    a. depression.
    b. mania.
    c. compulsive behavior.
    d. It is still most effective in treating schizophrenia.

19. Electroconvulsive shock treatment
    a. is faster than many antidepressant drugs.
    b. can produce severe memory impairment.
    c. is generally used only after drug therapy has been tried.
    d. all of the above

20. In contrast to pharmaceutical approaches to mental illness, psychotherapy
    a. is much more effective.
    b. involves interpersonal interaction.
    c. is more relevant to the nature of psychopathology.
    d. none of the above

21. Orthodox (classical) psychoanalysis
    a. states that illness is a result of unconscious defenses against unconscious urges.
    b. states that most problems date back to childhood.
    c. was developed by Freud.
    d. all of the above

22. The cure for mental illness can be achieved by _____ according to the classical psychoanalysts.
    a. the victory of reason over passion
    b. a complete suppression of bad memories
    c. a reenactment of the cause of the problem
    d. none of the above

23. When a patient is asked to say whatever comes into his or her mind, it is believed that sooner or later the memory relevant to the disorder should appear. This technique is known as
    a. resistance.
    b. repression.
    c. free association.
    d. role playing.

24. Psychoanalysts believe the emotions are a principal part of therapy. One means for bringing emotions into play involves the relationship between the patient and therapist. The patient begins to behave as if the analyst were an important figure in her life. This is known as
    a. blinding.
    b. transference.
    c. resistance.
    d. intellectualization.

25. Modern day practitioners of psychoanalysis
    a. emphasize interpersonal factors rather than sexual development.
    b. subscribe to neo-Freudian views.
    c. focus on the patient's present rather than his or her past.
    d. all of the above

26. Behavior therapists argue that
    a. the theoretical notions of psychoanalysis are untestable.
    b. the therapeutic effectiveness of psychoanalysis is unclear.
    c. neurosis is caused by maladaptive learning.
    d. all of the above

27. The behavior therapist tends to emphasize
    a. giving the patient insight into the origins of his or her problems.
    b. righting improper behavior patterns without regard for underlying causes.
    c. curing the patient by a variety of means, including free association.
    d. enabling the patient to reach a full realization of his or her human potentialities.

28. For behavior therapists, fear
    a. is a classically conditioned response.
    b. has its roots in early childhood.
    c. is a manifestation of emotional traumas.
    d. is an operantly conditioned response.

29. In systematic desensitization, the patient first learns muscular relaxation and then constructs an anxiety hierarchy of fear-evoking situations. The next step is
    a. to imagine the least fearful situation while relaxed.
    b. to experience the least fearful situation while relaxed.
    c. to imagine the most fearful situation and then relax as the conditioned link is extinguished.
    d. to give the patient homework assignments involving exposure to fear-evoking stimuli.

30. Systematic desensitization relies on which of the following principles?
    a. extinction
    b. operant conditioning
    c. counterconditioning
    d. none of the above

31. The pairing of an unpleasant stimulus with an undesirable behavior is known as
    a. paired associate learning.
    b. cognitive therapy.
    c. response-produced anxiety.
    d. none of the above

32. Token economies
    a. are ineffective with inpatients.
    b. are a form of instrumental conditioning.
    c. are a form of classical conditioning.
    d. are based on the use of extinction.

33. All of the following are operant techniques used in therapy except
    a. token economies.
    b. aversion therapy.
    c. systematic desensitization.
    d. contingency management.
    e. b and d
    f. b and c
    g. a and d

34. A therapist confronts a depressed patient with the irrationality of his belief that he cannot get a good job because he thinks he is incompetent despite evidence to the contrary. This therapist is most likely to be a proponent of
    a. modeling.
    b. cognitive therapy.
    c. desensitization.
    d. could be any of the above.

35. Cognitive therapies
    a. focus on the patient's beliefs and attitudes.
    b. are not primarily concerned with the patient's history.
    c. do not rely heavily on behavior modification.
    d. all of the above

36. One of the features on which cognitive therapies concentrate is
    a. the behaviors exhibited by patients.
    b. the automatic thoughts that patients seem to have.
    c. the irrationality of beliefs that patients have.
    d. more than one of the above

37. Interpersonal therapy concentrates on the treatment of
    _____ by addressing the _____
    relationships of patients.
    a. schizophrenia, intellectual
    b. schizophrenia, emotional
    c. depression, intellectual
    d. depression, social
    e. all of the above

38. It seems as if the different forms of psychotherapy concentrate on different aspects of the problem. In particular,
    a. cognitive therapy concentrates on the patient's thoughts.
    b. psychoanalysis concentrates on the patient's understanding of his or her past.
    c. humanistic therapy concentrates on the patient's feelings.
    d. all of the above

39. Psychoanalysis can be summarized by the word *unconscious* in the same way that behavior therapy can be represented by *conditioning*. What word best summarizes humanistic therapy?
    a. cause
    b. feeling
    c. directive
    d. rational

40. All of the following are common to the various therapeutic schools except
    a. interpersonal learning.
    b. self-knowledge.
    c. emotional defusing.
    d. therapy as an all-or-none process.

41. Recently psychotherapists have been advocating the use of "technical electicism" in treating patients, which amounts to
    a. token economies.
    b. doing what works.
    c. psychoanalysis.
    d. behavior therapy.
    e. none of the above

42. A major difference between shared-problem groups and group therapy is
    a. that shared-problem groups involve more interpersonal interaction.
    b. that shared-problem groups work on a single problem that is common to the group members.
    c. that shared-problem groups incorporate a greater amount of self-knowledge of the problem in question.
    d. that shared-problem groups involve a more gradual therapeutic process.

43. One of the differences between family therapy and classical psychoanalysis is
    a. family therapists deal with a group of individuals, not just one.
    b. family therapists concentrate on relationships, not individual mental health.
    c. family therapists do not concentrate on the developmental history of each individual.
    d. all of the above

44. Evaluating couples therapy is difficult because
    a. the patients who decide to see a therapist may not be the most troubled.
    b. the patients who decide to see a therapist may need the most individual therapy.
    c. the individuals will not get therapy on their own, just in a group.
    d. group sessions do not allow one to separate out the effect that the therapist has on any single person.

45. Relative to an untreated control group's scores on a test of emotional well-being, the scores of a post-treatment group are
    a. always at least slightly better.
    b. seldom significantly different.
    c. more variable.
    d. less variable.

46. Meta-analysis provides a way to compare treatment effectiveness across a wide variety of different treatments and outcomes by
    a. comparing the percentage of patients who benefit from the treatment of each different kind.
    b. comparing the percentage of treated patients who fall above the average of untreated patients.
    c. comparing the percentage of success of each of the treatment regimens.
    d. comparing the percentage of treated individuals who fall above the treatment average.

47. A patient gets worse following therapy. This is known as
    a. spontaneous remission.
    b. the deterioration effect.
    c. the placebo effect.
    d. desensitization.

48. One reason there are deterioration effects is that
    a. the variability in post-treatment scores is larger than the variability in pretreatment scores.
    b. the variability in pretreatment scores is larger than the variability in post-treatment scores.
    c. the mean of post-treatment scores is higher than the mean of pretreatment scores.
    d. any of the above

49. Evidence that psychotherapies are effective not merely because patients expect them to be effective includes
    a. the fact that patients given placebos score worse than the average score of patients given psychotherapy.
    b. the fact that patients given one form of psychotherapy improve about as much as patients given another form of psychotherapy.
    c. the fact that behavioral and cognitive therapies seem to produce more improvement than other techniques.
    d. the fact that there are no significant placebo effects when it comes to psychotherapies.

50. If psychotherapy's only effect is nonspecific
    a. it may nevertheless have value in providing a shoulder to lean on.
    b. it will have proved largely an ineffective treatment course.
    c. it will then, by definition, be just a placebo effect.
    d. it will be more effective than if its effect had been specific.

51. The notion that specific therapies may be most effective for particular mental maladies is called
    a. the Dodo bird verdict.
    b. prescriptionism.
    c. existentialism.
    d. none of the above

Answer Key for Self-Test

1.	c	27.	b
2.	d	28.	a
3.	c	29.	a
4.	d	30.	c
5.	e	31.	d
6.	a	32.	b
7.	c	33.	f
8.	d	34.	b
9.	d	35.	d
10.	a	36.	d
11.	c	37.	d
12.	a	38.	d
13.	a	39.	b
14.	c	40.	d
15.	d	41.	b.
16.	d	42.	b
17.	b	43.	d
18.	a	44.	a
19.	d	45.	c
20.	b	46.	b
21.	d	47.	b
22.	a	48.	a
23.	c	49.	a
24.	b	50.	a
25.	d	51.	b
26.	d		

Investigating Psychological Phenomena

DEMONSTRATION OF ROLE PLAYING

Equipment: None
Number of participants: Yourself and one other
Time per participant: Thirty minutes
Time for experimenter: Thirty minutes

All of the treatment options discussed in the text, whether behavior therapy, cognitive therapy, psychodynamic therapy, or drug therapy, require a trained and skilled practitioner to administer. Because of this, it is impossible to conduct an exercise that illustrates any of these treatments. However, one technique that is sometimes employed by therapists can be illustrated: role playing. Therapists use this technique to educate their patients about various aspects of interpersonal relations. This technique requires at least two people to assume the roles of individuals other that themselves in a particular social situation. In so doing, the hope of the treatment is that the participating individuals will gain some insight about the feelings, emotions, and cognitions of the persons whose roles are being played.

Although the technique sounds simple enough in principle, in actual practice it is a bit tricky. As the following quote illustrates, role-playing participants frequently lapse back into their own personalities and have to be reminded about their role-playing activities.

> [The therapist] says "Tom, do you really care for me?" Tom says "I would say to her that I do, but she'd complain." Therapist: "Don't tell me what you *would* do. I'm Jane. Talk to me. Tom, do you really care for me?" Tom (turning away, looking slightly disgusted): "Yes." Therapist (still as Jane): "You don't say it like you mean it." Tom: "Yeah, that's what she says, and I usually . . ." Therapist (interrupting): "You're again telling me *about* what you'd say. I'm Jane. Tom, you don't say it like you mean it." Tom: "It's very hard for me to answer her when she says that." Therapist: "OK, I'm Jane. Tell me how you feel." Tom: "Jane, when you do that it really turns me off. Maybe if you didn't ask me so often I'd be able to say it spontaneously without feeling like a puppet . . . (then, in a tone that indicates he is now talking to the therapist as therapist) Gee, I wonder what would happen if I really said that to her" (Wachtel, 1977, pp. 234–35).

You can try role playing on your own to discover some of its features. Solicit the participation of a fellow student of the opposite sex from your introductory psychology class and set up the following situation.

The two of you are married and have just graduated from college. Each of you has very well-defined career plans, and you have each been skillful and lucky enough to have been offered very attractive first jobs that fit precisely the career lines that you have planned. The problem is that your job offers are in cities 1,000 miles apart. How do you decide what to do?

You should go through two sessions: first, have a discussion about this problem with your partner with each of you playing yourselves. Write down each of your responses on paper. Second, switch roles and try having the discussion again. In each case, put yourselves in the other's situation. Again, write your responses on paper.

After you have finished playing both roles, talk about differences in the conversations that resulted from your playing the male versus the female role. Compare the transcripts of each session. Did this help you gain a different perspective on the problem?

At this point, you might want to try another role-playing exercise in which the two roles are quite different from one another. This will allow you to take two very different perspectives on a scene. Try out the following scene:

One of you should assume the role of an instructor for a course you are both taking (perhaps introductory psychology) while the other plays the role of a student. The issue is that the student has scored poorly on the midterm examination, but feels that at least part of the reason for his or her poor performance is that he or she was graded unfairly by the instructor. In addition, the student was faced with taking four midterm exams within three days, so his or her performance was bound to suffer. Now imagine that the student has come in to talk with the instructor about these issues. The person playing the role of the instructor should really try to assume the personality and attitudes of the real instructor in the course as much as possible. After you have acted out a scene, switch roles. This time, to add some variety, have the student role be one of a very aggressive student who is determined not to leave the instructor's office without a change of grade. Again, after each scene, write down your impressions so that you can later discuss and evaluate them.

Having finished this scenario, think about some of the following questions: Was it more difficult to assume the role of the instructor or student? Was it difficult to stay in character without lapses? What insights have you gained about instructor-student relationships? Would this be a useful exercise for students and instructors to try in general? How was this role-playing exercise different from the first one?

Reference

Wachtel, P. L. (1979). *Psychoanalysis and behavior therapy: Toward an integration.* New York: Basic Books.

Statistics: The Description, Organization, and Interpretation of Data

Learning Objectives

1. What is the topic of statistics about? Why are statistical tests needed in psychological research?

DESCRIBING THE DATA

2. What is scaling? Why is it important to understand the types of number scales?

Categorical and ordinal scales

3. Understand what categorical and ordinal scales are. Be able to describe the arithmetic operations permitted and not permitted with each. Give examples of these scales.

Interval scales

4. What is the important feature of an interval scale? Give examples.

Ratio scales

5. What defines a ratio scale? What are some examples of ratio scales?
6. How do interval and ratio scales differ? What arithmetic operation is permitted with ratio scales?

ORGANIZING THE DATA

The frequency distribution

7. How is a frequency distribution created from the raw scores in an experiment? To get practice in constructing a frequency distribution, plot one for the following heights (in inches) of males in a small class: 72, 72, 68, 66, 74, 73, 69, 69, 70, 67, 66, 73, 72.

Measures of central tendency

8. What is a measure of central tendency and why is it useful? Describe the three measures of central tendency that are commonly used. Calculate these three quantities for the scores given above.
9. What does it mean for a distribution to be skewed or symmetrical?

Measures of variability

10. Describe what the range of a group of scores is, and describe why the range has limited utility. What is the range for the scores given in Question 7 above?
11. What is the variance of a set of scores? Why is it a useful measure of variability? Calculate the variance and standard deviation of the scores given above.

Converting scores to compare them

12. How are percentile ranks calculated, and how do they permit comparison of scores obtained from different distributions?
13. What is a z-score? Why is it useful for comparing scores from two distributions?
14. How are z-scores and percentile ranks similar?

The normal distribution

15. What are the characteristics of a normal distribution?
16. Be able to convert a z-score into a rank for a variable that has a normal distribution.
17. Understand the principle that can explain when a variable will be distributed normally. To do this you should roughly understand how a repeated two-alternative event will approximate a normal distribution.

DESCRIBING THE RELATION BETWEEN TWO VARIABLES: CORRELATION

Positive and negative correlation

18. What is the meaning of positive and negative correlation?
19. How is a scatter plot constructed? What does it show? What does a line-of-best-fit have to do with a scatter plot?

The correlation coefficient

20. Understand what various values of r mean.
21. How is a correlation coefficient computed? Do you understand the logic of this computation?

Interpreting and misinterpreting correlations

22. Give examples of cases for which a correlation cannot be interpreted in terms of one variable causing changes in another. What is the danger in interpreting correlations in terms of cause-effect?

INTERPRETING THE DATA

Accounting for variability

23. What does it mean to account for variance?
24. Understand how variance is acounted for in actual experiments, such as the examples given in the text.
25. How does one account for variance in correlational data?

Hypothesis testing

26. Describe the procedure by which you could determine whether a particular test score does or does not belong to a distribution of scores.
27. What are null and alternative hypotheses? How do critical ratios allow us to rule out one of these hypotheses?
28. What trade-off is involved in the decision about where to set the cut-off for the critical ratio?
29. Be able to describe how hypotheses about differences between means can be tested using a critical ratio.

30. What is the relationship between a sample mean and a population mean?
31. What is a standard error, and what role does it play in testing hypotheses about sample means?
32. Be sure to follow the statistical analysis of the imagery experiment presented in the text.
33. Explain what it means to be reasonably confident that the mean of the population will fall within a specified interval.

Some implications of statistical inference

34. Explain how statistical conclusions are probabilistic. How does this affect these conclusions both about population means, and about individuals?
35. Based on your knowledge of how to compute a critical ratio, describe how sample size affects a statistical conclusion. When may statistical and psychological significance differ?

Programmed Exercises

1. The collection, organization, and interpretation of numerical data comprise the topic of _____.   statistics

DESCRIBING THE DATA

2. When all subjects in a group perform differently, or when the same subject performs differently on different occasions, we say that the data contain _____.   variability

3. Differences among subjects _____ groups and _____ groups are the two sources of variability that are analyzed by statistical methods.   between, within

4. The assignment of numbers to events is called _____.   scaling

5. The type of _____ that numbers represent is defined by which arithmetic operations are permitted on those numbers.   scale

6. The assignment of students in a school to the first, second, or third of three kindergartens would involve the use of a(n) _____ scale.   categorical (nominal)

7. If you ask someone to rank order four cola drinks from most to least preferred, you would be using a(n) _____ scale.   ordinal

8. The Fahrenheit scale of temperature is a(n) _____ scale as indicated by the fact that the difference between 30° and 35° equals the difference between 75° and 80°.   interval

9. The scale of length in feet is a(n) _____ scale; thus, we can say that a board of four feet is twice as long as a board of two feet.   ratio

ORGANIZING THE DATA

10. A _____ _____ of birthweight could be represented by a _____, a graph of the numbers of people in a sample who are born at various weights in the range to be studied.   frequency distribution, histogram

11. Investigators often organize data into _____ so that groups of observations that fall within a small interval are counted as the same value for a frequency distribution.   bins

12. There are three major measures of central tendency, the _____, _____, and _____.   mean, median mode

13. The distribution of reaction times in an experiment is likely to be _____, since there will be none below 0, many short ones, and fewer and fewer long ones.   skewed

14. The distribution of heights of males is _____ because there are just as many males with heights above the mean as there are males with heights below the mean.   symmetrical

_____ is a measure of variation that is defined as the difference between the highest and ~~_~s.~~   range

16. The _____ is a measure of variation that takes account of each score's deviation from the mean. Its square root is called the _____ _____.

variance
standard deviation

17. The _____ _____ of a score is the percentage of scores that lie below it.

percentile rank

18. A _____-_____ expresses scores in terms of units of standard deviations from a mean.

z-score (standard score)

19. The heights of females in a population form a _____ _____, one in which there are equal frequencies of heights on both sides of the mean.

normal distribution

DESCRIBING THE RELATION BETWEEN TWO VARIABLES: CORRELATION

20. If two dependent variables are related to one another, they are said to be _____.

correlated

21. If we ranked the top 10 runners in the world so that the top runner was ranked 1 and the 10th runner was ranked 10, and if we based these ranks on time to run the 1500 meter race, there would by definition be a _____ correlation between rank and time.

positive

22. On the average, the faster one can complete each item on an aptitude test, the higher will be one's score, assuming that one doesn't sacrifice accuracy. There is thus a _____ correlation between time per item and test score.

negative

23. Plotting two dependent variables, one on the abscissa and one on the ordinate, yields a graph that shows the relationship between the variables. This is called a _____ _____.

scatter plot

24. A line fit to the points of the graph described in Question 22 is called a _____-_____-_____-_____.

line-of-best-fit

25. A _____ _____ of –1 indicates that there is a perfect _____ correlation between two variables.

correlation coefficient, negative

INTERPRETING THE DATA

26. We say that we have _____ variance when we can attribute some of the variability in a set of scores to a particular factor.

explained (accounted for)

27. Squaring a correlation coefficient yields a proportion of _____ that is explained.

variance

28. The _____ _____ of a test statistic is usually set at 2 so that the probability of choosing the alternative hypothesis when the null hypothesis is, in fact, correct is quite small (one chance in twenty).

critical ratio

29. The standard deviation of a distribution of sample means is called the _____ _____.

standard error

30. The _____ _____ is the range within which we can be fairly confident the actual population mean will fall.

confidence interval

31. There are two important characteristics of statistical conclusions: they are affected by sample _____, and they are _____.

size, probabilistic

Self-Test

1. If there are 100 questions on a test, with each question worth one point, then the set of scores from 0 to 100 constitutes
   a. a nominal scale.
   b. an ordinal scale.
   c. an interval scale.
   d. a ratio scale.

2. Suppose you have three children and measure their heights: 49, 47, and 40 inches. These measurements constitute
   a. a nominal scale.
   b. an ordinal scale.
   c. an interval scale.
   d. a ratio scale.

3. If you assert that a jar has twice as much orange juice as another jar, you are making an implicit assertion about
   a. a categorical scale.
   b. an ordinal scale.
   c. an interval scale.
   d. a ratio scale.

4. There are ten digits on a touch-tone phone. If we compare two phone numbers, say 784-5183 and 982-2161, we must use which of the following scales to make that comparison?
   a. nominal scale
   b. ordinal scale
   c. interval scale
   d. ratio scale

5. The results of an examination are graphed so that each score is listed in order on the abscissa, and the number of students receiving that score is plotted on the ordinate. Such a graph
   a. is a frequency distribution.
   b. is a histogram of the scores.
   c. is not a scattergram.
   d. could be a normal distribution.
   e. all of the above

6. Suppose the graph in Question 5 turned out to look like the graph below. From this we could conclude that

   a. the mean is greater than the median.
   b. the mode is 50.
   c. the variance is 0.
   d. the test was statistically significant.
   e. none of the above

7. Suppose the graph in Question 5 turned out to look like the graph that follows. From this we could conclude that

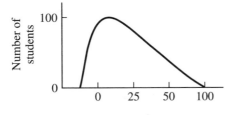

   a. the distribution is normal.
   b. the median is lower than the mean.
   c. the students with a score of 75 are in the 75th percentile.
   d. the mode is 100.
   e. none of the above

8. For the following five scores, 1, 2, 3, 4, 5,
   a. the median is 3.
   b. the mean is 3.
   c. the variance is 2.
   d. all of the above
   e. a and b but not c

9. Variability is to central tendency as variance is to
   a. correlation.
   b. z-score.
   c. mean.
   d. standard deviation.

10. All of the following could be measures of variation in a set of scores except
    a. mean-median.
    b. highest score-lowest score.
    c. sum of (each score-mean)^2.
    d. average of highest two scores-average of lowest two scores.

11. Consider two examinations: on one, the mean is 50, the standard deviation is 5, and your score is 65. On the other, the mean is 50, the standard deviation is 2, and your score is 60. Which of the following is true?
    a. Your percentile rank is higher on the second test.
    b. Your z-score is higher on the second test.
    c. You can meaningfully compare your z-scores on the two tests.
    d. You cannot meaningfully compare your raw scores on the two tests.
    e. All of the above.

12. If a set of scores on an exam has a mean of 75 and a standard deviation of 10, then
    a. the distribution must be normal.
    b. the distribution must be symmetric.
    c. a score of 50 corresponds to a z-score of –2.5.
    d. a z-score of 1.0 equals a test score of 75.

13. If SAT scores have a mean of 500 and a standard deviation of 100, and if IQ scores have a mean of 100 and a standard deviation of 15, then with an SAT score of 650 and an IQ score of 115
    a. the z-score for IQ will be higher than the z-score for SAT.
    b. the percentile score for IQ will be higher than the percentile score for SAT.
    c. both of the above
    d. the percentile score for IQ will be 84.
    e. the scores on the two tests will not be comparable since the tests differ.

14. If we found a correlation coefficient of –.88 between reaction time and performance on a test of motor skill, we could conclude that
    a. a high score on the test of motor skill predicts a fast reaction time.
    b. a high score on the test of motor skill predicts a slow reaction time.
    c. motor skill causes people to have faster reaction times.
    d. reaction time and motor skill are largely unrelated.

15. In the scatter plot shown below

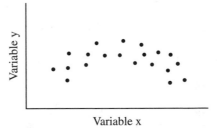

Variable x

    a. there is no relationship between x and y.
    b. the correlation coefficient is statistically significant.
    c. the correlation coefficient is close to 0.
    d. variable x is the independent variable.

16. If a line-of-best-fit for a scatter plot were flat, then
    a. the correlation would be 1.
    b. the correlation would be 0.
    c. the correlation would not be significant.
    d. we know nothing about the correlation until we calculate it.

17. Which of the following correlation coefficients shows the strongest inverse relationship between variables x and y?
    a. .82
    b. −.74
    c. 0
    d. −1.14

18. If the correlation between a parent's and his children's scores on a test of motor skills were .70, then we would know that
    a. 70 percent of the variability of the children's score is accounted for by the parent's scores.
    b. 70 percent of the variability of the parent's score is accounted for by the children's scores.
    c. children's motor skills are caused by the skills of their parents.
    d. none of the above

19. An experiment is performed to determine whether eating breakfast improves one's test performance. Two groups are given tests, one group after eating a good breakfast, one after no breakfast. Consider the following hypothesis: eating breakfast has no effect on test performance. This hypothesis
    a. can be evaluated only probabilistically.
    b. is called the "alternative" hypothesis.
    c. cannot be evaluated in this experiment.
    d. is assessed by examining within-subject variability.

20. In the experiment of Question 19 which of the following would be necessary in order for us to believe that eating breakfast enhances test performance?
    a. The sample must be normal.
    b. The sample must be statistically significant.
    c. The between-subject variance must be larger than the within-subject variance.
    d. all of the above
    e. none of the above

21. Suppose you were to discover a hospital in which there were eight new births each day, and you wished to test the hypothesis that this hospital had more births per day than the average hospital of its size. To do this we would need to know
    a. the correlations among births at all the hospitals in question.
    b. the mean, standard deviation, and number of hospitals in the comparison group.
    c. only the standard error of the births in the comparison group.
    d. none of the above

22. Two hospitals report eight births per day average with a standard deviation of ten births. For hospital A, this average was computed over 25 days; for hospital B, it was computed over 400 days. The standard errors of births in these hospitals
    a. are equal.
    b. are 2 in hospital A and .5 in hospital B.
    c. are not comparable because of the difference in number of days.
    d. none of the above

23. If a sample mean is 20, its standard deviation is 30, and the number of participants in the sample is 9, then
    a. you can be fairly confident that the sample is normal.
    b. a participant with a score of 25 is in the fifth percentile.
    c. a score of 17 would be equal to a z-score of 1.
    d. you can be fairly sure that the population from which this sample was drawn has a mean greater than 0.

24. Suppose you're trying to predict whether a Republican or Democratic candidate will win a particular senatorial race. You conduct a poll of the relevant voters and discover that 53 percent would vote for the Republican and 47 percent for the Democrat. Who do you think will win?
    a. You can be reasonably confident that the Republican will win.
    b. You can be reasonably confident that the Democrat will win.
    c. Given the polling data, it's not clear who will win.
    d. There isn't enough information to make a prediction one way or the other.

Answer Key for Self-Test

1.	d	13.	d
2.	d	14.	a
3.	d	15.	c
4.	a	16.	b
5.	e	17.	b
6.	e	18.	d
7.	b	19.	a
8.	d	20.	c
9.	c	21.	b
10.	a	22.	b
11.	e	23.	d
12.	c	24.	d

Investigating Psychological Phenomena

APPLYING STATISTICAL CONCEPTS

This exercise provides an opportunity for you to apply some of the statistical concepts described in the text. Reconsider the experiment described in the text in which participants are tested for recall performance on lists of twenty words with and without instructions to form images. Imagine that twenty participants had been run in this experiment—the ten described in the text plus ten others. The data of all these participants are presented in Table 1 below. In the first column are the recall scores with imagery instructions; the second column contains recall scores when no imagery instructions were provided; the third column is the difference between the first two, the amount of improvement. Finally, the fourth column contains the results of a test of imagery ability that was given to each of the participants in this hypothetical experiment (scores on this test could range from 0 to 40). Using the data in this table, perform the following tabulations and analyses.

TABLE 1

Participant	Score with imagery	Score without imagery	Improvement	Test of imagery ability
Alphonse	20	5	15	30
Betsy	24	9	15	26
Cheryl	20	5	15	27
Davis	18	9	9	21
Earl	22	6	16	33
Fred	19	11	8	26
Germaine	20	8	12	32
Hortense	19	11	8	38
Imogene	17	7	10	30
Jerry	21	9	12	27
Kerry	17	8	9	29
Linda	20	16	4	24
Moe	20	10	10	26
Nicolas	16	12	4	22
Orry	24	7	17	36
Penelope	22	9	13	32
Quarton	25	21	4	23
Ronald	21	14	7	26
Steven	19	12	7	24
Terry	23	13	10	28

1. Create frequency histograms for the recall data on the two unlabeled sets of axes below. The left graph is for the recall scores with imagery instructions, and the right is for recall scores without imagery instructions. Note that you must decide what specific values to place on each axis for each graph.

Frequency histograms

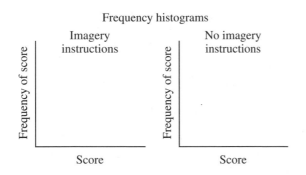

2. Calculate the mean, median, and mode of each of the distributions whose scores you have plotted above.

3. Calculate the range and standard deviation of each of these distributions.

4. Analyze the improvement scores to test the hypothesis that imagery instructions lead to better recall performance than no imagery instructions. To do this, you must compute a critical ratio that evaluates the sample mean of the improvement scores against the population mean for the null hypothesis (no improvement). Is this critical ratio larger than 2.0? If so, how do we interpret the improvement scores?

5. Examine the relationship between the improvement scores and performance on the test of imagery ability in two ways. First, create a scatter plot on the axes presented below. Second, compute a correlation coefficient between these sets of scores. Is there a relation between the variables? How would you interpret this relation psychologically?

Now that you have completed your analyses, you should turn to the next page to examine the correct answers and compare them to your own answers.

Answers to Statistical Exercise

1.

Imagery instructions

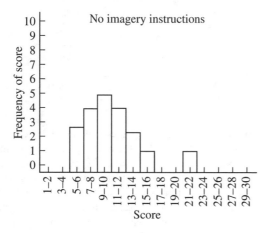

No imagery instructions

2. Imagery instructions
      Mean = 20.35
      Median = 20
      Mode = 20
  No imagery instructions
      Mean = 10.10
      Median = 9
      Mode = 9

3. Imagery instructions
      Range = 9
      Standard deviation = 2.46
  No imagery instructions
      Range = 16
      Standard deviation = 3.89

4. Critical ratio =

$$\frac{\text{sample mean} - \text{population mean by null hypothesis}}{\text{standard error of the mean}}$$

standard error of the mean

$$= \frac{\text{standard deviation}}{\sqrt{N}}$$

$$= \frac{4.05}{\sqrt{20}}$$

$$= .91$$

$$\text{critical ratio} = \frac{10.25 - 0}{.91}$$

$$= 11.26$$

This critical ratio is much larger than 2.0; therefore, we may conclude that there is a statistically significant improvement in recall scores comparing no imagery to imagery instructions.

5. Scatter plot

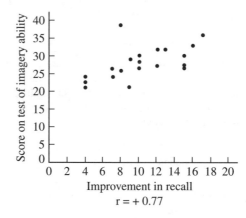

$$r = + 0.77$$

The correlation coefficient, r, is + 0.77.

Both the scatter plot and the correlation coefficient indicate that there is substantial relationship between the variables. We might propose the following hypothesis to account for this relationship. Participants with a better imagery ability are better able to form mental images in the memory task, and thus perform better. Our hypothesis must remain tentative, however, since we are not permitted to draw cause-effect conclusions from correlational data.

APPENDIX 2

Report Sheets

On this and the following pages you will find report sheets for several of the experiments in the preceding chapters. If your instructor wants to collect the data for these experiments, use these report sheets. You can cut them out and hand them in to your instructor.

Chapter 1

REPORT SHEET—CONSISTENCY OF JUDGMENT OF FACIAL EXPRESSION

	Female Subjects	Male Subjects
Female ecstatic		
Female happy		
Female sad		
Female shocked		
Female frightened		
Female disgusted		
Female calm		
Female resigned		
Female disappointed		
Female angry		
Female resolute		

	Female Subjects	Male Subjects
Male ecstatic		
Male happy		
Male sad		
Male shocked		
Male frightened		
Male disgusted		
Male calm		
Male resigned		
Male disappointed		
Male angry		
Male resolute		

Chapter 2

REPORT SHEET—NERVE IMPULSE

Practice   Trial 1 ankle = Time in seconds*

Part I   Trial 1 ankle = _____

           Trial 2 ankle = _____

           Trial 3 ankle = _____

           Trial 4 ankle = _____

           Trial 5 ankle = _____

Part II   Trial 1 upper arm = _____

           Trial 2 upper arm = _____

           Trial 3 upper arm = _____

           Trial 4 upper arm = _____

           Trial 5 upper arm = _____

Test
Part III   Trial 1 ankle time = _____

           ÷ 25 = _____ (a)

           Trial 2 upper arm time = _____

           ÷ 25 = _____ (b)

           Trial 3 upper arm time = _____

           ÷ 25 = _____ (c)

           Trial 4 ankle time = _____

           ÷ 25 = _____ (d)

$\dfrac{a + d}{2}$ = _____ (average ankle time)

$\dfrac{b + c}{2}$ = _____ (average upper arm time)

Average ankle time – average upper arm time = _____ (difference 1)

(1) Distance of ankle to base of neck

    (for third tallest person) = _____

(2) Distance of upper arm to base of neck

    (for third tallest person) = _____

    Distance 1 – distance 2 = _____ (difference 2)

$\dfrac{\text{difference 2}}{\text{difference 1}}$ = (speed of nerve impulse)

*Record time accurate to .1 second.

Chapter 3

REPORT SHEET—HEART RATE

Data from three participants (A, B, and C)

Instruction and time	A	B	C
"Begin and relax"			
00:00–0:30			
0:45–1:15			
"Increase physical activity"			
1:30–2:00			
2:15–2:45			
"Relax"			
3:00–3:30			
3:45–4:15			
"Increase mental activity"			
4:30–5:00			
5:15–5:45			
"Relax"			
6:00–6:30			
6:45–7:15			

List for each participant the basic situation that he or she imagined in the "increase" minutes.

	Physical	Mental
A	_____	_____
B	_____	_____
C	_____	_____

Chapter 4

REPORT SHEET—LEARNED TASTE AVERSIONS

Number of participants questioned _____

Number of participants with aversions _____

Number of participants who confirm Garcia's notions _____

Summarize the results from all of your participants below. You decide which questions are relevant to each feature of learned taste aversion and summarize your results with respect to each of the features listed below.

BELONGINGNESS Relevant questions (Nos.)

_____

_____

_____

ONE-TRIAL LEARNING Relevant questions (Nos.)

_____

_____

_____

LONG CS-US INTERVAL Relevant questions (Nos.)

_____

_____

_____

NOVELTY EFFECT Relevant questions (Nos.)

_____

_____

_____

"IRRATIONALITY" Relevant questions (Nos.)

_____

_____

_____

OTHER INTERESTING RESULTS

_____

_____

_____

Chapter 4

REPORT SHEET—MAZE LEARNING

Trial	Time	Number of errors
1	_____	_____
2	_____	_____
3	_____	_____
4	_____	_____
5	_____	_____

(using paper
with cut-out hole)

Chapter 5

REPORT SHEET—MEASURING BRIGHTNESS CONTRAST

Background values:	1	3	4	5	7	10
Matching value 1:	_____	_____	_____	_____	_____	_____
Matching value 2:	_____	_____	_____	_____	_____	_____
Matching value 3:	_____	_____	_____	_____	_____	_____
Total matching value:	_____	_____	_____	_____	_____	_____
Average matching value:	_____	_____	_____	_____	_____	_____

Chapter 7

REPORT SHEET—IMAGERY INSTRUCTIONS

Answer sheet for List 1	Answer sheet for List 2
1. _____	1. _____
2. _____	2. _____
3. _____	3. _____
4. _____	4. _____
5. _____	5. _____
6. _____	6. _____
7. _____	7. _____
8. _____	8. _____
9. _____	9. _____
10. _____	10. _____
11. _____	11. _____
12. _____	12. _____
13. _____	13. _____
14. _____	14. _____
15. _____	15. _____
16. _____	16. _____
17. _____	17. _____
18. _____	18. _____
19. _____	19. _____
20. _____	20. _____

Chapter 8

REPORT SHEET—THE STROOP EFFECT

Experiment 1

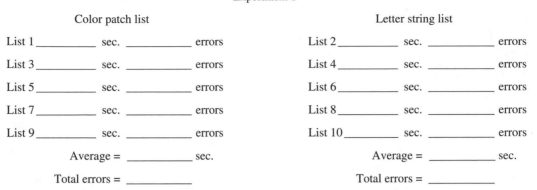

Color patch list

List 1 _____ sec. _____ errors

List 3 _____ sec. _____ errors

List 5 _____ sec. _____ errors

List 7 _____ sec. _____ errors

List 9 _____ sec. _____ errors

Average = _____ sec.

Total errors = _____

Letter string list

List 2 _____ sec. _____ errors

List 4 _____ sec. _____ errors

List 6 _____ sec. _____ errors

List 8 _____ sec. _____ errors

List 10 _____ sec. _____ errors

Average = _____ sec.

Total errors = _____

Experiment 2

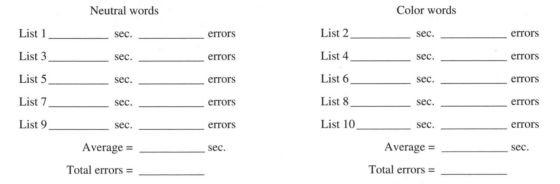

Neutral words

List 1 _____ sec. _____ errors

List 3 _____ sec. _____ errors

List 5 _____ sec. _____ errors

List 7 _____ sec. _____ errors

List 9 _____ sec. _____ errors

Average = _____ sec.

Total errors = _____

Color words

List 2 _____ sec. _____ errors

List 4 _____ sec. _____ errors

List 6 _____ sec. _____ errors

List 8 _____ sec. _____ errors

List 10 _____ sec. _____ errors

Average = _____ sec.

Total errors = _____

Experiment 3

Neutral words

List 1 _____ sec. _____ errors

List 3 _____ sec. _____ errors

List 5 _____ sec. _____ errors

List 7 _____ sec. _____ errors

List 9 _____ sec. _____ errors

Average = _____ sec.

Total errors = _____

Color referent words

List 2 _____ sec. _____ errors

List 4 _____ sec. _____ errors

List 6 _____ sec. _____ errors

List 8 _____ sec. _____ errors

List 10 _____ sec. _____ errors

Average = _____ sec.

Total errors = _____

Chapter 9

REPORT SHEET—IMPLICIT LEARNING

1. _____	9. _____	17. _____
2. _____	10. _____	18. _____
3. _____	11. _____	19. _____
4. _____	12. _____	20. _____
5. _____	13. _____	21. _____
6. _____	14. _____	22. _____
7. _____	15. _____	23. _____
8. _____	16. _____	24. _____

Participant's statement of rule: _____

_____

_____

_____

_____

_____

_____

_____

_____

Number of correct responses out of 24: _____

Chapter 10

REPORT SHEET—IMPRESSIONS

	Percent of participants checking favorable adjective at left			
	Asch's data		Your data	
	Group A	Group B	Group A	Group B
Adjective pair	(24 students)	(34 students)	(__ students)	(__ students)
generous	24	10		
wise	18	17		
happy	32	5		
good-natured	18	0		
humorous	52	21		
sociable	56	27		
popular	35	14		
reliable	84	91		
good-looking	74	35		
serious	97	100		
restrained	64	9		
honest	80	79		

Chapter 11

REPORT SHEET—PERSONAL SPACE

One person elevator	Number of cases with participants in predicted place (7 or 9)	_____/15
Two person elevator	Number of cases with participants in predicted place (7 or 9)	_____/15
Two person elevator	Number of cases with participants in noncontiguous squares	_____/15

Chapter 12

REPORT SHEET—CONSERVATION OF NUMBER

1. More blue _____
   More red _____
   Both equal _____
2. More blue _____
   More red _____
   Both equal _____
3. More blue _____
   More red _____
   Both equal _____
4. More blue _____
   More red _____
   Both equal _____

5. More blue _____
   More red _____
   Both equal _____
6. More blue _____
   More red _____
   Both equal _____
7. More blue _____
   More red _____
   Both equal _____
8. More blue _____
   More red _____
   Both equal _____

Chapter 13

REPORT SHEET—SEX DIFFERENCES

	Your data* (combined with classmates' data)			
	Males		Females	
Item	#	%	#	%
1. Killing cockroach	_____	_____	_____	_____
2. Queen Anne's lace (correct answer: flower)	_____	_____	_____	_____
3. Using word "shit" (fewer than 5 times)	_____	_____	_____	_____
4. Sew clothes	_____	_____	_____	_____
5. Intercourse only after spiritual love	_____	_____	_____	_____
6. Nude in locker room	_____	_____	_____	_____
7. Crying frequently (very often, often, or only with good reason)	_____	_____	_____	_____
8. Feel like smashing things	_____	_____	_____	_____
9. Chest measurement	_____	_____	_____	_____
10. Change tire	_____	_____	_____	_____
11. Playing radio	_____	_____	_____	_____
12. Prefer dominance in relationship	_____	_____	_____	_____
13. Overweight	_____	_____	_____	_____
14. Washing hair when depressed	_____	_____	_____	_____
15. Sleep in nude	_____	_____	_____	_____
16. Closest parent (mother)	_____	_____	_____	_____
17. Keep room neat	_____	_____	_____	_____

*Tabulate your results below in the following way. For the "yes" or "no" questions (e.g., Item 1), add up the number of participants who answered "yes." Then calculate what percentage answered "Yes." For the "true" or "false" questions (e.g., Item 8), record those who answered "True." For other items (e.g., Item 2), add up the number of participants whose answers are the same as those indicated in parentheses under "Item" (e.g., Item 2—flower).

List the femaleness scores of all of your participants:

Males: _____ _____ _____ _____ _____ _____ _____ _____ _____

_____ _____ _____ _____ _____ _____ _____ _____ _____

Females: _____ _____ _____ _____ _____ _____ _____ _____ _____

_____ _____ _____ _____ _____ _____ _____ _____ _____

Chapter 16

REPORT SHEET—DEPRESSION

Self-rating of mood now (enter number) _____

Self-rating of mood over last twelve months (enter number) _____

Number of negative events recalled _____

Number of positive events recalled _____

Negative minus positive events _____

Negative plus positive events _____

Credits

Grateful acknowledgment is made to: F. Garb, A. Stunkard, and the *American Journal of Psychiatry* to adapt from Garb and Stunkard, "Taste aversions in man," *American Journal of Psychiatry* 131 (1974):1204–1207; W. Epstein, I. Rock, and the *American Journal of Psychology* to adapt from Epstein, W., and Rock, I., "Perceptual set as an artifact of recency," *American Journal of Psychology* 73 (1960):214–228; J. R. Stroop and the *Journal of Experimental Psychology* to adapt from J. R. Stroop, "Studies in interference in serial verbal reactions," *Journal of Experimental Psychology* 18 (1935): 643–662; A. S. Reber and the *Journal of Verbal Learning and Verbal Behavior* to adapt from A. S. Reber, "Implicit learning of artificial grammars," *Journal of Verbal Learning and Verbal Behavior* 6 (1967):858–863; S. E. Asch and the *Journal of Abnormal and Social Psychology* to adapt from S. E. Asch, "Forming impressions of personality," *Journal of Abnormal and Social Psychology* 41 (1946):258–290.

Illustrations

Page 13 *bottom* and page 34 Keeton, W. T., *Biological science*, 4th edition. New York: W. W. Norton & Company, Inc., 1986. Copyright © 1986, 1980, 1979, 1972, 1967 by W. W. Norton & Company, Inc.

Page 20 Hodgkin, A. L., and Huxley, A. F. "Action potentials recorded from inside nerve fibers," *Nature* 144 (1939):710–711. Adapted by permission.

Page 32 Harlow, H. F., "Learning and satiation of response in intrinsically motivated complex puzzle performance in monkeys," *Journal of Comparative and Physiological Psychology* 43 (1950):289–294.

Page 41 Reproduced by permission of the publishers from Köhler, W., *The mentality of apes*, London, England: Routledge & Kegan Paul Ltd., 1976.

Page 42 *bottom* Pavlov, I. P., *Lectures on conditioned reflexes*, vol. 1. New York: International Publishers, Co., Inc. 1928. Adapted by permission of International Publishers Co., Inc.

Page 44 From Spooner, A., and Kellogg, W. N., "The backward conditioning curve," *American Journal of Psychology* 60 (1947): 321–334. Copyright © 1947 by The University of Illinois Press. Reprinted by permission of the publisher.

Page 68 From James J. Gibson, *The perception of the visible world*. Boston, Mass.: Houghton Mifflin Co., 1950.

Pages 69 and 72 Boring, E. G., "A new ambiguous figure," *American Journal of Psychology* 42 (1930): 444–445; and Leeper, R. W., "A study of a neglected portion of the field of learning: The development of sensory organization," *Journal of Genetic Psychology* 46 (1935):41–75.

Page 113 Festinger, L., and Carlsmith, J. M., "Cognitive consequences of forced compliance," *Journal of Abnormal and Social Psychology* 58 (1959):203–210. Copyright 1959 by the American Psychological Association. Reprinted by permission.